Touraj Atabaki is Senior Research Fellow at the International Institute of Social History, Amsterdam and the author of *Post-Soviet Central Asia* and *Azerbaijan: Ethnicity and the Struggle for Power in Iran* and the editor of *The State and the Subaltern: Modernization, Society and the State in Turkey and Iran*, *Iran and the First World War: Battleground of the Great Powers* and *Iran in the 20th Century: Historiography and Political Culture* (all published by I.B.Tauris & Co. Ltd).

Erik J. Zürcher is Professor of Turkish Studies at the University of Leiden and the author of *Turkey: A Modern History*, *The Young Turk Legacy and Nation Building: From the Ottoman Empire to Atatürk's Turkey* and the editor of *Arming the State: Military Conscription in the Middle East and Central Asia, 1775–1925* (all published by I.B.Tauris & Co. Ltd).

Men of Order
Authoritarian Modernization under Ataturk and Reza Shah

Touraj Atabaki and Erik J. Zürcher

I.B. TAURIS
LONDON · NEW YORK

New paperback edition published in 2017 by
I.B.Tauris & Co. Ltd
London • New York
www.ibtauris.com

First published in hardback in 2004 by I.B.Tauris & Co. Ltd

Copyright © 2004 Touraj Atabaki and Erik J. Zürcher

The right of Touraj Atabaki and Erik J. Zürcher to be identified as the editors of this work has been asserted by the editors in accordance with the Copyright, Designs and Patents Act 1988.

All rights reserved. Except for brief quotations in a review, this book, or any part thereof, may not be reproduced, stored in or introduced into a retrieval system, or transmitted, in any form or by any means, electronic, mechanical, photocopying, recording or otherwise, without the prior written permission of the publisher.

Original cover design by Brian Roberts.

References to websites were correct at the time of writing.

ISBN:	978 1 78453 706 7
eISBN:	978 0 85773 207 1
ePDF:	978 0 85771 469 5

A full CIP record for this book is available from the British Library
A full CIP record is available from the Library of Congress

Library of Congress Catalog Card Number: available

Contents

	Introduction	1
I	State and Society under Reza Shah	13
II	The Caliphate, the Clerics and Republicanism in Turkey and Iran *Some Comparative Remarks*	44
III	New Iran and the Dissolution of Party Politics under Reza Shah	65
IV	Institution Building in the Kemalist Republic: The Role of the People's Party	98
V	Some Views on the Turkish Single-Party Regime During the İnönü Period (1938–45)	113
VI	The Army, Civil Society and the State in Iran: 1921–26	130
VII	The Army and the Founding of the Turkish Republic	164
VIII	Dress Codes for Men in Turkey and Iran	209
IX	Language Reform in Turkey and Iran	238
X	Putting the Record Straight: Vosuq al-Dowleh's Foreign Policy in 1918/19	260
	Index	283

Introduction

Touraj Atabaki and Erik Jan Zürcher

For more than two hundred years the model of European modernity has been perceived in non-European societies such as Turkey and Iran as the exclusive model for adopting modernisation. Although from the start of the twentieth century onwards, Japan has been an inspiring example of how a non-Western country can 'catch up with the West' and even beat it, its influence as a model has remained limited indeed. To become modern was to have a strong, centralised state, on the model of post-Napoleonic France, based on an industrial society. However, the majority of those endeavouring to implement a European process of modernisation in their own societies had only an indistinct vision of modernisation and the course it had taken while being established in Europe. The majority of Persian and Ottoman enlightened circles, both inside and outside the establishment, neither had an inclusive perception of European modernity nor the means to enable them to implement those indispensable changes, which in Europe transformed a traditional, rural and agrarian society into an urban, secular and industrial one.

The age of modernity in Europe began with a new era in which the basic unit in the structures of modern society was the individual rather than, as with agrarian or peasant society, the group or community. Conveniently, the individualism that was embodied in the liberty and autonomy of the individual provided a new definition embracing the new association between the individual and the polity. According to this new association, the individual in a modern society, in principle at least, was not any more the subject and agent of a particular king or priest, sultan, shah or sheikh, endowed with divine or prescriptive authority. The individual rather acted according to rational and impersonal precepts formulated in laws. The investiture of new juridical and political rights, including the right of representation, was indeed the conclusion of this new association.

The emerging commercial and industrial urban middle class was inextricably linked to this individualism.

However, if in European society the process of modernisation was associated with the gradual development and expansion of critical reason compiled by the gradual embodiment of individual autonomy, and with the emergence of a civil society, in Ottoman Turkey and Iran the reverse was true. There, modernisation was embraced by an intelligentsia made up of bureaucrats and military officers, who identified their own interests with those of the state. The emerging commercial and industrial bourgeoisie, composed overwhelmingly of members of non-Muslim minorities, who enjoyed foreign protection, was increasingly seen as alien and eventually as a threat to the survival of the state. Consequently, the rights of the individual and his relationship with the state were of marginal rather than central significance in the eyes of Middle Eastern modernisers, and critical reason and individual autonomy seemed to have little relevance. The main reason for such discrepancy lay in the fact that the development of modern European societies was synchronised with and benefited from the age of European colonialism and imperialism and wars against the Orient. Modernisation in the Middle East was a defensive reaction.

In 1774, following the six-year Russo-Turkish War of 1768–74, the Ottomans defeated by the Tsarist Empire signed the treaty of Küçük Kaynarca, which in addition to territorial loss provided a pretext for future Russian intervention in the internal affairs of the Ottoman Empire. An attempt by the Ottomans to reverse their fortunes in a second war of 1787–92 ended in disaster and the conquest of Egypt by General Bonaparte's expeditionary force in 1798, was another humiliation for the empire. Similarly, in the two successive treaties of Gulestan (1813) and Turkmanchay (1828), which were imposed on Iran following its defeat in a long-lasting war with Russia, Tsarist interests became an enduring component in any social development, as well as in the political reorganisation of Iran. It was indeed in reaction to these humiliating treaties that the call for change and reform was first heard both in Ottoman Turkey and Iran. The fact that an Ottoman officer of Albanian extraction, Mehmed Ali Pasha, managed to grab power in Egypt after the defeat of the French, and subsequently monopolised the resources of the country so successfully that he could build the first modern army of the Middle East and conquer most of the Arab lands, served as an example of what could be achieved by the imposition of European models.

Although the original motive for the reforms was undoubtedly the desire to build an efficient European-style army, the modernisation process soon spread well beyond purely military affairs. The rebuilding of the army brought with it a need for an effective centralised monopoly of power, for the development of new skills, for more efficient extraction of surplus resources, for population censuses and land registration. By the middle of the nineteenth century increasing attention was being paid to the legal and political structures that underpinned the military and economic power of the European states. In both countries there were groups of enlightened individuals who, inspired by a complex conjunction of social egalitarianism, liberalism and romantic nationalism, strove to import and implement European rules and laws in order to resist the colonial and imperialist pressure from outside, as well as the centrifugal forces within their ethnically mixed states. For them, as Nipperdey correctly points out, romantic territorial nationalism provided the driving force for political action: 'cultural identity with its claims for what ought to be, demanded political consequences: a common state, the only context in which they [the people] could develop, the only force that could protect them and the only real possibility for integrating individuals into a nation'.[1]

The long-lasting endeavours of this group of intelligentsia have been well recorded in many chronicles written on the history of both these countries. However, one should realise that what was common amongst these intelligentsia, both inside as well as outside the ruling establishment, was indeed their search for a rather swift remedy to solve their countries' escalating problems. There was a real sense of urgency to their debates and what mattered, was, to use the oft-quoted Young Turk dictum: 'How can the state be saved?', not any utopian vision for society. From the 1860s onwards, the modernist intellectuals by and large supported the call for the establishment of parliamentary and constitutional rule in their respective countries, but it is no exaggeration to say that for them, constitution and parliament were a *means* to further the modernisation process by making the subjects into stakeholding citizens, rather than an *end* in themselves. This helps to explain why, when faced with the choice between strong government and swift reforms on the one hand, or, on the other, broader political freedoms that could benefit the opponents of reform, as in the Ottoman Empire after 1913 and in Turkey and Iran from 1925 onwards, most intellectuals tended to support the former.

The fact that the modernists saw in an enlightened intelligentsia, which availed itself of the power of the state machinery to push through reforms, as the only possible engine of change meant that ultimately many of them were prone to accept the view that only the ruling institutions coordinated by a potent and persuasive leader were able to instigate the overall needed change and reform in order to modernise the society. Although there were some unsuccessful attempts to initiate change and reform from below, the majority of enlightened individuals, both in Ottoman Turkey and Iran – even those who were known as outspoken critics of the establishment – were convinced that in a world divided amongst the colonial powers, each intent on expanding its realm, any attempt of examining change and reform from below tended to undermine the country's integrity and sovereignty.

It is highly significant that those members of the intelligentsia – an increasingly large group – who actually went to Europe as students, refugees or political activists or, most commonly, a combination of these, felt attracted by authoritarian ideologies of the political right. This had several reasons. Firstly, the fact that leading positivists had quite a high opinion of Islam as a religion, which was supposed to be much less opposed to 'reason' and 'science' than Christianity, was of course attractive to Muslim intellectuals. Secondly, the emphasis put by positivists on orderly progress in a regimented society, in which each professional group was assigned a place, tallied rather well with traditional Middle Eastern views on social organisation. Thirdly, the positivist vision of a society led by an aristocracy of the mind, by 'enlightened men', naturally appealed to those who were both servants of the state (and nearly all Ottoman and Persian intellectuals made their living in the service of the state) and members of the intelligentsia.

By the end of the nineteenth century, when Ottoman and Persian intellectuals (and young members of the Muslim elites of Russia) were frequenting the salons and cafes of Paris, positivism, although originally an idealistic ideology, had merged with Büchnerian biological materialism to produce a mindset that can best be called 'scientism': an unshakeable belief in progress through science (witness Atatürk's later dictum that 'the only true spiritual guide in life is science'). Darwinism and also social Darwinism were very much part of this mindset.

Although the Middle Eastern intellectuals of the late nineteenth century, with very few exceptions (such as the Ottoman sociologist Mehmet Ziya Gökalp), were eclectic rather than systematic and picked up fragments from many different European thinkers (Comte, Spencer, Darwin, Büchner, Tönnies, Renan and Durkheim among others), the one that stands out was the 'father of crowd psychology', Gustave LeBon. LeBon, who was recognised as their source of inspiration both by the founders of the *Action Française* and by Benito Mussolini, was immensely popular among younger military officers, not only in France, but in the Balkans and the Middle East. His works were translated into Arabic and Turkish and gained wide circulation. What attracted the Middle Eastern intellectuals who read him, was not only LeBon's popularised positivism and scientism, but also his authoritarian slant. A deep distrust of the 'crowd' (*foule*), of the 'masses', became part and parcel of the thinking of Ottoman and Iranian reformers, and the resistance they encountered when they tried to implement their modernisation programme, for instance in the counter-revolution in Istanbul in 1909, the anti-republican insurgence in Tehran in 1924, the Kurdish insurrection in 1925, or the 'Menemen incident' of 1930, tended to confirm their suspicions.

The practice of authoritarian modernisation in post-World War I Turkey and Iran was embedded in the perceived failure of the earlier attempts to introduce modernisation, both from below as well as above, in their two neighbouring countries. After all, the efforts of the nineteenth century and early twentieth century reformers had not protected these countries either from the separatism of minorities or from occupation by European powers. The setback that the Iranian constitutional movement (1905–11) suffered in the years before the outbreak of World War I, the political disintegration and partial occupation of Persia during the war; the traumatic loss of the European provinces of the Ottoman Empire in the Balkan War and its subsequent defeat in the war; the threat of imminent disintegration after the war: all of these left the middle classes and the intelligentsia in these countries with no other option than to look for a *man of order*, who, as agent of the nation, would install a centralised, powerful (though not necessarily despotic) government that would be capable of solving the country's growing problems of underdevelopment, while at the same time safeguarding its unity and sovereignty.

Whereas social egalitarianism, liberalism and romantic territorial nationalism had inspired the earlier generations of intellectuals in their efforts at initiating change and reform throughout the country, for the intelligentsia of the post-war world – who were more preoccupied with the ideas of modern and centralised state building – political authoritarianism, linguistic and cultural nationalism became the indispensable driving force in accomplishing their aspirations.

Despite the diversity of their political views, what singled them out from the previous educated or learned individuals was the model of society that they took for granted. The European model presupposed a coherent society, which by definition was organised around the distinctive concepts of *nation* and *state*. They were convinced that only a strong centralised government would be capable of implementing reform, while preserving the nation's territorial integrity. Likewise, they believed that modernisation and modern state building in Turkey and Iran would require a low degree of cultural diversity and a high degree of ethnic homogeneity. Along with ethnic and linguistic diversity, the existence of classes, too, was rejected. In Turkey, the ideas on 'solidarism' (*tesanütçülük*) of the Young Turk period eventually evolved into the 'Populism' (*halkçılık*) that became one of the pillars of the programme of Atatürk's ruling party. Only when the country fulfilled the preconditions for a nation-state as defined by the nationalists, when 'empirically almost all the residents of a state identify with the one subjective idea of the nation, and that nation is virtually contiguous'[2], could they realistically cherish hopes of safeguarding territorial integrity and gaining a respected place in the world. Some even argued that *Muasirlaşma* (in Turkish) or *Emrouzi budan* (in Persian), which meant being contemporary, or modernised, was attainable only by an 'ideal dictator' who, by retaining power and concentrating his political authority through 'banning the press, dismissing the parliament, and restricting the power of the clerics, sets up the country for a social revolution'.[3] In the societies where the exercise of arbitrary rule had a long record, it was not surprising that such calls soon found adherents, although it has to be said that there were always those among the modernist intelligentsia who rejected this solution. Critical journalists like Hüseyin Cahit in Turkey, for instance, saw in the emerging dictatorship of Mustafa Kemal Pasha in the mid-1920s a repeat of the authoritarian (and ultimately disastrous) policies of the wartime leader Enver Pasha, but these were exceptions. In Iran it was Mosaddeq who, during a session of the Iranian parliament in October 1925, warned the deputies in the following words:

> Today you Deputies of the Majles wish to make Sardar-e Sepah, Reza Khan, a King. The honourable gentleman is now not only Prime Minster, but Minster of War and Commander-in-Chief of the armed forces as well. Today our country, after twenty years of widespread bloodshed, is about to enter a phase of retrogression. One and the same person as king, as Prime Minster, as Minister of War, as Commander-in-Chief? Even in Zanzibar no such state of affairs exists![4]

Mustafa Kemal and Reza Shah's policy of centralising government power and implementing modernisation in Turkey and Iran was in a sense a reaction to this widely felt need for authoritarian reform. The process of political and cultural centralisation, which was flavoured with secularism, Westernism and meritocratism, generally enjoyed the support of many members of the intelligentsia, especially those with progressive and left-wing leanings. The Persian periodicals such as *Kaveh* (1916–22), *Farangestan* (1924–25), *Iranshahr* (1922–27), and *Ayandeh* (1925–26), which dominated the ideological environment of the time, were pioneers in publicising and promoting these policies. Kazemzadeh argued in an editorial that by getting rid of religious superstitions, by the separation of religion and the state, and by accepting religious principles in accordance with the parameters of modern society, a society should be liberated from the yoke of the clerics.[5] Taqizadeh, the editor of *Kaveh*, believed that salvation from long-lasting misery is only possible by blind submission to the Western civilisation: 'Iran must outwardly as well as inwardly, physically as well as mentally be westernised'[6]:

> By absolute submission to Europe, through adaptation and promotion of European civilization, with no reservation and condition one could hope that our country would eventually become prosperous.[7]

The editor of *Ayandeh*, Afshar, in an editorial entitled *Gozashteh – Emruz – Ayandeh* (Past – Present – Future), after expressing his concern for Iranian unity, displays his perception of modernisation in the following terms:

> What I mean by the national unity of Iran is a political, cultural and social unity of the people who live within the present day boundaries of Iran. This unity includes two other concepts, namely, the maintenance of political independence and the geographical integrity of Iran. However, achieving national unity means that the Persian language must be established throughout the whole country, that regional differences in clothing, customs and such like must disappear, and that *moluk ot-tavayef* (the local chieftains) must be eliminated. Kurds, Lors, Quashqa'is, Arabs, Turks, Turkmen, etc., shall not differ from one another by wearing different clothes or by speaking a different language. In my opinion, until national unity is achieved in Iran, with regard to customs, clothing, and so forth, the possibility of our political independence and geographical integrity being endangered will always remain.[8]

And by way of eliminating ethnic divisions and fostering national unity, he adds:

> Thousands of low-priced attractive books and treatises in the Persian language must be distributed throughout the country, especially in Azerbaijan and Khuzestan. Little by little the means of publishing small, inexpensive newspapers locally in the national language in the most remote parts of the country must be provided. All this requires assistance from the state and should be carried out according to an orderly plan. Certain Persian speaking tribes could be sent to the regions where a foreign language is spoken, and settled there, while the tribes of that region, which speak a foreign language, could be transferred and settled in Persian speaking areas. Geographical names in foreign languages or any souvenirs of the marauding and raids of Genghiz Khan and Tamurlane should be replaced by Persian names. The country should be divided from an administrative point of view if the goal of national unity is to be achieved.[9]

In the same manner, the famous reforms of Atatürk in the 1920s and 1930s, the adoption of European family law, clock and calendar, measures and weights, clothing and alphabet, as well as suppression of religious orders and shrines, had all been proposed long before he came to power. Two influences were paramount in the case of Kemalist Turkey: that of the Turkists and that of the Westernists. The most prominent Turkist ideologist was Mehmet Ziya Gökalp. Basing himself on German romantic nationalist thinkers in this, Gökalp made a distinction between an original Turkish culture (*hars*), an organic set of customs, values and beliefs transmitted within the family, and a consciously acquired Islamic (and partly Byzantine) civilisation (*medeniyet*). He advocated strengthening Turkish culture, while simultaneously exchanging the 'outmoded' and 'sterile' Islamic civilisation for the contemporary European one. Gökalp's anticlericalism (which was shared by almost all Young Turk thinkers) and his ideas on the Turkification of religion and language were certainly influential, but it goes too far to designate him as the sole spiritual father of the Kemalist reform programme. In many ways Mustafa Kemal Atatürk went farther than Gökalp (who died in 1924) and came closer to the ideas of the Westernists (*garbcılar*), a small group of Young Turk intellectuals who had rejected the dichotomy of culture and civilisation and advocated adoption of a completely European lifestyle, down to the wearing of hats and a prohibition of the veil. Atatürk's view that there was only one world civilisation – the European one – and that it had to be accepted lock, stock and barrel if Turkey was to survive in the modern world echoed the ideas of the Westernists. Thus, long before Atatürk and Reza Shah attained power, the blueprint for their future programme of reforms and changes throughout the country was there.

During his 20-year rule (1921–41) Reza Shah carried out with remarkable consistency most of the demands voiced by such intellectuals as Kazemzadeh, Taqizadeh and Afshar. His policy of authoritarian modernisation gradually changed the traditional social, as well as political, setting of Iran. New institutions such as a national standing army, a national monetary system and a secular educational curriculum were founded and even the judicial system was secularised. Moreover, to achieve greater national uniformity, the policy of centralisation that included such harsh and disruptive measures as transferring tens of thousands of nomads and forcing them to settle on the land was pursued. Atatürk, of course, had an incomparable advantage where the process of state building was concerned. The creation of a national standing army of conscripts, a national monetary system, a nationwide communication network of railways and telegraph lines, a large and self-confident bureaucracy and a secular judicial system (except for family law) had all been achieved in the nineteenth and very early twentieth centuries. Under the republic, this heritage was built on and the authority of the state was extended (primarily through the Gendarmerie) to every corner of the territory, but it remains true that, where Reza Shah had to build a state, Atatürk, during his 15-year rule (1923–38) could transform an existing one.

We should not, however, allow ourselves to think that because these two reforming dictators drew on the ideas of a number of leading modernist intellectuals, they were merely executing their prescripts. Academics, journalists and writers were there to be used for a purpose – to feed the leaders with ideas (as during Atatürk's famous all-night drinking bouts, where the problems as well as the future of the country were constantly debated) or to spread their messages. Those who were too independent-minded soon found themselves ostracised. Increasingly, Atatürk and Reza Shah relied on a younger generation of intellectuals who owed their position to a regime. If in Atatürk's Turkey losing favour usually meant isolation, surveillance and the need to find a job outside the educational system or the media, in Reza's Iran the situation was different. Within a couple of years of his accession, Reza Shah's dictatorship was evolving into autocracy and soon afterward it turned into arbitrary rule. While some intellectuals were forced to accept political retirement, others were imprisoned or executed. Only a few could find shelter in exile and were therefore unable to witness the fulfilment of their aspirations.

It is in this gradual transition, first to autocracy and then to arbitrary rule, that the major difference between the developments in the two countries can be found. There can be no doubt that Atatürk was a dictator. After 1928 he distanced himself more and more from daily politics, concentrating instead on the great 'modernisation campaigns', but he remained very much in control, appointing and dismissing members of parliament and cabinet ministers at will (and sometimes without informing the prime minister). From 1926 onwards, with the appearance of the first statues of Atatürk in Turkey, a personality cult was developed around him and grew increasingly extreme. Nevertheless, Atatürk left the political institutions – the national assembly, the party – sufficiently alone to

INTRODUCTION   11

allow them to develop a solid identity. This allowed his regime to be institutionalised to the extent that it could continue without major difficulties after his death. In contrast to Atatürk's performance in Turkey, it was the development of arbitrary rule that gradually alienated Reza Shah from his earlier urban social bases. Fascinated by technological aspects of modernisation, Reza Shah left no room for society or for his own supporters to enjoy practising rationalism, critical reasoning and individualism.

The contributions to this volume were accomplished, with some exceptions, as a result of a workshop on 'Authoritarian Modernization in Turkey and Iran', which we organised at the International Institute of Social History in the spring of 1999. By pursuing this project, it was intended to have a comparative, contrasting and inclusive historical study of modernisation in the post-World War I Turkey and Iran. Hence, Touraj Atabaki in 'The Caliphate, the Clerics and Republicanism in Turkey and Iran' examines the impediments facing two authoritarian rulers in Turkey and Iran in consolidating their rule. Homa Katouzian, in his chapter on 'State and Society under Reza Shah', observes the gradual change in rulership of Reza Shah from a dictatorship to an arbitrary rule. The study of political parties and party politics in Turkey and Iran is the subject of Erik-Jan Zürcher's chapter on 'Institution Building in the Kemalist Republic', of Matthew Elliot's 'New Iran and the Dissolution of Party Politics under Reza Shah' and of Cemil Koçak's essay on 'Some Views on the Turkish Single-Party Regime during the İnönü Period'. Cultural innovations are the subject of chapters by Houchang Chehabi and John Perry. In 'Dress Codes for Men in Turkey and Iran', Chehabi compares the attitudes of the Turkish and Iranian regimes in adopting European traditions and codes, while Perry contrasts Mustafa Kemal and Reza Shah's endeavours in 'Language Reform in Turkey and Iran'. The building of new social institutions such as an army, and its accommodation in Turkey and Iran, is the premise of Stephanie Cronin's chapter on 'The Army, Civil Society and the State in Iran' and of the late and lamented Dankwart Rustow's on 'The Army and the Foundation of the Turkish Republic'.

Rustow's chapter is a reprint of his classic article of 1959. It became obsolete almost immediately after its first appearance, as his main thesis was that in Turkey, unlike the Arab countries, the army had been successfully disengaged from the political leadership and was therefore unlikely to interfere in politics. The *coup d'état* of

27 May 1960 of course put paid to that notion, but Rostow constructed his argument on the basis of an analysis of the historical role of the Ottoman army, or rather its officer corps, in the establishment of the Turkish Republic; this is still extremely informative and offers a good basis for comparison with the Iranian case.

Finally, Oliver Bast in his chapter on the Iranian statesman, Vosuq al-Dowleh, examines the background of Iran's foreign-policy making in the post-World War I period.

It is hoped that, taken together, these texts will allow the reader to 'compare and contrast' the developments in Iran and Turkey after World War I. The model of authoritarian development strategy put into practice by Atatürk and Reza Shah has not, so far, been the object of a great deal of comparative analysis, and that is a pity. The regimes of these reforming generals can be seen as a unique mixture between the nineteenth-century tradition of the 'reforming pasha' (which started with Egypt's Mehmet Ali) on the one hand and the more modern European (particularly Mediterranean) dictatorships of the inter-war period on the other. Understanding the way Atatürk and Reza Shah shaped their respective states and societies is essential for an understanding of the different ways in which the two countries developed after World War II.

Notes

[1] Nipperdey, T., 'In Search of Identity: Romantic Nationalism, its Intellectual, Political and Social Background', in Eade, J. C. (ed.), *Romantic Nationalism in Europe*, Australian National University, 1983, p. 11.

[2] Linz, J. J. and Stepan, A., *Problems of Democratic Transition and Consolidation, Southern Europe, South America, and Post-Communist Europe*, Johns Hopkins University Press, London, 1996, p. 25.

[3] *Farangestan*, 1924, nos. 4 and 5.

[4] From a speech by Musaddeq during a session of the parliament, concerning the change of dynasty, 31 October 1925.

[5] *Iranshahr*, 1923, no. 1.

[6] *Kaveh*, 1920, no. 1.

[7] Ibid.

[8] Mahmoud Afshar, 'Aghaz-nameh', *Ayandeh*, 1925, no. 1.

[9] Ibid., p. 6.

CHAPTER I
State and Society under Reza Shah
Homa Katouzian

Society *versus* the state

Before the Constitutional Revolution, Iran had been run by arbitrary rule. This was not just another variant of absolute or despotic government, as it is known from European history. First, arbitrary rule had been the normal (and was seen as the natural and inviolable) form of government in Iran throughout its history, whereas absolutism reigned for a maximum of four centuries, for the European continent taken as a whole. The second and much more important difference between the two systems was that the absolutist state depended on the propertied and influential classes and was (therefore) bound by a certain legal framework, whereas the arbitrary state was independent from all social classes, standing not just at the head but above the society. Hence its will was not limited by any inviolable law or tradition, but merely by the extent of its physical power, which varied – sometimes drastically – in different circumstances. In other words, the state was able to do whatever it willed, including the arbitrary destruction and confiscation of the life and property of the highest men in the land, so long as it had the physical power to do it. This was well beyond the reach of even the strongest absolutist rulers of Western and Central Europe. The Russian Tsars were more powerful than they were, but even they did not and could not rule arbitrarily.

Because European rulers and states had had a social base, representing the important social classes, their revolutions were therefore revolts of the lower and less privileged parts of the society against their ruling classes. On the other hand, because the state in Iran was apart from the society, that is, was not based on any of the social classes, Iranian revolts had been rebellions of the society (*mellat*) against the state (*dowlat*) itself. They were led against an 'unjust' arbitrary ruler in the hope of replacing him with a 'just' one. When successful, the collapse of the state had invariably led to destructive conflict, disorder and chaos until a new arbitrary rule was established. This led to the cycle of 'arbitrary rule–chaos–arbitrary rule'.

In the latter half of the nineteenth century, acquaintance with European society suggested the value of a political system based in law as opposed to arbitrary rule. Therefore, for the first time in Iranian history, the Constitutional Revolution – while still being a revolt of the whole of the society against the state – was aimed, not just against an unjust arbitrary ruler, but at the destruction of the ancient arbitrary rule itself and its replacement by lawful government. It ended by establishing a constitution, which, besides providing a legal basis for the state, created parliamentary government along basic democratic principles.

Ideally, this might have resulted in the formation of a new state representing an extensive social base. Yet the radically new situation had no cultural roots, and the ancient traditions of chaos resulting from the fall of the state were as strong as ever. Therefore, the teens of the last century, which followed the victory of the revolution, witnessed growing destructive conflict both at the centre and in the provinces. It almost looked as if the country would disintegrate, as it had done after the fall of the Safavid state in the eighteenth century. Foreign intervention and occupation during the First World War encouraged the chaotic trends, but domestic factors had been independently at work, and had their roots in the long Iranian tradition of disorder following upheaval.

Thus, although the foreign factor was important especially during the war, the pattern was familiar, and the domestic forces needed little encouragement to engage in destructive conflict, which both created and perpetuated chaos. It is very important to note that – contrary to common belief – these conflicts were not just nomadic, ethnic and regional; they existed right at the centre, in the Majlis, among the factions and parties, and within the ranks of the competing political magnates. Indeed, had there not been such rift and chaos at the very centre of politics, it is unlikely that such powerful centrifugal forces would have been released, or been so effective, in the provinces. For it is characteristic of the country's history that whoever has the centre also has the periphery.[1]

Shortly before the end of the war, Vosuq al-Dowleh formed a ministry with active British support. Almost all the leading politicians felt the need for a strong government that would organise a unified army, reorganise the country's financial system and stamp out disorder. Some of them were opposed to Vosuq, but Vosuq had his own personal supporters within the political hierarchy, by far the most effective and influential among whom was Sayyed Hasan Modarres.[2]

In his first year of office, Vosuq managed to bring some order to government and administration. These measures did not change the hearts of his radical opponents, but they did tend to soften the attitude of some of his critics among popular politicians and moderate constitutionalists. During the same year, he and his two closest allies within the cabinet negotiated the Anglo-Iranian agreement, which was signed in Tehran in August 1919. Both inside and outside the country, the Agreement was denounced as an instrument for turning Iran into a British protectorate, and was rejected by the political public with growing resentment and vehemence. Even Modarres went over to the opposition.[3]

The Agreement had been the brainchild of Lord Curzon and the Foreign Office alone. Moreover, it had met with strong opposition from the government of India, the India Office, the Treasury and the War Office, the first two being opposed to extensive British involvement in Iran, while the latter two were wary of its financial and military implications. The document that finally came into being was the result of much debate and disagreement, and took considerable account of the British critics of Curzon's policy. Nevertheless, India maintained its opposition, and the other departments returned to their critical position as soon as the Agreement faced serious trouble.

It was not so much the text of the Agreement that led to the stormy reaction against it, but the secret manner (on which Curzon and Cox had insisted) of conducting the negotiations. Curzon managed even to exclude the official Iranian delegation from the Paris peace conference, and to keep France and America more or less in the dark about the negotiations in Tehran. Rumours (later confirmed) that British money had been paid to help smooth the Agreement's passage made matters much worse.

When the Agreement was announced, Bolshevik Russia – which had hitherto issued several unilateral declarations of the abrogation of Tsarist privileges in Iran – violently denounced it. This was enough to seal the opposition of Iranian radicals to it. But the strongly worded public attack by the United States, and the campaign against it by the French press, left little doubt in the minds of even most of the moderates that the country had been 'sold out to Britain'.[4] This encouraged another upsurge of Kuchik Khan's Jangal campaign, which, however, was driven back by a combined operation of Iranian Cossacks and the British Norperforce (North Persia Force) with its headquarters at Qazvin. Yet Vosuq followed this by an appeasement policy and, for a while, a permanent settlement between the government and the Jangalis looked likely. The policy had been largely encouraged by the fact that Iranian Bolsheviks both in the Caucasus and in Iranian Azerbaijan were making friendly overtures to Kuchik and his men, while the attitude of Colonel Staroselsky, the Russian chief of the Iranian Cossacks, was far from reassuring.[5]

The fear of a Bolshevik thrust across the frontier was indeed growing by the day. Vosuq and Firuz wisely thought of talking directly to Moscow, but – while stressing that he would not veto such a move – Curzon effectively stopped it. He did, however, support (and even help) their decision to recognise the newly formed non-Bolshevik Republic of Azerbaijan (formerly Russian Transcaucasus), and send an official delegation – led by Sayyed Zia – for a trade and cultural agreement. By the beginnings of April 1920, when the draft agreement reached Tehran, Shaikh Mohammad Khiyabani led his successful revolt in Tabriz. Three weeks later, the Azerbaijan Republic fell to the local Bolsheviks. On 18 May, a Russian fleet landed at Enzeli, and the Norperforce units retreated to Rasht. A few days later, Norperforce received orders from London to retreat further to their base at Qazvin. On 4 June, Kuchik entered Rasht and, together with Iranian Bolsheviks and their Soviet advisers, declared the Soviet Socialist Republic of Iran and a coalition government headed by himself.

Vosuq resigned and, in July 1920, Moshir al-Dowleh, a popular constitutionalist, became prime minister. He declared the Agreement as being in abeyance, and persuaded Kuchik to part company with the Gilan Bolsheviks. Soon after, he sent Mokhber al-Saltaneh to Azerbaijan as governor-general, and this quickly led to the downfall of Khiyabani and his revolt. At the same time he sent a large force of Iranian Cossacks, led by their Russian commander, Colonel Staroselsky, to fight the Gilan Bolsheviks. At first they had a lightning success, but later suffered a major setback. However, before they could mount a counterattack, Staroselsky was dismissed by the Shah under strong pressure from General Ironside – the newly arrived

GCO of Norperforce – and Herman Norman, the British minister in Tehran. The decision having been taken against Moshir's advice, he resigned, and early in November Sepahdar-e A'zam (Fathollh Khan Akbar) formed a cabinet.

By January 1921 there were genuine fears of a successful attack by the Gilan Bolsheviks on Tehran. These fears were shared both by the Shah and his government and by the British legation and the Foreign Office, to the extent that various contingency plans, particularly that of moving the capital to Isfahan or Shiraz, were discussed. Meanwhile, the government was in even more dire financial straits than before, and chaos everywhere had reached its highest level. Sayyed Zia, together with a couple of Gendarme officers, collaborated with Ironside and a couple of other British officers and diplomats to organise a coup by bringing 2,000 Cossacks from Qazvin to Tehran. They chose Reza Khan as their commander, although at least one other candidate had been approached before him and had turned it down.

The coup took place on 21 February 1921. Sayyed Zia became prime minister and Reza Khan commander of the Cossacks, although shortly afterwards he took over the ministry of war and, not long afterwards, the Gendarmerie as well. The British legation supported Sayyed Zia and tried to convince Lord Curzon and the Foreign Office to approve their policy. Curzon, however, rejected such pleas with contempt, for a number of reasons, not least because the Sayyed had formally abolished the 1919 Agreement. Given that Sayyed Zia had imprisoned, offended and alienated large numbers of the notables, once the Shah, who intensely disliked the Sayyed, and Reza Khan, who wanted him out of the way, realised that he did not have British backing, he had no base or power on which to depend. He was dismissed and sent into exile just over three months after the coup.

State *versus* society

The period 1921–25 was a period of dual sovereignty and power struggle between the three main political trends in the country: (a) the forces of chaos; (b) their antithesis, those of dictatorship, and later arbitrary government; (c) the constitutionalists, both conservative and democratic, who wished to have order without arbitrary rule but did not know how to achieve it, and quarrelled too much among themselves. But given the fact that they, and the classes they represented, were also wholly in favour of ending the chaos, it was relatively easy, once there was the will – of which Reza Khan had plenty – and the military instrument, which he quickly created. In 1926, there was dictatorship within a broadly constitutional framework. By 1931 there was arbitrary rule.

What is remarkable, and true to the pattern of Iranian history, is the speed with which chaos was turned into subjection. It had been a feature of Iran's arbitrary society that an arbitrary regime that one day seemed to be eternal could be overthrown the next day, if for some reason the public felt that it had lost its grip. By the same logic, a state of chaos that might have persisted even for decades could be ended almost abruptly, once the will was there to end it. Shah Isma'il I, Shah Abbas I, Nader Shah and Aqa Mohammad Khan were welcomed when they stamped out chaos, at least for a while.

Chaos in most regions and provinces came to an end even before Reza Khan became Shah. The further, relatively minor, rebellions that surged up in the first couple of years following his coronation were more often products of a backlash against the arbitrariness with which Reza Khan's army divisions behaved towards nomads, ethnic communities and provincial magnates. Yet in the first couple of years, not only the ruthless suppression of rebellion and brigandry, but also the subjugation of regional magnates and notables was very popular, at least with the urban public.

The matter was very urgent, hence it was the only achievement of Reza Khan that was acknowledged and admired by friend and foe alike. In the constituent assembly of December 1925 that made him Shah, Solaiman Mirza, the Socialist leader, mentioned Reza Khan's 'services in stamping out the *Moluk al-Tavayifi* system, his centralisation of power, destruction of rebels and those who did not recognise the central power . . .'[6]

Earlier, Taqizadeh had said – in his speech in the Majlis against the motion for making Reza Khan temporary head of state – that his most important reason for supporting Reza Khan as prime minister was 'the security which he has created'.[7] But, Mosaddeq who delivered the longest and most impassioned speech against Reza Khan becoming Shah (arguing that it would result in dictatorship) went much further:

> I doubt if there is anyone who is unaware of the services that [Reza Khan] has rendered to the country. The situation in this

country was such that, as we all know, if someone wished to travel he did not have security, and if someone was a landlord he had no security, and if he had an estate, he had to employ a few riflemen to protect his produce . . . And, for the sake of protecting my own home, my own family and my own people, I naturally wish to see the man called Reza Khan Pahlavi to be prime minister in this country. Because I wish to see security and stability; and it is true that – in the past couple of years – because of that man we have had such a thing, and so we have been able to get on with public works, and serving the interest of the society . . . And thank God that, due to the blessing of his being, we would now like to get on with some fundamental work . . .[8]

There certainly was some criticism of the attempt by provincial army divisions to dominate provincial life completely, but these were few and usually muted. The credit was given to Reza Khan for stamping out the chaos, which might have cost the country's integrity in the absence of an alternative way of dealing with it. Indeed, as Mosaddeq implied in the above-quoted speech, it was the rapid and successful ending of chaos that provided the basis for a steady increase in trade, and higher public and private investment and growth, just as had happened when the Qajars had stamped out several decades of chaos at the end of the eighteenth century.

Premiership and campaign for presidency

It took only two years and a few months, from June 1921 to November 1923, for Reza Khan to become prime minister in addition to minister of war and chief of the army. What happened in-between was typical of the politics of chaos. There were no fewer than five ministries, even though many of the constitutionalist politicians – both conservative and popular – were becoming increasingly alarmed at the rising autonomy of Sardar Sepah and his army.

The traditional politicians were still busy wearing each other out, and accusing one another of being some foreign power's agent, reactionary, Bolshevik, atheist, etc., almost all of which appellations were either untrue or highly exaggerated. This increased the conviction of the younger nationalists and modernists that they were utterly incapable of improving the country's situation. On the other hand,

Reza Khan was deeply engaged in creating his army, and using ever-increasing funds, both legally and illegally, to extend and improve its numbers, weaponry, organisation and training. At the same time, he cultivated friendship with all types of politicians, posed as an honest broker in politics and made himself look indispensable as the keeper of order and stability.

He also established excellent relations with foreign envoys, but especially with the British minister, Loraine, who thought he was indispensable for ending the chaos; and the Soviet ministers, Rotstein and Shumiyatsky, who saw Reza Khan as a 'bourgeois nationalist' leader trying to put down 'feudal reactionaries', most of whom were also 'agents of imperialism'. Reza Khan was able to manipulate many on the road to power. The fact that he managed to obtain Soviet and British sympathy or acquiescence is one of the most notable examples of his extremely rich talent for underhanded diplomacy.[9]

In November 1923 Reza Khan replaced Moshir al-Dowleh as prime minister. He brought down Moshir's government, and negotiated his own premiership, at a single stroke by bringing criminal charges against Qavam al-Saltaneh, who was his most serious rival. I have discussed the charge against Qavam elsewhere and it is now virtually impossible to know the truth. What is clear, however, is that it was used, if not designed, to bring down Moshir's government, to drive Qavam out of the country and to make Reza Khan prime minister.[10] Yet he had considerable support among the modern middle-class elite, including the Young Iran Club, which had been set up by foreign-educated young men such as Dr Ali Akbar Siyasi and Dr Mahmud Afshar. Ali Akbar Davar, the able and honest future minister of justice and finance, who in 1937 took his own life under pressure from Reza Shah, was openly advocating the need for a dictatorship in his newspaper. Leading younger journalists such as Zainol'abedin Rahnama joined Reza Khan's campaign. Together with a newly set-up group, Independent Democrats of Iran (known in the Majlis as the Tajaddod faction), led by Sayyid Mohammad Tadayyon, they began to advocate the change of regime to a republic, and obtained the support of Solaiman Mirza's Socialists as well.[11]

The campaign collapsed largely because the campaigners were in too much of a hurry, and partly because Modarres played his hands astutely. The Shah had become increasingly unpopular, especially after his recent journey to Europe, commonly being described as

'Ahmad the Wondering Trader' (*Ahmad-e Allaf*). There was an upsurge of his popularity as a result of these events. Seizing the moment, he sent a telegram to the Majlis that he no longer had confidence in Reza Khan, and sought their advice for a new government. Reza Khan resigned and went to one of his estates near Damavand.[12] The Independent Democrat group (the Tajaddod faction of the Majlis) issued dire statements that the country would be lost without Reza Khan.[13] Ali Dashti wrote a leading article in his newspaper entitled 'the country's father has gone'.[14]

Reza Khan's generals in the provinces began to issue threatening statements, with two of them – Ahmad Aqa and Hossein Aqa – openly threatening that they would march on Tehran. The Tajaddod, Socialist and other factions, who now made up the Majlis majority, voted for Reza Khan to return, and sent a top-heavy delegation, including Mostawfi al-Mamalek, Moshir al-Dowleh, Solaiman Mirza and Mosaddeq, to bring him back with ceremony.[15]

Reza Khan returned. As it happened, the great *ulema* – for example, Hajj Mirza Hossein Na'ini and Sayyed Abolhasan Isfahani – who had been recently exiled from the *atabat*, had just been allowed to return to Iraq. Reza Khan rushed to Qom to see them off, and they advised him to abandon the republican campaign, because they had been alarmed by developments in Turkey under Atatürk. That he did, and redoubled efforts to look like the defender of the faith by organising official religious congregations, and personally leading various processions in the annual mourning for the martyrs of Karbela. He was duly rewarded by the religious establishment, who not only sent gifts from the treasury of the sacred shrines to be publicly and ceremoniously delivered to him,[16] but also acquiesced in his elevation when he made a bid to become Shah and to establish his own dynasty.

Modarres was still leading the Majlis opposition. Popular and respected constitutionalists like Mostawfi al-Mamalek, Moshir al-Dowleh, Mosaddeq – known in the Majlis as the Independents – had so far avoided open opposition to Reza Khan, although there is contemporary evidence that they were far from happy with the prospect of military dictatorship and disruption of lawful government. But the Majlis was now solidly in Reza Khan's hands, largely because of the efficient manipulations of Davar, Taimurtash and Firuz.

The fall of the Qajars

As the summer of 1925 began, it looked as if there were no further impediments to Reza Khan's elevation to the supreme position in the land. Meanwhile, all the main Majlis factions other than the Modarres group and the Independents had been brought into line by the new triumvirate, which on 31 October 1925 made Reza Khan 'temporary head of state', pending the decision of a constituent assembly to be elected forthwith. Both the Soviet and British envoys thought that it might still be the first step towards the declaration of a republic.[17]

The Majils decision had strong backing from nationalists (to be distinguished from democratic patriots such as Mosaddeq), modernists and Socialists, and among the army and the higher civil service. The religious establishment neither campaigned for it nor opposed it, and a significant number of the *ulema* voted later in the constituent assembly. Only Modarres and four of the Independents, including Taqizadeh and Mosaddeq, opposed the original vote in the Majlis, others of their kind preferring to stay away or defect.[18]

It is difficult to know how widely the event had been supported among the general public at the time. But in the elections for the sixth Majlis only the Tehran elections (held in June 1926) were free, and not a single deputy who had voted for the change of dynasty was elected – not even Solaiman Mirza, a long-standing darling of the Tehran electorate. Instead, they elected those, like Modarres, Mosaddeq and Taqizadeh, who had formally opposed it, and others, like Mostawfi al-Mamalek, Moshir al-Dowleh and Mo'tamen al-Molk, who were known to have been opposed to it.[19]

The response in the provinces was far from enthusiastic. The British legation had remained neutral throughout, and had instructed their provincial consulates to do the same. Nevertheless, they had asked the consulates to send reports of the public response to the great change. There were 13 reports altogether. In Isfahan, 'Population apparently entirely disinterested'. In Mashad, there was little enthusiasm for the celebrations, and the public regarded the change of dynasty 'as a British triumph and Russian defeat'. In Tabriz, there was indifference by mass of the population. In Shiraz, a 'chilly reception', the people saying that the telegrams sent earlier to demand the change of dynasty were the 'work of a small clique'. In Kerman, 'no one dared express any unfavourable opinion', though they thought it was the Qajar's own fault, but were apprehensive at 'further strengthening of military power'. In Rasht, there was 'no excitement', in Bushire, quiet dissent, while in Yazd, the change 'appears to be popular'. Only in Sistan was the news received 'with every expression of rejoicing on the part of military and civilian'.[20] The light-hearted folk in Tehran almost took it as a joke, singing, 'that which they've put on your head, they've just been pulling your leg'.[21] On the whole, it appears that the ordinary people did not regret the fall of the Qajars, but neither did they view the rise of the new dynasty with enthusiasm.

This was the moment at which Reza Shah enjoyed the broadest social base ever of his career between 1921 and 1941. And relative to Iranian circumstances and traditions, the state and society had reached a certain equilibrium that could have prevented chaos without, at the same time resulting in a complete monopoly of power. No wonder that there was neither much hostility towards nor great enthusiasm for the new state by the society. In fact, the Shah's social base was even stronger than it would appear from the spontaneous responses of the ordinary people. As in similar situations anywhere, it was the influential classes and groups of society that mattered most.

Reza Khan had beaten all opposition on the way to becoming Shah. He was in direct control of the army that had been largely his own creation, and enjoyed its complete loyalty. He had a majority in the Majlis and most of the journalists on his side, and the support of many of them was still genuine. Many, if not most, middle- and upper-class young people were looking forward to a period of peace, prosperity and modernisation. He was almost idolised by most of the young and foreign-educated men, like those who had set up the Young Iran Club, but who were quickly advised by himself to close it down, since he himself would implement their ideas.[22] Of even more practical importance was the admiration, support, good will – or at least acquiescence or submission – of large sections of almost every establishment and elite of the society, including some leading Qajar noblemen.

Iranians, like many other people, are good at jumping on the bandwagon. Yet in the case of Reza Khan there was no sudden conversion on the part of large numbers of people. It was a relatively slow process, not so much among 'the masses', or even the urban crowds, but the politically intelligent public. And it was largely due to his establishment of peace in the country, and the prospect of modernisation, plus the glaring absence of a real alternative for a strong, stable and modernising government.

The most informative single document regarding Reza Shah's position among the commanding heights of the society at the time of his accession is the proceedings of the constituent assembly: voting was secret, yet no one voted against the motion for the change of dynasty. Among members of the Assembly there were many of the important *ulema*, both from Tehran and the provinces. Imam Jom'eh-yi Kho'i, Hajj Aqa Jamal Isfahani and Sayyed Mohammad Behbahani did not attend the meetings regularly and did not participate in the voting. Others, such as Ayatollh-zadeh-ye Khorasani, Ayatollah-zadeh-ye Shirazi, the Imam Jom'eh of Shiraz and Sayyed Abolqasem Kashani attended more regularly, and most of them were present at the time of voting. Kashani was quite active in the discussions.

Leading and influential merchants were also present. They included Hajj Mohammad Hossein Amin al-Zarb and Hajj Mohammad Taqi Bonakdar, who had played such important roles in the Constitutional Revolution. Apart from Solaiman Mirza, there were other old radical Democrats in the Assembly. Sadeq Sadeq (Mostashar al-Dowleh II) was elected chairman. Another member was Hajj Mohammad Ali Badamchi, one of the two or three closest lieutenants of Khiyabani and a leading figure in his revolt.[23] Another constitutionalist figure was Mirza Mahdi Malekzadeh, son of the famous Malek al-Motekallemin, the leading constitutionalist preacher who had been executed on Mohammad Ali Shah's orders after his coup against the Majlis.

Two well-known and active members of Sayyed Zia's Committee of Iron – Soltan Mohammad Khan Ameri and Adl al-Molk (Hossein Dadgar), both of whom had later been included in Zia's small cabinet – were among the constituents. So were some of those who had recently defected from the camp of Modarres, including Shokrollah Khan Qavam al-Dowleh, Mirza Hashem Ashtiyani and Sayyed Abolhasan Hayerizadeh.

Landlords and provincial magnates included Qavam al-Molk-e Shirazi, Sadrdar Fakher (Reza Hekmat), Moshar al-Dowleh (Nezam al-Din Hekmat), Ali Asghar Hekmat, Mortezaqoli Khan Bayat, Mohammad Khan Mo'azzami, Lotfollah Liqvani and Mohammad Vali Khan Asadi (Mesbah al-Saltaneh), who was very close to Amir Shawkat al-Molk (Ibrahim Alam) and was to be executed in 1935 on charges of fomenting the revolt in Mashad against the enforcement of the European bowler hat (see below).

The religious minorities were represented by well-known figures such as Arbab Kaikhosraw (Zorastrian), Alex Aqaian and Aleksandr Tomaniantz (Christian), and Hayem, the Jewish deputy and community leader who was later to be executed on the Shah's order for unknown reasons.

There were more than 270 representatives, and therefore many of the old pro-Reza Khan activists were there. Davar, Taimurtash the Bahrami brothers, Rafi', Tadayyon, Sayyed Ya'qub (Anvar), Rahnama, his brother Reza Tajaddod and others.[24] Never before or since could Reza Shah claim such a broad support among the country's various influential elites. It would not be misplaced to compare the event with the assembly in the Moghan Steppe 190 years before, which legitimised Nader Shah's accession to the throne.

When, in November 1925, the Majlis was considering the removal of the Qajars and election of Reza Khan to the status of Shah, pending the decision of the constituent assembly, Lancelot Oliphant, no doubt echoing the view of many a European observer, could not believe that it would be easy for such a 'usurper' to get away with it. He wrote in some minutes:

> It is difficult for anyone who remembers the old regime to believe that the old princes and their supporters can tamely accept such a usurper. Even if it appears to work at first it will be surprising if a reaction does not follow . . . There are difficult times ahead.[25]

These words do not reflect opposition by Oliphant to the change – although neither do they reflect support for it – since the British government was neutral in the matter. They reflect, rather, the experience of European society and history, where there was a *continuous, long-term* aristocracy, which was not only independent from the state, but the state tended to depend on it and on other influential classes. And a society where legitimacy, based on a traditional line of descent and acknowledged by those important classes, was necessary for a new monarch, or a new monarchy, to succeed.

This was absent from the arbitrary state and society in Iran, and the existing nobility and hierarchy at any time was quite aware of the rules of the game and of the transient nature of their positions, both as individuals and as a collective body. Certainly, there could be no resistance on grounds of dynastic legitimacy, as it is known from the experience of Europe. In any case, an Iranian ruler, even one who had succeeded as 'legitimately' as possible, would in fact himself build up his own power and thereby his own legitimacy. That is why, far from resisting the accession of Reza Shah, some of Oliphant's 'old princes' actively campaigned for it, and others submitted stoically, if not humbly.

This was therefore never a serious cause of lack of legitimacy for Reza Shah. The later jibes at his being 'the son of a stable boy', or in Bahar's angry verse, having come from 'the depth of the stable' – which in any case was an exaggeration about the Shah's relatively humble origins – was a sign of his unpopularity, that is, a sign of his losing what legitimacy he had made for himself, in very traditional Iranian style, in the earlier years of his career.

Indeed, the later attack on Reza Shah's legitimacy was much more potent when the vast majority of all colours and creeds firmly, although incorrectly, believed that he was no more than a paid agent of British imperialism. But even that belief, the conviction with which it was held and the vehemence by which it was used to condemn him, was largely due to the extreme unpopularity that resulted from his arbitrary and harsh rule in the 1930s.

From the moment of the 1921 coup, many, if not most, influential people thought that Britain had organised it (although, as noted above, while the British government had not been involved in it at all, some individual British officers and diplomats in Iran had been). Indeed, the matter was apparently so well known, and regarded with such equanimity at the time, that Reza Khan himself once told a few important politicians – including Mostawfi al-Mamalek, Moshir al-Dowleh, Taqizadeh, Mosaddeq and Dawlat-Abadi – that 'the British brought me'. And he added, either that 'I nevertheless served the country', or that 'they did not know whom they were dealing with', phrases whose basic meanings are quite similar.[26] Understandably, he too believed that the British government had been involved in the coup. But, if anything, this confirms the view that the British involvement – even if, as he and the others believed, it had been due to a long-term plan by the British government – was far from proof for Reza Khan's lack of legitimacy in 1923–24, when he was reaching the height of his success with large numbers of the political elite and modern intelligentsia.

It was his growingly autocratic, and then arbitrary – as well as harsh – rule, which later made this the most important weapon for denying any legitimacy for him, and arguing that all of his positive achievements, too, had been carried out on orders from Britain, because somehow they were in British interests. The best example cited by those who believed Reza Shah was a British agent was the 1933 oil agreement that he concluded. But that too, as has been shown by this author, was fundamentally a product of arbitrary government.[27]

The rise of autocracy

We now come to the second phase, the phase of autocracy. By the end of 1925, the life of the Majlis had come to an end, and Forughi had been holding the fort as acting prime minister while the constituent assembly put the ceremonial touches on the change of dynasty. Now Modarres thought of establishing a dialogue with the new Shah. He still had considerable popular following and carried a good deal of weight within the political establishment. There is no record of the negotiations, although Loraine was of the opinion that the Shah had abolished the office of military governor of Tehran 'under pressure from Modarres'.[28] The evidence strongly suggests that Modarres was hoping for a settlement whereby the Shah would have the army and security forces as well as a considerable amount of say in civil administration, but would leave some real role for political pundits in the Majlis.

The two men decided on a cabinet headed by Mostawfi al-Mamalek. The two most important appointments were those of Vosuq as minister of finance and Taqizadeh as minister of foreign affairs, but the latter declined the offer. Mostawfi was reluctant to accept office, and he told Mokhber al-Saltaneh that Modarres had pressured him to co-operate.[29] According to Bahar, Modarres had told them that they had done what they could, and 'now we should go along with the Shah and the [new] state, hoping they would serve the country'. 'And that is exactly what happened', adds Bahar, 'and we gave up our opposition' to the new regime.[30]

Mosaddeq did not accept this argument. He declined Mostawfi's offer of the post of foreign minister, saying that it was not possible to work with the Shah.[31] In the following Majlis debate, Modarres showed that he had been party to a deal. He said, in reply to

Mosaddeq's attack on the new cabinet because of its inclusion of Vosuq and Foroughi:

> After all that has happened we would like to use these men in the service of the country. After all this chaos [*enqelabat*] we would like to use them to do important things.

Then, in a brief diversion, he revealed the logic of his new policy towards the Shah:

> If I could manage to serve a *constitutional* monarch I would do it; if not [i.e., if he was not constitutional] I would fight him. Today our agenda is the constitution. We should [all] act according to that . . . And the constitution is our [ultimate] ruler and must be applied without exception [emphasis added].[32]

The attempt by Modarres to reach a compromise with the Shah, principled though it was, cost him much popularity. In twentieth-century Iranian politics, compromise (*sazesh*) was at best seen as 'collaborationism', and at worst as a 'sell-out'.

Mostawfi's new cabinet had been introduced to the Majlis in September when the above speeches were made. By November, Nicolson, then British chargé in Tehran, reporting the terrorist attempt on Modarres's life to Chamberlain, said that Modarres, having lost much popularity because of his rapprochement with the Shah, had lately become popular again since he had said that government must be constitutional:

> I have already, in my despatch of 10th September last, indicated how *the 6th Majlis had reacted against the supremacy of Modarres imagining that he was but an agent of the Shah*. The former has of late succeeded in retaining a large portion of his influence by adopting an arrogantly domocratic [sic] attitude and in a recent speech he stated baldly that he for his part would only support the Shah so long as His Majesty acted constitutionally [emphasis added].[33]

It was in October 1926, shortly after delivering that speech, that Modarres survived the gun attack by three assassins one early morning when he was going to teach at the Sephsalar College. There was popular outcry, and in the Majlis friend as well as foe condemned the attempt, although few would have imagined that it had been made without the Shah's knowledge and approval. Nevertheless, the cooperation of Modarres with the government continued until Mostawfi finally resigned – as he had already tried to, a couple of times earlier – in May 1927. Mostawfi met with Mosaddeq shortly after his resignation and told him that he had advised Mokhber al-Saltaneh, his successor, to be careful not to be humiliated even more than he himself had been.[34]

The strategy of Modarres failed because the Shah did not keep his end of the bargain. It is clear, at least with hindsight, that if the Shah could not reach a *modus operandi* with a self-respecting but flexible and disinterested Mostawfi as prime minister, there could be little hope for anyone else. The popular constitutionalists were thus quickly eliminated as a group. Then came the turn of the loyal politicians.

From dictatorship to arbitrary rule (1930–41)

Within a couple of years of his accession, the Shah's dictatorship was turning into autocracy, and soon afterwards into arbitrary rule. It was this that robbed him of his not very widespread, but important and influential, social base, which was comparable to that of Atatürk at the time and to that of Franco in Spain later. In the earlier phase there was, so to speak, a bridge between the state and the society, which maintained the personal loyalty of ministers and other officials while at the same time making them responsible as members of the executive. Atatürk never lost legitimacy, at least in his own constituency and among the secular, modernist or modernising strata of Turkish society, however critical some of them may have become of some of his policies. Reza Shah's position was quite comparable to this at the beginning of his reign, but a few years later he began to lose it when he moved from the position of an authoritarian dictator to that of an absolute and arbitrary ruler. The change was therefore absolutely crucial. Arbitrary rule and harsh behaviour undid even his useful contributions to stability and modernisation.

During the rise of dictatorship, which dated back to Reza Khan's premiership, there had of course been growing deviations from some basic tenets of the country's constitution. But government was still constitutional *in so far as it was not purely personal*, and there still was a considerable amount of ministerial discretion and parliamentary argument, checks and balances. This, after all, is what distinguishes a dictatorship, even an autocracy, from arbitrary government.

There had been arbitrary behaviour, especially in the regions and provinces, in the earlier period. But it had not been systematic, and had not begun to spread to the centre before the seventh Majlis. Mokhber al-Saltaneh (Hedayat) who was Reza Shah's prime minister for more than six years, and was by no means a hostile critic, wrote in his memoirs about the years beginning in 1929:

> In this period the [parliamentary] immunity of some Majlis deputies – Javad Emami, Esma'il Araqi, E'tesamzadeh and Reza Rafi [all of them old pro-Reza campaigners] – was withdrawn [and so they went to jail]. The minute anyone so much as mentioned the Shah's name they would grab him and ask him what he meant. Sometimes they would make up a story for it, and this would help to line up the pockets of agents of the police . . . *We have reached the point that the Shah expects to be worshipped* [emphasis added].[35]

He went on to say, about ministerial power and responsibility in a system of absolute rule:

> Under [Reza Shah] Pahlavi, no one had any independent power. Every business had to be reported to the Shah, and every order issued by him had to be carried out. Unless there is some degree of independence, responsibility would be meaningless . . . and no statesman would be left with a will of his own.[36]

In 1929, Firuz, who was minister of finance, was suddenly and inexplicably arrested while he was leaving a public gathering side by side with the Shah himself. The fall of Firuz was the first ominous sign that thenceforth no one was immune from arbitrary arrest. The fall and then the murder in jail of Taimurtash in 1933 made that fact clear and unexceptionable. Sardar As'ad quickly followed him both in prison and in death. It was no longer even felt that a sham trial was necessary. When, early in 1937, Davar committed suicide for fear of a similar fate (Firuz had been rearrested shortly before, and was to be killed shortly after) hardly anyone of any past stature and independence was left in the government and at the court.[37] Many other faithful defenders and leading pillars of the Pahlavi regime were killed, disgraced, jailed and/or banished, for example, Abdolhosin Diba Mohammad Vali Khan Asadi, Forughi, Taqizadeh, Farajollh Bahrami (Dabir-e A'zam), Hossein Dadgar (Adl al-Molk), Brigadier Mohammad Dargahi, General Habibollah Shaibani and General Amanollh Jahanbani, the brothers Rahnama and Tajaddod, and so on.

The alienation of the loyal politicians and administrative elite was mirrored by the alienation of the social classes. By the late 1920s hardly any trace had been left of nomadic rebellion and brigandry, and, moreover, the nomads had been largely disarmed. It was precisely after such pacification that extreme force was used to break up tribes and 'settle' them in strange environments, which often led to large-scale deaths in the process. Those in charge of such operations looked upon the nomads almost in the same way that many American whites viewed native Americans in the nineteenth century. Soltan Ali Soltani, who had been a Majlis deputy for Behbahan, for many years under Reza Shah, said in a long speech, a couple of months after the Shah's abdication:

> The Qahsqa'i, Bakhtiyari, Kuhgiluya and other nomads ... not only has their property been looted, but group after group of these tribes have been executed without trial. Only in one case they killed several groups of [Kuhgiluyeh nomads] whom they failed to find guilty in military courts, claiming that they were trying to escape ... They killed 97 of the Bahrami tribe ... in one day, including a thirteen year old boy, and they jailed four hundred of them in Ahvaz, of whom three hundred lost their lives. They brought khans of the Boyr Ahmad to Tehran with pledge of immunity, and then killed them saying they were rebels ... The way they settled the tribes was the way of execution and annihilation, not education and reform. And it is precisely this approach that has sapped the strength of the Iranian society and weakened the hope of national unity.[38]

Sawlat al-Dowleh, paramount chief of the Qashqa'is, and his son Naser, were jailed in Tehran, and the former died or was killed in jail in the 1930s. Speaking of Sawlat al-Dowleh, the Shah had told

Taqizadeh that 'these people must be destroyed (*ma'dum shavand*)'.³⁹ Several of Bakhtiyari leaders were killed or imprisoned, along with other leaders from the Khamaseh federation of the Fars nomads, and others from elsewhere. When the Shah left the country, almost all of those nomads who had survived the ordeal went back to their former way of life, and many of them adopted an angry, vengeful and rebellious attitude towards the state.

Private property, especially in land, was once again weakened in economic and, perforce, political terms similar to the old arbitrary tradition. While land was now registered according to the new law of property registration, in practice both the Shah and the army could confiscate, or buy by force at nominal prices, agricultural and other property. When the Shah left the country, he owned about 10 per cent of the agricultural estates, but since these were of the highest quality, their value and annual income was much greater than 10 per cent of the total.

Landlords were also alienated, because the state monopoly of trade in important commodities such as wheat was against their interest as well as that of the peasants, and because they had lost much political power even in their own provinces. Merchants were angry generally because of the ever-increasing *étatisme* and economic interventionism, and especially because of the trade monopoly acts of 1931 and 1932, which made all foreign and some of the most important domestic trade a state monopoly. Ali Dashti, who was a Majlis deputy at the time of abdication, said in a long speech, while the Shah was still in the country:

> The right of private property is one of the oldest and most noble rights in civilised societies. But it was violated in these last twenty years to the utmost limit . . . They have taken the people's property by force and it must be returned to them . . . What is surprising is that this violation of property was done by government departments as well . . . What then is the difference between a highwayman and a department of the state?

Regarding the state monopolies, he went on to say:

> [I]t is twenty years now that we have intervened in the economy in the most ignorant manner, and every child realises that, in

our hands, the merchants' wealth was destroyed, the country's treasury and everything [else] was ruined.[40]

No doubt there was some exaggeration in all this, but it does reflect the losses borne by landlords and merchants and, moreover, the anger and alienation that arbitrary rule had created in their midst.

The attack on the religious community, especially the enforced changing of men's hats to the European bowler hat, and the enforced prohibition of not only the *chador*, but also scarves, aroused very strong feelings among the public. Abdollah Mostawfi, a modern and secular high bureaucrat of the period, who defends Reza Shah on many grounds, nevertheless disowns what he describes as Reza Shah's attack on religion.[41]

Until the late 1930s it was strictly a matter of social propriety for all men, regardless of rank and class, to cover their heads in public, as well as indoors on formal occasions. At the beginning of Reza Shah's rule a hat fashioned after his own military cap (which had been adapted from the French military kepi and police cap) became in vogue among politicians and state officials, and was compulsory among military officers. This was later made compulsory for all men, and the compulsion was, on the whole, taken with good humour. The officially registered and recognised *ulema* and preachers could still wear the turban.

Suddenly, in the summer of 1935, the Shah ordered all men to wear the bowler hat, which was European *par excellence*, and which no one except for a few had even seen before. There was revulsion, and the non-violent resistance in Mashad was put down by bloodshed, followed by the execution of Asadi, the trustee of Imam Reza's shrine, an office that was in the Shah's gift. Asadi's sons were married to the daughters of Forughi and Amir Shokat al-Molk 'Alam. Forughi's mediation to save his life led to his own dismissal and disgrace.

Here may be noted an example of the important distinction between dictatorship, even autocracy, and arbitrary rule, in that it is very difficult to imagine that even Hitler's or Stalin's regime would have suddenly ordered all the men to wear top hats (let alone the Chinese hat) from the following day.

Mokhber al-Saltaneh, the former prime minister, still had occasional private audiences with the Shah. On one such occasion following the change of hats, the Shah revealed his real motive for this compulsory order to Iranian men:

In an audience, the Shah took my [bowler] hat off and said, Now what do you think of this. I said it certainly protects one from the sun and rain, but that [Pahlavi] hat which we had before had a better name. Agitated, His Majesty paced up and down and said, *All I am trying to do is for us to look like [the Europeans] so they would not laugh at us.* I replied that no doubt he had thought this to be expedient, but said to myself, It is what is under the hat, and irrelevant emulations, which they laugh at [emphasis added].[42]

This explains the most important motive for the compulsory removal of women's *chadors* as well as scarves a few months afterwards. Women were ordered to take off their *chadors*, without being allowed to wear a scarf instead. The effect on most women – almost all those above the age of 40 – was as if European women had been suddenly ordered to go topless in the streets in 1936. The subject of removing the *chador* was not new. All modern, and some not so modern, intellectuals had been campaigning for permission and protection of its *voluntary* removal for one or two decades, but they had not dreamed of forcing all women to remove it, without even the right to wear a scarf.

Only imported European hats were allowed, which only upper-class women had both the means and culture to wear. One major problem for most urban women was that they simply lacked the sartorial experience of appearing in public without a bodily cover, and in any case buying hats was very expensive for them at the time. They also lacked the culture of a public hairdo and, apart from that, would have felt much less embarrassed if they could cover their hair with a scarf.

Compulsory district parties were ordered to which men had to bring their wives without the *chador*. Scarves were torn off women's heads by the police in the streets and alleys. There was much social and cultural violence and some suicides. Many women simply stopped going out of their homes, only once a week going out covertly to go to the public bath through the connected flat roofs of the houses in most Tehran districts at the time. The result was that, outside the modern middle-class women, almost all put their *chadors* back on after the Shah's abdication.[43]

Literary and cultural progress, which had begun before the Constitutional Revolution and had continued since through the works of poets such as Bahar, Iraj, Aref and Eshqi, prose and fiction writers like Dehkhuda, Jamalzadeh, San'ati-zadeh and Moshfeq Kazemi, and scholars such as Qazvini, the Forughi brothers (Mohammad Ali and Abolhasan), Tonokaboni and Taqavi, was further stimulated – especially among the young modern elite – by the stability and optimism of the mid-1920s.

But while higher education expanded, the University of Tehran was founded in 1933 and traditional scholarship was to continue openly, creative and critical work – even though it was not critical of the regime – began to dry up from the early 1930s. Hedayat wrote his first work (in Paris in 1929) and continued writing and publishing fiction and other literary works, although he did so at his own expense. But in 1935 he had to give a written pledge to the censors to stop publishing altogether. It was shortly after this that he went to Bombay, staying there as long as he could and returning with great reluctance. While he was there, he reproduced in 50 copies his handwritten new novel, *The Blind Owl*, sending most of them to Jamalzadeh in Switzerland to distribute among their Iranian friends abroad. Remarkably, this first 'edition' of the best Persian novel of the century carried the notice, 'The publication and sale of this book in Iran is forbidden', so that if a copy of it somehow fell into the hands of the censors the author would not be persecuted for having published again. He wrote other stories that were published in the collection of short stories, *Sag-e Velgard* (*Stary Dog*) after the Shah's abdication. It included the short story, 'The Patriot', which is a scathing attack on the Shah and the new official literary chiefs, and containing a devastating mockery of official cultural propaganda, especially the proceedings of Farahangestan, the official academy.[44]

This academy had been set up to replace foreign, particularly Arabic, loan words by largely invented words of Persian origins, which were then sent to the royal court for the Shah's approval before it became mandatory to use them. This offended the sensibilities, not only of young critics such as Hedayat (he was to publish his ridiculing review of one of its volumes after the Abdication), but also of established and loyal literati like Taqizadeh and Ali Asghar Hekamat, the minister of education himself! It was at the latter's suggestion that Taqizadeh sent an article from Berlin, mildly critical of the academy's proceedings, which threw the Shah into such a rage that made Taqizadeh vow never to return to Iran as long as the Shah was in power.[45]

Of the leading poets and writers of the 1920s, Eshqi was assassinated by agents of the police while Reza Khan was still prime minister.[46] Abolqasem Lahuti had led a revolt of the Gendarme's in Tabriz, in 1923, on the failure of which he had fled across the border to the Soviet Union, eventually ending his days in Tajikistan.[47] Iraj died of natural causes also in the 1920s.[48] Aref, who had conducted a very effective campaign for Reza Khan and against the Qajars, died in depression and destitution in a village near Hamadan in 1933,[49] and Farrokhi Yazdi, who decided to cooperate with the regime and even became a Majlis deputy at one stage, spent many years in jail, where he died or was killed in 1939.[50]

Bahar was arrested and banished several times, for no obvious reason and despite the fact that he had given up all political activity. An important result of this was his long *mathnavi*, *Karnama-ye Zendan* (*Life in Prison*), which was to remain unpublished until the 1950s. So were many other poems that he wrote against the Shah and the regime, although – after he wrote and published a panegyric for the Shah and was finally released from banishment – he occasionally wrote and published panegyrics in praise of the Shah and his achievements to ensure his own freedom.[51]

Jamalzadeh virtually ceased to publish any more fiction until 1941, after his most successful *Yeki Bud va Yeki Nabud*. Nima Yushij also virtually ceased to publish poetry in the period, although he was not naturally much inclined to publish his works even in better times. Apart from Hedayat, of the younger writers who emerged in the early 1930s, Bozorg Alavi stopped publishing about 1935, and went to jail early in 1937 as a member of the well-known young and modern-educated 53 prisoners, who were arrested on the charge of belonging to a Marxist organisation. While in jail, Alavi wrote – secretly, on scrap wrapping paper – his next collection of short stories, *Prison Scrap-notes* (*Varaq-pareh-ha-ye Zendan*), which was published after the Shah's abdication, when he was released from jail.[52]

In fact, there had been no organisation at all, and most of the young prisoners had barely heard of Marxism, although many were converted to it after they were condemned as Marxists. Their leader, Taqi Arani, who had been a romantic nationalist in the 1920s – he had even written a long poem about 'the motherland' – had now become an intellectual Marxist, even though he had no political affiliation.[53]

This was the process whereby the society (*mellat*) was completely alienated from the state (*dowlat*) during the latter phase of Reza Shah's rule. The state then stood above and apart from the society much more than it had been under Naser al-Din Shah. Although such total, absolute and arbitrary rule had existed in the past, it was without the benefit of modern military weaponry and technology, roads and railways.

The fall of Reza Shah

The Shah, as we saw, started in 1926 with considerable political legitimacy and a firm, although not popular, social base, when he had the explicit or tacit approval of the commanding heights of the society. At that time, his opposition among the political establishment and the modern middle classes had dwindled to a relatively small number of politicians and intellectuals, who were particularly concerned about the likelihood of the return of arbitrary government.

But for all the reasons discussed above, which were, indeed, largely the result of the restoration of arbitrary state in modern form, by the time the Allies invaded Iran in 1941 the Shah was virtually isolated. He did not have the approval of any of the social classes and communities as such; almost all of them had turned against him long before, and sought his downfall.

Furthermore, there were very few men of any real standing, either civilian or military, who were genuinely committed to him and his rule. Abbasquli Golsha'iyan, who had been a successful high official under Reza Shah and was an important minister during the allied invasion of 1941, wrote in his diaries *at the time* that men like himself had been worried that the Shah would fall by assassination. It is clear that their concern was about the ensuing absolute chaos and also their own fate; as Golsha'iyan wrote, almost joyfully, they could not have anticipated his fall by foreign invasion:

> Thus was the fall of Reza Shah Pahlavi, and so ended the worry everyone had as to what would happen to the country after Reza Shah's death. Since no one anticipated his abdication. And – given the way he ruled – they expected that, if he did not die of natural causes, he would certainly be killed. But he would have fallen one way or another, and the country would have faced terrible chaos and revolution, except in this way

[i.e., an abdication enforced by the Allies] which was outside everyone's imagination.[54]

It is also clear that the Shah would not have had to abdicate had the state and society not fallen apart so much by that time. Indeed, all the evidence shows that his abdication was the one event following the occupation of Iran that the vast majority of the people welcomed. The people's great fear of him suddenly gave way to relief, ridicule, abuse and a desire for vengeance. It would have been very difficult to keep him on the throne even if the Allies had wished to. The public outcry against him was very strong indeed. Neither the loyal Forughi nor the Majlis deputies believed that the Shah would keep to a promise to observe constitutional government, and many of them feared that they would pay for their reformist demands handsomely the minute he was in a position to renege on his commitment.[55]

Apart from that, it would not have been possible for the Shah to try and play the role of the constitutional monarch under the Allies' watchful eyes (even if he had wanted to), because of the irresistible pressure for the rectification of the injustices committed, which directly implicated him. If the Allies had tried to keep him on by sheer force, they would have earned the double hatred of the people both for invading the country and keeping Reza Shah as their ruler.

It is therefore clear that the Shah's abdication was not inevitable, that is, he would not have had to abdicate had he enjoyed a certain amount of political legitimacy and a reasonable social base among his own people, especially as by then he had offered full cooperation to the Allies, who were physically present to ensure that he would keep his word.

It was noted at the outset that, according to the general pattern of major change in Iranian history, the fall of an arbitrary state is followed by chaos. Its most recent occurrence had been during and after the Constitutional Revolution, which had led to great popular disappointment in constitutionalism, and thus to a generally welcome reception for the 1921 coup and its aftermath. This pattern was repeated again in the 1940s, with chaotic and disintegrative trends appearing, once again, both in the centre of politics and in the provinces. If it was significantly less marked, this was, *inter alia*, largely due to the physical presence and later the considerable influence of the Allies in the country. Therefore, again true to the pattern, many – especially among the political establishment and modern middle classes – began to feel and even to express nostalgia for Reza Shah's rule after a few years. The pattern was familiar from the long history of Iran, and was to be repeated in comparable forms later in the twentieth century.

The whole experience proved, although not quite for the last time, that the integration of the state with the society and, with it, a *lasting* stability, development and accumulation for the people of Iran would not be possible under arbitrary rule or, even more obviously, under chaos (the other side of the coin), each of which, from the sociological viewpoint, has justified the return of the other throughout Iran's long history.

Notes

[1] For an analysis of the Constitutional Revolution, see Homa Katouzian, 'Liberty and Licence in the Constitutional Revolution of Iran', *Journal of the Royal Asiatic Society, Series 3*, 8, 2, 1998. For the theory of arbitrary rule, see Homa Katouzian, 'Arbitrary Rule: A Comparative Theory of State, Politics and Society in Iran', *British Journal of Middle Eastern Studies*, 24, 1997: 49–73; idem, 'Problems of Political Development in Iran: Democracy, Dictatorship or Arbitrary Government?', *BJMS*, 22, 1995: 5–20; idem, 'The Aridisolatic Society, A Model of Long Term Social and Economic Development in Iran', *International Journal of Middle East Studies*, July 1983: 259–81; idem, *The Political Economy of Modern Iran*, London and New York: Macmillan and New York University Press, 1980, chs. 1–4; idem, 'Nationalist Trends in Iran, 1921–1926', *IJMES*, November 1979. For evidence of rift and chaos after the revolution, see W. J. Olson, *Anglo-Iranian Relations During World War I*, London: Frank Cass, 1984; Ervand Abrahamian, *Iran between Two Revolutions*, Princeton, NJ: Princeton University Press, 1982.

[2] See, for example, Abdollah Mostawfi, *Sharh-e Zendegani-ye Man*, vol. 2, Tehran: Zavvar, 1964; Yahya Dawlat-Abadi, *Hayat-e Yahya*, vols. 3 and 4, Tehran: Attar and Ferdawsi, 1983; Malek al-Sho'ara Bahar, *Tarikh-e Mokhtasar-e Ahzab-e Siyasi dar Iran*, vol. 1, Tehran: Jibi, 1978; Javad Shaikholeslami, *Sima-ye Soltan Ahmad Shah Qajar*, vol. 1, Tehran: Nashr-e Goftar, 1989; Olson, *Anglo-Iranian Relations*.

[3] The references can be numerous. See, for example, the documents in the British Public Record Office files, F.O. 371/3558, F.O. 371/3859, F.O. 371/3860, and *British Documents on Foreign Policy*, vol. iv; William J. Olson, 'The Genesis of the Anglo-Persian Agreement of 1919', in Elie Kedourie and Sylvas G. Haim, eds, *Towards a Modern Iran*, London: Frank Cass, 1980; Shaikholeslami, *Sima-ye . . .* ; Houshang Sabahi, *British Policy in Persia*,

1918–1925, London: Frank Cass, 1990; James Balfour, *Recent Happenings in Persia*, London: Blackwood, 1922.

⁴ See Homa Katouzian, 'The Campaign Against the Anglo-Iranian Agreement of 1919', *British Journal of Middle Eastern Studies*, 25 (1), 1998. Martin Sicker, *The Bear and the Lion, Soviet Imperialism in Iran*, New York: Praeger, 1988; Aryeh Y. Yodfat, *The Soviet Union and Revolutionary Iran*, London: Croom Helm, 1984; *Documents on British Foreign Policy*, vols. iv and xiii.

⁵ See Homa Katouzian, 'The Campaign Against the Anglo-Iranian Agreement of 1919'; and also Ebrahim Fakhra'i, *Sardar-e Jangal*, Tehran: Javidan, 1978; Cosroe Chaqueri, *The Soviet Socialist Republic of Iran: Birth of the Trauma*, Pittsburgh: Pittsburgh University Press, 1995. But for the specific point in hand, see especially Major C. J. Edmonds's reports to Cox for the months of October 1919 to May 1920, The Edmonds Papers, St Antony's College, Oxford.

⁶ Hossein Makki, *Tarikh-e Bistsaleh-e Iran*, Tehran: Elmi, 1995, vol. 3, p. 591.

⁷ See Hossein Makki, *Doktor Mosaddeq va Notq-ha-ye Tarikhi-ye U*, Tehran: Elmi, 1985, p. 130.

⁸ Ibid., p. 139.

⁹ See, for example, Loraine to Curzon, 21/5/23, 23/5/23 and 28/5/23, F.O. 248/1369. Curzon warned Loraine not to be overoptimistic, since he thought that Reza Khan was 'quite capable of talking sweet and acting sour', but Loraine was sure of his view, and expressed it in private letters to friends in England as well; see Gordon Waterfield, *Professional Diplomat, Sir Percy Loraine*. See further, Katouzian, *State and Society in Iran, The Eclipse of the Qajars and the Emergence of the Pahlavis*, London and New York: I. B. Tauris, 2000, chapters 10–11.

¹⁰ See ibid. ch. 10, and Loraine to Curzon, 2/10/23, F.O. 248/1369.

¹¹ See Katouzian, *State and Society*, chapter 10 and the relevant sources therein.

¹² For a humorous and critical, but basically accurate, account in verse of the campaign for a republic see Bahar's long *mosammat*, 'Jomhuri-nameh', which he wrote in the wake of the campaign's collapse, in Mohammad Malekzadeh (ed.), *Divan-e Bahar*, vol. 1, Tehran: Amir Kabir, 1957, pp. 359–66. For Eshqi's several poems against the campaign, which he thought to be a British plot, see *Kolliyat-e Mosavvar-i Eshqi*, ed. Ali Akbar Moshir Salimi, first edition, Tehran: Moshir Salimi, n.d., Books Six and Eight. The full account of the campaign seen as a British plot has been given in the long *mathnavi* on pp. 277–80. For similar poems and articles by Hossein Kuhi Kermani, published in his newspaper *Nasim-e Saba*, see *Bargi as Tarikh-e Iran Ya Ghoghai-ye Jomhuri*, Tehran: Kuhi Kermani, 1952.

¹³ See the full text of the long communiqué in *Reza Shah* (Khaterat-e Solaiman Behbudi . . .) ed, Gholamhossein Mirza Saleh, pp. 498–501.

STATE AND SOCIETY UNDER REZA SHAH   41

[14] Quoted in Poet Laureate Bahar, *Tarikh-e Mokhtasar-e Ahzab-e Siyasi*, vol. 2, Tehran: Amir Kabir, 1984, pp. 667.

[15] See Hossein Makki, *Tarikh-e Bistsaleh*, vol. 2, p. 576.

[16] See, for example, Bahar, *Tarikh-e Mokhtasar*, vol. 2, and Makki, *Tarikh-e Bistsaleh*, vols. 2 and 3. See, in particular, the letter of the famous Marja', Mirza Hossein Na'ini in Makki, vol. 3, p. 46.

[17] 'PERSIA', Foreign Office minutes, 11/11/25, F.O. 371/10840; Katouzian, *Political Economy*, chapter 5.

[18] See Homa Katouzian, *Mudaddiq and the Struggle for Power in Iran*, second paperback edition, 1999, chapter 3, and *State and Society*, chapter 10.

[19] For the list of the new Tehran deputies, see Baqer Aqeli, *Ruzshomar-e Tarikh-e Iran, Az Mashruteh ta Enqelab-e Islami*, Tehran: Nashr-e Goftar, 1995, vol. 1, p. 210.

[20] See 13 consular reports to Loraine, 5–8/11/25, F.O. 248/1372.

[21] It read in the Persian original: 'In keh sarat gozashtan [gozashteh-and] / Sar beh sarat gozashtan [gozashteh-and]'.

[22] See the memoirs of a leading figure among them, Ali Akbar Siyasi, *Gozaresh-e Yek Zendegi*, London: Siyasi, 1988. See also letters by friends to another leading figure, Mahmud Afshar, *Nameh-ha-ye Dustan*, ed. Iraj Afshar, Tehran: Bonyad-i Mawqufat-e Doktor Mahmud Afshar, 1996.

[23] For Badamchi's radical democratic credentials, see, for example, his long article in *Iranshahr*, no. 14, 1926 (special issue on Shaikh Mohammad Khiyabani), reprinted in *Entesharat-e Iranshahr*, Tehran: Eqbal, 1972. See further, Homa Katouzian, 'The Revolt of Shaykh Mohammad Khiyabni', *IRAN* (published by the British Institute for Persian Studies), XXXVII, 1999.

[24] For the complete minutes of the constituent assembly, see Hosin Makki, *Tarikh-e Bistsaleh*, vol. 3, pp. 547–655.

[25] See PERSIA, Foreign Office minutes, 11/11/25, F.O. 371/10840.

[26] This was said in Mosaddeq's house in one of the weekly meetings of Reza Khan and the popular voluntary counsellors (all of them Majlis Independents) whom he had chosen shortly before his final bid to become shah. See Dawlat-Abadi, *Hayat-e Yahya*, vol. 4, p. 343; Mohammad Mosaddeq, *Taqrirat-e Mosaddeq dar Zendan*, Jalil Bozorgmehr/Iraj Afshar (eds), Tehran: Farhang-e Iranzamin, 1980, p. 102. For Reza Khan's regular meetings with his 'special counsellors', see Katouzian, *State and Society*, chapter 10.

[27] See Katouzian, ibid. ch. 11, *Musaddiq*, particularly chapter 3, and *Political Economy*, particularly chapter 7.

[28] Loraine to Chamberlain, 11/3/26, F.O. 371/11481.

[29] See Mokhber al-Saltaneh, *Khaterat va Khatarat*, Tehran: Zavvar, 1964, p. 370.

[30] See Makki, *Tarikh-e Bistsaleh*, vol. 5, pp. 144–45. The whole of Bahar's series of articles in *Khandani-ha* have been reprinted in this source.

[31] See Mohammad Mosaddiq, *Musaddiq's Memoirs*, ed. and intro. Homa Katouzian, tr. S. H. Amin and H. Katouzian, London Jebeh, 1988.
[32] For the full text of Modarres' speech, see Hossein Makki, *Doktor Mosaddeq va Notqha*, pp. 204–5. For a wider discussion of the circumstances, see Homa Katouzian, 'The Campaign Against the Anglo-Iranian Agreement of 1919', *British Journal of Middle Eastern Studies*, 25, 1, 1998, and *State and Society*, chapter 5.
[33] Nicolson to Chamberlain, 4/11/26, F.O. 371/11481.
[34] See Mosaddeq, *Taqrirat-e Mosadde*.
[35] Mokhber al-Saltaneh, *Khaterat va Khatarat*, p. 397, emphasis added.
[36] Ibid., p. 402. See further Homa Katouzian, 'The Pahlavi Regime in Iran', in H. E. Chehabi and Juan J. Linz (eds), *Sultanistic Regimes*, Baltimore and London: Johns Hopkins University Press, 1998.
[37] The sources on these events are numerous. See, for example, 'Taimurtash', 'Davar', 'Amir Tahmasebi' and 'Dashti' in Ebrahim Khajeh Nuri, *Bazigaran-e Asr-e Tala'i*, Tehran: Jibi, 1978 (and 'Amir Khosravi', 'Ayrom', etc, in the first, complete, edition, Tehran, 1942. Iraj Afshar (ed.), *Zendegi-ye Tufani: Khaterat-e Sayyed Hasan Taqizadeh*, Tehran: Elmi, 1993. Nasrollh Saifpur Fatemi, *Ay'ineh-ye Ebrat*, vol. 2, London: Jebheh, 1990. Alireza Arouzi (ed.), *Khaterat-e Abolhasan Ebtehaj*, vol. 1, London: Ebtehaj, 1991. Makki, *Tarikh-e Bistsaleh*, vols. 5 and 6.
[38] For the full text of the speech, see 'Proceedings of the Majlis on Sunday 13 December, 1941', in Kuhi Kermani, *Az Shahrivar-e 1320 to Faje'eh-ye Azerbaijan*, vol. 1. Tehran: Kuhi, n.d., pp. 222–29.
[39] See Taqizadeh, *Zendegi-ye Tufani*, pp. 232–33.
[40] See Khajeh Nuri, *Bazigaran*, pp. 188–91.
[41] See his *Sharh-e Zendegani-ye Man*, vol. 3, Tehran: Zavvar, 1964.
[42] See his *Khaterat va Khatarat*, p. 407.
[43] For a documentation of the official persecution over the removal of the *chadors*, see Sazaman-e Madarek-e Farhangi-e Enqelab-e Eslami, *Vaqaye'-e Kashf-e Hejab*, Tehran: Mo'assese-ye Pazhuhesh-ha va Motle'at-e Farhangi, 1992.
[44] See Homa Katouzian, *Sadeq Hedayat, The Life and Legend of an Iranian Writer*, London and New York: I. B. Tauris, 1991; *Buf-e Kur-e Hedayat*, Tehran: Nashr-e Markaz, second impression, 1998, *Sadeq Hedayat va Marg-e Nevisandeh*, Tehran: second impression, 1995, and *Tanz va Tanzineh-ye Hedayat* (Arash: Stockholm, 2003). After 1941, Hedayat wrote some very scathing attacks in his fiction on Reza Shah and life under his regime, especially in the novel *Hajji Aqa*, the allegorical fable, 'The Case of the Anti-Christ's Donkey', and the dramatic satire, *Tup-e Morvari*. See the author's books on Hedayat cited above.
[45] See further, Katouzian, *State and Society*, chapter 11, and Taqizadeh/Afshar, *Zendegi-ye Tufani*, pp. 569–76.
[46] See Eshqi/Moshir Salimi, *Kolliyat-e Mosavvar*; Mohammad Qa'ed,

Mirzadeh-ye Eshqi, Tehran: Tarh-e Naw, 1998; Bahar, *Tarikh-e Mokhtasar*, vol. 2.

[47] See Kaveh Bayat, *Kudeta-ye Lahuti*, Tehran: Shirazeh, 1997; Mokhber al-Saltaneh, *Katerat va Khatarat*.

[48] See *Divan-e Kamel-e Iraj Mirza*, ed. Mohammad Ja'far Mahjub, third edition, sixth impression, America: Sherkat-e Ketab, 1989; Gholamhosain Riyazi, *Javdaneh Iraj*, Tehran: Riyazi, 1976.

[49] See *Divan-e Aref*, ed. Abdorrahman Saif-e Azad, Tehran: Amir Kabir, fourth impression, 1963.

[50] See *Divan-e Farrokhi*, ed. Hossein Makki, Tehran: Amir Kabir, 1978; Khalil Maleki, *Khaterati-e Siyasi-ye Khalil Maleki*, ed. and intro. Homa Katouzian, second edition, Tehran: Enteshar, 1989.

[51] For Bahar's *Karnama-ye Zendan*, in Bahar/Malekzadeh, *Divan*, vol. 2; for the panegyric *qasidehs*, see ibid., vol. 1. These volumes also include some of the poetical attacks on the Shah and the regime written in the period. Bahar's collected works, edited by his son Mehrdad and published after the revolution of 1977–79, contain more of these as well as some of the anti-Reza Shah poems written in the wake of his abdication.

[52] See Bozorg Alavi, *Khaterat-e Bozorg Alavi*, ed. Hamid Ahmadi, Sweden: Nashr-e Baran, 1997, and *Panjah va Seh Nafar*, Tehran: Ulduz, 1978.

[53] See further, Khalil Maleki/Katouzian, *Khaterat-e Siyasi*; Anvar Khameh'i, *Panjah Nafar va Seh Nafar*, Tehran: Entesharat-e Hafteh, 1983.

[54] See 'Yaddasht-ha-ye Abbasqoli Golsha'iyan', in *Yaddasht-ha-ye Doktor Qasem Ghani*, ed. Cyrus Ghani, London: Ghani, 1984, p. 604.

[55] See the full text of Forughi's radio broadcast in Makki, *Tarikh-e Bistsaleh*, vol. 8, pp. 179–85.

CHAPTER II

The Caliphate, the Clerics and Republicanism in Turkey and Iran
Some Comparative Remarks

Touraj Atabaki

In pursuing modernization, reform and change in twentieth-century Turkey and Iran, the heart of the dispute between the reformist camp and their conservative opponents was the question of individual rights and autonomy and of public representation in general, rather than the form of the government in particular. In establishing a representative government, the reformists aimed to install an elected parliament, or any form of formal process of selecting individuals for public office that would ultimately make the executive power responsible and accountable. The possible form that this new representative institution would adopt, whether a republic or a constitutional monarchy, was not yet the reformists' concern.

On the other hand, the conservative clerics and their laymen followers in both countries were anxious that any change and reform would be a preliminary step towards creating a secular state. Furthermore, on the question of the form of government, although in Islamic jurisprudence there was no consensus as to a preferred form of government, nevertheless, in an analogy with France's political upheavals and revolution, the clerics generally identified the republican form of government with secularism or even atheism.

With the gradual shift in political power in both Turkey and Iran, where across-the-board changes with perceptible features of secularism seemed inevitable, the question of the form of government became the main concern of the majority in the conservative camp. The conformist clerics saw themselves on the brink of a critical and crucial event in Islamic history, where an individual whose 'origin of authority is in the will of the nation'[2] could be elected by the nation rather than the sultan or caliph. In societies with a long tradition of arbitrary rule, it was indeed the caliph, sultan or caliph-sultan who enjoyed the divine blessing as being the shadow of God on earth. For such clerics, the legitimacy of power of the temporal ruler was seriously dubious.

In this chapter, while the background of republicanism in the Ottoman Empire and Qajar Iran has been reviewed, an attempt has been made to compare and contrast the endeavours by the Kemalist and Pahlavi secularist elites in Turkey and Iran to install a republican form of government in the lands that emerged after the fall of the Qajar and Ottoman Empires.

On studying secularism in Turkey and Iran, it is commonly conceded that Mustafa Kemal Atatürk's endeavours at modernization and secularization were parallel to those of his contemporary, Reza Shah Pahlavi in Iran. Nevertheless, in the matter of religion, if Atatürk's reforms were more sweeping, since he was able to divest Islam of its traditional form and to reduce it to a sort of rationalistic monotheism,[3] in Iran, 'Reza Shah's reforms were more difficult to achieve', since the clerics, in contrast to Turkey, 'continued to play an important role in the political life of the country'.[4] In explicating these arguments, references have often been made to the success of Kemal Atatürk in terminating the Sultanate/Caliphate and establishing a republic in Turkey, and to the failure of Reza Shah in his earlier attempt to abolish the Qajar's rule by establishing a republic in Iran. Contrary to these arguments, there are scholars who, by highlighting the fractions amongst the clerics, deny any role played by them in restoring the monarchy in Iran.[5] The purpose of the present paper is to contest the validity of the above arguments, by examining Atatürk's practices in proclaiming the Turkish Republic in contrast to Reza Shah's failure.

Among the six famous principles of Kemalism aimed at cultural manipulation and social change in Turkey – republicanism, secularism, nationalism, populism, *étatisme* and revolutionism[6] – it was indeed republicanism that was the cornerstone laid by Mustafa Kemal in his long campaign of political as well as social change. The separation of the Sultanate from the Caliphate and the abolition of the former, were announced in November 1922.[7] A year later, in October 1923, Mustafa Kemal declared the Republic of Turkey and finally, in March 1924 he abolished the House of the Caliphate.

In Iran, although Reza Shah never advocated any principles for his wide-ranging reforms, one could nevertheless characterize three main trends along which Reza Khan/Shah advocated his programme for change. These trends were secularism, nationalism and *étatisme*. He never believed in populism and if one observes some populist policies he initiated during the early years of his rule as Minister of War and as Prime Minister, these were to a large extent the initiatives and interpretations of some left-oriented political groups such as the Socialist Party, both inside and outside the Majles. Furthermore, considering his endeavour to establish a republican regime in Iran, his project, as we shall see in the following pages, was soon aborted, even before it took its earliest shape.

In Turkey, the idea of establishing a republican regime, or, as it was translated to Turkish *cumhuriyet*, had not originated from Mustafa Kemal. As early as the *Tanzimat* period, the notion of *cumhuriyet* was referred to and discussed amongst the learned circles in the Ottoman Empire. However, those who employed the term *cumhuriyet* in their political discourse were mostly referring to the notion of democracy rather than a particular form of government. Indeed, when 'Mustafa Reşit Pasha was accused by some of his disparagers of wanting to proclaim a republic, by this they meant that he aimed at organizing a constitutional régime that would have considerably decreased the Sultan's power'.[8]

In the 1870s, the word *cumhuriyet* 'gradually acquired a more subversive connotation [and] it turned up in the writings of several intellectual liberals of the Young Ottomans'.[9] Ali Suāvi, the famous publicist, 'openly pleaded in favour of a republican regime' and 'during his exile in Paris, he had briefly published a newspaper called *La République*'.[10] However, among the Young Ottomans, the one who endeavoured to adopt republicanism combined with Islamic jurisprudence was Nāmik Kemal. In a series of articles published in 1868 in the newspaper *Hūrriyet* (Liberty), he went so far as to claim that 'the monarchical system is not necessarily the only possible Islamic political regime'.[11] He goes on from there to make the statement that, in fact, the early Islamic state was 'a kind of republic at its inception'. In his own words:

> What does it mean to state that once the right of the people's sovereignty has been affirmed, it should also be admitted that the people can create a republic? Who can deny this right?[12]

Nevertheless, despite frequent references to the term *cumhuriyet* in political discourses during the late Ottoman period, the common perception of the notion was confined to the call for inaugurating a regime that observes the rule of law and order in society. As Dumont argues:

> Yet none of the Young Turks dared pronounce himself openly for the abolition of the Sultanate and the Caliphate. The *cumhuriyet* they advocated was a kind of constitutional monarchy based on the principle of people's sovereignty. The word itself eventually acquired so subversive a connotation that it was rarely used in the political vocabulary. Well-advised people preferred to employ such words as *meşrutiyet* (constitutional régime) or *meşveret* (consultation), which did not call into question the institution of the Sultanate and could consequently be used with less danger.[13]

In Iran, the earliest reference to republicanism dates back to the early nineteenth century. Mīrzā Sāleh Shīrāzī, one of the pioneers of advocating change and reform in Qajar Iran, in his widely read travel account compiled during his early travels to Europe (1815–19) gives a descriptive account of the French Revolution, which, according to Mīrzā Sāleh, in its early stages aimed at establishing 'a state without the king'.[14] Half a century later, in 1870, Yusef Khan Mostashār al-Dowleh, another Iranian *munavvar al-fikir* (enlightened), while posted as the Iranian government's chargé d'affaires in Paris,[15] compiled his well-known book on politics, *Resaleh-e Mosumeh beh Yek Kalemeh* (A Treatise Entitled 'One Word'), where he advocated and promoted the idea that: 'The origin of the authority of the *dowlat* (the state) is the will of the *mellat* (the nation).'[16] For these *munavvar al-fekrs*, the main task was indeed how to impose the authority of the *mellat* through a constitutional government with a 'parliamentary order'. As stated by Mīrza Mohammad Khan Zoka al-Molk, 'for the people, the government form of republic or monarchy does not make much difference'.[17]

Amongst those Iranians who explicitly presented the diverse forms of government and endeavoured to give a detailed account of each of them was Mirza Aqa Khan Kermani, an enlightened essayist residing in Istanbul, where he published the renowned periodical *Akhtar* (The Star). In one of his treatises known as *Takvin va Tashri'* (The Creation and the Legislation), Kermani, by referring to *Republic of Athena*, while praising 'the Athenians for not letting an individual impose his sole authority on the executive power', admits that the republican form of government on its own, as it was seen even in Athens, is unable to secure the practice of democracy in a country: 'the republicanism in Greece was not always in accordance with the country's progress'.[18]

On the eve of Iranian Constitutional Revolution (1905–11), next to piles of *resalehs* (treatises), written on the *favayed-e mashruteh* (the advantages of constitution), there was also a considerable number written in favour of *estebdad* (arbitrary rule).[19] In almost all these latter treatises, those calling for change and reform in the country were accused of being *jumhurikhah* (republican) and of aiming to undermine the Islamic *shari'a*. Agha Sayyed Hossein Musavi, in his *resaleh* of *Tashkil-e Mellat-e Motemaden* (The Formation of a Civilised Nation) condemns the constitutionalists as:

> The idle chatterers of the earth who call themselves republicans and liberals, in every country commence composing fine phrases of established rhetoric, and in different languages, denying the existence and the need for absolute monarchy as form of government. Gradually even in their propaganda they have reached a point where they argue that if the Prophet (May God send him blessings and peace!) would seek help from other experts in founding the ground for the religion and in reasoning his argument, he would then have had a solid base for Islam. Such nonsense culminating disturbs the mind of all learned elites from different communities ... if they could present with republicanism a better regulation for Islamic jurisprudence, why they haven't done it up till now and why they hesitate to do so? The art of rulership is a gift donated by God to certain people. Nobody can learn this art ... The people of France for many years were engaged in regulating their society according to a republican form of government. But up till now they have failed to succeed.[20]

Although, the authors of such treatises attempted to mobilize the crowds by portraying the opposition as heretical and their actions as anti-religious, nevertheless in their arguments they hesitated to give a reference to a Koranic *nas* (text), or *sunnat* (deeds and utterance of the prophet Mohammad). Indeed, the Koranic *nas* of: 'Do obey God and do obey his messenger and those who have the command',[21] only refers to the ruler and does not distinguish the type of the ruler, president or sultan. Accordingly, the supporters of the republican form of government in Iran employed this notion in their argument. In a series of articles, published in the periodical *Habl al-Matin* (The Firm Cord), under the heading of *Lozum-e Jomhuriyyet va tafkik-e Qowa-ye Rohani dar Iran* (On the Necessity of Republic and the Separation of Divine Rule in Iran), the anonymous author, by referring to Islamic jurisprudence, endeavoured to allegorize that all forms of government are accepted in Islam.[22] Moreover, as believed by some republicans, besides *nas* and *sūnnat* it is also *'orf* (tradition) in Islam, which includes *ijma'* (consensus of community), that observes the collective conscience of the Muslim community. For example, Zia Gökalp, as one of the earnest advocates of republicanism in the late Ottoman Empire, often quarrelled that *qiyas* (analogy) and *'orf* should be used for explanation and might replace *nas*.[23]

Neither in the movement that eventually ended with the proclamation of the constitutional regime of 1906 in Iran, nor in the Ottoman Empire during the political upheaval that paved the way for *Ittihad ve Terakki* (The Committee of Union and Progress – CUP) to come to power in 1908, can one find the call for establishing a republic. In Iran, it was following the inauguration of the first Majles and the anti-constitutional stands of Mohammad 'Ali Shah, that some papers openly called for the monarchy to be replaced by a republic. For example, in April 1908, in an editorial in his paper *Musavat* (Equality), Mohammad Reza Musavat, by comparing the king to a pharaoh who has been caused to faint by the God, glorified the republican form of government as the one where the right of *mellat* has been more respected.[24]

The outbreak of the First World War left no room for any debate on the possible change of the form of government in the region. Nevertheless, the political configuration of the world that came out of the war was different from 1914. Imperial Czarist Russia was forced to leave the region's political scene and instead a Soviet Socialist Republic raised its flag on the dome of the Kremlin. In the southern region of the old Czarist Empire, for the first time in a Muslim land, the Azerbaijani Musavatists established a republican form of government in 1918. The collapse of the Romanovs and the formation of the Musavati government soon had considerable repercussions on political development in the region. In the northern Iranian province Gilan, in 1920–21, a short-lived 'Soviet Republic' was formed. Although it could not entirely rely on popular support, nevertheless it was not confronted by substantial aversion either.[25] Besides Gilan, in Fars province one of the Bakhtiyari Khans formed a Bakhtiyari Soviet and published a 'manifesto of sorts aimed at more equal and egalitarian relations within the tribe'.[26] In the northern Iranian province of Azerbaijan, Shaikh Mohammad Khiyabani, by calling the province Azadistan, challenged the authority of the Qajar Shah and appealed for an introduction of constitutional reforms for the country and more autonomy for the region.[27] Likewise, with reference to the question of the republican form of government, Khīyābāni acknowledged that:

> We are neither monarchist nor republican. At this stage, our main goal is to have a Majles, democratically elected, where the deputies can decide on the future form of the government.[28]

And again:

> The will of people should be superior to every other will. If the people wish, they should be able to depose a king and choose a new one. They have a right even to call a republic.[29]

In the Ottoman Empire, following the Mondros Armistice in October 1918, when the Allies expanded their occupation, a series of local nationalist societies such as the 'Eastern Anatolian Society for the Defence of Rights', which later became the 'Anatolian and Rumelian Society for the Defence of Rights', were established, aimed at preventing the rapid disintegration of the Empire. A year later, in a congress held in Erzurum in July–August, the Nationalists proclaimed their national pact and elected Mustafa Kemal as president of the Standing Committee. A month later, the Sivas Congress met and a stronger version of the national pact was agreed upon and published. It has been reported that in both these two nationalist gatherings, the notion of a republican form of government for what remained of the Ottoman Empire was discussed for the first time.[30] Mustafa Kemal too in his memoirs refers to a political society known as *Trakya Paşeli Jem 'iyeti* (The Trakya Paşaeli Society), which in the same period in Edirne and adjacent area, by seeking support from the British or French governments, was hoping to establish a 'Trakya Republic'.[31]

By the end of 1919, the core of nationalist activities moved to Ankara, where some months later, on 23 April 1920, the Grand

National Assembly met and formed a new cabinet of ministers under the chairmanship of Mustafa Kemal. Moving the political capital to Ankara enabled Mustafa Kemal to dissociate himself from the old establishment. Contrary to Reza Khan, who by residing in Tehran had to cope with the existing political establishment and had to harmonize his activities with political activists, Mustafa Kemal, by setting up an independent, parallel establishment in Ankara, and by challenging the authority of the Istanbul Sultanate, left no room for the half-hearted Turkish intelligentsia, either in Istanbul or Ankara. Among those who readily opted for Istanbul was the Empire's new Shaikh al-Islam. On 11 April 1920, 'Abdullah Dürrizade, while holding the title of Shaikh al-Islam in the third cabinet of Damad Ferid, issued four *fetwas* (injunctions in Islamic law), of which the main one referred to Ankara as the citadel of:

> 'Certain civil persons [who] have allied and united and chosen for themselves leaders . . . with fraud . . . are deceiving . . . the loyal Imperial subjects and without authority are rising up to enlist soldiers from the populace; and to this end are imposing, in contravention of the sacred law and against high orders, certain dues and equipping these soldiers but really by reason of [their own] greed for worldly goods . . .'. Among many other specific accusations it charged these same persons with 'treason' and with being 'rebels' (*bughat, baghiler*), who in accordance with religious law were to be killed (*katl ü kitālleri meshrū' we fard olur*) one at a time or as a group. The briefer subsidiary *fetwas* obliged Muslims to head the Sultan's call to arms against the rebels and threatened eternal punishment for deserters from any such army and earthly penalties for those disobeying orders in this fight against the rebels.[32]

Ankara's reaction was swift and unequivocal. Rifat Efendi, the influential mufti of Ankara, speedily reacted to Dürrizade's injunction and by issuing a counter-*fetwa* declared Istanbul's decree void. Besides the political outcome of Rifat Efendi's swift reaction, his counter-*fetwa* was an explicit step challenging the legitimacy of Istanbul as the House of the Caliphate. Ankara, as the headquarters of the new regime, had its own views, even on religious decrees.

On 10 August 1920, the Istanbul government signed the Treaty of Sèvres, which effectively eliminated Turkey's sovereignty. Ankara's reaction was swift: the Grand National Assembly issued a declaration calling the signatories of the treaty traitors. Furthermore, during the following months, Ankara decided to design its own international link. The Treaty of Gümrü, which fixed the Turko-Armenian border, was the first such step. Some months later, on 16 March 1921, the Moscow Agreement was signed between the Grand National Assembly and the Soviet government. Furthermore, by autumn that year France recognized the Ankara government. By then the Ankara government had established its legitimacy throughout the entire country, and when in September 1922 the nationalist troops raised the Turkish flag at Kadifekale in Izmir, nobody could doubt that the days of the Sultan were numbered. Preparation for the peace conference made Mustafa Kemal tighten his grip on Istanbul. Now Gazi Mustafa Kemal threatened Istanbul by issuing an ultimatum stating that only the Grand National Assembly could represent the Turkish State. Furthermore, to avoid the Sèvres Treaty experience, the Grand National Assembly endeavoured to limit Istanbul's authority. On 1 November 1922, the Assembly ratified the law proclaiming the separation of the Caliphate from the Sultanate and announced the abolition of the latter.

The reaction to the dissolution of the Sultanate was mixed. While there were some within intellectual circles in Istanbul who felt that the abolition of the Sultanate was the first step towards the elimination of the Caliphate, the Grand National Assembly did not encounter any serious resistance, and when the Sultan Vahidettin fled the country aboard the English warship *Malaya*, still claiming to be Sultan of the Ottoman Empire and Caliph of the *Muslimun* of the World, nobody shed tears for him. 'Even if Atatürk had wanted to retain the monarchy, he could not have done so without compromising his entire revolution.'[33] Almost all Turkish intelligentsias now were behind Atatürk's republican agenda. Even those like Ziya Gökalp, who till 1918 was advocating a constitutional monarchy in the Ottoman Empire, was now 'unburdened by any romantic notion that Kemalist "republican democracy" represented plebiscitarian democracy, [and] regarded Atatürk's charismatic leadership as the focal point for future socioeconomic developments, which could emerge in Turkey only when the centre of the new political system was in the hand of an authoritative leader.'[34]

On 29 October 1923, when the Republic of Turkey was proclaimed by means of a constitutional amendment and Gazi Mustafa Kemal was elected as President, in Iran Reza Khan was forming his first cabinet as the country's Prime Minister, following his coup of 1921.

Reza Khan's reputation had been on a steady rise from the very first day after the coup. His supporters had every expectation that having become Prime Minister he would be able to complete what he had started. He now would take the final step to unify the country and advance bold plans for an economic revival.[35]

Nevertheless, the fulfilment of this assignment, as was proved during the days to come, was not an easy task. Although the loyalty of the military was auspicious, nevertheless, among the country's intelligentsia he was not yet accepted as a trusted politician. Although, they respected and appreciated Reza Khan's record during his short period in office, they were sceptical about offering him their unconditional support.

The news of the setting up of a republican government in Turkey caused distinctive reactions in Iran. While the traditional establishment, represented by the court, adopted a more cautious position and confined itself to sending a telegram to Gazi Mustafa Kemal, congratulating him on retaining the new position,[36] the radical-modernist camp was clearly in disarray. On 20 January 1924, a newspaper in Istanbul came out in favour of a republic in Iran.

The article was well received in Tehran by newspapers that were supporters of Reza Khan. A Tehran journalist tried to determine what Reza Khan thought of the article. Reza did not answer directly and was non-committal. He was quoted as saying, 'the progress of a country depends less on its form of government than on the morale of the people. Take Greece and Great Britain. Both are monarchies. One is decadent and decayed; the other great, vibrant and prosperous.' Mexico and France were similarly contrasted as republic.[37]

As the events of the following months confirmed, Reza Khan was not sincere in his apparent impartiality on the form of government. Ghani presents valid arguments in his assessment that:

> The idea of a republic was probably strengthened in Reza Khan's mind during the course of his negotiations with Ahmad

Shah to become Prime Minister. Not only was he convinced of the uselessness and cowardice of the Shah and his indifference to the fate of the country, but also of the Shah's capacity to intrigue against him. Furthermore, the generation of politicians who had ruled Iran during 1909–1921 had proven to be incompetent and had lost all self-respect. They had been incapable of independent action and were treated as paid agents by their European sponsors. A republican form of government would change everything and the old crowd of self-seeking unpatriotic notables would be discarded. Reza Khan's principal advisers were all of the same mind and encouraged the idea of a republic.[38]

In early 1924, in the absence of the Shah who was in Europe, apparently enjoying his luxurious life, Reza Khan soon orchestrated a hasty campaign aiming at establishing a republic in Iran, for which he was not well prepared. By contrast, in Ottoman Turkey, it took almost four years for Mustafa Kemal Pasha to change the political order in what was left of the fallen Ottoman Empire and to proclaim the new republic of Turkey in 1923. During this period, especially from the date of abolishing the Sultanate to the date of declaring the Republic, it took more than a year for Mustafa Kemal to rally the reformist camp, pacify the half-hearted politicians of the so-called Second Group – all influential political figures such as Rauf (Orbay), Ali Fuat (Cebesoy), Kazim Karabekir, Refet (Bele), Adnan (Adıvar), Hūseyn Cahit (Yalçin) and Ahmet Emin (Yalman) – and to eventually form his People's Party. On the other hand, for Reza Khan this period was no longer than even a month. He hastened to declare the republic before 21 March 1924, the date of Iranian New Year, *Nowrūz*. Traditionally, it was at the New Year that the Shah presided over the customary reception for government officials and notables. By calling the republic before the New Year, Reza Khan was very anxious to stop the Crown Prince presiding over the reception, which, according to him, was nothing more than a demonstration of homage to the Qajar dynasty. Then he would hold the reception for himself as the new President of the Republic of Iran.

Subsequently, in mid-February 1924, a vigorous campaign began in the press in support of republicanism. 'Articles in favour of the republic and in abuse of the Shah occurred daily with no evident steps to prevent them.'[39] Republican Committees were formed and telegrams from provinces poured into the capital. Some conventional political parties changed their old statutes in favour of accepting the republican form of government. The Independent Democrat Party of Iran, following a meeting of its board of leadership, declared the following points:

1 From now on, by opting for the republican form of government in Iran, we announce the monarchy and rule of Qajar dynasty in Iran illegitimate.
2 We call the Majles to adopt a new Constitution, altering the form of government in Iran from monarchy to republic.
3 We call on our members and supporters throughout Iran to utilize their ultimate power in order to fulfil this call.
4 In the Majles, the Independent Democrat Party's fraction ought to adopt necessary measures facilitating the ratification of new bills.[40]

At this time, even a new political party known as the *Hezb-e Jomhuri-ye Iran* (The Republican Party of Iran), was formed.[41] In its published manifesto it dated its founding to four years earlier, when it published its first programme calling for an end to Qajar rule in Iran, 'when such a call apparently caused their arrest and imprisonment'.[42] In their 'new' manifesto, the 'governing body' of the party 'once more', by accusing the Qajar's nobles and notables of 'the misery they caused for Iranians', calls on all co-patriots 'to follow the Germans' and Turks' pattern and bring down the tyrannical rule of Qajar'. However, what made the Republican Party of Iran's manifesto different from the former one and from earlier groups' political stands was its odd reference to the Qajar dynasty's ethnic background. Calling the Qajar a Turkic tribe, the manifesto 'wondered that how a Turkic dynasty could ever reign [over] a non-Turkic country?':

> Today's civilized world does not accept the reign of crowned rulers. The Germans and the Turks both brought an end to the reign of Kaiser and Sultan. But here in Iran we ought not still to be suffering the yoke of an alien Turk's dynasty. The rule of this dynasty does not accord with Iranian dignity and is a disgrace.[43]

In late nineteenth- and early twentieth-century political discourse in Iran, there is no trace of such ethnic identification. With no reference to their ethnic background, the Qajar rulers were often blamed for advancing a tyrannical rule in Iran and for hindering the necessary political change in the country. The Iranian territorial nationalists in this period, who were also the pioneers of advocating change and reform in the country, themselves come from an Azerbaijan Turkic background. One could refer to the Republican Party of Iran's anti-Turkic stand as the early sign of what in a few years time became the dominant feature of Iranian nationalism – linguistic nationalism.[44]

In the uproar about republicanism in Iran, the role of the periodicals was significant. Divided into pro- and anti-republican camps, they endeavoured as much as possible to manipulate public opinion in accordance with their political agenda. On the other hand, the clerics' reaction to the uproar was mixed. While the clerics preferred to keep quiet, watching the public sentiment, the mullahs began to manifest different reactions: Haji Sheykh Javad *mujtahed*, made a speech in the shrine of Shāh 'Abd al-Azim, in south of Tehran, on 15 February protesting at the Shah's behaviour in Europe and exhibiting a photograph of him in European costume, which was also printed in several newspapers.'[45] Haj Aqa Jamal held a conference on 18 February to ascertain the general feeling on the issue, and it was decided to seek guidance from Ayatullah Khalesi in Mashhad.[46]

On 11 February, the fifth session of parliament was officially convened. The main task of this Majles was to draft a bill abolishing the monarchy and constituting the republic. The supporters of Reza Khan in this session were divided into three camps. The faction of *Tajaddod* (the Revivalists) with some 40 deputies, headed by an ex-cleric, Sayyed Mohammad Taddayon; the *Socialist Unifiyeh* (the United Socialist Party) of Qajar Prince Solyman Mirza Eskandari and with some 12 to 13 members; and some 10 to 15 deputies who presented themselves as independents.

The opposition camp, headed by Sayyed Hasan Moddarres, an excellent parliamentarian, had some 12 members including the most experienced and influential deputies. From the first day that the new session of the Majles was convened, it was evident that the anti-republican opposition to Reza Khan, although a minority, nevertheless took the lead in all of the parliamentary debates. The tactics of prolonging the debate on the deputies' mandates that was adopted by Moddarres's faction lasted for more than a week and had a clear twofold objective: openly provoking the other camp into pacifying Reza Khan's non-partisan deputies and postponing the discussion on the issue of republic until after the Persian New Year.

Effort by Reza Khan and his supporters to bring pressure on the opposition had negative repercussions. Pressure on Moddarres to co-operate with Reza Khan led some neutral deputies to join his side, and ordinary people outside the Majles, resenting the implied intimidation, turned against republicanism.[47]

Almost contemporaneous with the republican uproar in Iran, the Grand National Assembly in Ankara on 3 March 1924 decided to abolish the Caliphate, expelling the members of the Ottoman dynasty from the Turkish Republic, abolishing the Ministry of *Shari'a* and Pious Foundation and passing a law for the unification of secular education (*Tevhid-i Tedrisat Kanunu*). As Jacob Landau remarks:

> Just as the abolition of the Sultanate had been intended to vest all state authority in the Grand National Assembly, that of the Caliphate was meant to conform with the new political ideology with which Mustafa Kemal wished to endow the young Republic of Turkey.[48]

Within a week, the news of Ankara's Grand National Assembly's new decisions reached Tehran. The pro-republican newspaper of *Shafaq-e Sorkh* (The Red Twilight) presented the events by stating that:

> Mustafa Kemal Pasha in his public speech while referring to the necessity of separation of politics from religion added that the education and juridical matters should be freed from all influences and be secularised.[49]

The anti-clerical measures adopted by Ankara had an ample repercussion for the Iranian religious establishment. Although the world of Shi'ism had never appreciated the legitimacy of the Ottoman Caliphate, nevertheless, for the Shi'i clerics, the consensus between daily politics and the Islamic jurisprudence was non-negotiable. The clerics acknowledged that the introduction of the Civil Code in Turkey was the ultimate conclusion of sequences of events and movements there, which had begun with the separation of the Sultanate from the Caliphate, had been followed by the elimination of the Sultanate, and now saw the abolition of the Caliphate and secularization of the state. In a leaflet distributed in Tehran, the republicans were condemned of attempting to eliminate Islam by calling for the change of the regime:

> The republicans are intending to uproot the Shi'i Islam from this country. They are intending to do the same as their colleagues did in the Ottoman land [*Mamlekat-e Osmani*]. In the name of republic, they abolished the Caliphate and took off the turban from the heads of clerics.[50]

To demonstrate their displeasure, the high-ranking *ulema* turned to their traditional ally, the bazaar, for help. On 19 March, the bazaar took to the street protesting against republicanism. Three days later on 22 March, the day on which the Majles was due to discuss the proposal to change the constitution and establish a republic, 'a crowd of around 5,000 clerics, merchants, guildsmen and ordinary people gathered round the Majles building shouting pro-Shah and anti-republic slogans. Moddarres was reported to have the solid backing of the Tehran merchants'.[51] Furthermore, 'a large meeting was organized in the Shāh Mosque, where sermons were preached against Reza Khan and republicanism'.[52] When Reza Khan sent two regiments to the Majles to disperse the protestors, his harsh reaction caused more dissatisfaction among the deputies. Some deputies, including the head of the Majles, Mo'tamen al-Molk, accused him of using force against the people. Reza Khan soon retreated. Later on, following some consultation and intervention, he agreed to 'relinquish the republican cause, release about 200 jailed demonstrators and promised to respect Islam'.[53]

The following day Reza Khan set off for Qom to meet with high-ranking *ulema*, where he was asked to refrain from republicanism, which 'is not in the people's interest and does not correspond with the country's needs'.[54] Coming back to Tehran, he issued a statement, asserting:

> In my meeting with the highly respected ulema in Qom, once more I confirmed my commitment that preservation of Islam had been one of the most important duties of the army from the beginning. Moreover, we reviewed the events of the last few days and I would like to ask everybody to abandon the demand for a republican form of government.[55]

THE CALIPHATE, THE CLERICS AND REPUBLICANISM   59

Consequently, the republican movement in its early days was aborted by an alliance of the clerics and the bazaar.

In studying this episode in the history of modern Iran, there are those who deny the role of clerics, by arguing that, since 'the ulema were not united ... they did not enter the conflict of their own accord'.[56] Many Persian monographs written on Reza Shah's early history endorse this argument. On the other hand, other scholars overestimate the role played by clerics, and present the then Iranian religious establishment as an anti-republican establishment.

The Iranian clerics in the early stages of the republican campaign demonstrated a certain degree of indifference, at least in public, to the debate that was aiming to change the form of government. They did not perceive the change as a threat to their traditional social position. Nevertheless, in encountering the Turkish political developments, when the question of conjunction of secularism and republicanism became more evident, they did not hesitate to jump into the scene and call on their traditional collaborator, the bazaar, to pour into the street and impede the movement. Thus the repercussions of the abolition of the Caliphate and the introduction of secular measures by the Turkish Grand National Assembly should not be underestimated.

Furthermore, one can find the reasons for Mustafa Kemal's success and Reza Khan's failure in establishing a republic in their respective countries, not only in the role of Iranian clerics, even though performed at the final stage, but also, and more importantly, in the performance of the two leaders and the procedures by which the change was conducted in the two countries.

In Turkey, thanks to the parallel political institutions set up by Mustafa Kemal in Ankara, the committed and united intelligentsia and the army both supported Kemal's cause. Moreover, the lack of purpose together with the severe political mistakes on the part of his antagonist, the Sultan Vahidettin, made it possible for the abolition of the Sultanate to be accomplished rather smoothly. The new President, Mustafa Kemal, was not even anxious to inform his colleagues on his scheduling:

> While we were eating I said: tomorrow [by sealing the last chapter of the history of Sultanate], we declare the Republic ... I did not even find it necessary to inform the closest allies and colleagues. I was quite confident of their reaction.[57]

However, the abolition of the Caliphate proved to be not an easy task. Here Kemal's prudence and performance became incisive. He 'coordinated strategy and politics in preparing for retrenchment'.[58] For example, to impede any possible opposition by the religious circles and to disarm them ideologically, he formed a committee at the time of abolition of the Caliphate with a task of backing up his view. The committee 'pointed out that the Ottoman claim to the Caliphate was illegitimate and had ceased to exist in 1258 when the Mongols conquered Baghdad. Nevertheless, there appears to be more evidence for the view that the abolition was engineered primarily by Kemal himself and the clerics on the committee were handpicked by him' to stamp his decision.[59] Nevertheless, there were a few activists, even in Kemal's own party, such as Halit (Akmansü) who deserted him over the Caliphate issue. The Kurdish revolt of 1925 lead by Shaikh Sa'id was another example of the Caliphate being a more sensitive issue compared to the Sultanate:

> With the abolition of the Caliphate the most important symbol of Turkish-Kurdish brotherhood disappeared. It became possible to condemn the Ankara government as irreligious, an accusation that seemed to be confirmed by other measures it took. This argument carried more weight than any other with many of the Kurds, who were strongly committed to Islam.[60]

Reza Khan, on the other hand, did not wish to maintain independent institutions, nor did he enjoy the complete support of the reformist circles in Iran. In his camp were those such as Ali Akbar Davar, with strong affinities with *étatisme*, who admired him as a man of order, and agreed with much of his reform programme, such as expansion of education and creation of a modern army and bureaucracy. Nevertheless, on the question of republicanism, they sincerely believed that the country 'was not yet ripe for a republic'.

On the issue of his dependence on a modern army, which proved to be Kemal's backbone in his performances, it should be noted that the only modern military institution in Iran at that time was the newly created Gendarmerie, which in contrast to the country's other military institutions had gathered the most reform-minded officers and personnel. However, Reza Khan was not one of the Gendarmerie's men. Coming from the old-style Cossack Brigade himself, Reza's relations at that time with the Gendarmerie were not very auspicious. Even within his own brigade there were some officers who, during the republican movement, preferred to keep a distance from him.[61]

Finally, on the failure of the republican movement in Iran, reference should be made to Reza Khan's indiscreet behaviour. In contrast to Mustafa Kemal, whose 'resourcefulness, careful exploration of alternatives, and keen sense of timing'[62] were all contributory factors to his ultimate success, Reza Khan's lack of these qualities gradually persuaded some of his most ardent admirers to reconsider their support for his cause.

Reza Khan's failure to assume power by calling for a republic in Iran drove him to employ more traditional tactics in pursuing his cause. Rather than relying only on the Majles and street politics, he secured a functional network within the old establishment, which eventually allowed him to obtain a bill from the Majles on 31 October 1925 terminating the Qajar dynasty. He was appointed as head of the provisional government pending a decision on a permanent basis for Iran's future. On 12 December that year, the Majles voted by 257 to 3 to lay the foundation of a monarchy to be conferred upon Reza Khan. Later in the following year he was formally crowned as the first Shah of the Pahlavi dynasty.

The assumption of political power by Mustafa Kemal in Turkey and Reza Shah in Iran put a new pace on the process of authoritarian modernization in two neighbouring countries. Both Turkey and Iran went through a basic scheme of secular reforms, as a result of which the traditional political structure in both countries was significantly changed. However, as far as public representation was concerned, neither in Turkey nor in Iran was it fully practised. In the Republic of Turkey, Mustafa Kemal stayed in power as uncontested President until his death in 1938, while in Iran, Reza Shah Pahlavi consolidated his authoritarian regime by practising arbitrary rule up until his abdication in 1941. All in all, the form of government, republic or monarchy, was not embedded in a democratic culture in which individualism and public representation would be observed in either country.

Notes

[2] Yousef Khan Mostashar al-Dowleh, *Resaleh Mosumeh beh Yek Kalameh*, Paris, n.p., n.d., p. 14.

[3] For a stereotype example of such arguments, see Wilhelm Haas, *Iran*, New York, Columbia University Press, 1946, p. 142.

[4] Vida Garoussian, *The Ulema and Secularisation in Contemporary Iran*, unpublished Ph.D. thesis, Michigan, Ann Arbor, 1976, p. 21.

[5] Vanessa Martin, 'Modarres, Republicanism and the Rise to Power of Reza Khan Sardār-i Sipah', *British Journal of Middle Eastern Studies*, vol. 21, no. 2, 1994, pp. 202–10.

[6] For a critical analysis of the Kemalist principles, see Akural, Sabri, M., 'Kemalist view on Social Change', in Jacob M., Landau (ed.), *Atatürk and the Modernization of Turkey*, Boulder, CO, Westview Press, 1984, pp. 125–52.

[7] For a short review of the event, see Halil Inalcik, *The Caliphate and Atatürk's inkilāp*, Turkish Review Quarterly Digest, Ankara, 2/7 (Spring 1987), pp. 25–36.

[8] Ibid.

[9] Ibid.

[10] Ibid.

[11] Şerif Mardin, *The Genesis of Young Ottoman Thought, A Study in the Modernization of Turkish Political Ideas*, Princeton, NJ, Princeton University Press, 1962, pp. 296–97.

[12] Ibid.

[13] Paul Dumont, 'The Origin of Kemalist Ideology', in Landau, J. M. (ed.), *Atatürk and the Modernization of Turkey*, p. 28.

[14] Gholamhusayn Mirza Saleh (ed.), *Majmueh-e Safarnameh-ha-ye Mirza Saleh-e Shirazi*, Tehran, Nashr-e Tarikh-e Iran, 1985, p. 253.

[15] Fereydun Adamiyat, *Fekr-e Azadi va Moqaddameh-e Nehzat-e Mashrutiyyat*, Tehran, Sokhan, 1961, p. 186.

[16] Yusef Khan Mostashar al-Dowleh, *Resaleh-e Mosumeh beh Yek Kalemeh*, p. 38.

[17] Fereydun Adamiyat, *Ideology-e Nahzat-e Mashrutiyyat-e Iran*, Tehran, Payam, 1976, p. 211.

[18] Fereydun Adamiyat, *Andisheh-ha-ye Mirza Aqa Khan Kermani*, Tehran, Payām, 1978, p. 117.

[19] For a good collection of such treatises, see Musa Najafi, *Bonyad-e Falsafeh-e Siyasi dar Iran ('Asr-e Mashrutiyyat)*, Tehran, Markaz-e Nashr-e Daneshgahi, 1997. Another collection is Zargarinezhad (ed.), *Rasa'el-e Mashrutiyyat*, Tehran, Kavir, 1995.

[20] Fereydun Adamiyat, *Ideology-e Nehzat-e Mashrutiyyat-e Iran*, Tehran, Payam, 1976, p. 202.

[21] 'Ati'ū llāh wa- ati' ūl-rasūla wa- uli 'l-amri minkum', the Koran, al-Nisa, 59.

22 M. Mohammad, 'Lozum-e Jomhuriyyet va Tafkik-e Qowa-ye Rohani dar Iran', *Habl al-Matin*, 27 October and 3 November 1924.
23 Taha Parla, T., *The Social and Political Thought of Zia Gökalp, 1876–1924*, Leiden, Brill, 1985, p. 39.
24 *Musavat*, 3 April 1908.
25 For a detailed study of the 'Soviet Republic' in Gilan, see Cosroe Chaqueri, *The Soviet Socialist Republic of Iran, 1920–1921: Birth of the Trauma*, Pittsburgh and London, University of Pittsburgh Press, 1995.
26 David Brooks, 'The Enemy Within', in Richard Tapper (ed.), *The Conflict of Tribe and State in Iran and Afghanistan*, London, Croom Helm, 1983, pp. 358–59.
27 Touraj Atabaki, *Azerbaijan, Ethnicity and Autonomy in the Twentieth-Century Iran*, London, I. B. Tauris, 1993, pp. 46–51.
28 'Ali Azari, *Qiyam-e Sheykh Mohammad Khiyabani dar Tabriz*, Tehran, Safi'alishāh, 1975, p. 341.
29 Ibid., p. 428.
30 Dumont, 'Origin', p. 28.
31 Gazi Mustafa Kemal, *Nutuk*, Ankara, 1927, pp. 511–15.
32 *The Encyclopaedia of Islam*, new edition, vol. II, Leiden, Brill, 1965, p. 630. For the text of the *fetwas*, see Takwim-i Wekayi', no. 3834, 11 April 1920.
33 Walter F. Weiker, *Political Tutelage and Democracy in Turkey: The Free Party and its Aftermath*, Leiden, Brill, 1973, p. 11.
34 Sabri Akural, 'Kemalist view on Social Change', in Landau (ed.), *Atatürk and the Modernization of Turkey*, p. 141.
35 Cyrus Ghani, *Iran and the Rise of Reza Shah, From Qajar Collapse to Pahlavi Rule*, London, I. B. Tauris, 1999, p. 307.
36 In the absence of the king, the heir to the throne, Hasan Mīrzā, signed the telegram. See Hossein Makki, *Tarikh Bist Saleh-e Iran*, vol. 2, p. 437.
37 FO 371/144, 35 February 1945 and FO 371/10145, 1 April 1945, cited by Ghani, *Iran*, p. 308.
38 Ghani, *Iran*, p. 308.
39 FO 416/74 No. 110, 22 Feb. 1924, cited by Martin, 'Modarres', p. 203.
40 *Setareh-e Iran* (Iran's Star), no. 149, 17 March 1924.
41 *Setareh-e Iran*, no. 144, 10 March 1924.
42 Ibid.
43 Ibid.
44 For a detailed study of territorial and linguistic form of nationalism in early twentieth-century Iran, see Touraj Atabaki, 'Recasting Oneself, Rejecting the Other', in Willem van Schendel and Erik Jan Zürcher (eds), *Opting Out of the Nations*, London, I. B. Tauris, 2000.
45 FO 416/74, No. 129, March 1924. Cited by Martin, 'Modarres', p. 204.
46 Ibid.

⁴⁷ 'Abdollah Mostowfi, *Sharh-e Zendegi-e Man ya Tarikh-e Ejtema 'i va Edari-ye Qajariyyeh*, vol. III, Tehran, Zavvar, 1964, pp. 407–8.
⁴⁸ Jacob M. Landau, *The Politics of Pan-Islam, Ideology and Organization*, Oxford, Oxford University Press, 1990, p. 181.
⁴⁹ *Shafaq-e Sorkh*, 10 March 1924.
⁵⁰ Mansoureh Taddayonpour (ed.), *Asnad-e Rohaniyat va Majles*, vol. 3, Tehran, Markaz-e Asnad-e Majles Showray-e Eslami, 1997, p. 40, document 12.
⁵¹ FO 416/74, No. 165, 26 March 1924. Cited by Martin, 'Modarres', p. 206.
⁵² Martin, 'Modarres', p. 206.
⁵³ Malek al-Sho'ara Bahar, *Tarikh-e Mokhtasr-e Ahzab-e Sīyasi Iran*, vol. II, Tehran, Amir Kabir, 1984, p. 54. Ervand Abrahamian, *Iran Between Two Revolutions*, Princeton, NJ, Princeton University Press, 1982, p. 134.
⁵⁴ Mostowfi, *Sharh-e*, p. 601.
⁵⁵ Hossein Makki, *Tarikh-e Bist Saleh-e Iran*, vol. II, Bongāh-e Tarjomeh va Nashr-e Ketab, 1980, p. 520.
⁵⁶ Martin, 'Modarres', p. 210.
⁵⁷ Kemal, *Nutuk*, p. 495.
⁵⁸ Dankwart Rustow, 'Atatürk as founder of a state', in *Philosophers and Kings, Studies in Leadership*, *Journal of the American Academy of Arts and Sciences*, Summer 1968, p. 801.
⁵⁹ Hugh Poulton, *Top Hat, Grey Wolf and Crescent: Turkish Nationalism and the Turkish Republic*, London, Hurst, 1997, pp. 91–99.
⁶⁰ Martin van Bruinessen, *Agha, Shaikh and State, The Social and Political structure of Kurdistan*, London, Zed Books, 1992, p. 281. For a detailed study of the Kurdish rebellion, see Martin van Bruinessen, 'Popular Islam, Kurdish nationalism and rural revolt: The rebellion of Shaikh Said in Turkey (1925)', in János M. Bak and Gerhard Benecke (eds), *Religion and Rural Revolt*. Manchester: Manchester University Press, 1984, pp. 281–95. Also Robert Olson, *The Emergence of Kurdish Nationalism and the Sheikh Said Rebellion, 1880–1925*. Austin, University of Texas Press, 1989.
⁶¹ Martin, 'Modarres', p. 205.
⁶² Rustow, 'Atatürk', p. 811.

CHAPTER III

New Iran and the Dissolution of Party Politics under Reza Shah[1]

Matthew Elliot

New Iran (*Iran-e Now*)[2] was the name of a Persian political party whose active life lasted just three months. Yet the appearance in 1927 of *Iran-e Now* and its longer-lasting parliamentary offshoot, Progress (*Taraqqi*),[3] marked a turning point in party and parliamentary politics under Reza Shah. Western diplomats and newspapers immediately grasped the significance of *Iran-e Now*, which they described as a party organised 'on Fascist lines',[4] and successive diplomatic despatches recorded the importance of *Taraqqi* during the years 1927–32. The history of Persia as written in both Farsi and English, however, has virtually forgotten it.

Some general observations will help to set the *Iran-e Now* episode within the political history of modern Persia and the inter-war Middle East. The first concerns the tradition of royal absolutism in Persia. This tradition, which the Qajar dynasty maintained alongside its nineteenth-century reforms, was weakened by the Constitutional Revolution of 1906. However, it recovered during the reign of Reza Shah Pahlavi.[5] An important difference between the absolutism of the Qajars and that of Reza Shah was that the former possessed the style, but little of the substance, of absolute rule whereas Reza's regime demonstrated both. Although unfettered by any constitution before 1906, the Qajars exercised relatively little control over Persia as a whole, and indeed, owing to their weak administrative and military apparatus, lacked the means to collect much revenue or to impose drastic changes upon the country. Reza, on the other hand, established a strong central government and army with which he enforced high taxes and radical reforms. Consequently, Reza's state weighed far more heavily on Persia than that of his Qajar predecessors.[6]

Secondly, the character and record of the parliamentary and party system as established in Persia after the Constitutional Revolution should be taken into account. The electoral franchise was heavily weighted in favour of the higher ranks of society and a two-stage system of elections in the provinces (which facilitated local and administrative manipulation) further restricted the circle of political influence.[7] Some of the larger factions that formed within the Majlis represented identifiable social groups with distinct elements of policy, but most represented only the personal followings of individuals or the temporary coalitions of interested individuals. None were genuine national political parties with mass memberships and electoral campaigns based on firm manifesto commitments.[8] Indeed, Persian liberal politics conformed, in its limited social ambit and factionalism, to the pattern in the Arab Middle East.[9] However, the inter-war years witnessed not only a growing disillusionment with representative government in the region and in continental Europe, but also the emergence of new, alternative, authoritarian models. This inclined some countries, particularly those in conditions of stress, towards authoritarian solutions.[10] Persia, whose experience of parliamentary rule between 1906 and 1921 was particularly disastrous, belonged to this category. Its weak and faction-ridden governments failed to pass significant reforms, lost control over the provinces and watched helplessly as the Great Powers turned the country – despite its natural status – into a battleground during World War I.

Thirdly, Reza's regime did not spring suddenly into existence, but gradually evolved. His military *putsch* of February 1921 made little impact on Persia's constitutional system, although it secured him the position of army commander and a place in the Cabinet.[11] Reza then added to his authority and powers through successful military campaigns against rebel movements in the provinces and by cultivating influence amongst the different political factions (particularly those who claimed an interest in reforms). While vulnerable to other powerful and potentially hostile political institutions and individuals, he benefited from dissatisfaction with the liberal political system and the associated desire for a strong man who could take decisive action to revitalise the country. However in December 1925, Reza's election as Shah (Ahmad, the last Qajar Shah, was deposed) by a Constituent Assembly made him effectively secure. At this point he enjoyed great popularity and prestige in Persia and could have decided, as many Persians and foreign observers hoped he would, to preside over a process of reform in cooperation with Parliament and the country's leading politicians.

That did not happen. Instead, Reza Shah Pahlavi continued to acquire power and to strip it away from other institutions and individuals, relying increasingly on methods of coercion and arbitrary action. One important facet of this policy can be seen in his treatment of Parliament and of Iran's politicians. During the first year and a half of his reign he sponsored few reforms, but appears instead to have tried to weaken and discredit Parliament, as my analysis of the parliamentary developments between December 1925 and mid-1927 will demonstrate. Thereafter, the establishment of *Iran-e Now* and *Taraqqi* struck a fatal blow at the remaining elements of independent-mindedness amongst Persian politicians and within Parliament. Some of Shah's 'sultanist' tendencies are already evident at the period described by this chapter: gross personal misbehaviour; arbitrary arrests and extra-judicial killings; and land-grabbing on a vast scale.[12] His allocation of the high public offices, notably the premiership, to loyal mediocrities showed a characteristic contempt for the spirit of constitutional rule.[13] Such a ruling style was not out of keeping, however, with the absolutism of Persia's pre-constitutional government.

Persia under Reza Shah, like the Soviet Union, Fascist Italy and Republican Turkey, preserved the institutions of representative government while driving out their liberal spirit. The formation of *Iran-e Now* and *Taraqqi*, Western diplomats and newspapers agreed, meant the adoption of modern authoritarian party methods in Iran. These observers described *Iran-e Now* as Fascist on the basis of articles in the Persian newspapers and public statements by the party leader, Minister of Court Taimurtash,[14] as well as – in the case of the British Embassy – his private conversations with the Oriental Secretary, Godfrey Havard.[15] *Iran-e Now*'s objectives were twofold: first, the creation of a powerful, pro-Shah party intended to form a disciplined majority in parliament and to ensure that radical, reforming proposals could be passed into law; and second, the mobilisation or organisation of army officers, officials and some elements of the wider public behind the Shah through a large-scale membership.[16] Taimurtash appears to have conceived of both *Iran-e Now* and *Taraqqi*, but consulted closely with and received the Shah's approval.

Was there a definite link with Italy? The position there, where

Mussolini and the Fascist Party gradually constructed an authoritarian, centralised regime within the existing framework of a constitutional monarchy, bore some resemblance to the situation in Persia after Reza's military *coup d'état*. But Taimurtash did not pay an official visit to Mussolini until 1928.[17] Moreover, the definition of a Fascist Party employed here could equally suggest that the Communist Party in the Soviet Union or, most likely of all, the Republican People's Party in Turkey served as a model. Taimurtash, who had been educated in Russia, spent part of 1926 negotiating a trade agreement in Moscow and Mustafa Kemal received him that year in Turkey.[18] In other words, Taimurtash could draw on a range of experiences. Reza himself already showed a keen interest in Mustafa Kemal's achievements.[19] Furthermore, some evidence of Reza's personal interest in the concept of a 'Fascist' Party appeared at the time of *Taraqqi*'s eclipse in 1932,[20] but he himself did not visit Turkey until 1934.

Why, if *Iran-e Now* failed within the space of a few months, is it worth considering? Partly because of the sense in which it failed. *Iran-e Now* set out to mobilise support for the Shah in the country at large, and in this respect had no real successor. Reza's lack of a mass party backing, such as that enjoyed by Mustafa Kemal in Turkey, is often regarded as a major weakness of his regime. However, *Iran-e Now* is also worth considering because of the sense in which it, or rather its offshoot *Taraqqi*, succeeded. *Taraqqi* had taken control of the Majlis by the end of 1927 and continued to serve the Shah, under the instructions of Taimurtash, until its dissolution in 1932. This destroyed the representative character but restored the legislative function of Persia's parliament:[21]

> Although there are a few independent members of Parliament, as distinct from those who are members of the *Taraqqi* or Government party, there is no minority party in the House... The *Taraqqi* party comprises more than 95 per cent of the total Deputies, and is so well shepherded by the Minister of Court that Bills presented to the Majlis by the Government pass without any trouble.

Indeed, Taimurtash justified *Iran-e Now* (to the British Embassy) in part as a way of bringing discipline to Iran's chaotic Parliament. He argued that Persia's Parliament and liberal political system had failed, and that a further concentration of authority was necessary in order to overcome faction and dissent and to push through the reforms required by the country.

Moreover, the affair is interesting because while the British, Americans, Germans, French and Italians noticed *Iran-e Now* and marked it out as a special type of party, as far as we know Persian politicians did not.[22] Some did, however, attack *Iran-e Now* at the time on the grounds of being an anti-religious or anti-clerical party and as the perceived faction of Taimurtash.[23] In retrospect, *Iran-e Now* seemed even less significant to retired Persian politicians and historians: Prime Minister Hidayat's memoirs,[24] although fairly detailed, do not trouble to mention it, nor does Bahar's two-volume *Short History of the Political Parties*.[25] Bagher Agheli's biography of Taimurtash devotes some lines to *Iran-e Now*, but also confuses it with *Iran-e Javan*, while Hossein Makki's well-known eight-volume work, *Twenty Years of Iran's History*, refers only to the dissolution of *Taraqqi*.[26] Some additional confusion has ensued from the report that the Shah dissolved *Taraqqi* because of its republican tendencies – almost certainly a false pretext for dissolving a formation that had long served the Shah but whose lead, Taimurtash, was now discredited.[27] In part the lack of attention paid to *Iran-e Now* derives from the low esteem in which Persian political parties have been held for the reasons cited above. Other prominent contemporary issues – the abolition of capitulations, legal reforms, and conscription – also tended to overshadow the apparently minor *Iran-e Now* controversy and the unopposed formation of *Taraqqi*.

Yet the tale of *Iran-e Now*'s rise and fall is a fascinating one. It shows, for example, the extraordinary manoeuvring and double-dealing of Reza. When *Iran-e Now*'s political opponents manifested themselves in the country, as well as in the Majlis and even in the Cabinet, Reza Shah responded with Byzantine skill. He permitted his Chief of Police to take over the running of another party, the so-called Anti-Foreigner (*Zedd-e Ajnabiha*)[28] group, which marshalled and led resistance to *Iran-e Now*. In this way he secured an indirect control over the opposition elements. Reza then left for a tour of his northern provinces, while the contending parties fought themselves to a standstill. On returning to the capital, he restored calm by ordering *Zedd-e Ajnabiha* to disband and then forbade state employees and officers from membership of any political party including *Iran-e Now*.[29] This latter move marked a concession to conservative clerical and public feeling, whose initial hostility towards *Iran-e Now* had by now widened into a campaign against recent secular reforms of the judicial system and the existing conscription law.[30] *Iran-e Now* went into decline. Meanwhile *Taraqqi*, which had quietly hatched out in September, went on to fulfil its objectives.

Some further words about sources. British Foreign Office General Correspondence (FO371) and the derivative Confidential Print (FO416)[31] at the Public Record Office in Kew provide the main diplomatic basis for this study, which, however, also draws on German, Italian and United States diplomatic records. The United States dispatches contain regular summaries from a number of Persian newspapers. Other sources include the Persian newspaper *Ittilâ'ât*, memoirs and secondary literature in Farsi, and summaries of contemporary newspaper reports from *Oriente Moderno* and the *Revue des Études Islamiques*. However the paucity of information, and above all of comment in Farsi sources, makes this a very Western account of the *Iran-e Now* episode.

Although the quoted British sources appear severe on certain Persian politicians (notably three Prime Ministers) and on Reza Shah, the reader would be mistaken to regard these remarks as either poorly based or a reflection of the overall British attitude. The criticisms of Foruqi, for example, are founded on concrete indications of his poor performance provided by, amongst others, Persians and Americans, and were balanced in his and the other Prime Ministers' cases by British expressions of regard for their personal manners and culture (left largely unquoted).[32] The German Minister, Graf Friedrich Werner von der Schulenburg, could be equally critical.[33] Similarly, the British remarks made about Reza Shah in 1926 seem harsh, but they are made in the context of the particular period of his illness and do not necessarily reflect a longer-term British view of him.

Iran-e Now

At the end of July 1927 the British Minister in Tehran, Robert Clive, briefly observed in his fortnightly Intelligence Report that 'A party on Fascist lines has been formed in Tehran with the Shah's approval, calling itself "Iran-i-No".'[34] His next Intelligence Report added little to this: 'the "Iran-i-No" party has been treated to a certain amount of press propaganda, and it is reported that the party is viewed with favour in high quarters'.³⁵ In the course of August, however, *Iran-e Now* expanded rapidly and the extent of its backing amongst the regime's leading personalities became apparent:³⁶

> The promoters of this party are a few of the younger and more advanced Persian politicians, like Taimourtach [sic], Minister of Court; Prince Firuz, Minister of Finance; Daver, Minister of Justice; together with a sprinkling of the younger Deputies and higher officers of the army. His Imperial Majesty the Shah is said to be the honorary president.

Taimurtash emerged as the party's official leader around the time of its first public meeting, held on 28 August. There he outlined *Iran-e Now*'s objectives:³⁷

> The independence of Persia under the banner of Pahlavi; the progress of Persia through the power of Reza Shah to civilisation and modernity; resistance to foreign influence; opposition to all reactionary and subversive ideas;³⁸ [and] honesty and devotion in public administration.

In the course of the same speech Taimurtash expressed himself in 'strongly anti-clerical, if not actually anti-Islamic' terms.³⁹ His party's unfriendliness towards the clergy became explicit in the requirement that members should adopt the peaked Pahlavi hat as a token of their obedience to the Shah. For religious reasons concerned with the brim and injunctions against imitating the infidel, such a proposition offended pious individuals as well as most of the *ulema*. The *ulema* also considered that they could not themselves adopt Pahlavi hats without abandoning a fundamental element of independence from the monarchy, and therefore felt deliberately excluded by the new party.⁴⁰ Such anti-clericalism actually attracted the Young Iran (*Iran-e Javan*) activists, whose group merged with *Iran-e Now*, while the newspaper *Tufan* argued that hats and dress had little to do with Islam.⁴¹ Minister of Justice Davar, who dissolved his Radical Party into *Iran-e Now*, himself struck a blow against clerical influence in the judiciary by instructing all ministry employees to wear peaked caps.⁴²

However, there was a deeper motive behind the creation of *Iran-e Now*, as Taimurtash made clear in a conversation with the British

Embassy's Oriental Secretary. He argued that Persian attempts to operate a liberal parliamentary system had failed:[43]

> Persia, after twenty years of so-called Constitutional Government, had made very little progress, and it had, so far, failed to grasp even the principles of Constitutional Government. Everything had to be started over again. There was one person around whom a political group could gather and that was the Shah. His Majesty longed for Persia to progress along modern lines and [that] all who were of the same idea should gather round him. There was no discipline in Persian political life to-day, and without discipline there was no hope. We had seen how the elections were run and how hopeless the Deputies were when they were safely ensconced in their chairs for two years. Elected on no programme and on no principle, their acts were devoid of reasoning and sense. It was every one for his own personal profit. They formed parties of mushroom growth, which grew unwieldy, split up, merged into other parties and disappeared almost before they had grown up. The reason was that personal interest was paramount ... A homogeneous and disciplined party, grouped around a personality and working through that personality for the good of the country, was the only hope for the future. The Iran No [sic] would scrutinise closely the record of would-be members, and he hoped that by the time when the new elections were due they would be in a strong position. If, as he hoped, they succeeded in acquiring a majority of seats, they could then go ahead with reforms of all kinds, even of a constitutional nature, which were so necessary. He instanced the difficulties which confronted the Government today in the face of an unruly and undisciplined Parliament by referring to the claim of His Majesty's Government for the debt owing by the Persian Government. He said that really no Government could be sure that the Majlis, as it was today, would even discuss this or similar questions in a spirit of fairness, because no Government could even be said to have a definite majority in the House. No ties of order, discipline, or principles of sympathy bound the two bodies together and thus we had Governments coming and going simply at the whim and caprice of a group of unscrupulous Deputies.

In short, conflicts within Parliament as well as between Parliament and the Cabinet were preventing the settlement of government business and the passage of reforms. Taimurtash was only too well aware of this state of affairs, because Reza Shah had given him the responsibility for managing relations between Parliament and the government.[44] Clive himself had expressed similar criticisms, and stressed a need for greater governmental and parliamentary discipline in his Annual Report for 1926.[45] Taimurtash's proposal, however, indicated a one-party solution.

Resistance to *Iran-e Now*

Almost as soon as it began to expand, *Iran-e Now* encountered resistance from some mullahs and rival politicians. Clive recorded the formation around mid-August 1927 of an unspecified new party largely dedicated to confronting *Iran-e Now*.[46] The new organisation might have been the *Zidd-i Ajnabîhâ* group, which Clive later described as being 'run by Khalisseh Zadeh and the Chief of Police'.[47] At any rate it appears to have served as an umbrella or linking structure for several elements of the opposition to *Iran-e Now*. The Education Minister Tadayyon and his existing Revival (*Tajaddud*) Party, for example, together with a number of lesser parliamentary factions, featured prominently amongst the opposition.[48] For a time in late August it looked as if the Shah would clamp down on them: Tadayyon left Tehran 'on a mysterious journey to Tabriz and rumour suggested that he has been sent there and will go from there to Europe, in disgrace for refusing to disband his party and join the new party [*Iran-e Now*] himself'.[49] In addition, Prime Minister Hidayat issued a stern public warning against the exploitation of religion for political ends.[50] By now, however, resistance to *Iran-e Now* was making itself felt in the country at large. Several *ulema* not only preached against *Iran-e Now* and the Pahlavi hat but went on to attack Minister of Justice Davar's legal reforms, the conscription law and even the Shah himself:[51]

> Incited partly by the formation of the Iran-i-No party, and partly by other indications of a growing disregard for their authority on the part of Young Persia, the mullahs have begun to agitate. They have singled out as objects for attack the reformation of the Courts of Justice, the official approval of

the wearing of the Pahlavi hat (an ordinary Persian kullah with a peak) and the Pahlavi costume (coat and trousers with collar and tie), which are now almost compulsory for Government employees, and, as far as the first is concerned, almost universally worn by Young Persians. Some violent sermons have been preached which, in their denunciation, did not clearly distinguish between the Shah and his Government, leading in some cases to the arrest of the preachers, followed by minor disturbances on the part of the crowd, amongst whom the mullahs have still many supporters. More serious disturbances occurred at Isfahan ... The mullahs of Isfahan seized the occasion of the arrest of a preacher, who had criticised the Shah and certain actions of the present regime, to organise a demonstration of protest. For eight days the Isfahan bazaars were closed, and crowds assembled at the telegraph office to send telegrams to Tehran. The offending priest was released, but the mullahs did not cease their agitation until the chief of police had been removed from his post.

In an atmosphere of continuing agitation the Shah himself left for Tabriz on 29 August, where, among others, he received Tadayyon. Taimurtash flew to the same city by Junkers on 1 September while Tadayyon received leave to return to Tehran.[52] His reappearance heartened the enemies of Taimurtash and *Iran-e Now* and redoubled their efforts:[53]

> Opposition to the party [*Iran-e Now*], which comes from various quarters, is strengthening and combining. The priests are solidly against it, and it has many opponents also in Parliament, led by Tadayun, the Minister for Public Instruction. A very active member of the Opposition is the Chief of Police, an entirely submissive servant of the Shah. It is as unlikely that he joined the Opposition without the Shah's consent, as that the Minister of the Court joined the new party against the Shah's wishes.

Many of the *ulema* believed that their livelihoods and influence were under serious threat from the regime and that they must take what opportunity was available to make an effective stand.[54] As indicated above, this campaign and the outcome of the Isfahan incident widened out into clerical protests against legal reforms (which affected many of their livelihoods), the lack of clerical representation in Parliament,[55] and above all over conscription, the issue of most concern to the general public and the merchants. Public feeling was such that a large group of *ulema*, headed by the *mujtahid* Haji Agha Norullah, did indeed rally a national protest movement around a sit-in at Qum. While that protest falls mainly outside the scope of the present study, it marked a serious challenge to the regime's authority and took several more months to settle.[56]

The Shah's role in the *Iran-e Now* affair, and his having a hand in both camps, gave rise to considerable speculation amongst leading Persian politicians and at the British Embassy as to what would happen on his return. As Clive observed, 'On the one side there is his Minister of the Court, on the other his chief of police, inciting the Opposition. Neither of these is likely to be acting without his orders. It is generally anticipated that the struggle will result in the crushing of some person or some faction.'[57] When he did arrive back in Tehran on 26 September,[58] Reza rebuffed 'various deputations of mullahs, who came to complain of the actions of "Iran-i-No"', and ordered the disbandment of *Zidd-i Ajnabîhâ*. However, he also issued an edict stating that no member of the court, or any official or officer, should join a political party. This meant that Taimurtash could no longer act as the official leader of *Iran-e Now* and many of its more influential supporters were obliged to withdraw. In addition, the Shah reached a compromise with Tadayyon and 'recommended the leaders to compose their party differences'.[59]

According to Clive, the Shah's action against *Iran-e Now* formed part of his negotiation with the more turbulent *ulema*:[60]

> Having somewhat clipped the wings of the Iran No, the Shah felt he could listen to the petition of the Clerical party, and sent some of them word that their wishes in connection with the agitation against the Iran No had been accomplished. The Clericals in Tehran have passed this on to their confrères in Meshed, and the Shah had asked Haji Agha Jemal, one of the principal Tehran mujtahids, to telegraph in this sense to Haji Agha Norullah . . .

Taraqqi

The Sixth Majlis (summer 1926–summer 1928) contained a group of factions whose number and composition varied and to which roughly nine-tenths of the deputies belonged. Their frequent shifts in membership and alignment, and occasional disappearances, appearances or changes in title, are still more obscure than those of the official parties. In June 1927, however, a few weeks before the foundation of the *Iran-e Now* Party, the chamber contained the following groups (in order of size): Independent (*Mustaqill*), Unity (*Ittihâd*), Radical (*Radîkâlî*), Free (*Âzâd*), National Cooperation (*Ta'âwun-i Millî*) and Progress of Iran (*Taraqqi-yi Iran*). Education Minister Tadayyon led the Independent grouping, which included deputies belonging to his Revival (*Tajaddud*) Party, while Justice Minister Davar ran the smaller Radical faction.[61]

Signs of a fundamental shift in the organisation of Parliament began to appear in early September, when the newspapers *Ittilâ'ât* and *Kûshish* noted that deputies were abandoning their existing groupings and contemplating fusion into one or more new parties.[62] Indeed the Radical, Independent, Unity and Free groupings dissolved themselves. However their anticipated amalgamation into an official party or parties did not take place; instead there arose another parliamentary grouping, the new *Taraqqi* faction (not to be confused with *Taraqqi-ye Iran*).[63] Clive described *Taraqqi* as the intended counterpart of *Iran-e Now* and 'sympathetic to its ideals'.[64] Thus it seems that the Shah and Taimurtash initially intended to incorporate the various parliamentary groupings into *Iran-e Now*, but in the face of continued agitation against that party decided to set up *Taraqqi* instead.[65] The fact that *Taraqqi* not only survived the Shah's intervention against *Iran-e Now* but continued to grow, reinforces the impression that he abandoned *Iran-e Now* for tactical reasons and transferred his support to *Taraqqi*. While *Iran-e Now* 'eked out a moribund existence', the *Taraqqi* faction became 'the strongest party in the Majlis. It is run by Taimourtache and is kept together by promises of the re-election of its members to the next Majlis.'[66] Significantly, *Taraqqi* absorbed the remainder of Tadayyon's Revival (*Tajaddod*) Party deputies by late October 1927. Tadayyon himself was sacked from his ministry and arrested shortly after the conclusion of the Qum crisis.[67] Meanwhile *Taraqqi* had begun to prove itself:[68]

NEW IRAN AND THE DISSOLUTION OF PARTY POLITICS 77

The energetic Minister of Court, who formed the Iran No party, also formed its counterpart – the Taraqqi party – in the Majlis, and he has kept the heterogeneous members of that party well in hand, with the result that the Majlis has actually been brought to pass some Bills which the Government greatly desired to have ratified. Before this shepherding took place, the Majlis had wasted its time in abortive discussions . . .

Elections to the Seventh Majlis (winter 1928–winter 1930) confirmed *Taraqqi*'s leading position in Parliament, which continued on into the Eighth Majlis (winter 1930–winter 1932).[69] Taimurtash remained throughout at the head of *Taraqqi*, whose demise accompanied his own fall from grace in 1932. Although the party had no successor, it would be misleading to insist that Persian party politics ended in 1932: liberal party politics effectively ceased after the formation of *Taraqqi*.[70]

The Context: Reza Shah and Parliament

Taimurtash's criticisms of the Majlis when setting out the case for *Iran-e Now* (as quoted above) sound less convincing if one considers the record of high politics since Reza's accession in December 1925. This record, as outlined below, shows that Reza Shah's own behaviour contributed significantly towards Parliament's poor legislative performance, bad relations with ministers and general unruliness over that period.[71] Indeed, his actions were so negative, in political conditions so propitious for positive initiatives (the period of grace and goodwill after his accession), as to raise suspicions regarding the Shah's attitude towards parliamentary independence and to suggest that, consciously or unconsciously, he acted thus in order to weaken the prestige of this institution before moving to impose his will on it.

Reza Shah's accession raised high hopes of reform amongst Persians and foreign observers (notably the British, American and German Embassies and the American Financial Mission headed by Dr Millspaugh) that were thoroughly dashed in the course of 1926. The Shah was understandably concerned with the political reliability of appointees to positions of authority, but his brooding, violent and suspicious character made it difficult for him either to trust or stimulate a sense of loyalty amongst others. Consequently he tended to appoint the incompetent or the semi-competent to important governmental and military posts instead of men of ability, whom he more often sought to discredit or destroy:[72]

> The Shah since his accession has thought only of maintaining his position . . . While hesitating to govern himself, he has permitted no one else to do so . . . He has not controlled the army; he has selected and kept in office two successive Prime Ministers who, even in Persia, are notorious for fecklessness and incompetence; internal security has not been maintained; he has quarrelled with the Majlis; he has quarrelled with the American mission; his main energies have been devoted to discrediting all possible rivals, and to amassing by questionable methods enormous private estates.

For example, Persia's written constitution entitled the Shah to choose as well as officially appoint his Prime Minister, and Reza did so. The Majlis, however, had become used to making the choice itself under Sultan Ahmad Shah and believed that Reza was reneging on an earlier promise to continue this practice. But what caused great disquiet amongst the deputies, the public and the foreign embassies was his manner of proceeding in the adoption of a candidate for the opening premiership of his reign:[73]

> With the choice limited to these two candidates, it was soon very apparent that, if public political opinion was to be the sole arbiter, only one of them could be considered to be in the running, and that one was Mirza Hassan Khan Mushar. He enjoyed the confidence and was assured of the active support of 75 per cent of the Deputies of the Majlis, and hardly one politician outside the Chamber could be found who was in favour of his rival. When about two days previous to the accession, it was learnt that His Majesty was in favour of Foruqi [the other candidate] becoming Prime Minister, there was a general feeling of astonishment mingled with dismay. Foruqi, although he possesses considerable culture, is a man of no political personality whatever, and, moreover, is lacking in decision and energy. In this respect he is the very antithesis of Mirza Hassan Khan Mushar, and it was felt that the choice of such a man to guide the affairs of the country was anything but

a happy augury for the beginning of the new regime. It was, of course, well known that His Majesty placed great confidence in Foruqi, as on the three occasions when, during his premiership, he had been obliged to leave the capital he had entrusted the direction of affairs of State to Foruqi. The reason of His Majesty's confidence in former times seems to have been that he knew Foruqi was incapable of doing anything either good or bad in his absence, and that he was sure on his return to find affairs exactly in the same position as they had been when he left. This negative sort of confidence may have been comforting, and undoubtedly gave him a feeling of security in those times, but with the present changed condition of affairs it seemed at this time quite unnecessary, if not actually disadvantageous.

Indeed, Reza's prime ministerial appointments displayed a consistent preference for mediocrity and political reliability: Foruqi ('politically he is incapable and a nonentity') between December 1925 and May 1926,[74] Mostafi ('of weak character and incapable of taking a decision on the most unimportant matter') between June 1926 and June 1927,[75] and for several years subsequently Hedayat ('now old and addicted to opium . . . has lost much of his former energy').[76] Able, independent-minded politicians such as Mushar and Vossuk, who looked quite capable of mustering a majority in the Majlis, were passed over for this position.[77] Reza Shah also interfered in the selection of ministers, without, however, exercising any quality control.[78] Clive, for example, described the situation in early 1927 as follows:[79] 'The Cabinet, with Mostowfi-el-Mamalek, now for the sixth time Prime Minister, was composed of the usual collection of futile mediocrities.' The Fifth and Sixth Majlis thus became increasingly frustrated at a policy which infringed their prerogatives, clashed with the majority of their members' wishes and produced ineffectual governments. It responded by criticising ministers, holding up business and seeking to bring cabinets down. This led to the frequent dissolution and reconstitution of cabinets, but to little change in their character.[80]

Although Reza and the conservative politician-cleric, Modarres, had clashed over the proposal to establish a republic in 1924 and over Reza's substitution for Shah Ahmad in 1925,[81] they collaborated in Parliament for the remainder of the Fifth Majlis (spring

1924–spring 1926) and in managing elections to the Sixth (summer 1926–summer 1928).[82] Modarres exercised a say in the composition of cabinets and in return lent them his parliamentary and public support, although he intervened in May 1926 to insist (successfully) on Foruqi's resignation.[83] However the Sixth Majlis, which opened in July, turned on both the new Prime Minister (Mostowfi) and Modarres:[84]

> A block was formed against Modarres, two or three of his henchmen were unseated, and in fact imprisoned, and the mandates of those who had resisted his influence were confirmed. Having thus manifested their independence, the block directed a frontal attack on Modarres by combining against the Mostowfi Cabinet.

According to the British Embassy, the Majlis acted in this way because it regarded Mostowfi as the stooge of Modarres and Reza.[85] Parliament was now 'solidly anti-Shah'.[86] Modarres reacted by attempting to distance himself from Reza. But on 30 October he suffered an attempted assassination (apparently by members of the secret police acting on the Shah's orders):[87]

> Modarres, who realised that his prestige as a demagogue was suffering from his alliance with the Shah, took occasion to make a daring speech, in which he stated that he would only support His Majesty so long as he acted constitutionally. Three weeks later a determined attempt was made upon the life of Modarres in circumstances which implicated the secret police. The Majlis appear to have been momentarily cowed by this attempted murder, and Modarres himself, on his return from hospital, adopted a less arrogant tone. Towards the end of the year, however, the attacks upon the Mostowfi Cabinet were redoubled, and the debates in the Assembly became as hectic, as egoistic, and as futile as ever.

Very little was achieved during the first year of Reza's reign. Clive noted in his Annual Report that 'neither the Foruqi nor the Mostowfi Cabinets which ruled Persia during 1926 have done any constructive work whatsoever. Such Bills as have been proposed were due to the American mission working through the Ministry of Finance.'[88]

The Shah's Illness and Recovery

In the course of 1926 British and German diplomats came to believe that Reza was suffering some form of mental malaise:[89]

> his energy appears for the moment to have deserted him; his faculties have been clouded by the fumes of opium, which have distorted his judgement and induced long spells of sullen and secretive lethargy punctuated by nightmare suspicions or by spasms of impulsive rage. He appears bewildered, and even afraid . . . This apparent degeneration has bewildered his most fervent admirers, who are inclined to attribute it to the effects of opium. His insane suspicion, his sudden outbursts of rage, and his inability to see things in their correct proportions may, indeed, be attributable to his indulgence in narcotics. But his persistent inaction, his apparent indifference to his own reputation and popularity, his somewhat shameless cupidity, must be due to less adventitious causes, and constitute a psychological problem of great interest which only his subsequent development can solve.

Reza also showed little hesitation in unleashing his violent and capricious temper in public. One example among many will suffice:[90]

> As an illustration of his petulance, a recent visit that he paid to the cadet school may be cited. When His Majesty arrived the band was playing; he did not like the drummer's action, so he stopped the band, cursed the unhappy man until he shook with fear, and ended by putting his foot through the drum. He then made the cadets march past; two of the budding officers did not appear to him to have a sufficiently martial bearing, and as they passed he walked up to them frowning. They lost step from fear. He then laid hold of them and shook them until they were limp. Such is the way in which he himself was treated by the old Russian N.C.O.s of the quondam Cossack brigade when he first joined it as an awkward private soldier. When his temper gets the better of him he forgets that he has left the barrack room for the palace, but his victims, their relations and friends, see in him the King, and when such unkindly behaviour is noised abroad, it is hardly calculated to raise the

Royal prestige or to engender love of their sovereign in the hearts of his subjects.

Since Reza had exhibited some of these traits in the past, diplomats such as Harold Nicolson continued to hope for an improvement. Indeed, towards the end of 1926 Reza showed signs of recovery.[91] Around this time, however, the new British Minister (Clive) began to perceive an underlying strategy in the Shah's political behaviour:[92] 'It is much to be feared that his [the Shah's] sole aim is to discredit not only the elder statesmen, but parliamentary government itself. He seems to be working towards a military autocracy.'

It is difficult to establish what precise role the return of Taimurtash to Persia at the very end of 1926 played in the Shah's recovery. However, Clive believed that Taimurtash helped to jolt Reza out of his lethargy.[93] Similarly, Taimurtash had an important hand in most of the political and legislative initiatives which occurred during 1927, but he worked in close cooperation with the Shah.[94] He certainly enjoyed extraordinary political privileges:[95]

> As Minister of the Court he has acquired the position of the Shah's most intimate political adviser. His influence is ubiquitous, and his power exceeds that of the Prime Minister. He attends all meetings of the Council of Ministers, and one might compare his position with that of Reich Chancellor, except that he has no direct responsibility.

Conclusion

In view of the above and what we know about the different capacities of Taimurtash and Reza Shah, it seems that Taimurtash produced the *Iran-e Now* scheme in response to what he perceived as the inclinations of the Shah, and that this proposal met with the Shah's approval. *Iran-e Now* did have a predecessor, the *Tajaddod* party, which Taimurtash co-founded with Davar and Tadayyon and which served the Shah in the Fifth Majlis (spring 1924–spring 1926). During the Sixth Majlis (summer 1926–summer 1928), however, *Tajaddod* no longer represented their combined forces but belonged exclusively to Tadayyon. Even so, *Tajaddod*'s originally secular credentials cast doubt on Tadayyon's religious objections to *Iran-e Now*, just as the breakdown of collaboration over *Tajaddod* suggests political rivalry as Tadayyon's principal motivating factor. It is clear that jealousy and personal dislike motivated others among the opposition.[96] As to whether Persian politicians recognised *Iran-e Now* as a 'Fascist' party, that remains uncertain. At the time it was certainly safer to express dissent in a religious form than in directly political terms of opposition to dictatorship.[97] Some members of the *ulema* found that religious arguments succeeded in stirring up public feeling against the regime, but the controversy over *Iran-e Now* and legal reforms roused the public far less than the issue of conscription (although that too had a religious aspect).

Who then was to blame for the 1926–27 parliamentary crisis, which the *Iran-e Now* scheme (or rather *Taraqqi*) resolved? The evidence cited shows that Reza's extremely negative attitude was at least partly responsible. One might indeed go further and suppose that the Shah was content to see the situation in Parliament deteriorate until conditions were ripe for radical intervention. That not unfamiliar tactic apparently operated in the case of the law reforms, where the existing system was allowed to degenerate and fester thoroughly before Davar received the signal to step in with secularising changes. Potential opposition to these legal reforms was also undercut by associating them with the abolition of capitulations.[98]

Yet there is no doubt that the deputies in the Majlis operated in a confused and selfish manner, as Clive observed:[99]

> The Sixth Majlis has proved itself during the year to be a very unintelligent, ignorant and obstructive body; such party organisation as exists has been of a kaleidoscopic nature, and the groups coalesce and then again dissolve for purely personal and incidental causes. The majority of the Deputies are rabidly Nationalist, and anti-British feeling is very vocal and may be intense. They are not pro-Russian, but it is always possible that they may from fear or cupidity adopt a Russian point of view. The Assembly as a whole has no conception of the difference which should exist between the Legislature and the Executive, and every Deputy claims the right to interfere in the most trivial executive matters, and to annul whatever undertakings the Government or the Departments may have contracted. Not only are they jealous and suspicious of the Government and the Departments, they are equally jealous and suspicious of each other. Blackmail and corruption are universal, and the

Deputies are apt to attack the rights of foreign companies in the sole hope that they may thereby receive a bribe for silence. It is to be feared that unless the Shah is able to impose some discipline upon the Majlis the machinery of government will be completely obstructed.

The frequent bitter outbursts and personal feuds between members of the Majlis also indicate a lack of political maturity.[100] Indeed, the extraordinary business of Tadayyon as well as the Chief of Police attacking *Iran-e Now* illustrates the extent to which personal rivalries and jealousies could bypass discipline and the duty of obedience to the Shah. Rigged elections and a packed Parliament were the logical solution to this parliamentary and political chaos. They were also the natural corollary of choosing a strong man like Reza to save the country.

This chapter has illustrated some of the genuine difficulties encountered by Persia, like many other countries, in attempting to run a parliamentary system, and thus helped to explain their interest in modern authoritarian solutions. Taimurtash presented one such solution, *Iran-e Now*, which set out to organise Parliament as well as significant sections of Persia's population. In practice, he achieved only the parliamentary domination afforded by *Taraqqi*, and the Shah succeeded in managing the Majlis without it after 1932. The failure to establish a ruling national party, an important point of difference between inter-war Turkey and Iran, may or may not have made it easier for the older tradition of absolute rule to reassert itself in Reza Shah. But Reza's inclinations were despotic, whereas Mustafa Kemal would be better described as a dictator. The authoritarian Turkish Republic had several other advantages over Persia: skills and pride inherited from the Ottoman Empire, a century of relatively effective reforms and development behind it, and a cohesion between regime and people arising from the successful War of Independence.

Notes

[1] The author wishes to thank Houchang Chehabi, as well as the British Institute of Archaeology at Ankara, the British Institute of Persian Studies, the Public Record Office (PRO), the Auswärtiges Amt Politisches Archiv (AA) and the Archivio Storico del Ministero degli Affari Esteri (ASMAE).

[2] *Iran-e Now*, founded in July 1927, should not be confused with the

earlier newspaper of the same name or with *Hizb-i Iran-e Nuwîn* (post-1965).

³ This *Taraqqi* party, which was founded in September 1927, can easily be confused with an already existing parliamentary faction of a very similar name. See *Confidential United States Diplomatic Post Records: Middle East, Iran 1925–1941* (Frederick: University Publications of America, 1984) (henceforward *USDPR*), Reel 4, No. 456, Tehran, 8 October 1927, 'Shafagh-i Sorkh (September 23): publishes a notice signed by the so-called *Taraghi-i-Iran* Party (Progress of Persia) having no connections with the new group formed in the Majlis. *Taraghi-i-Iran* requests the new group to change its name'; *Oriente Moderno* (henceforward OM) (Roma: Istituto per l'Oriente), 1927, 274, referring to *Setareh-e Iran*, 29 May–3 June 1927, and to *The Times*, 4 June 1927.

⁴ PRO, FO371, 12286, E3559 Sir Robert Henry Clive, Tehran, 29 July 1927; FO371, 12286, E3914 Clive, Tehran, 27 August 1927; FO371, 12293, E3909 Clive, Tehran, 26 August 1927; FO371, 13069, E2897 Clive, Tehran, 21 May 1928; AA, Abt. III, R78145 Graf Friedrich Werner von der Schulenburg, Tehran, 11 August 1927; ASMAE, Rapporti Politici, Pacco 1471, Giulio Daneo, Tehran, 26 June 1929; *The Times*, 1 September 1927: 'A party has been formed in Persia under the name of the Irani Noh (New Persians) with a policy modelled upon that of the Fascisti. It is rumoured that the movement has the approval of the Shah'; OM, 1927, 501; Ervand Abrahamian, *Iran Between Two Revolutions* (Princeton, NJ: PUP, 1982), 138.

⁵ Reza Khan adopted the name Pahlavi at the time of the abolition of titles and adoption of surnames in 1925, OM, 1925, 376–77, referring to *Temps*, 29 June 1925; Bagher Agheli, *Taimurtash* (1377), 207; A. C. Millspaugh, *The American Task in Persia* (New York: Century, 1925), 167–69. In practice it was some time before nomenclature came into alignment with the law, even in the case of ministers, OM, 1926, 530. Indeed, Hidayat's government introduced an additional system of political titles in 1927, Agheli, *Taimurtash*, 236.

⁶ Abrahamian, *Iran*, 41–42, 47, 51–58; A. C. Millspaugh, *Americans in Persia* (Washington DC: Brookings Institute, 1946), 29–31, 34.

⁷ Abrahamian, *Iran*, 86, 88, 101; J. M. Landau, 'Madjlis', *Encyclopaedia of Islam* (henceforward *EI*), 2nd ed. (Leiden: Brill, 1986), 5:1042–44.

⁸ Banani, 'Hizb', *EI*, 2nd ed. (Leiden: Brill, 1986), 3:527–30.

⁹ Elie Kedourie, 'Political Parties in the Arab World', in his *Arabic Political Memoirs and Other Studies* (London: Cass, 1974), 28–58; Philip S. Khoury, *Syria and the French Mandate: The Politics of Arab Nationalism, 1920–1945* (London: Tauris, 1987), 219–42, 563–618; Patrick Seale, *The Struggle For Syria* (London: Tauris, 1987), 24–32.

¹⁰ Nor did authoritarian rulers such as Mussolini hesitate to criticise parliamentary factionalism: Ismail Sidqi, *Mudhakkirâtî* (My Recollections) (Cairo: Dâr al-Hilâl, 1950), 58: 'He [Mussolini] began to speak with me and

I perceived that the man had a violent detestation for the parliamentary system which obstructed – in his view – the progress of countries due to the [harm] arising from personal differences between those involved in politics . . .' (translation). On Mussolini's Middle East policy, see Renzo De Felice, *Il Fascismo e l'Oriente: Arabi, Ebrei e Indiani Nella Politica di Mussolini* (Bologna: Mulino, 1988).

[11] Abrahamian, *Iran*, 118.

[12] On the theory of sultanism, see Huochang E. Chehabi and Juan I. Linz (eds), *Sultanistic Regimes* (Baltimore: Johns Hopkins University Press, 1998), 3–48. Millspaugh, *Americans in Persia*, 26–27, 34, 36–37, summarises some of the worst aspects of Reza Shah's regime. Mohammad Turkman, 'Negah-I beh Amval-e Manqul va Ghay-e manqul-e Reza Shah' (A Survey of Reza Shah's Movable and Immovable Property), in *Tarikh-e Mo'aser-e Iran*, Book 7, Spring 1374/1995, 101–68, looks at the Shah's acquisitions. Eventually the Persian Parliament became little more than a rubber stamp, PRO: GFM36/507 Ministero degli Affari Esteri, Iran: Situazione Politica Nel 1937.

[13] Mohammad Reza Shah appeared to follow a similar policy of appointing relatively weak personalities as Prime Minister after the fall of Musaddiq in 1953.

[14] Mirza Abdul Hussain Khan Taimurtash was appointed Minister of Court by a firman issued on 28 Zahar 1304 (19 December 1925), that is, shortly after Reza Shah's election to the throne, Agheli, *Taimurtash*, 211, 215; FO416, 81, No. 36, Clive, Gulhek, 13 July 1927.

[15] FO371, 12285, E883 Clive, Tehran, 28 January 1927; FO371, 12286, E3737 Clive, Tehran, 13 August 1927; FO371, 12293, E3909 Clive, Tehran, 26 August 1927; AA, Abt. III, R78145 Schulenburg, Tehran, 11 August 1927: 'Offenbar schwebt Seiner Majestät und seinen Helfern das Beispiel der Faschistenpartei oder das der türkischen Regierungspartei vor'; Ittilâ'ât, 9 Shahrîvar 1306 (31 August 1927), 'Notq-e Aqa-ye Taimurtash Vazir-e Darbar' (Speech of Taimurtash the Minister of Court).

[16] AA, Abt. III, R78145 Schulenburg, Tehran, 11 August 1927; ASMAE, Rapporti Politici, Pacco 1471, Daneo, Tehran, 26 June 1929: 'sarebbe assai migliore la via per la quale il Teymourtache avrebbe inteso incamminare la Persia e cioè la creazione di un forte partito nazionale, analogo al Fascista, che costituisce una base solida su cui appoggiare il programma di riforme che è in animo del Sovrano e da cui si potessero trarre uomini energici, non venduti ad alcun Governo straniero ma patriottici e sinceri partigiani del nuovo regime'; Agheli, *Taimurtash*, 238; OM, 1927, 501, referring to *Tribune d'Orient*, 18 October 1927.

[17] *The Times*, 11 and 14 August 1928. Taimurtash returned to Italy in 1931, Agheli, *Taimurtash*, 258, 273.

[18] FO416, 81 No. 36, Clive, Gulhek, 13 July 1927; FO371, 12296, E870 Clive, Tehran, 26 January 1927; Agheli, *Taimurtash*, 217–20. Taimurtash

also visited France, Germany and Switzerland in 1926. According to *USDPR*, Reel 4. No. 432, Tehran, 10 September 1927, quoting *Shafaq-i Surkh*, 31 August, Taimurtash compared the Shah to both Mussolini and Mustafa Kemal in his speech at *Iran-e Now*'s first public meeting. However the version of his speech in *Ettela'at*, 9 Shahrivar 1306 (31 August 1927), 'Notq-e Aga-ye Taimurtash Vazir-e Darbar', does not mention either. Many Persian intellectuals admired Mussolini, who was seen as a strong man uniting and modernising Italy, Abrahamian, *Iran*, 124.

[19] Agheli, *Taimurtash*, 229.

[20] FO371, 16967, E2439 Hoare, Tehran, 22 April 1933: 'With the temporary eclipse of its founder Teymourtache in August, followed by his fall on 22 December, the Tarraqi party has to all intents and purposes disappeared. His Majesty, in a speech to certain Deputies, who had come to one of his receptions on 17 October, alluded to the desirability of forming a national party for the furtherance of national aims in Persia, somewhat on the lines of the Fascist party. The idea may be to replace the defunct Taraqqi party by something more universal; or it may foreshadow a genuine attempt to instil into the population at large some of the ideas of duty and responsibility which are being painfully instilled into the official and military classes. Nothing more was heard of the new party by the end of the year. In a Majlis the members of which are chosen beforehand by the Government it does not appear likely that any party will arise in opposition to the Shah's expressed wishes'; AA, Abt. III, R78147 Von Blücher, Tehran, den. 22. Oktober 1932: 'Der Schah hat beim letzten Wochenempfang der Deputierten einige Äusserungen fallen lassen, die hier lebhaft kommentiert werden. Er hat gesagt, es rücke jetzt der Zeitpunkt heran, in dem man in Persien eine oder mehrere politische Parteien gründen müsse, um das Leben des Parlaments zu befruchten. Er sei selbst bereit, das Ehrenpräsidium dieser Partei bezw. dieser Parteien zu übernehmen. Er erwartete, dass ihm die Deputierten nähere Vorschläge unterbreiteten . . .'

'. . . In persischen Kreisen zerbricht man sich den Kopf, in welcher Weise die Anregung in die Praxis umzusetzen sei. Was dem Schah vorschwebt, glaube ich aus einer vertraulichen Mitteilung eines hiesigen italienischen Faschisten schliessen zu können. Dieser ist von persischer Seite, deren Beziehungen sehr hoch heraufgehen sollen, aufgefordert worden, ein Exposé über das Wesen des Faschismus und insbesondere über seine Organisation aufzustellen.'

[21] FO416, 113 (E2445) Clive, Tehran, 30 April 1930; FO371, 13799 E3676 Clive, Tehran, 14 July 1929; FO416, 113 (E3067) Clive, Tehran, 22 May 1931; FO416, 113 (E3354) Hoare, Tehran, 12 June 1932.

[22] In truth it is difficult to know because of the contemporary restrictions on free speech and publishing, which did not apply to diplomats.

[23] Tadayyon and his party *Tajaddod* played a leading role in rallying

parliamentary as well as public opposition to *Iran-e Now* and Taimurtash. This was ironic considering that Tadayyon, Taimurtash and Davar had jointly founded *Tajaddud*, a party with secular principles. The role undertaken by *Tajaddud* in the Fifth Majlis foreshadowed that envisaged by Taimurtash for *Iran-e Now* in the Sixth, Peter Avery, *Modern Iran* (London: Benn, 1965), 265; Abrahamian, *Iran*, 121–26, 132–38.

[24] Mokhber al-Saltaneh Hedayat, *Khaterat va Khatarat* (Memories and Perils) (Tehran, 1361/1982).

[25] Malik Sha'ra'i Bahar, *Tarikh-e Mokhtaser-e Ahzab-e Siyasi-ye Iran* (A Brief History of Iran's Political Parties), 2 Vols (Tehran: 1343). I have also consulted Hasan 'Azam Qudsi, *Ketab-e Khaterat-e Man* (The Book of My Memoirs), 2 Vols (Tehran: 1368).

[26] Hossein Makki, *Târikh-i Bîst Sâlah-yi Iran* (20 Years of Iran's History), 8 Vols, (Tehran, 1362/1983), 5:239; Agheli, *Taimurtash*, Contents page and 238. Agheli's *Nasrat al-Dowleh Firuz* (Tehran, 1994), does not mention *Iran-e Now*.

[27] Abrahamian, *Iran*, 138–39; Homa Katouzian, 'The Pahlavi Regime in Iran', in Chehabi and Linz, *Sultanistic Regimes*, 192; Agheli, *Taimurtash*, 238, states that the Shah disliked *Iran-e Now* because 'the party was inconsistent with dictatorship'. Donald N. Wilber, *Reza Shah Pahlavi: The Resurrection and Reconstruction of Iran* (New York: Exposition, 1975), pp. 122, 255, gives some accurate but also some inaccurate information about *Iran-e Now* and *Taraqqi*.

[28] Apart from references in FO371 files and a bare citation in Banani, 'Hizb', *EI*, 2nd ed., 3: 528, I have no information about this party.

[29] FO371, 12286, E4503 Clive, Tehran, 8 October 1927.

[30] FO371, 12293, E4506 CLive, Tehran, 8 October 1927; FO371, 12293, E4735 Clive, Tehran, 21 October 1927; FO371, 12286, E4109 Clive, Tehran, 10 September 1927; FO371, 12286, E4742 Clive, Tehran, 22 October 1927; FO371, 12286, E4982 Clive, Tehran, 5 November 1927; FO371, 12286, E5206 Clive, Tehran, 19 November 1927.

[31] FO416 consists almost entirely of selections from FO371. In addition, I have cited FO248 and a captured Italian diplomatic document from GFM36.

[32] FO416, 78 No. 18 (E391) Sir Percy Loraine, 30 December 1925, 'a scholarly man and a jurist . . . He has translated Sykes's "Persia" into Persian and is very fond of books. As a Minister of State he is extremely lazy and has never shown any decision or initiative. As Minister for Foreign Affairs he was passively obstructive, and official letters often remained unanswered for months. As Minister of Finance he was a dummy, simply occupying himself with signing letters prepared for him by the American adviser, often without taking the trouble even to read them. His compatriots have dubbed him "the signature machine". His two good qualities are scholarship and honesty, but politically he is incapable and a nonentity.' Foruqi's reputation

later improved as a result of his statesman-like behaviour after the Anglo-Russian invasion of 1941.

33 AA, Abt. III, R78145 Schulenburg, Tehran, 18 June 1927, 'Der Innenminister Samii ist eine Null, ebenso der neue Kriegsminister Serdar Assad Bakhtiari'.

34 FO371, 12286, E3559 Clive, Tehran, 29 July 1927.

35 FO371, 12286, E3737 Clive, Tehran, 13 August 1927; FO371, 12293, E3909 Clive, Tehran, 26 August 1927: 'The Tehran press has . . . been busy telling its readers how advantageous for the country it would be to have properly constituted political parties, founded on real political principles and imbued with a desire for Persia's progress'; AA, Abt. III, R78145 Schulenburg, Tehran, 11 August 1927.

36 FO371, 12293, E3909 Clive, Tehran, 26 August 1927; Agheli, *Taimurtash*, 238. Wilber, *Reza Shah Pahlavi*, p. 122, also cites 'General Murtiza Yazdanpanah and Faraj Allah Bahrami, the private secretary of Reza Shah' among the founder members.

37 FO371, 12286, E4109 Clive, Tehran, 10 September 1927; *Ittilâ'ât*, 9 Shahrîvar 1306 (31 August 1927), 'Notq-e Aqa-ye Taimurtash Vazir-e Darbar'.

38 In other words, opposition to the excessive influence of religion in politics and to Communism.

39 FO371, 12286, E4109 Clive, Tehran, 10 September 1927; *USDPR*, Reel 4, No. 432, Tehran, 10 September 1927. At an earlier meeting with the Minister, Taimurtash had described *Iran-e Now*'s principles as 'devotion to the Shah, maintenance of sovereign rights, and opposition to Socialism, Communism and the domination of the clergy' (FO371, 12293, E3909 Clive, Tehran, 26 August 1927). For further information on relations between the state and the ulema at this time, see Shahrough Akhavi, *Religion and Politics in Contemporary Iran: Clergy–State Relations in the Pahlavi Period* (Albany: State University of New York Press, 1980); Mohammad H. Faghfoory, 'The Ulama–State Relations in Iran: 1921–1941', *International Journal of Middle Eastern Studies*, Vol. 19, 1987, 413–432; Faghfoory, 'The Impact of Modernization on the Ulama in Iran, 1925–1941', *Journal of the Society for Iranian Studies*, Vol. 26, 1993, 277–312.

40 FO371, 13069, E2897 Clive, Tehran, 21 May 1928; FO371, 12293, E3909 Clive, Tehran, 26 August 1927; Matthew Elliot, *The Modernisation of Male Headgear in the Inter-War Middle East*, Ph.D. Thesis, Univ. of London (SOAS), 1998, 52–65.

41 *Ittilâ'ât*, 7 Shahrîvar 1306 (29 August 1927), 'Dar Majma'-i Iran-e Javan' (At the meeting of Iran-e Javan); FO371, 12293, E4113 Clive, Tehran, 10 September 1927; FO371, 12286, E4109 Clive, Tehran, 10 September 1927; *USDPR*, Reel 4, No. 417, Tehran, 27 August 1927; *USDPR*, Reel 4, No. 442, Tehran, 24 September 1927.

⁴² *Ittilâ'ât*, 30 Amurdâd 1306 (21 August 1927), ''Ilâ az taraf-i Vizârat-i 'Adliyah' (Announcement by the Ministry of Justice); FO416, 81, No. 36, Clive, Gulhek, 13 July 1927; FO371, 12293, E3909 Clive, Tehran, 26 August 1927; OM, 1927, 274 referring to Sitârah-i Iran, 29 May–3 June 1927, and to *The Times*, 4 June 1927, given a figure of 19 radical deputies at that date in the Majlis; *Revue des Études Islamiques*, 1927, 591; *USDPR*, Reel 4, No. 417, Tehran, 27 August 1927. Mirza Firuz Mirza (title: Nusrat al-Dowleh), another supporter of *Iran-e Now*, had already demonstrated his loyalty to the Shah and his commitment to modernisation by replacing his kulah with a Pahlavi hat, *USDPR*, Reel 4, No. 385, Tehran, 2 July 1927.

⁴³ FO371, 12293, E3909 Clive, Tehran, 26 August 1927. During the second half of 1926 Taimurtash visited Turkey, Russia, Germany, Switzerland and France (OM, 1926, p. 610, referring to *Temps*, 23 November 1926) but not, apparently, Italy.

⁴⁴ Agheli, *Taimurtash*, 221–24.

⁴⁵ FO371, 12296, E870 Clive, Tehran, 26 January 1927.

⁴⁶ FO371, 12286, E3914 Clive, Tehran, 27 August 1927, 'a rival party, whose object is little more than to obstruct the progressive ideas of the other, has been formed by priests and some of the enemies of the Minister of the Court. Intimate and loyal followers of the Shah are to be found in both parties.'

⁴⁷ FO371, 12293, E4506 Clive, Tehran, 8 October 1927.

⁴⁸ FO371, 12286, E4309 Clive, Tehran, 24 September 1927; FO371, 12293, E1008 Clive, Tehran, 11 February 1927; FO371, 12293, E4506 Clive, Tehran, 8 October 1927; AA, Abt. III, R78145 Schulenburg, Tehran, 27 October 1927; OM, 1927, 274, referring to *Sitârah-i Iran*, 29 May–3 June 1927, and to *The Times*, 4 June 1927; *Revue des Études Islamiques*, 1927, 590–92, referring to *Sitârah-i Iran*.

⁴⁹ FO371, 12293, E3909 Clive, Tehran, 26 August 1927; *USDPR*, Reel 4, No. 432, Tehran, 10 September 1927.

⁵⁰ Makki, *Tarikh-e Bist Saleh-ye Iran*, 4: 396–97; FO371, 12293, E3909 Clive, Tehran, 26 August 1927; *USDPR*, Reel 4, No. 417, Tehran, 27 August 1927. After Tadayyon's return from Tabriz the opposition boldly rejected the Prime Minister's declaration, *USDPR*, Reel 4, No. 432, Tehran, 10 September 1927. Mahdi-Quli Khan Hidayat is sometimes referred to by his title, Mukhbir al-Sultana.

⁵¹ FO371, 12286, E4109 Clive, Tehran, 10 September 1927; FO371, 12293, E3909 Clive, Tehran, 26 August 1927; FO248, 1384, 301c/14 No. 241, 23 September 1927.

⁵² *Ettela'at*, 9 Shahrîvar 1306 (31 August 1927), 'Mosaferat-e Shah' (The Shah's Journey); *Ettela'at*, 11 Shahrivar 1306 (2 September 1306), 'Mokeb-e Shah' (The Shah's Procession); *USDPR*, Reel 4, No. 432, Tehran, 10 September 1927, citing *Iran* and *Kushesh*; FO371, 12286, E4309 Clive,

Tehran, 24 September 1927: 'During the absence with the Shah in Tabriz of Taimourtache {sic]...'; *USDPR*, Reel 4, No. 432, Tehran, 10 September 1927: '(September 4): Announces the arrival in Tehran of Tadayon, Minister of Education. (Note: He had been absent for a fortnight apparently out of royal favor).'; FO248, 1384, 301c/12 British Consulate, Tabriz, 18 September 1927; FO248, 1384, 301c/13 British Consulate, Tabriz, 27 September 1927.

[53] FO371, 12286, E4109 Clive, Tehran, 10 September 1927; *USDPR*, Reel 4, No. 432, Tehran, 10 September 1927: 'Shafagh-i-Surkh (September 7): It is reported that Tadayon, Minister of Education, made a speech last night in the club of the Tajadod Political Party against the Iran-i Now Party'; FO371, 12293, E4113 Clive, Tehran, 10 September 1927, 'Teymourtache ... has many enemies. His very methods of directness and plain speaking invite opposition. Politicians of the old school like Mukhber-es-Sultaneh, the Prime Minister, and Tadayun, a former Sayyid, the Minister of Education, while no doubt loyal to the Shah, are not in sympathy with the shock tactics of the Minister of Court. The chief of police, in whom the Shah has great confidence, hates him. In Isfahan and Shiraz the mullahs look upon him as their declared enemy. In the Majlis the Deputies are much divided, and but a few at present have joined the new party'; FO371, 12293, E4506 Clive, Tehran, 8 October 1927, 'Taimourtache's absence in Tabriz left the Iran No party somewhat weak, and Tadayun's return from Tabriz, whilst Taimourtache was still absent, gave renewed vigour to the Tajaddud party and weakened the Iran No. Tadayun lost no time in attacking the Iran No along the whole line, and the Clericals in Tehran, Isfahan and Meshed launched a regular campaign against the Iran No and its leaders, Taimourtache, Firuz Mirza and Daver. The important ulema in Tehran threatened to leave the city, those of Isfahan threatened to go into a sort of bast at Qum, and those at Khorassan appealed to their colleagues at Tehran to show themselves men and extirpate the Iran No.'

[54] FO371, 12293, E4506 Clive, Tehran, 8 October 1927: 'the anger of the Clerical party is not so much against the Iran No as against the present Minister of Justice and the reforms which he has been and is still trying to enforce in that Ministry. In a word, these so-called reforms have had the immediate result of depriving a host of the turbaned gentry from earning their daily bread. Practically every little mullah had a miniature religious court of law where notarial acts were performed and where matters relating to personal status were arranged. The new Ministry of Justice has centralised a court for these matters and Daver has become very unpopular. This is a sore that will continue to fester, and even Daver himself is said to be very anxious about the success of his reforms'; FO371, 12286, E4742 Clive, Tehran, 22 October 1927: 'The mullahs, having no longer the Iran-i-Now party as an easy object against which to arouse hostility of the masses, and realising that the present trend of events, particularly the reform of the

justice Department, is so threatening their old privileges that, if they are to retain any of them, they must make a stand now, have taken advantage of the latent opposition of the people of the towns, particularly trades' guilds, to conscription, to arouse a fresh agitation. The mullahs of Isfahan took the lead in organising opposition to conscription, followed by Tehran, Meshed, Kazvin and Shiraz'; FO371, 12293, E4735 Clive, Tehran, 21 October 1927: 'the opposition of the mullahs is stubborn, and it does not appear that they will easily give way where their existence is at stake'; *USDPR*, Reel 4, No. 478, Tehran, 5 November 1927, '(October 26): In the Parliamentary session of October 25, Davar, the Minister of Justice, presented an urgent bill . . . This bill met with determined opposition from the clergy. If it passes, the fees now collected by the clergy for the authentification of titles, deeds, etc. will go to the state, and the clergy will be practically devoid of revenue.'

[55] FO371, 12293, E5207 Clive, Tehran, 19 November 1927.

[56] FO371, 12293, E4506 Clive, Tehran, 8 October 1927; FO371, 12293, E5207 Clive, Tehran, 19 November 1927; FO371, 13069, E2897 Clive, Tehran, 21 May; Makki, *Tarikh-e Bistsaleh-e Iran*, 4: 396–439, 478–99; Hedayat, *Khaterat va Khatarat*, 375–78; OM, 1927, 610–11, referring to *Sitârah-i Iran*, 23 November 1927; *USDPR*, Reel 4, No. 472, Tehran, 22 October 1927; *USDPR*, Reel 4, No. 478, Tehran, 5 November 1927; *USDPR*, Reel 4, No. 503, Tehran, 16 December 1927.

[57] FO371, 12286, E4309 Clive, Tehran, 24 September 1927; FO416, 81 No. 99, Clive, Tehran, 17 September 1927; FO371, 12293, E4506 Clive, Tehran, 8 October 1927.

[58] *USDPR*, Reel 4, No. 456, Tehran, 8 October 1927.

[59] FO371, 12286, E4503, Tehran, 8 October 1927; *The Times*, 5 October 1927; FO371, 12293, E4506 Clive, Tehran, 8 October 1927; FO371, 12296, E4742 Clive, Tehran, 22 October 1927; Abrahamian, *Iran*, 153.

[60] FO371, 12293, E4506 Clive, Tehran, 8 October 1927.

[61] OM, 1927, 274, referring to *Sitârah-i Iran*, 29 May–3 June 1927, and to *The Times*, 4 June 1927; *Revue des Études Islamiques*, 1927, 590–92, referring to *Sitârah-i Iran*; Makki, *Tarikh-e Bistsaleh-e Iran*, 4: 144; Agheli, *Taimurtash*, 224. There are some discrepancies between these sources and it is possible that another parliamentary faction, Economy (*Eqtesad*), still existed in June 1927.

[62] *Ettela'at*, 13 Sharivar 1306 (4 September 1927), 'Fraksiyon-ha-ye Majlis' (Groups in the Majlis); *USDPR*, Reel 4, No. 432, Tehran, 10 September 1927; *USDPR*, Reel 4, No. 456, Tehran, 8 October 1927; *USDPR*, Reel 4, No. 472, Tehran, 22 October 1927.

[63] *Ettela'at*, 2 Mehr 1306 (24 September 1927), 'Dar Majlis: Tashkil-e Fraksiyon-e Taraqqi' (In the Majlis: Formation of the Taraqqi Group), which lists the names of the 42 deputies who had already joined Taraqqi and gives Tabataba'i Diba as the presumably nominal or temporary leader; *USDPR*,

Reel 4, No. 456, Tehran, 8 October 1927, referring to *Kûshish*, 26 September 1927.
⁶⁴ FO371, 13069, E2897 Clive, Tehran, 21 May 1928.
⁶⁵ FO371, 12286, E4309 Clive, Tehran, 24 September 1927: 'Several parties in the Assembly are pledged to oppose it [Iran-e Now], and the new party has not yet by any means achieved its aim of securing a parliamentary majority. The Opposition is composed of factions with little cohesion, unlikely to show a united front for long.'
⁶⁶ FO371, 13069, E2897 Clive, Tehran, 21 May 1928.
⁶⁷ *USDPR*, Reel 4, No. 472, Tehran, 22 October 1927, 'Koushesh (October 19): Reports the dissolution of the parliamentary group Tajadod which had sunk down to three or four members who have joined the Taraghi group'; *USDPR*, Reel 4, No. 514, Tehran, 12 January 1928: 'The reasons are not fully known; it is conjectured that, because Tadayon tried to make political capital out of the clerical disturbances, he became persona non grata when those disturbances were quieted. The immediate cause of his disgrace, however, is known to result from his failure to defend the Shah when Mr Mossadegh criticized the latter in the Medjlis'; *USDPR*, Reel 4, No. 503, Tehran, 16 December 1927.
⁶⁸ FO371, 13069, E2897 Clive, Tehran, 21 May 1928; FO371, 13799, E3676 Clive, Tehran, 14 July 1929: 'For the last few months of its two-year sitting the Majlis seems to have been more alive to its duties and amenable to reason.'
⁶⁹ FO371, 13799, E3676 Clive, Tehran, 14 July 1929: 'The Taraqqi party, which was created by the genius of the Minister of Court, formed, as time went on, a more and more solid block ready to carry out the wishes of the Shah as expressed through his Minister of Court. There were mutual advantages to both sides in this association, for in return for the party's obedience to the Royal wishes, the individual members of the party were promised re-election to the next term of the Majlis. This promise was kept and the members of the party were duly re-elected and the Taraqqi forms in the seventh term of the Majlis the majority party . . . The Iran No party has completely disappeared, but its counterpart in the Majlis, the Taraqqi party, is flourishing and a large majority of the Deputies of the Seventh Majlis belong to it. It is directed by the Minister of Court, who convenes it whenever he wishes to expose it to certain projects and plans which will ultimately require the approval of the Majlis'; FO416, 113 (E3067) Clive, Tehran, 22 May 1931; FO416, 113 (E3354) Hoare, Tehran, 12 June 1932: 'The Taraqqi party . . . This party, to which about 90 per cent. of the Deputies belong, has continued to support the Government in the Majlis. All laws and Bills which are to be brought to the Majlis are discussed in the party sittings before coming before the House, and in this way the Government is always sure of obtaining parliamentary sanction for its

proposals without too much debate. The Minister of Court is generally present at the sittings of the party, and keeps its members well in hand.' Even so, Taimurtash had to cope with some elements of dissent in the House, Agheli, *Taimurtash*, 238-45.

[70] FO371, 16967, E2439 Hoare, Tehran, 22 April 1933; Abrahamian, *Iran*, pp. 138-39. Taimurtash suffered arrest, trial, imprisonment and death in 1933, 'The Rise and Fall of Teymourtache' [sic], *Journal of the Royal Central Asiatic Society*, 1934, Vol. 21 No. 1, 93.

[71] Taimurtash's sarcastic comment on Persia's Sixth Majlis elections (FO371, 12293, E3909 Clive, Tehran, 26 August 1927, 'We had seen how the elections were run . . .') likewise omits to mention that Reza Shah and Modarres were principally responsible for their manipulation (FO371, 12296, E870 Clive, Tehran, 26 January 1927: 'The elections to the Sixth Majlis were engineered by the Shah, working through the provincial army commanders, and by Modarres working through the clergy'). Schulenburg further noted that Parliament's apparent inability to ratify certain agreements was often convenient for and willed by the regime: AA, Abt. III, R78145 Schulenburg, Tehran, 29 June 1928.

[72] FO371, 12296, E870 Clive, Tehran, 26 January 1927; FO416, 79 No. 34 (E4553) Nicolson, Gulhek, 17 July 1926.

[73] FO416, 78 No. 19 (E392) Loraine, Tehran, 30 December 1925.

[74] FO416, 78 No. 18 (E391) Loraine, Tehran, 30 December 1925; FO416, 81 No. 36, Clive, Gulhek, 13 July 1927.

[75] FO416, 81 No. 36, Clive, Gulhek, 13 July 1927. Notes on Leading Personalities in Persia, 'He [Mostowfi] is a typical old-time Persian gentleman, fond of hawking and hunting, but a man of weak character and incapable of taking a decision on the most unimportant matter. Completely bereft of any qualities of organisation, he has entirely whittled away the great wealth he inherited from his father . . . His feeble character has not gained any strength by the experience of years, and if he is still incapable of doing bad he is equally incapable of doing good.' Some contemporary newspaper reports attributed Mostowfi's replacement by Hedayat to the rupture of Anglo-Soviet relations consequent upon the Arcos affair, OM, 1927, 273-74, referring to *Sitârah-i Iran*, 29 May-3 June 1927, and to *The Times*, 4 June 1927, but Persian sources provide little support for this view.

[76] FO371, 12293, E2734 Clive, Tehran, 30 December 1925; FO371, 12293, E878 Clive, Tehran, 27 January 1927, 'Vossuk-ed-Dowleh . . . told me that . . . If he wished he could be Prime Minister to-morrow, as he could count on the support of at least 80 per cent of the Majlis. The difficulty lies in his relations with the Shah.'

[78] FO416, 78 No. 18 (E391) Loraine, Tehran, 30 December 1925: 'Mirza Mehdi Khan Fatemi (Emad al-Saltaneh), the Minister of Justice, is another person who has absolutely no qualifications for the post which he is called

upon to fill ... He consumes a large quantity of opium daily, and the Ministry of Justice, so much in need of reforms and reorganisation, is likely to remain in the same deplorable state as heretofore.' Despite his attitude over the premiership the Shah often preferred to have talented men in the Cabinet, possibly because this left them less scope for independent political activity than as ordinary deputies in the Majlis; FO416, 78 No. 18 (E391) Loraine, Tehran, 30 December 1925: 'Mirza Hassan Khan Mushar (Mushar-ul-Molk) ... was very unwilling to serve as Foreign Minister under Foruqi, but fear of offending His Majesty, who had expressed a personal wish that he should continue to occupy that post, obliged him to accept the charge. A man of energy and decision he has nothing in common with the Premier [Foruqi], whose general laziness and dilatory methods he often finds most trying'; FO416, 79 No. 127 (E5746) Nicolson, Gulhek, 25 September 1926: 'Mirza Hassah Khan Vossuk takes the portfolio of Justice ... As I have already reported, it was the desire of Vossuk to resign his Cabinet post and to acquire as a private Member that contact with his fellow Deputies which would prepare the way for his own assumption of the premiership. The fact that he was forced by pressure of the Shah to remain in the present scapegoat Ministry suggests that His Majesty wishes to discredit Vossuk, of whom, I regret to record, he is acutely and increasingly jealous.'

[79] FO371, 13069, E2897 Clive, Tehran, 21 May 1928. Mostowfi al-Mamalik held the post of Prime Minister in 1910–11, 1914–15, 1915, 1918, 1923 and 1926–27. He held the last post between June 1926 and May 1927, when he resigned (FO416, 81 No. 36, Clive, Gulhek, 13 July 1927).

[80] AA, Abt. III, R78145 Schulenburg, Tehran, 18 June 1927.

[81] Vanessa Martin, 'Modarres, Republicanism and the Rise of Rezaâ Khân, Sardâr-i Sipah', *British Journal of Middle Eastern Studies*, Vol. 21 No. 2, 1994, 200–10; FO416, 81 No. 36, Clive, Gulhek, 13 July 1927: 'Modarres, more than any individual Persian, caused the failure of the republican movement in 1924', Millspaugh, *The American Task in Persia*, 206.

[82] FO416, 78 No. 103 (E2084) Loraine, Tehran, 11 March 1926; FO371, 12296, E870 Clive, Tehran, 26 January 1927.

[83] FO416, 79 No. 7 (E4076) Loraine, Gulhek, 15 June 1926.

[84] FO416, 79, No. 111 (E5539) Nicolson, Gulhek, 10 September 1926; FO416, 79 No. 69 (E4824) Nicolson, Tehran, 31 July 1926.

[85] FO371, 12296, E870 Clive, Tehran, 26 January 1927, 'The Sixth Majlis ... showed strong opposition to the Mostowfi Cabinet, whom they regarded as creatures of Modarres and the Shah ... It at once became evident that the Deputies, having secured their election, were determined to turn against Modarres, and by implication against the Shah.'

[86] FO416, 79 No. 127 (E5746) Nicolson, Gulhek, 25 September 1926; ASMAE, Rapporti Politici, Pacco 1469, Galli, Tehran, 26 September 1926: 'Questo Gabinetto è il risultato del contrasto non fra il precedente e il

Parlamento, ma fra Parlamento e Scià' . . . 'non è lieve sintomo del disagio e della inquietudine generale' . . . '[la crisi] investe lo stesso Scià che ha deluso molte aspettative e perduto molta popolarità'; Agheli, *Taimurtash*, 221.

[87] FO371, 12296, E870 Clive, Tehran, 26 January 1927; Makki, *Tarikh-e Bist Saleh-ye Iran*, 4: 201–6; AA, Abt. III, R78145 Schulenburg, Tehran, 15 November 1926; Makki, *Modarres: Qahreman-e Azadi (Modarres, Hero of Freedom)*, 2 Vols (Tehran, 1359), 2: 727–28; FO416, 79 No. 150 (E6467) Nicolson, Tehran, 4 November 1926; FO416, 79 No. 161 (E6828) Clive, Tehran, 20 November 1926. Modarres recovered sufficiently to play an active part during the last months of parliamentary politics: OM, 1927, 274–75, referring to *Sitârah-i Iran*, 8 June 1927.

[88] FO371, 12296, E870 Clive, Tehran, 26 January 1927.

[89] FO371, 12296, E870 Clive, Tehran, 26 January 1927; FO416, 79 No. 34 (E4553) Nicolson, Gulhek, 17 July 1926; AA, Abt. III, R78162 Wipert Von Blücher, Tehran, 27 October 1933; FO371, 13783 E98 Clive, Tehran, 18 December 1928.

[90] FO371, 13069, E2897 Clive, Tehran, 21 May 1928.

[91] FO416, 79 No. 59 (E4808) Nicolson, Gulhek, 24 July 1926; FO371, 12296, E870 Clive, Tehran, 26 January 1927.

[92] FO371, 12296, E870 Clive, Tehran, 26 January 1927; FO371, 12285, E883 Clive, Tehran, 28 January 1927, '[Tehran] A strong campaign is now being waged by the newspapers subsidised by the Shah and the Russians against all the better-known statesmen, against the Deputies in Parliament, and, under a thin veil, against parliamentary government'; AA, Abt. III, R78145 Schulenburg, Tehran, 11 August 1927.

[93] FO371, 13069, E2897 Clive, Tehran, 21 May 1928; FO371, 12293, E1237 Clive, Tehran, 25 February 1927; USDPR, Reel 4, No. 278, Tehran, 25 February 1927.

[94] FO416, 81 No. 36, Clive, Gulhek, 13 July 1927; FO371, 12293, E1237 Clive, Tehran, 25 February 1927; FO371, 13069, E2897 Clive, Tehran, 21 May 1928; Agheli, *Taimurtash*, 236, lists the legislation inspired by Taimurtash.

[95] FO416, 81 No. 36, Clive, Gulhek, 13 July 1927; FO371, 13069, E2897 Clive, Tehran, 21 May 1928; AA, Abt. III, R78145 Schulenburg, Tehran, 18 June 1927; ASMAE, Rapporti Politici, Pacco 1470, Bordonaro, Londra, 1 August 1928: 'Come noto a Vostra Eccellenza, Termoutache è una specie di Eminenza grigia in Persia, la persona attualmente più influente presso lo Scià e avente rango superiore anche al Primo Ministro'; Hidayat, *Khâtirât û Khatarât*, 371; Agheli, *Taimurtash*, 233–35.

[96] FO371, 12293, E4113 Clive, Tehran, 10 September 1927; AA, Abt. III, R78145 Schulenburg, Tehran, 27 October 1927.

[97] ASMAE, Rapporti Politici, Pacco 1471, Daneo, Tehran, 31 December 1928: 'Nella discussione del progetto al Majlis vi è stata qualche eco di

tali preoccupazioni di ordine religioso, ma pochi deputati hanno osato manifestare un' aperta opposizione.'

[98] FO371, 12293, E1225 Clive, Tehran, 21 February 1927; FO416, 80 No. 146, Clive, Tehran, 7 May 1927; FO371, 12293, E2523 Clive, Tehran, 20 May 1927, FO371, 12293, E4735 Clive, Tehran, 21 October 1927. Schulenburg was also sceptical about the value and purpose of Davar's legal changes: AA, Abt. III, R78145 Schulenburg, Tehran, 18 June 1927: 'Justizminister Dawar, der aus Anlass seiner Justiz-"Reform" die biserigen Richter durch ebenso unfähige Leute aus seiner Verwandtschaft und Freundschaft ersetzt hat.'

[99] FO371, 12296, E870 Clive, Tehran, 26 January 1927.

[100] FO416, 79 No. 127 (E5746) Nicolson, Gulhek, 25 September 1926.

CHAPTER IV

Institution Building in the Kemalist Republic: The Role of the People's Party

Erik-Jan Zürcher

In spite of the striking ideological and programmatic similarities between the regimes of Atatürk and Reza Shah in the 1920s and 1930s, their short-term successes and long-term legacies have been very different. This is undoubtedly caused in part by the very different degrees to which the two leaders were able to institutionalize their personal authoritarian rule and to transfer authority to collective bodies that were able to survive the death, or in the Iranian case, deposition, of the founding father. In discussing this issue of institutionalization in Iran and Turkey, one has to distinguish carefully between *state* building on the one hand and the underpinning of a particular kind of *regime* and policies on the other.

In terms of state building, the degree to which the characteristics of the modern centralized state had been established, there was a world of difference between the late Ottoman Empire and Qajar Iran. While it is undoubtedly true that there was an old tradition of a state in Iran and a widely shared consciousness of belonging to the realm of the Shah, the indispensable attributes of a modern state, such as efficient taxation, a bureaucratic administration by salaried officials with clear divisions of power and a distinct hierarchy, military conscription and a census enabling both conscription and taxation were all practically non-existent. In the Ottoman Empire, on the other hand, all of these had gradually been developing during a century of reforms, which preceded the coming to power of Mustafa Kemal Pasha.

When looked at from an Ottoman perspective, therefore, the task that faced Reza Khan, and his accomplishments, resemble those of the reforming Sultan Mahmud II (1808–39) as much as they do Atatürk's. Certainly in his early years his main accomplishments were the building of a unified army and of a degree of centralized control, which contrasted sharply with conditions in the late Qajar Empire, where the ruler had very little effective power outside his own capital. Mustafa Kemal Pasha, on the other hand, could build on a century of achievement in this field. To take just one example: where Reza Khan's main effort in the 1920s was to build a national army out of such disparate elements as the Cossack corps, tribal forces and the Gendarmerie, and then to introduce modern conscription (as opposed to the traditional *bunichah* system),[1] the Ottoman Empire had had military conscription and a unified army since 1844.

If the Ottoman imperial heritage is relevant to the greater success of Mustafa Kemal, one has of course to assume that a large degree of continuity can be established between the late Ottoman Empire and the Kemalist republic. To what extent this continuity can indeed be assumed has been a matter for debate in the historiography of the republic. The Kemalist republic itself had powerful incentives for emphasizing the differences between itself and the empire. Firstly, Mustafa Kemal emerged gradually as the undisputed leader of the national resistance movement (which fathered the republic) in the years 1919–22, and in doing so he took over a movement that had been started by the leadership of the Committee of Union and Progress, to which he himself had also belonged, but in whose circles he had played only a minor role. Depicting himself as a *deus ex machina* who created the new Turkey out of nothing, without any reference to the Young Turk heritage, was an important weapon in his elimination of political competitors.[2] Secondly, as Mustafa Kemal himself remarked at the time, the essential novelty of Kemalist Turkey, and its rejection of the Ottoman past, were very important for Turkey's prestige in Europe. European public opinion had had very little confidence in Ottoman readiness to reform, but Mustafa Kemal's radically new departure had a lot of credit.

The essential novelty of the Kemalist republic and its making a clean break with the Ottoman past was the theme, not only of Kemalist historiography itself, but of literally dozens of books published in the West from the 1920s onwards. It was often (and as recently as Feroz Ahmad's *Making of Modern Turkey*) expressed as a contrast between the decay of the 'old Turkey' and the dynamism and youthful vigour of the 'new'.[3] From the 1950s onwards (a period coinciding with the establishment of multiparty politics in Turkey and the partial dismantling of the Kemalist state), a different approach has become influential, one associated with the names of political scientist Tarik Zafer Tunaya and sociologists Niyazi Berkes and Serif Mardin in Turkey, and with Bernard Lewis and Stanford Shaw in the West. This school, if we can call it that, acknowledges the debt of the republic to its immediate predecessors, the *Tanzimat* reformers of the nineteenth century, and particularly the Young Turks of the second constitutional period (1908–18), characterized by Tunaya as the 'laboratory of the republic'.

Both schools, the traditional Kemalist and the 'revisionist' one, have tended to concentrate on questions of policy and ideology – primarily the issues of modernization and national identity. Interesting and complicated though these are, I would like instead to concentrate on the question of institutional links between empire and republic. Here a picture of almost total continuity emerges. This is true first of all of the army. The success of the nationalist movement in Anatolia was ultimately based on the strength of the remains of the Ottoman army. Although by the end of World War I in October 1918, the army had an effective strength of only some 100,000[4] (down from a peak of around 800,000 in 1916) and was plagued by war weariness and enormous numbers of deserters, it is nevertheless true that it remained intact as an organized, indeed a disciplined, body. It did not disintegrate, nor was there a tendency for leading officers of the regular army to establish themselves as warlords. As Rustow has shown, the main body of officers, those who were now in their thirties and forties, who had been educated in the Western-style military schools and academy and had gained experience and rapid promotion during the years of the Balkan War (1912–13) and World War (1914–18), supported the national struggle.[5] Once the top officers like Kâzim Karabekir and Ali Fuat accepted Mustafa Kemal's leadership (even after he had been sacked) they were in a position to carry out his strategy, because the chain of command remained intact. The forces raised by the Sultan's government in Istanbul, called *Kuva-yi Inzibatiye*, even when (rather halfheartedly) supported by the British, never were able to mount a serious challenge to the nationalists. The army of the national movement continued practically without change under the republic. Until Turkey's entry into NATO in 1952 its doctrines and organization were very little changed, and as late as the 1960s it was still commanded by officers who were the product of the Ottoman military academy and had gained their first command experience in World War I (officers like republican presidents Cemal Gürsel and Cevdet Sunay and the founder of the Justice Party, Ragip Gümüşpala).

When we turn to the civilian bureaucracy we see almost the same picture. In the early years of the national struggle, the nationalists weeded out members of the provincial bureaucracy who were considered unreliable because of their links to the Istanbul government. The persons concerned were mostly provincial and district governors (*valis* and *kaymakams*), who had been political appointees. On the lower levels the provincial administration remained intact, and this enabled the nationalists to conscript soldiers and raise taxes in the areas under their control. As is well known, the main communications network, that of the Ottoman telegraph service, proved highly dependable and rendered sterling service to the nationalists.

In the field of finance, the republic inherited two separate bureaucratic structures from the empire. The one was the regular ministry of finance, which had been thoroughly modernized under the Young Turk finance minister Cavid Bey, and the administration of the Ottoman public debt, which since 1881 had taken control of the collection of taxes, duties and excises in areas such as the sale of tobacco and tobacco products, salt and fisheries on behalf of the European creditors of the Empire. Although the new Turkey shouldered part of the Ottoman debt at the Treaty of Lausanne in 1923, the autonomous operation of the Public Debt Administration was terminated and the tobacco monopoly was taken over by the Turkish state in 1925. This provided vital income for the new state in the 1920s and 1930s.

There were no wholesale purges of the bureaucracy after the nationalists' victory. At the peace conference of Lausanne in 1923, the Turks first resisted Allied demands for a general amnesty after the conclusion of peace, then they gave in but reserved the right to ban 150 undesirable Ottoman Muslims from the country. The number of 150 was completely arbitrary and the names were only filled in (with some difficulty) more than a year after the conclusion of peace. There were a number of army officers and bureaucrats among those banned, but obviously it concerned only a very small number of people. The early years of the public witnessed political purges within the leadership (notably in the show trials of 1926), but the attempts to purge the state apparatus were rather limited: Law

347 of 25 September 1923 prescribed the expulsion from the armed forces of those officers who had stayed abroad or declined to serve in the 'national forces', while Law 854 of 26 May 1925 did the same for civil servants. The number of people affected seems to have been small, however, and two years later, on 24 May 1928, the passing of Law 1289 gave those officers and civil servants who felt they had been wrongfully sacked the opportunity to appeal.[6] The one major occasion when many civil servants left government service had nothing to do with political purges: when the (then still very small and extremely uncomfortable) town of Ankara was declared the permanent seat of government in October 1923 an important part of the staff of the ministries in Istanbul declined to move with their departments to Ankara.

Of all the branches of the state bureaucracy, the one to undergo the greatest change under the republic was undoubtedly the religious institution. The passing of the law on the unification of education in 1924 and the introduction of a European-style family law in 1926 meant that the secular state now took direct control of these important fields and that the role of the religious establishment contracted accordingly. The abolishing of the Caliphate and the simultaneous replacement of the office of the *Sheykh ul-Islam*, the highest religious authority, by a directorate under the prime minister, certainly meant that the top of the religious establishment lost much of its room for manoeuvre. On the other hand, the fact that Mustafa Kemal Pasha could push through these reforms almost without opposition from within the clergy is testimony to the degree to which the Ottoman religious establishment had already been bureaucratized and brought under state control in the Ottoman Empire. This is the reason why, in the Turkish case, unlike that of Pahlevi Iran, opposition to the new secular regime was lead by the dervish brotherhoods (*tarikat*) and not by the clergy.

Not only the important branches of the state were inherited by the republic, the means of reproducing these branches also remained virtually unchanged. The great schools of the empire, modelled on the French *grandes écoles*, which had bred the officers and civil servants of the Tanzimat, Hamidian and Young Turk eras, continued to do so under the republic. The Military Academy and General Staff College were relocated to Ankara in 1923, but remained essentially unchanged. The same is true for the Civil Service Academy (*Mülkiye*), which was reconstituted as the School of Political Science in 1935 and relocated to the new capital soon after. It continued to provide the state with its governors, diplomats and administrators. In time, both institutions also became centres of Kemalist indoctrination, where nationalism, republicanism and secularism were articles of faith for staff and students alike – a situation that continues to this day. The reproduction of religious learning was severely affected by the closure of the *medreses* in 1924. The decline in the level of religious learning only became apparent when the older Ottoman-educated generation started to fade, however, something that can be roughly dated from the mid-1940s.

If the Kemalist republic was the receiver of such a rich institutional inheritance from the Empire, what were the Kemalists' own particular contributions to the institutions of the republic? In other words: if the building of a Kemalist *state* was no longer a priority, what instruments did the Kemalists create for the institutionalization of their *regime*? Here, I think, the answer can be quite unequivocal: that instrument was the party created by Mustafa Kemal in 1923: the People's Party (*Halk Fırkası*).

Mustafa Kemal announced his intention to transform the Defence of Rights Group, the majority faction in the first National Assembly (1920–23), into a political party on 6 December 1922. At the same time he announced the new party's name, which was remarkable in two respects. *Fırka* was the most commonly used term for political party at the time, but the term had distinctly negative connotations. It recalled the bickering of factions in the parliaments of the second constitutional period and sounded very different from *cemiyet* (society), the word used in the title of the Society for the Defence of the National Rights, in whose name the independence war had been fought and whose president Mustafa Kemal still was. Both in this context and in the earlier one of the Committee of Union and Progress (which was often called a *cemiyet-i mukaddes* or 'holy society' by its members, a term also used by Mustafa Kemal for the People's Party in his speech in Trabzon on 16 September 1924[7]), 'society' seemed a more prestigious as well as a more inclusive term than 'party'. Had not the delegates to the congress in Sivas (September 1919) sworn, each one of them, to work 'free from party strife' (*fırkacılık amâlinden münezzeh*)?[8]

The fact that *fırka* was associated with party strife and the defence of group interests made the choice of the other word in its name, *halk*, even more remarkable. As Tuncay has pointed out,[9] this term had gained currency in leftist circles, where it meant the mass of the population (peasants and workers). In nationalist circles at the time the word *millet* was the more common one to denote the (Muslim) population as a whole. The name of the new party therefore aroused the suspicion that it had leftist leanings and might embrace the idea of class struggle. Mustafa Kemal was quick to dispel any such thoughts, however, during his tour of the country in early 1923 and especially during the extensive interviews and speeches he gave in Eskişehir and Izmit on 15–17 January 1923. He emphatically stated that large landowners and capitalists were so rare in Turkey that there was no reason why improving the living standard of the peasants should be at their expense. Industrial workers, he said, did not number more than 20,000 in all of Turkey, so they could not form the basis of a political party either. The new party would be a party for all sections of society, preaching harmony and not class struggle.[10]

What Mustafa Kemal had in mind in founding the party was, on the one hand, to create a disciplined and reliable majority in the second National Assembly after the 1923 elections (discipline which had been notably lacking in the first assembly), and on the other, to unite all 'enlightened' elements in the country as a vanguard for the social and cultural revolution he wanted to accomplish. Although Mustafa Kemal himself and the party always claimed to represent the national will and to act in harmony with the wishes of the population at large, his campaign in the spring of 1923 seems to have been aimed rather at uniting the enlightened elite behind him.

The elections in the summer of 1923 took place before the official founding of the new party, but a kind of rudimentary party programme, the Nine Principles (*Dokuz Umde*) was published by Mustafa Kemal and only candidates who subscribed to them were given the support of the Defence of Rights Groups in the elections. The Nine Principles were a concoction of very broad statements on issues like national sovereignty on the one hand, and very specific proposals, designed to win the support of different social groups on the other.

After the elections, the newly elected members of the Defence of Rights Group in the national assembly (which comprised all but one of the deputies), reconstituted themselves as the People's Party (PP) on 9 August 1923. Shortly afterwards, they formally declared that the PP was the only heir to the Society for the Defence of the National

Rights of Anatolia and Rumelia and that it took over all its assets. The local branches of the Defence of Rights organization were not consulted on this move, but neither they nor those politicians who had been equally active in the national resistance movement, but who had not been included in Mustafa Kemal's slate for the elections, were in a position to protest. The spurious pedigree thus created for the new party was emphasized at the 1927 party congress, which called itself the second congress of the PP, stating that the first national conference of the resistance movement, that of Sivas back in September 1919, had been its first.

It is no exaggeration to say that the creation of the PP was one in a chain of events, through which Mustafa Kemal gradually established a power monopoly in 1923–25. Other links in this chain are change in the High Treason Law in April 1923,[11] the promulgation of the republic with Mustafa Kemal as first president in October, the abolition of the Caliphate in March 1924 and the suppression of the liberal and socialist opposition from March 1925. From June 1925 onwards the PP was the only legal party in Turkey. Within this single party, Mustafa Kemal Pasha's position was unassailable. The internal structure of the party, as described by the statutes of 1927, gave him almost unlimited power: he was permanent chairman of the party and he appointed the two other functionaries, the vice-chairman and the secretary-general, who together with him made up the party leadership. The party leader alone was entitled to name candidates for the National Assembly.[12] Since the split in the party in November 1924 new disciplinary measures were in force, which prevented individual deputies from venting dissident opinions in the National Assembly. All debate was now limited to the closed sessions of the parliamentary party. One could be excused for thinking that, with complete control over the only legitimate political party, Kemal would turn it into the main vehicle for enforcing Kemalist policies. But in March 1925 the parliamentary party agreed to give the government (whose prime minister, İsmet İnönü was appointed by Mustafa Kemal in his other capacity as president of the republic) dictatorial powers under the Law on the Maintenance of Order (*Takrir-i Sükûn Kanunu*), which remained in force for four years. During these years, which saw the enactment of all the most famous Westernizing and secularizing measures, which together constitute the Kemalist 'revolution', the party, therefore, played hardly any political role at all. One can therefore say that, having helped to create a secure platform for the president to execute his policies, the party had more or less served its purpose.

The party certainly did not function as an instrument for mass mobilization on the pattern of socialist or fascist parties in Europe in this era. In the first six years of its existence (1923–29) the party publicly defended the policies of the government, but it made very little effort to actually drum up support for the Kemalist policies or to encourage grassroots activism. This picture changes from 1930 onwards, when the PP began to play a much more active role in these fields. It became much more active in education and propaganda, and it is certainly no coincidence that the party school for orators was founded in 1931.

The changing role of the PP in the 1930s is directly linked to a change in the nature of the Kemalist regime, which – I would contend – underwent a transition from authoritarian to totalitarian rule, or at least an attempt at it. From the early 1930s onwards, the PP government organized a drive to eliminate all forms of civil society organizations that were not linked to the party. The best-known examples of organizations that were closed down were the Turkish Women's Union, the Freemasons lodges, professional organizations such as the Teachers Union, the Reserve Officers Society and the Society of Newspaper Journalists and the cultural and educational clubs of the Turkish Hearths (*Türk Ocakları*), which had survived from the Young Turk era and had been the main meeting place of supporters of cultural Turkish (and Turkic) nationalism since 1912. Istanbul University was reformed and purged.

These independent organizations were replaced with new ones, which, however, were completely under party control: the women's branch of the PP replaced the women's union and the People's Houses (*Halkevleri*) were founded in February 1932 as successor to the Turkish Hearths and took over the latter's assets, primarily its buildings. The People's Houses soon became by far the most significant vehicle for mobilization of the party.

The aims of the People's Houses were summarized by the party leadership as follows: to build national unity through the spread of culture and ideals; to bring villagers and town dwellers closer together; and to explain the principles of the People's Party to the masses. The organization was to fulfil these aims by activities in nine different fields: language and literature; fine arts, theatre, sports, welfare, educational courses, libraries and publications, village development and history. Membership was open to all. It was fully subsidized by the People's Party and the board of each People's House was appointed by the local party leadership, except for that of Ankara which was appointed by the national leadership. The number of houses increased dramatically. In total, 478 People's Houses were founded and from 1940 onwards a total of 4,322 of a rudimentary version of the same thing, called People's Rooms (*Halkodaları*) was created in villages. The People's Houses and the People's Rooms employed various means of communication to spread the message of Kemalist modernization: films, theatre productions, puppet shows, concerts, expositions and, most of all, lectures and speeches. In the villages, oral instruction and wall posters were used. The choice of these media shows that the party was well aware it was trying to spread a message in a country with an illiteracy rate of over 80 per cent. For those who were literate, the People's Houses also produced a large number of journals, of which *Ülkü* (Ideal), the journal of the Ankara People's House was the most important.[13]

It may be doubted, however, whether the People's Houses really succeeded in their mission of propagating the Kemalist ideals among the broader strata of the Turkish population. Contemporary accounts seem to indicate that, in spite of all the high-minded ideals, the Houses to a large extent remained a meeting place for intellectuals, teachers, professionals and bureaucrats, and very few peasants or workers ever set foot in them. The People's Houses' greatest success was probably in helping to build a dedicated middle class cadre for the Kemalists in the towns, rather than in gaining mass support for the reforms. Their efforts to encourage a European lifestyle and culture and the lack of interest in, and respect for, expressions of traditional cultures may actually have created resentment among the mass of the population.

One contemporary traveller who actually made a point of visiting the People's Houses was Lilo Linke, whose *Allah Dethroned: A Journey through Modern Turkey* appeared first in 1937. She describes the Samsun Halk Evi in some detail. According to her information one in 40 of Samsun's inhabitants was a member. At the time this would amount to about 800 people. 'Those higher up the social scale' were 'as good as obliged' to take up membership. She copied the week's timetable of activities of the People's House, which looked like this:

Monday:	Women's needlework class
	Football club meeting
	Drama group
	Reading and writing class for adults
	Free legal advice
Tuesday:	Turkish history group
	Choir practice
	Party meeting
	Bookbinding and handicrafts
Wednesday:	Committee meetings
	Women's dressmaking class
	Chamber music class
	Turkish language and art group
Thursday:	Military band practice
	Reading and writing class
	Girl's gymnasium group
	Museum and exhibition committee
Friday:	Orchestra practice
	Free medical advice
	Village group meeting
Saturday:	Sports clubs
	Foreign language classes
Sunday:	Lectures, concerts, conferences.

Clearly a provincial centre like Samsun had a sizeable core of activists, who devoted quite a bit of spare time to the spreading of the Kemalist values. Linke's description of the activities of the 'village group' that returned from what was clearly a routine visit to a number of villages, also makes clear why these activities may have created resentment in the countryside. The group (consisting of a student, a dentist, a teacher and the owner of the car in which they travelled) had given literacy classes and medical briefings, but they had also carried out the registration of villagers for the census and enforced the new law on family names. In the eyes of the villagers, the People's House delegation must have looked like just another bunch of state officials making incomprehensible demands.[14]

More than anything else, the development of the People's Houses mark the change of the People's Party from a fairly closed cadre party into an instrument for control and mobilization. Three reasons can be discerned for the changing role of the PP in the early 1930s.

Firstly, the world economic crisis with its attendant dramatic fall in the price of agricultural products severely affected Turkey from 1930 onwards. This in itself created a demand for a more active and interventionist government policy.

Secondly, Mustafa Kemal's short-lived experiment with a legitimate (but tame) political opposition in 1930 (the Free Republican Party or *Serbest Cumhuriyet Fırkası*) had shown up the discontent in the country and the unpopularity of the PP. When the experiment threatened to run out of control because of the enormous support shown to the opposition party, it was quickly terminated, but for many in the PP it had come as a rude awakening. Together with a particularly horrifying ritual murder of a junior officer (in Menemen near Izmir on 23 December 1930), which raised the spectre of religious reaction or *irtica*, this led to a realization within the PP that the party's message of social and cultural modernization had not yet got across to the mass of the population. This meant that more efforts had to be devoted to education and propaganda and that democratization had to be postponed indefinitely.

Thirdly, the seeming inability of the Western democracies to deal with the world economic crisis undermined their credibility as role models. The Soviet Union and Fascist Italy seemed to deal with the crisis much more effectively. The Soviet Union continued its expansionist programme of industrialization, and the Italian economic programme, which aimed at 'autarchy', or self-sufficiency, gained added impetus from the imposition of sanctions by the League of Nations in 1935.[15] The latter subsequently proved to be economically disastrous, but this was not so clear at the time and it is undeniable that the authoritarian regimes, like that of the Soviet Union, Italy and, after 1933, Hitler's Germany gained many admirers among the leading cadres of the PP. Already in 1932 a group of prominent intellectuals with PP connections had formed the 'Kadro' (Cadre) group, which advocated a much more active role for the party in all sorts of social and cultural spheres. Slightly later, in 1935, the very powerful secretary-general of the party, Recep Peker, proposed to put the party in charge of the country's administration. Peker's inspiration was Nazi Germany rather than the Soviet Union, as had been the case with the Kadro group.[16] His recommendations were rejected, as Atatürk preferred to put his trust in the state apparatus of army and bureaucracy, but the fact that Turkey was officially declared a one-party state a year later, with state and party functions being merged on all levels, certainly owed a great deal to the authoritarian examples in Europe.

The transition of the PP from a fairly closed, elitist, political organization whose activities were confined almost completely to the National Assembly, to one which attempted to monopolize cultural and social life in order to make the mass of the people aware of the Kemalist modernization programme is symbolized by the celebrations of the tenth anniversary of the republic in 1933. Whereas before that date, Mustafa Kemal Pasha usually addressed party caucuses at indoor venues (even for such a momentous occasion as his famous six-day speech of 1927), his speech of 1933 was held in an open-air stadium in Ankara, before a mass audience. The programme of the celebrations, with its parades and mass gymnastics, clearly resembled similar occasions in Fascist Italy in its imagery and choreography.

When we compare this development to that in Iran, we see that the examples of Kemalist Turkey and of Fascist Italy and Nazi Germany became increasingly important in Iran in the 1930s. There was a great deal of similarity between the manner in which Reza Shah employed history and linguistics in the service of nation building during the 'Vahdat-e Millî' campaign and the efforts of the Turkish History Society and the Turkish Language Society. The suppression of the Azeri Turks and the discrimination against Assyrians and Armenians recall the anti-minority polemics of PP stalwarts such as Mahmut Esat Bozkurt and Recep Peker. The denial of a Kurdish identity after 1928 in Iran echoes that in Turkey after 1926. The influence of the Kemalist example seems to have grown after the shah's 1934 state visit to Turkey. Nevertheless, there were important differences between the regimes. Where the PP became *more* important in the early 1930s as an instrument for mobilization and control, the parties that had been created by Reza Shah and his Minister of Court Taimurtash to replace the ones banned in 1927, first the *Iran-e Now* (New Iran) party, and then its successor, the *Hezb-e Teraqqi* (Progressive Party), although probably modelled on the Kemalist example, never gained a life of their own.

As the chapter by Matthew Elliot in this volume shows, the original aim of the *Iran-e Now* party was much the same as that of the PP in Turkey: to 'form a disciplined majority in parliament and ensure that radical, reforming proposals could be passed into law' (Elliot). But these parties never gained anything like the organizational strength, support or discipline of the PP. Reza Shah dissolved the *Hezb-e Teraqqi* in 1932. He seems to have relied on individuals who were totally dependent on his whim and deeply mistrusted institutions and collective bodies, even those created by himself. Mustafa Kemal, on the other hand, created a party, which, although it was undoubtedly an instrument for authoritarian and later even totalitarian policies, nevertheless formed the training ground where the politicians of the post-war multiparty democracy could learn their trade. It started out as an instrument for control of the National Assembly, but from about 1930 onwards it also began to give a corporate identity to an important section of the urban middle class that saw itself as the 'enlightened' vanguard of a social and cultural revolution. Ervand Abrahamian sums it up nicely when he says:

> Whereas Mustafa Kemal conscientiously channeled the enthusiastic backing of the intelligentsia into the Republican Party [obviously, the (Republican) People's Party is meant here, EJZ], Reza Shah gradually lost his initial civilian support, and, failing to secure social foundations for his institutions, ruled without the assistance of an organized political party.[17]

Notes

[1] Stephanie Cronin, 'Conscription and Popular Resistance in Iran (1925–1941)', in Erik-Jan Zürcher, *Arming the State. Military Conscription in the Middle East and Asia 1775–1925*, London: I. B. Tauris, 1999, pp. 145–68.

[2] This issue is debated in Erik-Jan Zürcher, *The Unionist Factor. The Role of the Committee of Union and Progress in the Turkish National Movement 1905–1926*, Leiden: E. J. Brill, 1984.

[3] On p. 77 of his *The Making of Modern Turkey* (London: Routledge, 1993), Feroz Ahmad says: 'The destruction of the Ottoman Empire proved to be a blessing, for the Turks were now free to rediscover themselves and to make a *fresh* start by abandoning a *decadent* past' (my italics).

[4] Maurice Larcher, *La guerre turque dans la guerre mondiale*, Paris: Chiron, 1926, appendices 44 and 50.

[5] Dankwart A. Rustow, 'The Army and the Founding of the Turkish Republic', *World Politics*, 11 (1959), pp. 513–52.

[6] Gotthard Jaeschke, *Türk İnkılâbı Tarihi Kronolojisi*, Istanbul: Millî Mecmua, 1939, vol. 1, p. 156; vol. 2, pp. 50, 73.

[7] *Hakimiyet-i Milliye*, 18 September 1924.

[8] Uluğ İğdemir, *Sivas Kongresi Tutankları*, Ankara: TTK, 1969, p. 3.

⁹ Mete Tunçay, T.C. 'nde Tek Parti Yönetimi'nin Kurulması (1923–1931), Istanbul: Cem, 1989 (1981), p. 48.

¹⁰ Arı Inan, Gazi Mustafa Kemal Atatürk'ün 1923 Eskişehir – İzmit Konuşmaları, Ankara: TTK, 1982, pp. 118ff.

¹¹ Michael M. Finefrock, 'From Sultanate to Republic. Mustafa Kemal and the Structure of Turkish Politics 1922–24', unpublished Ph.D. thesis, Princeton University, 1976.

¹² Tunçay, T.C. 'nde Tek Parti, p. 384.

¹³ Tevfik Çavdar, Halkevleri, in Murat Belge, ed., Cumhuriyet Dönemi Türkiye Ansiklopedisi, Istanbul: İletişim, n.d. [1984], Vol. 4, p. 878 gives all the essential information on the People's Houses aims and organization.

¹⁴ Lilo Linke, Allah Dethroned: A Journey through Modern Turkey, London: Constable, 1937, pp. 169–75.

¹⁵ Alan Cassels, Fascist Italy. Second Edition, Arlington Heights: Harlan Davidson, 1985, pp. 60–62.

¹⁶ Andrew Mango, Atatürk, London: John Murray, 1999, p. 501.

¹⁷ Ervand Abrahamian, Iran Between Two Revolutions, Princeton, NJ: Princeton University Press, 1982, p. 149.

CHAPTER V

Some Views on the Turkish Single-Party Regime During the İnönü Period (1938–45)

Cemil Koçak

The last years of the Ottoman state – that is to say, the short period that begins with the First World War and continues until the end of the National War of Independence – can probably be compared to the few years that followed the announcement of the Second Constitutional Period in terms of the expression of differing political views and of various political standpoints. In contrast to the military defeat, the 1918–25 term was a term in which political thought could be freely expressed and differing political standpoints could be defended. However, when compared to the short-lived atmosphere of political freedom of the Second Constitutional Period (1908–12), this term has lasted a little bit longer. The free political discussions both during the War of Independence in Istanbul and Ankara (here I refer to the differing political standpoints of the Anatolian movement), as well as before and after the announcement of the Republic, would continue until 1925. If one were to take into consideration the atmosphere of the First Assembly as well as the ensuing political atmosphere, it would not be at all easy during these years to foresee that Turkey would one day return to a dictatorial regime.[1]

The single-party period that started in 1925 continued until Atatürk's death in 1938, sometimes broadening, sometimes narrowing.[2] The most important political change during this period was when the so-called 'permanent' Prime Minister, İsmet İnönü, was dismissed from this post in autumn 1937 on the demand of Atatürk personally. The sudden removal of İnönü – victorious commander of the National War of Independence, hero of the Treaty of Lausanne

– from all the important political positions that were in his power, bore some similarity to the fate of Recep Peker, who, about a year before, had had to abandon the position of Secretary General of the Republican People's Party (RPP), except that İnönü's removal brought about a much deeper change: Not only was he being removed from his position of Prime Minister, but also from his duty as Acting Secretary General of RPP, which meant representing Atatürk within the party and being next in line to him.[3]

Of course, for public opinion and those who were outside political life, there was no way of finding out the reasons for this dramatic change.[4] What was not possible during those years is still not really possible even today. Nevertheless, it can be said that over a long period, Atatürk and İnönü shared very different views on three main issues.

The first cause of conflict was the intervention of Atatürk, President and Permanent Head of the RPP, in the government headed by İnönü. In violation of the constitutional system, Atatürk was inclined to exert control over the government (which was responsible to, or was supposed to be responsible to Parliament) and, if necessary, to meet with members of the government one by one and, again if necessary, to intervene in government policy – which turned out to be 'necessary' rather often. İnönü, for his part, did not hesitate to show at every opportunity that he was extremely sensitive as head of government to what he perceived to be direct interference with his authority and with his right to use initiative. Similar clashes were frequently seen during the 1930s and, moreover, although they usually ended with some type of compromise, there was no change in the general trend.[5]

The second area of conflict can be summarized as disagreements over foreign policy. During the second half of the 1930s, Atatürk tried to implement a foreign policy that was closer to England, and as a direct result set a distance from the Soviet Union. From time to time, this policy was very much against the general inclination of İnönü, who was always very cautious in foreign policy issues. The Hatay issue and the Lyon agreement are two important developments in foreign policy that played an important role in the severing of relations between the two men.[6]

The third issue, which may have constituted the last straw in the conflicts, was the disagreement concerning economic policy, or, to put it more precisely, the policy of statism. As İnönü was to point out very frankly years later, from the start Atatürk had doubts as to the success of statist policies and had never supported them with enthusiasm. These policies were more İnönü's preference. Indeed, in Atatürk's view this was the reason for the country's not being able to reach a more satisfying level economically, and it was now time to initiate economic arrangements that were more 'liberal'. Contrary to İnönü's narrow understanding of statism, Atatürk had made it clear he was in favour of another type of economic policy, of which Celâl Bayar was the 'symbol'.[7]

By 1937, all of these areas of disagreement had resulted in dramatic conflict and in separation. Official declarations, as well as official interpretations of the official declarations publicized by the media, rejected all allegations that there was any disagreement between Atatürk and İnönü, and claimed that nothing had changed between the two. According to these pronouncements, the recent developments had all taken place because of the health problems of the 'second man'.[8]

However, for those who were in the political arena, no matter how surprising these developments were – for no one could have imagined or wanted to imagine that the conflict could reach this point – they were not inexplicable. İnönü had had to withdraw and Atatürk had preferred the former Minister of the Economy, Celâl Bayar, as an alternative to him. The reason was that Bayar would implement an economic policy in compliance with Atatürk's preferences, and it was known that in matters of political conflict Bayar would act in accordance with the Chief's instructions. Upon reaching this peak of his political career, Bayar was no longer just Prime Minister, but at the same time Acting President of the RPP, that is to say, the second person in line after Atatürk within the Party. As for İnönü, it was almost as if he were totally erased from politics. He was no more than a simple deputy now.[9]

The fact that although there had been other people alongside Bayar who were much more senior than him in their political careers, none of them was chosen, is evidence that the main reason for Bayar's rise had to do with his economic policy preference. İnönü's traditional political rivals had won an important round.[10]

In November 1938, as Atatürk was about to die, a struggle for power that had been going on for over a year, but was totally unknown to those who were not in the political arena, was about to come to an end. Indeed, even today in Turkish political literature it is still considered a very natural and expected development that immediately after Atatürk's death – just the following day – İnönü was elected President with no rival candidate. But as a former politician who had been removed from power about a year before and kept at a safe distance from it, indeed, who was not only pushed out of political life altogether but virtually condemned to total solitude, İnönü's climb back to power should in reality be viewed as an unexpected and extraordinary development. If this last year is not reviewed under a political magnifying glass, it will not be possible to understand the true meaning of this development and the reasons for it.

İnönü's election as President immediately after Atatürk's death has always been regarded as a natural and normal development. However, this event deserves much more careful study.

Even though some political groups did attempt to remove İnönü completely from the political arena during the term of Celâl Bayar's government, none of these attempts was successful. It is worth emphasizing Prime Minister Bayar's approach during this period. The fact that those groups and persons who were against İnönü had been unable to find an alternative candidate to İnönü; the attitude of the Army; and the fact that no important changes had been made in the TGNA (Turkish Grand National Assembly) and in the government, all played an important role in İnönü's election as President.[11]

Immediately after he was elected, a short-term temporary government was set up with Bayar at its head. It should be pointed out that İnönü – in particular during the short, one-year absence from power – had focused on some incidents of corruption and had asked the relevant persons and administrators to account for them, and had also been completely removed by his opponents from the political arena. It is remarkable that the same İnönü who, during Atatürk's time when he was in the opposition, had been kept away from the political arena, now had to try to compromise with prominent political figures, and that he was in fact successful in simultaneously implementing these two contradictory policies. As İnönü was accepting the resignation of the second Bayar Government, which was now politically damaged because of recent incidents of corruption and related court cases, he was at the same time marking the end of the transition period.[12]

During this time, in order to fill the power vacuum caused by

Atatürk's death without losing any time and without a crisis, İnönü gradually increased his control and authority over political life – the party, the government and the TGNA.[13] It should also be pointed out that the single-party political system continued without any crisis after Atatürk's death.

During the period that Celâl Bayar was Atatürk's second and last Prime Minister – a period of over a year – it is possible to say that the problems that emerged during İnönü's term in that office were completely solved. Bayar displayed extreme sensitivity to the Chief's instructions. Trying to implement private initiative methods from a statist standpoint turned out to be one of the most important characteristics of this government.

Not only were political manoeuvres employed to completely liquidate İnönü from political life, but an assassination was even attempted. Sleeves were rolled up to find a Presidential candidate in lieu of İnönü, to succeed Atatürk. However, all these enterprises proved futile. During this process, his opponents were unable to reduce İnönü's influence either within the Party, or within Parliament, or in the bureaucracy. İnönü was able to find the opportunity to return to power, thanks in part to Bayar's important and positive contributions, but mainly as a result of the support of the army.[14]

The political paradox at this point was this: as the Prime Minister who had carried on his shoulders all the political responsibilities of the Atatürk period, and as the second man of the single-party government, İnönü could be regarded as a symbol of the political regime. But on the other hand, he had been kept away from power for more than a year. When he returned to power, there were many questions as to whether the Atatürk regime would continue or not. To a great extent, the regime bore Atatürk's personal seal, and with the replacement of the 'first man' by the 'second man' there was curiosity as to whether the regime would change and, if so, to what extent. This was the day that the political opponents of the Atatürk period had been waiting for.

At the start of his term in power, İnönü was to carry out a very sensitive political manoeuvre: he kept Bayar as Prime Minister as a sign that the system would continue as before. However, he did not show the same mildness to those who, during his period out of office, had tried to remove him from the political arena and even to liquidate him. These people were immediately removed from the government and the bureaucracy. The liquidation was not large-scale and was kept at a reasonable level. However, this process was to wound Bayar personally, because many of his close friends were involved, and after a short while he felt compelled to resign, voluntarily. By the time Refik Saydam's name was put on the agenda as Prime Minister for the new term – Refik Saydam, who was always at İnönü's side even when İnönü had fallen from power, who had refused to take place in Bayar's first government, but had assumed a position in his last cabinet – it had already become clear that the regime would continue to a great extent, although some areas would be modified.[15]

Years later, during the transition years to the new democracy in 1945/46, İnönü's speeches were interpreted as the first signs of democratic life, but in reality they were about new arrangements aimed at amending the single-party government system. One of the primary goals was to increase the RPP's political function and control within the government as a single party, and some measures were indeed taken for this purpose. However, in practice very little changed. There were many reasons for this. First of all, it was unclear whether the RPP had sufficient willpower for this role. Secondly, as an organization, the RPP seemed very far from possessing the identity of a political party that could put its name to such a function. Also, the state bureaucracy was very influential. No matter how much effort İnönü put into separating the state from the party – which had been 'merged' into each other by Atatürk – he was not successful. The same applies to the 'Independent Group', which was seen as another sign of transition to democratic life, and had been set up within the RPP in order to control the Parliament. In practice, this did not work, either.[16]

Another development that was to be expected was the initiation of an 'Atatürk' debate at the beginning of the term. This debate was put on the agenda by former elite politicians who had opposed Atatürk during his term and had therefore had to abandon politics, and whose 'honour' had finally been 'restored' by İnönü. Although İnönü was to vehemently oppose such initiatives, Atatürk's men were nevertheless removed from their posts.[17]

The development of the 'People's Houses' (*Halkevleri*) and the additional setting up of 'People's Chambers' (*Halk Odaları*), should be viewed as continuations or extensions of the single-party regime within society. Both organizations were propaganda tools with the goal of legitimizing the system within Turkey. It was through these organizations that the operations of the government were made known to various levels of society. The 'Village Institutes' (*Köy Enstitüleri*) as well were important for the continuity of the system. Teachers educated in accordance with the ideology of the single-party regime were needed to solve the problem of education in the vast rural areas. The Village Institutes should also be regarded as an important tool in training large numbers of teachers.[18]

Because the İnönü period, 1938–45, coincided with the years of the Second World War, they are stagnant years for the single-party regime. War and foreign policy concerns made it impossible to initiate any internal move. And at the end of the war, external factors were to play an important role in the preparations to end the single-party regime.[19]

It is hard to find any important difference between the single-party system of İnönü's time and that of Atatürk's era. As President, İnönü seemed to have forgotten all the complaints he once had about that office when he himself was Prime Minister, and he continued all of its traditions. It would not be an exaggeration to say that, as it was with Atatürk, İnönü had the last word on everything. The single-party regime of his time continued to control all the levers of society. To a large extent, this included the media. Another characteristic of the period was that the changes in the balance of military and political power between the countries at war during the war years, brought changes in the domestic politics of Turkey, a country caught in-between. In particular, the warmth in Turkish-German relationships caused the Turkish Nationalist and Racist-Turanist groups to gain strength; however, during the last stage of the war, all of these groups were liquidated. Leftist groups that had struggled politically against these groups were to share a similar fate. Throughout the single-party regime, the left was regarded as illegal.[20]

All of the questions posed in 1938 as to whether or not the single-party regime would continue, and if so, how, were answered within a short period of time. Under İnönü, the regime continued almost as before. If the extraordinary changes of 1945 had not taken place, it appeared that there would have been no reason for this regime not to continue.[21]

At this point, we can come to some general conclusions about the single-party political system and the RPP. The first striking feature in the structure of the RPP is that there is an unshakable authority and discipline starting from the top, going down to the bottom. The bottom level of the party organization and the provincial organization are absolutely dependent on headquarters, and headquarters exercises complete authority and control over the party's provincial organization. And at headquarters, the Chief's authority is definitive. At every level of the Party, a high degree of centralism and bureaucratism is evident.[22]

In principle, anyone can become a member of the RPP. However, becoming a member does not carry any important functional importance: activities within the party are kept at a minimum. It is only an outward appearance that the RPP's organizational structure seems so widespread. In reality, it would be very difficult to speak of an important and effective provincial organization.

The RPP's management and top-level executive organs are composed exclusively of members of parliament. The party's parliamentary wing enjoys complete superiority over the provincial organization. Even at party assemblies, the number of parliamentarians always exceeds that of delegates. It seems almost as if the RPP's central decision-taking organ is not the party assembly, but parliament itself. Party congresses are not forums of discussion, but places where decisions already taken by the administration gain legitimacy. In this sense, party congresses are similar to the function of parliament: the parliament approves decisions concerning the state and that have been taken by the administration; the party congresses and assemblies approve decisions concerning the party which, again, have already been accepted by the administration.

There is no indication that internal party elections are freer than the national elections of the country. Both national elections as well as those of the party, the candidates are determined and announced by the RPP executive administration. The RPP's top-level administrators themselves are all personally appointed by the 'Lifelong President'. In fact, the mechanism of 'appointing' applies to all important executive positions within the party. A committee comprised of the RPP's Lifelong President, the RPP's Vice-president and the RPP Secretary General, determine and announce the candidates for parliament. This announcement means that the candidate has been appointed as a parliamentarian.[23]

At this point, it is worth taking a look at the RPP's legal and actual ties to the government and the state. Particularly towards the end of the Atatürk period (1936–38), as a result of the party-state fusion, the RPP had been confronted with the danger and threat of completely losing its organizational autonomy. Indeed, it is open to discussion how separate and autonomous the party was from the state mechanism even before 1936. During the 1931–36 period, the RPP Secretary General, Recep Peker, had tried to strengthen the party organizationally as well as ideologically, and had not only been unable to find any support from within the party or from the party executives, but had finally been removed from his position in 1936 by Atatürk personally. Peker's isolation during this period shows that the administration did not want the RPP to show any initiative in this direction.[24]

During his term, İnönü tried to prevent the party-state fusion, which in practice meant the party's melting away within and into the state. With the intention of having the party assert itself, he tried to break off its legal and *de facto* ties to the state and government. However, his numerous initiatives were to remain insufficient and unsuccessful, and to produce no results whatsoever. Meanwhile, in terms of the government's 'supervisory' function, it is very obvious that the RPP was not able to perform this duty. During the İnönü period, therefore, the RPP was unable to become a party independent from the government and the state mechanism, but continued to be an unconditional supporter of the administration. In this context, it is hard, even impossible, to claim that the RPP was an independent political organization. As a political party, the RPP was being managed rather than managing, and as such it neither possessed the identity of a political party, nor performed its functions.

As is officially and openly stated in its programme, the RPP's ideology is Kemalism. However, Kemalism has not officially been developed, analysed and expounded as a doctrine, although the party itself was the only organization that had the means to do this. Ideologically, the RPP was an extremely weak party. It was undoubtedly an authoritarian single-party. However, the extent of its authoritarianism should be questioned as well. It has been claimed that the RPP is a 'trustee' party. But it should be pointed out that it is hardly, if at all, possible to find any similarity between the model created by the historical and political incidents studied here, and the 'trustee' single-party model put forward by those who claimed that the RPP belonged to this type.

It would be fair to say the following about the İnönü period:

during this period, the administration and the RPP had presented themselves to society as a single party, had done their best to propagate every kind of ideological declaration that legitimized the administration and the regime, and had given no indication or made no announcement that the single-party regime was temporary. Indeed, although it is not easy to find any written document to the effect that the administration regarded the single-party rule as temporary, it is possible to find many official declarations indicating attempts to legitimate this regime.

Another point that should be considered carefully is the compatibility between the view that the RPP is in reality a trustee party, and the views announced by the RPP itself during the transition period to the multi-party regime and in following years, when the party was proclaiming its views and recounting the history of the recent past.

While it is possible to reach some conclusions on the Turkish single-party system, to do so more fully it becomes necessary to study in greater detail the way the administration worked. It should be stated that during the single-party regime in Turkey (1925–45), all developments relating to foreign policy were carefully observed by Çankaya (the name of the district where the President's office is located, this word symbolizes the Presidency of the Republic and its apparatus) and that all important and basic decisions related to foreign policy, were, again, taken by Çankaya. Within this context, the government and Foreign Ministers were faithful implementers of foreign policy decisions, rather than playing a determining and executing role in foreign policy.

Foreign policy matters were generally neither raised nor discussed within the TGNA or within the RPP Parliamentary Group. Foreign policy decisions were always taken within a narrow circle in Çankaya with (Atatürk and) İnönü alone having the last say. The main guidelines of foreign policy were always drawn up at Çankaya. Decisions taken there would be brought to the RPP Parliamentary Group; parliamentarians would be given whatever information was regarded as necessary and sufficient and would have to be content merely with being informed. The government's proposals were always accepted at the RPP Parliamentary Group. However, from time to time important discussions did take place. But even in these exceptional times, the discussions and debates at the Parliamentary Group always resulted in the acceptance of the proposals brought to it by the administration. It is impossible to say that the RPP Parliamentary Group made any contribution to the decision-taking process in foreign policy. Nor did the TGNA play an important role or make any significant contribution to the decision-making process in foreign policy. The Parliament has always unanimously approved all foreign policy proposals brought to its agenda by the administration, without feeling the need for any debate or discussion. In other words, the TGNA constituted the last link in the official chain of the decision-taking mechanism, which legitimized foreign policy decisions and saw to it that those taken at Çankaya, after passing through the RPP Parliamentary Group, were, as a formality, turned into law.

While he was Prime Minister, İnönü had felt a strong reaction to President Atatürk's taking foreign policy decisions without consulting him as head of government, and having these decisions implemented through the Foreign Minister, leaving himself out of the picture. However, when he became President, İnönü did not change these methods, and the process of foreign policy decision-making continued as before. Generally speaking, it is probably correct to say that foreign policy issues were seen as fields of specialization in themselves, and were conducted accordingly.[25]

Turkish foreign policy during the İnönü period was in principle not much different from that of the Atatürk period. In fact, it was a consistent continuation of that policy. During the last years of the Atatürk period – that is, during the second half of the 1930s – a tendency had emerged in foreign policy to establish closer political relations with Western states. Immediately after Atatürk's death, as war loomed, this foreign policy naturally yielded the signing of a military alliance agreement. The fact that it was signed in such a short time shows that a lot had accumulated in terms of foreign policy. Indeed, if this policy had been new, it would not have been possible for such a development to result in a military alliance in such a short time, least of all during war!

Immediately prior to the Second World War, İnönü, seeing the approaching danger of war and the possibility of an attack on the country, concluded that Turkey's security could only be secured within a Western alliance and, availing himself of the distance covered by Turkish foreign policy especially during the second half of the 1930s, he ensured in a short time that Turkey took its place within the Western alliance. This decision shows that the country's foreign policy had reached its long-term goal in the face of the threat of war and of rapidly changing developments.

During the Second World War, the main aim and principle of Turkish foreign policy was to avoid taking part in it, no matter what happened. Indeed, Turkey would gain nothing by participating in the war. Turkish administrators had personally witnessed, and not forgotten, the consequences of the First World War and the state to which it had brought the country. İsmet İnönü, who occupied the most important decision-taking position in Turkish foreign policy during that term, was most acutely aware of this reality. His efforts to keep the country out of war should therefore come as no surprise.

All through the war years, the strategic goal of foreign policy was to keep the country away from war, and to achieve this various tactics were employed. However, the main one never changed: to try to keep out of the war and to gain time by using the various powers against each other, preventing the country from getting too close to any single one of them, all the while bearing in mind Europe's political and military balance of power. With this purpose, Turkey followed a policy – or perhaps one should say a game – of balance throughout the war years. As long as Turkey wished to take no part in the war, it always found excuses, political, military or otherwise, to keep out of it.

This balancing act on the part of Turkey was only possible by using the power relations and the conflicts of interest between the Axis countries, Germany and Italy, on the one side, and the Allied countries, Britain, France, the Soviet Union and the USA, on the other. To maintain this balance, Turkey not only skilfully used the frictions and conflicts between the Allied and Axis countries, but also those among the Allies themselves. Of course, the general military changes of power during the course of the war played an extremely important role in determining the main trend of Turkish foreign policy, and in the continuation of the game of balance. In this sense, one can say that Turkish foreign policy adjusted its tactics and diplomatic manoeuvres according to how the war developed.

From the point of view of achieving what was aimed for, the Turkish foreign policy pursued during the Second World War was a success. However, it should be emphasized that the main problems that emerged at the end of the war and after it was over are a direct continuation and result of this very policy: the policy kept Turkey out of the war, but the price paid was that in the new international political arena of the post-war years, Turkey was left alone. It was unable to find a place for itself within the Western alliance.[26]

The decision-making process for domestic policy differs somewhat from that of foreign policy issues. First of all, perhaps because during this period developments and problems related to foreign policy were continuous and of primary importance, Çankaya allowed the government more freedom in taking domestic policy-related decisions. Other than determining the main trend in domestic politics, İsmet İnönü hardly ever intervened in matters that could be regarded as details. Domestic policy was left more to the initiative of the government or the relevant ministers. However, it is known that İnönü did closely observe domestic policy developments.

Another important point that should always be borne in mind when studying the 'National Chief' period, is that during this time domestic and foreign policies were hard to separate from each other. This was a period when foreign policy developments seriously affected, and from time to time even determined, domestic policy.

The TGNA was unable – even in domestic policy – to constitute a platform for negotiation and debate, nor was it able, as the legislative body, to perform its duty of supervision. Until the end of the war, it remained an institution that always unanimously accepted the proposals (which were already-taken decisions) brought by the government, and that carried out whatever formality was necessary according to the Constitution. This does not mean that there were never any debates or criticism in Parliament. However, the rare criticisms were always expressed very gently and with careful wording. Since, according to the RPP regulations, it was compulsory in party discipline always to vote in accordance with the decisions taken by the RPP Parliamentary Group at the TGRN, even those who had criticized a certain decision were compelled to always vote in its favour in the end.

The TGNA performed its function of criticism within a very narrow framework, that of the RPP Parliamentary Group. This Group had a closer interest in domestic politics. Debates and discussions in this field were always much livelier than those related to foreign policy. However, discussions within the Parliamentary Group never reached the point where an important governmental proposal was rejected. Major decisions taken by the government were brought as proposals to the Parliamentary Group, were accepted here and voted into laws at the TGNA.

During the single-party regime, there were two totally different systems of government in Turkey. The first was the Constitution of 1924, which formally stipulates Turkey's mode of government. There is an enormous difference between the political system as seen theoretically from the point of view of the Constitution of 1924, and the 'Chief' system that was actually implemented. Therefore, throughout the single-party period, a parliamentary system based on the superiority of Parliament (as stipulated in the Constitution of 1924), that is to say, a Parliament elected by popular vote, and a government model stemming from this Parliament and responsible towards the assembly, never had a chance to survive. The President, according to the 1924 Constitution, was described as head of the executive organ, but thanks to the 'Chief' system in reality he possessed an extreme authority that was never mentioned in the Constitution, and he always used this authority. The 'Chief' system continued throughout the 1945–50 term, only gradually fading away, but retained its influence within the RPP for a long time. The Prime Minister and the government, which, according to the 1924 Constitution, had political responsibility, were always overshadowed by the President. So much so that governments always and without fail fulfilled the instructions of the President, and never dared to show any initiative against him.

The legislative body (the TGNA), which, according to the 1924 Constitution, was supposed to enjoy an extremely powerful and superior status, was never able to fulfil this role. Rather than being an organ that supervised government activities, the TGNA had instead largely taken on assisting the administration as its actual duty. As such, it served only to legitimize decisions taken by the government.

As a result of the legislative organ's loss of its supervising function, this role seems to have fallen to a large extent to the RPP Parliamentary Group. However, it will be hard to say exactly how far the RPP did fulfil this function until the Minutes of the RPP Parliamentary Group become accessible. It is clear, though, that the function of supervision was performed only at a minimum level. Even the 'Independent Group', which had been set up during İnönü's term of power, was never able to fill this gap when it became evident that the Parliament was unable to perform its actual duty.

Generally, it is hard to find any basic difference between the single-party regime of Atatürk's time and that of İnönü's time. Nor is it easy to see any indication that the 'National Chief' regime, İnönü and the RPP demonstrated any tendency towards liberalization in political life and in the political system. It is also apparent during this period that the regime continued to present the existing single-party political system and regime as justified and legitimate.[27] However, in 1945 a sudden decision was taken to return to multiparty political life. It could be said that this decision was taken within the framework of the new balance of power that came into being after the war had ended. However, such an interpretation, which takes only foreign policy as its basis, would be insufficient. Developments in domestic politics played a very important role in the taking and implementation of this decision. Judging from outward appearances, one could say that the 'National Chief' period came to an end in the spring of 1946. However, bearing in mind that this period came to an end gradually and followed a certain process, it would be more correct to say that the new transition started at the beginning of 1945, then gradually accelerated and continued until 1950, the year that, in a way, defines the end of the single-party period.

The Turkish single-party experience can be interpreted as a result of internal dynamics within the Ottoman political tradition and culture. However, the factor that brought about its end should be searched for externally rather than internally.[28]

(Translated into English by Gülayşe Koçak)

Notes

[1] Ahmet Demirel, *Birinci Mecliste Muhalefet: İkinci Grup*, İletişim Yayınları, İstanbul, 1994; *Birinci Meclis*, (ed. Cemil Koçak), Sabancı Üniversitesi Yayınları, Aralık, 1998; Erik Jan Zürcher, *Turkey: A Modern History*, I. B. Tauris, London-New York, 1993; Erik Jan Zürcher, *The Unionist Factor: The Role of the Committee of Union and Progress in the Turkish National Movement 1905-1926*, E. J. Brill, Leiden, 1984; Erik Jan Zürcher, *Millî Mücadelede İttihatçılık*, Bağlam Yayınları, İstanbul, 1987; Samet Ağaoğlu, *Kuvâyı Millîye Rûhu (Birinci Türkiye Büyük Millet Meclisi)*, İstanbul, 1973.

[2] Mete Tunçay, *Türkiye Cumhuriyeti'nde Tek-Parti Yönetiminin Kuruluşu (1923-1931)*, Târih Vakfı Yurt Yayınları, İstanbul, 1999; Hakkı Uyar, *Tek-Parti Dönemi ve Cumhuriyet Halk Partisi*, Boyut Kitapları, İstanbul, 1998; Erik Jan Zürcher, *Opposition in the Early Turkish Republic: The Progressive Republican Party 1924-1925*, E. J. Brill, Leiden, 1991; Erik Jan Zürcher, *Terakkiperver Cumhuriyet Fırkası*, Bağlam Yayınları, İstanbul, 1992; Cemil

Koçak, *Siyasal Tarih (1923–1950), Çağdaş Türkiye (1908–1980), Türkiye Tarihi*, (Editör: Sina Akşin), Vol. IV, Cem Yayınevi, İstanbul, 1989; Esat Öz, *Tek-Parti Yönetimi ve Siyasal Katılım (1923–1945)*, Gündoğan Yayınları, Ankara, 1991.

[3] Cemil Koçak, *Türkiye'de Millî Şef Dönemi (1938–1945)*, Vols I and II, İletişim Yayınları, İstanbul, 1996.

[4] *Ulus*, and *Cumhuriyet*, and *Tan* (Summer–Fall 1937).

[5] Mete Tunçay, 'Hatay Sorunu ve TBMM', *Türk Parlamentoculuğunun İlk Yüz Yılı (1876–1976) (Kânûnu Esâsî'nin 100. Yılı Sempozyumu*, Ankara; Koçak, Vol. I, op. cit., pp. 23–28; Fâlih Rıfkı Atay, *Çankaya*, Batez, İstanbul, 1980; İsmet Bozdağ, *Bir Çağın Parde Arkası: Atatürk-İnönü, İnönü-Bayar Çekişmeleri*, Kervan Yayınları, İstanbul, 1972; Yâkup Kadri Karaosmanoğlu, *Politikada 45 Yıl*, Bilgi Yayınevi, Ankara, 1968; Feridun Kandemir, *Siyasî Dargınlıklar (Atatürk-İnönü, İnönü-Mareşal Dargınlığı)*, Ekicigil Tarih Yayınları, İstanbul, 1955.

[6] Koçak, op. cit., Vol. I, pp. 23–28, 53–56; Ludmilla Jivkova, *İngiliz-Türk İlişkileri (1933–1939)*, Habora Kitabevi Yayınları, İstanbul, 1978.

[7] Koçak, op. cit., Vol. I, pp. 29–47; İlhan Tekeli ve Selim İlkin, *Uygulamaya Geçerken Türkiye'de Devletçiliğin Oluşumu*, ODTÜ İdari İlimler Fakültesi Yayını, Ankara, 1982, pp. 144–48; Korkut Boratav, *Türkiye'de Devletçilik*, Gerçek Yayınevi, İstanbul, 1974, pp. 181–201; Yahya Sezai Tezel, *Cumhuriyet Döneminin İktisadi Tarihi (1923–1950)*, Tarih Vakfı Yurt Yayınları, İstanbul, 1994.

[8] *Ulus*, *Tan* and *Cumhuriyet* (daily newspapers), (21 September 1937); *Tan* (26 September 1937); Ahmet Emin Yalman, 'Başvekâlette Değişiklik', *Tan* (26 September 1937) and *Tan* (27/28 September 1937), *Cumhuriyet* (28 September 1937), *Ulus* (29 September 1937) and Fâlih Rıfkı Atay, 'Başvekâlette', *Ulus* (29 September 1937).

[9] Şevket Süreyyâ Aydemir, *İkinci Adam*, Vol. 1, Remzi Kitabevi, İstanbul, 1968, pp. 515–18; Fâlih Rıfkı Atay, *Çankaya*, Bateş, İstanbul, 1980, p. 483; Sabahattin Selek, 'Ölümünün Birinci Yılında İnönü: Demokrasiye Geçiş: Atatürk-İnönü Ayrılığı', *Milliyet* (daily newspaper) (8 January 1975); Hilmi Uran, *Hâtıralarım*, Ankara, 1959, p. 303; Âsım Us, *Hâtıra Notları (1930–1950)*, Istanbul, 1966, pp. 205–13.

[10] Koçak, op. cit., Vol. I, pp. 66–76.
[11] Koçak, op. cit., Vol. I, pp. 97–137.
[12] Koçak, op. cit., Vol. I, pp. 139–44, 192–224.
[13] Koçak, op. cit., Vol. I, pp. 154–73.
[14] Koçak, op. cit., Vol. I, pp. 133–37.
[15] Koçak, op. cit., Vol. I, pp. 76–86.
[16] Koçak, op. cit., Vol. I, pp. 53–90.
[17] Koçak, op. cit., Vol. I, pp. 139–228 and Vol. II, pp. 13–53.
[18] Koçak, op. cit., Vol. II, pp. 53–126.

SOME VIEWS ON THE TURKISH SINGLE-PARTY REGIME 129

[19] Koçak, op. cit., Vol. I, pp. 229-713 and Vol. II, pp. 141-275.
[20] Koçak, op. cit., Vol. II, pp. 134-40.
[21] Koçak, op. cit., Vol. II, pp. 545-82.
[22] Koçak, op. cit., Vol. I, pp. 152-173 and Vol. II, pp. 53-115, 301-38.
[23] Koçak, op. cit., Vol. II, pp. 46-47, 285-300.
[24] Tunçay, op. cit.
[25] Koçak, op. cit., Vol. II, pp. 545-81.
[26] Koçak, op. cit., Vol. I, pp. 229-713, 141-274, 560-62; Cemil Koçak, *Türk-Alman İlişkileri (1923-1939) (İki Dünya Savaşı Arasındaki Dönemde Siyasal, Kültürel, Arkeri ve Ekonomik İlişkiler)*, Türk Tarih Kurumu Yayınlan, Ankara, 1991; Selim Deringil, *Denge Oyunu (İkinci Dünya Savaşı'nda Türkiye'nin Dış Politikası)*, Tarih Vakfı Yurt Yayınları, İstanbul, 1994; Selim Deringil, *Turkish Foreign Policy During the Second World War: An "Active" Neutrality*, Cambridge University Press, Cambridge, 1988; Türkkaya Ataöv, *Turkish Foreign Policy (1939-1945)*, Siyasal Bilgiler Fakültesi Yayınları, Ankara, 1965; Edward Weisband, *Turkish Foreign Policy 1943-1945: Small State Diplomacy and Great Power Politics*, Princeton University Press, Princeton, NJ, 1973; Edward Weisband, *İkinci Dünya Savaşı'nda İnönü'nün Dış Politikası*, Milliyet Yayınları, İstanbul, 1974; Mümtaz Soysal, *Dış Politika ve Parlamento (Dış Politika Alanındaki Yasama-Yürütme İlişileri Üzerinde Karşılaştırmalı Bir İnceleme)*, Siyasal Bilgiler Fakültesi Yayınları, Ankara, 1964.
[27] Koçak, op. cit., Vol. II, pp. 21-139, 275-363, 545-81.
[28] Kemal Karpat, *Turkey's Politics: The Transition to a Multi-Party System*, Princeton University Press, Princeton, NJ, 1959; Kemal Karpat, *Türk Demokrasi Tarihi*, İstanbul, 1967; Taner Timur, *Türkiye'de Çok Partili Hayata Geçiş*; İletişim Yayınları, İstanbul, 1991.

CHAPTER VI

The Army, Civil Society and the State in Iran: 1921–26

Stephanie Cronin

In 1921 Reza Khan arrived at the site of political power via a military coup. Appropriating the objectives of secular nationalism and constitutionalism, he embarked on the task of constructing a strong, modern, centralized state, at the heart of which would be a national army. He simultaneously began to establish his own personal ascendancy within the new army and state, crushing both civilian and military opposition, a process that was largely complete by his accession to the throne as Shah in 1926. In these years the military came to permeate the fabric of society. Reza Khan used the army as a focus of nationalism and officers were at the forefront of social and cultural change. By its work of national unification and the creation of an effective central authority the army, as well as the regime it served, achieved considerable popularity among the intelligentsia and nationalist circles. Yet problems were immediately evident in the relationship between the military and civil society. Particularly damaging both to the army and to the regime was the tendency, encouraged by Reza Khan, to perpetuate financial and administrative malpractices typical of the preceding era, but now magnified in significance by the enormously increased weight of the modern state and military in society generally. From the very beginning Reza Khan's regime exhibited arbitrary, erratic and unpredictable features which, after 1926 worsened into a new absolutism. The military roots of this absolutism lay in the early 1920s.[1]

The Historical Context

The construction of a strong army, as part of a general programme of defensive modernization, had been a central objective of Iranian reformers since the early nineteenth century. Awareness of the dangers attendant upon Iran's weakness and vulnerability, coupled with a desire to combat them rapidly, increased as the overall failure to renovate the structures of Qajar state and society led Iran to enter the twentieth century financially bankrupt, with a disintegrating and helpless central authority. Accordingly, for many of the participants in the constitutional revolution an important goal, even the primary goal, was the creation of a strong state with an effective army, capable of overcoming Iran's backwardness.[2]

Yet the ten years between the suppression of the Majlis in 1911 and the coup of 1921, were a period of anarchy and collapse in Iran. The constitutional revolution had destroyed the 'traditional centre of despotic power'[3] but had failed to create a viable alternative, and World War I saw the very existence of Iran as a political entity threatened. During the war the country experienced both foreign military intervention and extreme domestic political strife. By its end, provincial centrifugal, regional and tribal forces augured national disintegration, while at the centre stood only a weak Shah and a helpless government.[4] The war years had witnessed the rapid advance of nationalist thought and activity, and there was widespread disgust at the corruption and incompetence of the traditional elite.

In this environment the Cossack officer Reza Khan held a ready appeal. Although flagrantly disregarding constitutionalist critiques concerning the evils of tyranny and the benefits of the rule of law, he nevertheless attracted wide support due to his success in realizing the second cherished objective of the revolution: the creation of a strong, centralized state with a modern national army at its centre. The inclination of the early constitutionalists to search for a strong personality to carry out the state-building effort had been visible at a very early stage,[5] while the appeal of a charismatic leader after the exhausting fratricidal conflict of the period of revolution and war was irresistible.[6] During these years power was, as Homa Katouzian has put it, 'lying in the streets waiting to be picked up',[7] and, in these circumstances the source from which a leadership of sufficient decisiveness was most likely to emerge was the military.

In 1920–21 however, it was by no means clear which element within Iran's disparate military forces might posit itself as the instrument of national salvation. Although, as a result of the later consolidation of Pahlavi rule, Reza Khan's military pre-eminence by 1921 seems established, in fact military rivals to his ascendancy, both individual and collective, persisted. The creation of his own supreme power, both within the army as well as in the state and society generally, was still in 1921 a matter awaiting accomplishment. The liquidation of his most serious military rival, the Gendarme Colonel Mohammad Taqi Khan Pasyan, and the suppression of any overt challenge from the Gendarmerie, were key episodes in this process.[8]

In 1920–21 the Cossack Division and the Gendarmerie were contending for military supremacy in Iran. The Gendarmerie, imbued with the spirit of constitutionalism and with a strong nationalist record, offered a sharp contrast to the Cossack Division, long identified with the most reactionary tendencies in Iranian society. Yet the leadership that spearheaded the renovation of the Iranian state, exemplified by and grouped around Reza Khan, emerged from the latter environment. This clique of former officers of the Cossack Division had grown to political maturity in an atmosphere dominated by loyalty to autocracy and opposition to reform, and it was they who stamped their identity so strongly on Iranian history in the 1920s and 1930s.[9]

The traditions and aspirations represented by the Gendarmerie and the Cossack Division may perhaps be illustrated by a comparison of the two most famous officers to emerge from these forces. The Gendarme officer, Colonel Pasyan, and the Cossack Reza Khan were, in many respects, typical products of their respective corps. Although mortal political enemies, ideologically they had much in common. Both were charismatic leaders, nationalist, secular, even anti-clerical, and they shared a profound detestation of the traditional elite. Personally and politically, however, they were very different. Pasyan's intellectualism and his sophisticated acquaintance with European thought and culture contrast with Reza Khan's limited intellectual level, while the former's lifelong and active identification with constitutionalist ideals differs starkly from Reza's opportunism and adventurism.[10] It was only Pasyan's destruction in the autumn of 1921 that allowed Reza Khan to adopt unchallenged the mantle of nationalism among the military and to fashion both the army and the state in his own image.

Much of the justification, both contemporary and historical, for the early Pahlavi dictatorship has been predicated on notions of inevitability and necessity. It was, and is, argued that whatever the defects of the monarchist regime as it emerged in the 1920s, no serious alternative national leadership was available. Furthermore, in the context of the period, the regime's authoritarianism, martial temper and easy resort to force was unavoidable and even essential to any programme of reconstruction and reform.

Nevertheless, the type of regime that emerged in Iran during the 1920s owed much to Reza Khan's methods, habits and inclinations and clearly bore his personal imprimatur. To what extent Iran's history in the 1920s and 1930s might have been different had military leadership been grasped by Colonel Pasyan or any other officer more authentically representative of Iranian constitutionalism than Reza Khan, is a question which may only be answered speculatively. Perhaps instructive in this respect is a comparison with the development of Turkey under the rule of another modernizing army officer, Mustafa Kemal. Although Reza Khan and Mustafa Kemal were both authoritarian, even dictatorial, the systems that each established were very different, both in their day-to-day functioning and in their consequences for the future. In the early 1920s both men faced similar state-building tasks and many of the measures they adopted also bore a superficial similarity. However, Kemal was always careful to seek legitimation for his actions and to base them upon legal principles.[11] He removed the army from involvement in political life and created an enduring political party, the Republican People's Party, ultimately capable of relinquishing power, and enabled Turkey to avoid embroilment in World War II. He abstained from the temptation to use Islam in moments of crisis and, in the six arrows of Kemalism, tried to give his actions theoretical consistency. He was, furthermore, not personally corrupt. The patrimonial monarchy established by Reza Shah possessed none of these positive features. Iran's modernization, in any case much weaker than that instituted in Turkey, took place within the context of absolute and despotic personal rule, the main political change being the presence of a different royal family at the centre of the system. The officer corps of the Iranian Gendarmerie had undergone, in many respects, similar formative experiences to those of the Young Turks officers in the Ottoman army.[12] Perhaps under a leadership derived from the latter source Iran might have followed a path closer to that of Turkey under Kemal, building more solid institutions and achieving greater stability.

The Military–Monarchist Dictatorship

By 1922 Reza Khan had clearly emerged as the single most powerful personality within the Iranian army and was able to pose as the saviour of the Iranian nation, presenting a new-found, but undoubted, appeal to nationalist elements. His establishment of his personal ascendancy within the army went in tandem with his growing dominance over state and society.[13] By 1926 he had, by a combination of repression, co-option and manipulation, secured the foundations of his military–monarchical dictatorship.

In the years 1921–26 Reza Khan used the Iranian army both to intervene directly in the political process and also to manipulate, in a more subtle way, the political life of the country. His direct intervention began, of course, with the *coup d'état* itself, and continued with episodes such as the repeated cowing of the Majlis by the threat of armed force, in 1922 and 1924. As well as openly intimidating the Majlis at certain key moments, the military, with its increasing control over elections, had by 1926 fatally compromised the independence of that body. The army furthermore sponsored and orchestrated political movements, such as republicanism, and prepared the ground for constitutional change. Reza Khan, having by the early 1920s come to dominate the cabinet, reducing it largely to an appendage to his own position, systematically promoted the military at the expense of the civil authorities throughout the country. He also used the army to gain more comprehensive control over wider spheres of civil life, negatively, by introducing repressive measures often under the cover of martial law, and positively, by making the army a focus of nationalism and a pioneer of social progress, with military personnel leading the way in clothing reform, the abolition of titles, rudimentary town planning, linguistic reform, and so on. By 1926 the military character of the regime was as clear as it was novel.

The Cabinet and the Majlis

The *coup d'état* of February 1921 marked a sudden, and the first direct, intervention of the military in Iranian political life. Nevertheless, the new government formed by Sayyed Ziya remained largely civilian in character, the only army officer given a post being the Gendarme Major Mas'ud Khan Kayhan, who became Minister of

War. Reza Khan himself had no post in this cabinet, but was granted the title of Sardar-i Sipah and retained the *de facto* command of the armed forces, which he had assumed on taking control of the capital, under the nominal authority of the Shah.

Using his command of the Cossack force, particularly that element stationed in the capital, Reza Khan immediately embarked on his aggrandisement of power. First he refused to obey the Minister of War, Major Kayhan, and demanded to replace him while retaining active command of the army. In the circumstances Sayyed Ziya found himself with little option but to accede and in early May appointed him the new War Minister. By combining in himself the offices of War Minister and *de facto* Commander-in-Chief, Reza Khan made himself unquestionably the highest authority in the army, although the Shah remained constitutional head, and reduced the military's accountability to the civil power. Furthermore, as a member of the cabinet he could now insist on the claims of the army over the claims of any of the other ministries on the meagre resources at the disposal of the exchequer.

Reza Khan's next step was to secure his domination of the cabinet by ousting his main rival, Sayyed Ziya. Through a political intrigue, he quickly forced Sayyed Ziya into flight and exile, and his victory placed him in a pre-eminent position in the capital.[14] However, he still preferred to remain in the background. He did not yet demand the prime ministership himself, although he was able to determine to whom the Shah should offer that post, and in any case he was clearly the strongest figure in the cabinet.

The new government formed after Sayyed Ziya's exile was quickly made aware of the new reality of civil–military relations, the ministers intimidated by the War Minister's complete control over the armed forces in the capital and fearful of arrest.[15] During the latter part of 1921 Reza Khan's military successes in Mazandaran, and especially in Gilan against Kuchik Khan, increased enormously his power and prestige in the country. He had liquidated the independence of his most serious military rival, Colonel Mohammad Taqi Khan Pasyan, and he now more than ever resembled a military dictator, dominated the cabinet and was feared by the Shah. The dynamic relationship between Reza Khan and the army, whereby the former's personal advancement simultaneously depended upon and guaranteed the latter's interests and predominance, was now becoming clear. Indeed, it was in this period that the army increasingly identified itself, and was identified by the general population, as Reza Khan's own personal instrument.

Reza Khan fully realized that his position depended on keeping the army contented, yet by the close of 1921 the government was practically bankrupt while the War Ministry was in urgent need of cash, both to pay the troops and to mount operations against the Kurdish rebel, Simitqu, in Azarbaijan. In December Reza Khan insisted on the daily revenue of the customs and excise departments being paid into the military treasury. By the end of the month he was raiding all the civil revenues he could lay his hands on, had quarrelled with the Shah by demanding that the latter pay the troops out of his private fortune and was issuing all manner of threats to the Prime Minister, Qavam al-Saltanah, should the government continue to prove unable to provide him with sufficient funds.

On 10 February 1922 the Majlis passed the budget of the War Ministry, sanctioning an expenditure of nine million tumans on the army for the ensuing year, but without giving any indication as to how such a sum might be raised.[16] In March, facing a desperate financial crisis, Reza Khan took the drastic step of assuming direct control of all the revenue-bearing administrations of the country: Crown lands, Municipality, indirect taxes, roads, customs, excise, opium, etc., and diverted their funds to military purposes. In addition to appropriating money from the central Treasury, the War Minister also instructed his commanders to take similar action regarding the provincial revenues, naturally causing considerable friction between the military and civilian authorities in the provinces and also placing an almost unbearable strain on the provincial budgets.

During the first half of 1922 three cabinets had foundered, largely as a result of the War Minister's demands for funds for the army, and by the early autumn the fourth government of the year, headed by Mushir al-Dowleh, was running into difficulties. There had also been, in this period, a rapid and widespread growth of general opposition to Reza Khan, caused by resentment partly at his illegal appropriation of government money for the army, and also particularly by his eagerness to replace provincial civil governors by military officers, and open attacks on him were appearing in the press. The War Minister requested the government to take action to suppress one particular newspaper, but Mushir al-Dowleh refused and instead resigned. Reza Khan then took the law into his own hands and

THE ARMY, CIVIL SOCIETY AND THE STATE IN IRAN 137

personally punished the offending editor, subsequently complaining to the Majlis of the intolerable situation in which such attacks placed him. It was to general surprise that he took this step as, up to that point, he had largely ignored the Majlis, his attitude being only one of 'contemptuous toleration'.[17]

The Majlis, however, far from offering support to the War Minister, expressed in forceful terms its displeasure at his dictatorial methods. As a result of this expression of opinion Reza Khan, in a completely unexpected move, tendered his resignation in writing to the *vali'ahd* on 7 October. The same day he called his officers together to a conference at the War Ministry and announced to them his intention to resign. All the assembled officers expressed their loyalty to him and offered to close the Majlis and arrest the offending deputies should he so instruct them. Reza Khan replied that it was not in their interests to carry out such extreme measures at the present time, and that he wished to await the Shah's reply to his request to resign.[18] The assembled officers refused to agree to allow him to resign and swore to follow him in any course he cared to pursue to preserve his authority. The political situation in Tehran became extremely tense, as there were widespread fears concerning the reaction of the army should the Shah accept the War Minister's resignation.

In the event the *vali'ahd* refused to accept Reza Khan's resignation and negotiated a compromise solution to the crisis. Reza Khan agreed to withdraw his resignation and to continue in office, to withdraw certain military governors and to hand over control of the revenue-bearing administrations to the American financial adviser, Dr Arthur C. Millspaugh, on his arrival. As a result of this compromise, Reza Khan appeared to meet halfway the demands of the Majlis for more constitutional methods, while the Majlis thanked him for the services he had rendered to his country amid scenes of great enthusiasm. The War Minister's tussle with the Majlis had in fact strengthened his position, for, although he had conceded some points, the Majlis had publicly thanked him for his great services and thus ranged itself on his side. It actually seems extremely doubtful that he ever had any serious intention of resigning, and had orchestrated the whole episode in order to gauge his strength vis à vis his opponents.

By the end of 1922 Reza Khan had both demonstrated his ability ultimately to defy and intimidate the Majlis and had established his pre-eminence within any government that might be set up. In the frequent formation and dissolution of cabinets during 1922, the War Minister had been the one and only comparatively stable factor, for he had remained as War Minister in each of the cabinets that had come into existence during that year, and by alone refusing to resign his ministry he had filled the breach during the interval between the fall of one cabinet and the formation of another. In any case, no Prime Minister would or could take any decision without his consent.

During 1923 Reza Khan had no difficulty in dictating the primacy of military considerations in the programme of successive Prime Ministers. Nevertheless, towards the end of the year he apparently decided to abolish the fiction of an independent Prime Minister and to adopt that title himself. Following the flight abroad of the then Prime Minister, Qavam al-Saltaneh, after the discovery of an alleged conspiracy, Reza Khan grasped the opportunity to take over the now conveniently vacant post.[19] By combining in himself the offices of War Minister, Prime Minister and army commander, Reza Khan unified the military and civil authorities, at their apex, to an unprecedented degree.

Although the Majlis had been shaken by Reza Khan's show of strength during the 1922 resignation crisis, it retained considerable independence and was capable of blocking the legislation required by the War Minister for his military projects and took a critical attitude towards the army generally. In fact, Reza Khan's principal base of support in the Fourth Majlis, the conservative elements of the Reformers' Party, crumbled completely over his radical conscription proposals. He therefore determined to produce in the Fifth Majlis a working majority that could be counted on to support his reforms, using the military to manipulate the elections.[20] In this he met with considerable success, the army command exercising a strict, although by no means total, control over the election process.

Election procedures in Iran were naturally of an unsophisticated nature and prone to manipulation, particularly in the rural areas. Not only did the military intervene, but the civil authorities responsible for the conduct of the elections themselves interfered in the official procedure in a variety of crude ways, using methods of bribery, exerting undue influence, tampering with and substituting voting papers, etc. The elections for the Fifth Majlis, particularly in the provinces, entailed a protracted and complex struggle between the military, sponsoring certain candidates, and a variety of local civilian factions and individuals, all of whom resorted to illegal tactics.[21]

Despite the considerable success achieved by the military in its intervention in the elections, the Fifth Majlis was by no means a docile instrument of Reza Khan, as was demonstrated by the fierce, even violent scenes among the deputies during the republican agitation in 1923 and by their strong opposition to the subsequent imposition of martial law in Tehran.[22] But in fact, the Fifth Majlis was the last during the early Pahlavi period to retain any political viability. In the elections to the Sixth Majlis the army exercised much more effective and consistent control, reflecting the growing ascendancy of the military over civil society, resulting in a body of much greater docility.[23] Although the Majlis continued to exist and to engage in desultory debates, and was periodically dissolved and re-elected, in the years between 1926 and 1941 it functioned purely as a rubber stamp.

The Shah

Although the Cossack march on Tehran in February 1921 had been undertaken without Ahmad Shah's knowledge and to his considerable alarm, the leaders of the coup clearly proclaimed their loyalty to the throne. The Shah, nonetheless, apparently intuitively realized that the Cossack march on the capital was inaugurating a fundamentally new stage in his relationship with his erstwhile bodyguard.[24] At the prospect of the arrival of the Cossacks in Tehran he was reported to be in a very agitated state and to be talking of immediate flight. In the long run, his apprehensions regarding his security at the hands of his nominal subordinates were to be fully justified.

Immediately after the coup, the Shah, under duress, had issued a proclamation stating that he was entirely in agreement with the views of the army and appointing Sayyid Ziya as Prime Minister. But he never gave the new cabinet his genuine support and readily intrigued with Reza Khan to bring about the Sayyid's downfall. The Shah soon found that Reza Khan's new pre-eminence produced a situation not entirely to his liking. By December the Shah was in fear of his War Minister, and was eager to escape his predicament by leaving for Europe.

Although it is not clear exactly when Reza Khan decided to try to supplant the Shah, an important factor in that decision was the Shah's thwarting of his ambition to be fully recognized as Commander-in-Chief of the armed forces. In fact, shortly after the *coup d'état*, Reza Khan had adopted the habit of signing letters emanating from the army as Commander-in-Chief, *farmandeh-e koll*. This was in direct contradiction to the constitutional law, which invested that office in the person of the reigning sovereign alone. In April 1923 Reza Khan requested the Shah to appoint him formally as Commander-in-Chief, but the Shah refused. The Shah's apprehensions at what he regarded as the unbounded ambitions of his War Minister had recently revived, and he viewed this request as proof that his fears were justified. Reza Khan was not satisfied with the Shah's blunt refusal and further discussions ensued, the issue being shelved when the Shah appointed him Chief, *ra'is*, of the army. But the Shah evidently regarded this as another victory for Reza Khan and a defeat for himself, and resented in accordingly.[25]

It was in early 1924 that Reza Khan made a decisive move against the Shah by inaugurating the republican movement, in which the military played a leading role, both in the capital and in the provinces. Ahmad Shah had left for Europe in November 1923, and the republican agitation had opened in January 1924 with a press campaign of unrestrained republican propaganda and abuse of the Shah and the Qajar dynasty. The abuse of the Qajars was accompanied by the most flattering remarks and praise of Reza Khan, whom the newspapers proposed should be elected President of the future republic.

In the provinces, republican committees were formed and telegrams began to pour in to the Majlis demanding the abolition of the Qajar dynasty and the establishment of a republic. In some places people took *bast* in the telegraph offices, stating that they would not leave until Tehran granted their request for a republic; elsewhere the bazaars were closed in demonstration. Yet much of this activity appears to have been artificial, and inspired and even paid for by Reza Khan and his supporters, particularly the military authorities, with republicanism evoking little real support in the country.[26] At first the campaign, carefully orchestrated and managed by the military authorities, progressed smoothly, but towards the end of March opposition from a variety of sources began to gather steam. Political hostility to Reza Khan's growing dominance combined with religious dislike of the secular implications of republicanism to produce massive popular opposition.

Reza Khan, baulked by widespread discontent from a smooth transition to a republic again resorted to force. On 22 March the Majlis was due to debate the issue and a large crowd of anti-republicans, numbering more than 5,000, had entered the Majlis grounds and begun making speeches. When Reza Khan arrived he ordered two companies of the Pahlavi regiment to clear the grounds. This they did in a 'none too gentle' manner, inflicting bayonet wounds on several people and making many arrests.[27] Reza Khan then entered the Majlis, where the President, Mu'tamin al-Mulk, remonstrated with him for using military force against the crowd, and told him that he had no authority to do so in that place. He further told him that he had been chosen by the people and had no right to turn on them because he was afraid of being defeated. Mu'tamin al-Mulk even offered to call the deputies into session to denounce Reza Khan's action and, had he done so, there would almost certainly have been a vote of no confidence in the War Minister. The release of those arrested was demanded, Reza Khan acquiesced, and the President apologized to them on behalf of the Majlis. A conference then took place between the deputies, the ulema and Reza Khan, at which the latter sulkily agreed to abandon his republican project, but announced that he would resign as he could not work with either the Shah or the *vali'ahd*. A little later a sitting of the Majlis was held, at which it was decided that the Constitution must be upheld, and there could be no question of a republic.

As a result of turning his soldiers against the peaceful demonstrators in the Majlis grounds, Reza Khan had lost a good deal of what popularity he had left. His position had now become precarious and he seemed to be in a state of considerable indecision over the future of republicanism, apparently prepared to ditch it if this were necessary to preserve his own hold on power. On 26 March the War Ministry telegraphed to all divisions that the troops were to maintain a strict neutrality on the question of a republic. Also with effect from 26 March, the troops in Tehran were confined to barracks, the military authorities being anxious to isolate them from the opposition, who were making strenuous attempts to subvert them and with whom the rank and file had evinced considerable sympathy. By the end of March, as his consultations with various ayatallahs in Qom revealed, Reza Khan had finally made up his mind to drop the republican project.[28] The republican movement immediately collapsed, the military authorities receiving orders from Tehran to abandon it.[29]

Nevertheless, Reza Khan's enemies were making the most of the opportunity to bring him down. Many people now believed that he should give up the premiership and content himself with the War Ministry, or even only with the command of the army.[30] Furthermore, it seemed that even among his supporters, many were prepared to drop him if he persisted in his formerly expressed opinion that he could not work with the Shah or the *vali'ahd*. During the first week of April it was clear that Reza Khan, although he had dropped the republican movement, was in a state of desperate uncertainty regarding the best way of preserving his position. Some sort of showdown between him and the Shah seemed inevitable and, indeed, a telegram arrived from the Shah dismissing Reza Khan from the post of Prime Minister. Having failed to secure sufficient control over the Majlis by manipulating the elections, Reza Khan now tried to repeat the tactic of intimidation that had been so successful at the end of 1922. His response to his dismissal was to send a letter to the Majlis on 7 April saying that, in view of his extreme weariness, he was going to the country for a rest and was resigning from all his government responsibilities and also from command of the troops, a role that was to devolve on the General Staff.[31] A similar letter was read out to senior officers at the War Ministry by the Chief of the General Staff, Brigadier Amanallah Jahanbani. Reza Khan left Tehran the same day.

The next day, 8 April, the Majlis received telegrams from all the provincial army commanders, some expressing regret at Reza Khan's withdrawal and requesting the Majlis to bring him back, others, notably from the divisional commanders in the west and the east, Major-Generals Ahmad Amirahmadi and Hossein Khuza'i, holding the Majlis responsible for what had happened and threatening to march on Tehran at the head of their forces unless Reza Khan returned within 48 hours.[32] Local disturbances, orchestrated by the military authorities, also broke out in several provincial towns, bazaars were closed and crowds took refuge in the telegraph offices demanding Reza Khan's return. That evening the President of the Majlis read out the telegrams from the divisional commanders, causing considerable consternation among the deputies. The Majlis immediately passed a vote of confidence in Reza Khan, a deputation went to visit him in the country and he returned to Tehran on 9 April. He resumed all his posts and reformed his cabinet, which he presented to the Majlis on 13 April.

The action of the provincial army commanders had been so spontaneous that there was little doubt in Tehran that it was part of a prearranged plan.[33] The evident joy with which Reza Khan received the Majlis deputation, and the almost undue haste with which he complied with their invitation to return, confirmed this impression. The Majlis had been obliged to capitulate by the clear threat that, if Reza Khan were not reinstated constitutionally, the army would return him to power by force. By this spectacular manoeuvre Reza Khan not only resolved the deadlock resulting from the failure of the republican movement, but also demonstrated, once again, his ability to triumph over all other political forces by an ultimate recource to military strength.

Although the Fifth Majlis had been forced to humble itself by the threats of the army commanders following Reza Khan's resignation manoeuvre, many deputies remained resentful and angry, and they used the opportunity presented by the introduction to the Majlis of the new cabinet's programme, on 15 April 1924, to criticize the army. The programme was first criticized by Modarres, on general grounds and in moderate terms, but it was then attacked hotly and bitterly by another deputy, Abolhasan Ha'irizadeh.[34] The latter singled out the proposal to extend the army, saying that the army needed to be purged rather than enlarged, and that the money allocated for military purposes would be better spent in spreading education, so that better educated divisional commanders might acquire a livelier sense of their duty to the state, and not send threatening telegrams of the kind that had recently been received. Ha'irizadeh continued that it was clear to him that the army belonged to one man and not to the state, and asked why, in that case, the latter should contribute to its upkeep? Ha'irizadeh's sentiments were shared by many of his colleagues, even among those who had joined in the vote of confidence in Reza Khan, and many of them wished an example to be made of those commanders whose telegrams had been particularly threatening.[35] Nevertheless, the programme of the new cabinet was eventually accepted by the Majlis, undoubtedly signalling a triumph for Reza Khan.

Notwithstanding the War Minister's success in overawing the Majlis and his subsequent efforts to consolidate his position, in the months following the collapse of the republican movement the political situation in Tehran definitely seemed to be crystallizing in favour of the Shah, even though he was still in Europe. By early July the demand for Reza Khan's resignation from the premiership showed no signs of weakening; press criticism continued unabated, and evidence of popular discontent with military domination was accumulating from all parts of the country.[36] Reza Khan's position in the capital was serious and he seemed in danger of an eclipse. It was, in fact, not until the murder of the American consul by a mob allowed Reza Khan to declare martial law in Tehran, that he was able to regain the political initiative.[37] In fact the imposition of martial law, which then remained in force for the duration of the contest between Reza Khan and Ahmad Shah, was a key factor enabling the military authorities to engineer a political and constitutional outcome favourable to their chief.

The failure of the republican movement had not diminished Reza Khan's determination to get rid of Ahmad Shah. During the summer and autumn of 1924 he did not completely relinquish republicanism, but toyed with the idea of reviving the movement. But opposition remained strong, and by December Reza Khan's republican strategy had finally been superseded by his decision to make himself Shah, although his final struggle with Ahmad Shah was to endure for most of the following year. By mid-December a considerable amount of quiet work had restarted in Tehran to prepare the ground for a change in the Constitution. Propaganda was now directed not in favour of a republic, but rather towards creating discontent with the Shah. The principal directing force was the Military Governor and General Officer Commanding the Central Division, Brigadier Yazdanpanah.

However, Reza Khan apparently now decided that a direct move against the Shah would be premature. He ordered Yazdanpanah to cease his public campaigning, and adopted instead a different tactic, reviving his dispute with the Shah concerning their respective constitutional positions. On 8 February he again issued what was practically an ultimatum to representatives of various parties in the Majlis, renewing his demand to be officially recognized as *farmandeh-e koll*, Commander-in-Chief, of the army, making this a condition of his continuing in office.[38] He had, in practice, continued to arrogate to himself the powers of that post following the Shah's refusal to confer it on him formally, and this had been one of the principal causes of the suspicions that the Shah harboured regarding Reza's ambitions and which had led to the prolonged royal absence from the country. However, while remaining, even nominally, as Commander-in-Chief, the Shah had powers of appointment in and dismissal from the army. He could therefore, at any time, order the dismissal of Reza Khan, thus depriving the latter of, or at least rendering doubtful, the only real support, that of the army, on which he was able to depend.

Feverish discussions took place between the deputies and Reza Khan, whereby the former endeavoured to find some compromise that would satisfy the latter, preserve intact the constitutional law and save the honour of the Majlis.[39] A proposal to appoint him Commander-in-Chief was in fact defeated in the Majlis, and Reza Khan, seemingly apprehensive of the Shah's formal powers of dismissal, accepted with alacrity the resolution that was eventually framed to avert the constitutional crisis and that would, at any rate, place him beyond the possibility of removal by the Shah. On 14 February the Majlis passed a resolution that recognized the special claims of Reza Khan to the command of the armed forces, excepting the police, gave him full powers in that office within the laws of the State, and decreed that he could be dismissed only by the Majlis.

In the autumn of 1925 Reza Khan vigorously renewed his attack on Ahmad Shah and the military authorities again played a leading role, both in Tehran and the provinces, in organizing the anti-Qajar campaign. By mid-October Brigadier Yazdanpanah, the Military Governor of Tehran, was actively carrying out propaganda against the Shah, having already stated that there was this time no question of a republic, only of a change of dynasty. The anti-Qajar agitation was not confined to the capital. In Mashhad, Isfahan, Rasht, Kirman and especially in Tabriz, the military authorities made great efforts to organize demonstrations against the Shah. During the last week of October the agitation against the Shah rapidly grew in momentum. *Nahzat-e melli* (national committees) were formed to work for the deposition of the Qajars, and bombarded the Majlis with telegrams making this demand. Tabriz was particularly strident, the tone of its telegrams growing increasingly threatening, culminating in the announcement of the severance of relations with the capital and the formation of a nationalist army to march on Tehran. The moving spirit behind the Tabriz committee was the divisional commander, Brigadier Mohammad Hossein Ayrum, although he kept well behind the scenes,[40] but there also seems by now to have been some genuine popular support for the campaign.

On 31 October the Majlis duly voted the abolition of the Qajar dynasty and the establishment of a provisional government with Reza Khan at its head, pending the decision of a Constituent Assembly. However the military were already pre-empting any decision by the

Constituent Assembly by constantly referring to Reza Khan as *'ala hazrat* (his majesty) and newspapers and certain officials followed suit. The elections to the Constituent Assembly, held towards the end of 1925, were, like the Majlis elections, closely managed by the army. Martial law was abolished throughout the country for the period of the voting, although this did not seem to reduce greatly the level of military intervention. In some remote districts even the formality of an election was dispensed with, nominees being merely notified of their success and packed off to Tehran.[41] In early December the *nahzat-e melli* in the capital and the provinces were revived in order to urge on the Constituent Assembly the undesirability of any delay in establishing Reza Khan on the throne, and on 12 December the Assembly decided in favour of a hereditary Pahlavi dynasty. Reza Khan's success in using the military to pack the Assembly was illustrated by the unanimity of the vote. Of the 260 deputies, only three abstained from the decision to bestow the throne on the Pahlavi family.

Reza Khan, in making himself Shah, assumed the highest civil office in Iran. The morale of the army was markedly improved by the termination of the struggle between its commander and the erstwhile Shah. Furthermore, the elevation to the throne of the army's creator and commander raised military self-esteem to an unprecedented degree, and for this achievement the army took all the credit and expected a fair share of reward. The army rightly regarded itself as the first consideration of the new Shah, and firmly believed that it was the military which had both put him on the throne and would keep him there.[42] Despite Ahmad Shah's personal unpopularity, as long as he had remained monarch there existed at the apex of the political system a permanent focus for potential opposition to Reza Khan, both civilian and, more dangerously, military, and an authority to which any such opposition might appeal for legitimacy. With the Qajars gone, and the regime free of internal dissension, the new Shah was able to begin the implementation of a major social and cultural transformation.

The Military Ascendancy over the Civil Authorities

In the early to mid-1920s the army came to dominate the civil authorities throughout Iran, sometimes via the establishment of formal military government, sometimes through informal and unregulated mechanisms of pressure and control. Immediately after the coup of February 1921 martial law and military government had been established in Tehran and many of the provincial towns. Each military conquest of a recalcitrant area or population was invariably accompanied by the establishment of military government. Military officers were likewise appointed to replace traditional semi-autonomous rulers and tribal chieftains. For example, towards the end of 1923 Captain Hasan Khan, commanding the troops at Khui, was made governor of Maku, superseding Iqbal al-Saltaneh, the Sardar of Maku, who had recently been arrested. In 1925 Nasir Khan, the son of Sawlat al-Dowleh, was dismissed from the ilkhaniship of the Qashqa'i tribe and a military governorship created. These substitutions were typical of the extension of military control then taking place throughout the country.

The frequent declaration of martial law and the establishment of military government in both the capital and the provinces gave the military authorities the opportunity to tighten their control over all aspects of civilian life, especially political dissent. The two periods of military government in the capital, 1921–22 and 1924–26, were crucial to Reza Khan's rise to supreme power. Perhaps the most spectacular example of Reza Khan's use of the tactic of martial law to crush political opposition comes from the summer of 1924. After the failure of the republican movement, Reza Khan's position in the capital had deteriorated seriously. However, the murder of the American consul in Tehran by a mob on 18 July gave Reza Khan the opportunity to retrieve the situation by declaring martial law, which he did the following day. He was thus enabled to break through the restrictions of constitutional government and he took full advantage of this power. He appointed one of his most reliable officers, Brigadier Yazdanpanah, Military Governor, made numerous arrests, chiefly of those individuals who had been active in the recent campaign against him, deported some of the leading agitators, suppressed the most vocal of the anti-government newspapers and established a strict censorship of the press. Martial law continued in Tehran for some time, although it had largely achieved its object by mid-September, by which time the political situation in the capital had quietened.[43] To complete his grip on the capital, making assurance doubly sure, Reza Khan also, in 1924, placed the Tehran municipality under military control, appointing as director the ex-Cossack Colonel Karim Buzarjomehri.[44]

There was also considerable pressure from within the army to ensure that control, once established, remained in its own hands. Once in place, Military Governors proved very hard to get rid of. Even when achieved, the official abolition of military government often made little real difference to the location of power, owing to the increasing weakness of the civil administration.

A particular problem faced by the civil authorities in their efforts to preserve their position was the apparent ability of the military to delay, frustrate or veto the appointments of Governors-General. The military also took advantage of the long intervals between the departure and arrival of governors to usurp the functions of the civil authorities. Furthermore the military were often able to force insufficiently malleable or inconvenient governors to resign, by creating an environment frustrating and humiliating for the civil authorities. In July 1922, for example, Mohammad, Mosaddeq al-Saltanah, resigned as Governor-General of Azarbayjan owing to the refusal of the provincial military to obey his instructions.[45] In Fars, Brigadier Fazlallah Zahidi achieved the resignation of two Governors-General within a year, while in Gilan Brigadier Mohammad Hossein Ayrum also forced the resignation of two governors within a short space of time, himself replacing the second of these.

In these years, even when a provincial civil regime was officially in existence, the local military authorities encroached upon its sphere, appropriating its authority and many of its functions. Administrative chaos frequently resulted from the lack of clearly demarcated authority and the military's tendency to aggrandize power to itself, and there was constant friction between the civil officials and the military commanders. Notwithstanding the ensuing difficulties, the military's power continued to wax at the expense of the civil authorities and the army quickly established itself as the controlling power in the land. Practically the only effective civilian limitation on the powers of army commanders was the Finance Administration, controlled by Dr Millspaugh. Both in the capital and in the provinces the real authority lay with the military commanders and affairs were conducted mostly according to their wishes, the civil governors being little more than figureheads. The novelty of this situation, both in terms of the pre-eminence of the army and the possession of authority by individuals from outside the traditional elite and often lacking in conventional education, was widely remarked upon and frequently resented.[46]

From an early date the practice of appointing Military Governors aroused much opposition, both from those who thereby found their traditional perquisites jeopardized and from those who more generally feared the growth of military power and the threat it posed to constitutional government. There was, throughout these years, a general decline in the importance of the civil Governor-General *vis à vis* the military command. As Shiraz notables pointed out, following the resignation of Prince Sarim al-Dowleh as Governor-General of Fars, magnates of the first rank were unlikely in future to accept posts that exposed them to public humiliation at the hands of plebeian army officers.[47] Further blows were struck at the prestige of the civil authorities in these years by successive reductions in their salaries, while many informal sources of income were taken over by military officers and other officials. Furthermore, the Governors-General, at the same time as they were losing their power struggle with the provincial divisional commanders, were finding that their authority was also being whittled away by the increasing modernization and centralization of government. Formerly, control of all departments, revenue, judicial, etc., was vested in them. Now not only had the army, the *amniyyah* and (sometimes) the police been taken out of their hands but, for example, the collection of revenue was the responsibility of the Finance Department under Millspaugh, and justice was administered by the new *'adliyyeh* courts. From now on, governor-generalships were no longer coveted by powerful statesmen and wealthy aristocrats, but were posts occupied by functionaries drawn from a lower social stratum who lived modestly and whose work was purely bureaucratic in character.

The Military and the Civil Population

From the very beginning an ambiguity was apparent in the attitude of many Iranians towards Reza Khan and his army. Although his patriotism and nationalism were appreciated and his policies of centralization and strengthening of the state were applauded, there was also considerable resentment at his and his commanders' dictatorial methods and arrogant disregard for constitutional government. Of course, different elements within the population reacted differently to the extension and consolidation of military power, while the population generally responded differently to positive and negative aspects of the army's presence. The goodwill that the army gained by its suppression of disorder was often squandered as a result of its rapacity and corruption, and particularly in the period immediately after Reza's accession to the throne, anger and despair at the untrammelled abuse of power by the senior commanders was widespread throughout the society.

The restoration of peace and order to troubled areas and the reestablishment of government control had been widely welcomed after the chaos of the preceding period. Specific groups such as merchants were especially pleased at the setting up of security along the trade routes. However, many of the traditional elite, who saw their privileges jeopardized and their power diminished, were resentful and suspicious of the growth of military power. Particularly threatened were the tribal leaders and feudal lords, who vainly attempted to preserve their autonomy, including their armed strength, while the *ulema* disliked Reza Khan's modernizing reforms and were angered by the pronounced anti-clerical tendency of the officer corps.

Indeed, many of those very consequences of the extension of military power that alarmed the aforesaid groups, in fact assured Reza Khan's popularity and the prestige of the army amongst nationalist elements. This may be seen clearly in relation to southern Iran, where Reza Khan's attempts to establish the authority of the central government, to destroy the autonomy of feudal anachronisms such as the Shaikh of Muhammarah, and to remove the remaining British military presence, earned him the respect and support of modernizing circles both in the provinces and in Tehran. These elements encouraged the growth of the army and gave their political support to the War Minister and his military projects on the basis of his policies of centralization and national independence. They were rewarded, in southern Iran, by the suppression of the Shaikh of Muhammarah and the end of the threat of secession by the oil-rich province of Arabistan, by the reduction and eventual withdrawal of the British garrisons from the Gulf ports, and by the transfer of the responsibility for the protection of the oil-fields from the Shaikh and the Bakhtiyari khans to Iranian regular troops, all of which were regarded as victories for Iranian nationalism achieved by Reza Khan and his army. The campaign against the Shaikh of Muhammarah, in the latter part of 1924, was a particularly important focus for, and symbol of, Iranian national feeling, and provided Reza Khan with enormous political credit in nationalist circles, his victory over Shaikh Khaz'al going some way towards restoring his political position and the morale of the army, both of which had been seriously damaged by the recent failure of the republican movement. The aura of nationalism and modernization surrounding the army was reinforced in various ways in the early 1920s. Of course, the dismissal of British officers in 1921 and the steadfast rejection of any further foreign military missions provided an important boost for the nationalist credentials of both Reza Khan and his army. Various minor measures were also taken which contributed towards promoting this image of the army. For example, Reza Khan set up a military commission to Persianize the military terms in use in the army. Over a long period this commission worked on the production of a dictionary for the use of the army, from which all European and most Arabic words had been expunged. In 1923 the War Ministry issued orders that all officers must henceforward wear uniforms made of material of Iranian manufacture only. The army was also used as a pioneer of social progress generally, and military personnel, particularly the officer corps, led the way in the introduction of reforms into the wider society, setting an example and encouraging the acceptance of innovation. For instance, Reza Khan issued orders that all military offices were to give up their titles and were to be known in future by their personal and family names, himself giving up his title of Sardar-i Sipah and taking the ancient Iranian name of Pahlavi. Military personnel were the first to adopt clothing reforms, such as the introduction of the peaked *kulah* (cap). When, early in 1925, some young men appeared in Tehran wearing the *kulah* and thereby challenging the mullahs, who had declared this cap unfitting to Muslims as the peak prevented their foreheads from touching the ground during prayers, the opposition of religious elements to this innovation was weakened by the fact that the troops had adopted it some time previously. At times provincial military commanders took modernizing initiatives on their own account, such as Brigadier Mohammad Hossein Ayrum's encouragement of a 'Freedom for Women' movement in Rasht,[48] or the enthusiastic town planning of Brigadier Prince Mohammad Hossein Firuz, Chief of Staff of the Southern Division, whereby a good deal of property in Shiraz had been demolished, without compensation to the owners, to permit the widening of streets for carriages and cars, roads had been paved, and the main avenue laid out in boulevard fashion and a certain number of electric lights installed.[49]

At first, the renovation of the Iranian army under Reza Khan seems to have been a source of genuine national pride to many Iranians,[50] and the army was itself proud of its role as the chief instrument in the pacification and unification of the country. Nevertheless, as military control over the country tightened and its weight in financial and political terms became more burdensome to the population, resentment grew. By 1926 the demands of the army were breaking through conventional and acceptable limits and reaching levels that were popularly perceived as rapacious and corrupt. Accordingly, hatred of the army became widespread and intense.

Evidence of popular discontent with military domination of civil life first began to accumulate significantly after the failure of the republican movement in the spring of 1924. Examples multiplied from all over the country, both of general resentment at the army's behaviour and of specific grievances over such practices as requisitioning, particularly of transport animals, and labour conscription. Military recruiting parties were especially feared in rural areas, while the population of both town and country bitterly resented the army's recruitment of labour, sometimes on a temporary, *ad hoc* basis, sometimes for long-term projects, particularly of road construction.

The behaviour of the army towards the civilian population was naturally related to the state of discipline and morale inside the force. Conditions within the army deteriorated rapidly in late 1925–26[51] and there was, at the same time, a marked worsening in the army's relations with the civilian population. In the 18 months after the collapse of the republican movement, popular resentment at military domination hardened and deepened dramatically, to reach a crescendo in 1926. So great was the identification between the army and Reza Khan personally that these developments dangerously increased the unpopularity both of the regime and of Reza himself. Furthermore, Reza Khan fully reciprocated the civilian population's distrust, claiming that only in the army did he find any spirit of cooperation.[52] By 1926 the army's relationship with civil society had reached its lowest ebb yet.

In the first half of 1926 corruption among the senior military commanders reached unprecedented dimensions, particularly in connection with the new Shah's coronation celebrations and the elections to the Sixth Majlis.[53] At the end of May, Major Melvin Hall of the American Financial Mission described the activities of the most senior officer in Khorasan, divisional commander Brigadier Jan Mohammad Khan Davallu, which, he said, had:

extended to all manner of extortion, ranging from forced contributions for mythical orphanages to barefaced insistence on gifts in cash. The divisional commander had finally left to attend the coronation with sacks of bank notes crowded into his motor-car, and after his departure a serious shortage of metal and paper currency was observable in the bazaars.[54]

The example of the senior officers' extortion and corruption was irresistible to the unpaid rank and file, who pilfered and stole from each other and the civilian population more or less unchecked. In any case, the officers paid little attention to the activities of their subordinates or indeed to military duties in general, being preoccupied with acquiring wealth or intriguing against or warding off the intrigues of their rivals. In addition, the growing problem of the non-receipt of pay and rations by the troops had the inevitable consequence of forcing the army to maintain itself at the expense of local inhabitants, greatly increasing the latter's suffering.

One section of the population that suffered particularly from the army's methods was the tribes. The armed nomadic tribal confederations had always been a thorn in the side of Iran's urban modernizers, and brutality towards, and unnecessary provocation of, the tribal population were constant features of this period. There was of course some degree of contradiction between Reza Khan's centralizing policies and the traditional semi-autonomy of the tribes, although the nature and extent of the fundamental opposition between the new regime and the tribal populations and their leaderships has been considerably over-estimated and misunderstood.[55] In fact, in the 1920s the general approach of the nationalist elite, especially as represented by the army, frequently impeded rather than hastened tribal pacification. Initial successes in bringing the tribes under direct control were sometimes spectacularly reversed by the methods employed by the army, particularly acts of atrocity and the treachery and cruelty of certain senior commanders.

A clear example of the bungling of tribal pacification and the provocation of disorder by the corrupt activities of a senior commander is provided by General Amirahmadi's campaign against the Lurs in 1924.[56] Operations to disarm the Lurs had begun in 1923 and, despite the army's mixed fortunes, by early 1924 negotiations were proceeding with the tribal chiefs, who appeared to be resigning themselves to the new situation. A certain number of arms were being handed in and the establishment of military authority was progressing favourably. However, at that moment General Amirahmadi, then commanding the Western Division including the Luristan front, ordered the murder of a number of Lur chiefs who had surrendered themselves to him as hostages and to whom he had given a promise of a free pardon on a sealed Quran. These treacherous murders immediately sparked off a new conflagration. The Lurs launched a violent attack on the garrison of Khorramabad, which resulted in its serious defeat with heavy casualties and its being besieged in the town. Amirahmadi's iniquitous action cost the Iranian government dear in men and money and the authorities were forced to call a truce with the Lurs, leaving them their arms and their semi-independence for the time being.

The renewed rising in Luristan was undoubtedly due to the bitter resentment felt by the tribes at the execution of their chiefs.[57] Indeed, the Lurs themselves wrote to the Majlis saying that they were loyal Iranians but had been forced to fight by the actions of the commander of the Western Division.[58] The opinion was widely held, even within the army, that Amirahmadi was personally and directly responsible for the rising. A letter was written in May by Brigadier Mohammad Khan, the commanding officer of the advanced troops on the Luristan front, to the General Staff at Army Headquarters, attributing the Lurs' renewed unity and determination to fight to Amirahmadi's treachery in first promising the chiefs a free pardon and then robbing and executing them. Mohammad Khan concluded by asserting that all Iranian officers were enraged at Amirahmadi's actions.[59] Indeed, the dissensions between Amirahmadi and his senior officers became so serious that in September Reza Khan personally visited Khurramabad to enquire into the matter.

Although it seems that other senior officers in Luristan objected to Amirahmadi's methods, in fact the approach to tribal pacification embodied by this officer was very widespread throughout the army. Middle-ranking and senior officers made no secret of their belief in ruthless suppression. The military commandant at Dezful, for example, a Major Reza Quli Khan, expressed the conviction that Lur and Arab chiefs should be captured and executed by whatever form of treachery might suggest itself, and that affairs in Arabistan and Luristan should be arranged on the basis of the intimidation of all tribal leaders and the destruction of all local authority.[60]

The prevalence of these views may again be seen in the case of

Luristan, where Amirahmadi's treachery of 1924 was repeated in almost identical fashion the following year, although Amirahmadi himself had been removed from this command. By the summer of 1925 the pacification of Luristan had again to some degree been achieved; merchants had begun to send goods by the Muhammarah-Dizful-Khurramabad route, and in July numbers of troops were withdrawn, leaving normal peace-time garrisons in occupation of Khurramabad and in protection of the road from there to Dizful. The Lurs seemed reconciled to the new situation; the men had begun to surrender their arms and the more important chiefs had come in to military headquarters on safe-conduct to discuss the future. But then, in October, the military commander was guilty of an exact repetition of Amirahmadi's treachery and no fewer than 20 of the Lur chiefs, including nearly all the important tribal leaders, in Khurramabad on safe conduct were seized and hanged. The officer responsible for this step justified it by the argument that without leaders the tribes would be incapable of combination or of organizing a movement of any serious proportions in opposition to the government. This justification demonstrates clearly that such methods were not attributable simply to the brutality of individual commanders, acting on their own initiative, but were the product of attitudes widely held amongst the military, and apparently had official sanction from the highest levels of army and government.

A second major social category comprehensively alienated by the regime and the army in these years was the religious establishment. Certainly Reza Khan was prepared to resort to Islam in moments of crisis, for example after the republicanism fiasco. Yet the open contempt more typically demonstrated by Reza and his officers, senior and junior, for the susceptibilities of the *ulema* further estranged a still powerful group already resentful and fearful of the state's encroachments on its functions and privileges, and caused offence in wide civilian circles. Undoubtedly there existed among the ex-Cossack officers in the army a tradition of contempt for religious personnel, which continued to affect the conduct of many senior officers. Other elements within the army, particularly the ex-Gendarme officers, shared the dislike of Islamic orthodoxy and the influence of the *ulema* frequently found among Iranian reformers. These two perspectives combined to produce a widespread tendency among army officers to treat religious figures with deliberate and marked scorn and arrogance. Armed soldiers frequently stood guard over suspected mullahs as they preached, in case they made derogatory remarks about the government, while the military did not hesitate to imprison religious figures and caused widespread resentment by interfering with, and even prohibiting, traditional religious processions. The military also caused offence by violating the traditional right of sanctuary, forcibly removing deserters from mosques and shrines.

Although inevitably opposed to the major secularizing measures of the Pahlavi regime, the *ulema* were further irritated by the army's role in promoting minor social reforms and the often tactless and arrogant manner in which this was done. Provincial military commanders often took the initiative in minor measures of reform, and even orders from Tehran did not always succeed in modifying their anti-clerical zeal. In Rasht in 1925, for example, there was serious trouble when the army attempted to arrest a mullah who had preached a highly provocative sermon aimed principally at the then commander of the Northern Independent Brigade, Brigadier Mohammad Hossein Ayrum. The Brigadier had apparently incurred the wrath of the mullah by his advocacy of freedom for women, and by the disregard for religious susceptibilities with which he had driven an avenue through a graveyard. Although Reza Khan, at that moment anxious for political reasons not to antagonize religious circles, instructed the Brigadier to adopt more conciliatory tactics, nevertheless Ayrum exiled the offending mullah and wholly failed to make his peace with the *ulema*.[61] In 1925 Ayrum was transferred to Azerbaijan as the new commander of the North-Western Division. By the following year it was being reported that army officers in that province were arousing antagonism by their 'open flouting of religious prejudices',[62] while according to the Governor-General, Sharif al-Dowleh, the bulk of the population had been estranged specifically by Ayrum's attitude towards the religious establishment. It seems that Sharif al-Dowleh was only too pleased to make the most of the opportunity presented by Ayrum's tactless anti-clericalism to wage a campaign for his removal. The mullahs, for their part, had consistently returned Ayrum's hostility in full measure, having declared themselves greatly pleased at the arrival of a new civilian Governor-General in the spring of 1926 and expressing the hope that it would be the end of what they described as the looting of the province of Azerbaijan by the military authorities.[63]

1926 was a year of crisis for the new Shah. Mutinies within the army and the crumbling of civilian toleration for the new order began to threaten the unravelling of both the regime and the new dynasty. Yet within a year the political and military structures of the state had stabilized and consolidated themselves and had reasserted their control over society. In 1927 the government embarked on its most radical phase, launching a raft of centralizing, secularizing reforms, and implementing them in an aggressive manner. It was the two elements who had particularly been the object of nationalist enmity in the early 1920s, the *ulema* and the tribes, which, in 1927 and 1929 respectively, were to provide the foci for opposition to these reforms and to mount the most dangerous challenges to the new state.[64]

Conclusion

During the early 1920s the new army broadly continued the tradition established in an earlier period by the Cossack Brigade/Division: although of questionable conventional military capability, it was extremely successful in advancing the political ambitions of its chief and in safeguarding and extending his power. Indeed, by far the most important function of the new army was to ensure the survival of the regime or, more narrowly interpreted, of Reza Khan's personal position. This involved a two-pronged approach: firstly, the army had to establish internal security throughout the country; secondly, the military authorities had to enforce the subordination of all civilian political elements to their own rule. These tasks had to be accomplished, moreover, in tandem with Reza Khan's struggle to secure his own ascendancy with the army.

In the early 1920s therefore, the Iranian army embarked on a major effort to extend and maintain the authority of the central government throughout the country, a task involving the destruction of every type of autonomous local rule, including that of the tribes and traditional semi-feudal rulers such as the Shaikh of Muhammarah, that was capable, actually or potentially, of challenging the state's power. In this it met with a large degree of success, although pockets of resistance remained, the tribes were not fully disarmed and the end of the decade was still to see tribal upheavals of considerable magnitude, particularly in the south of the country. By 1926 the victory of the military authorities over civil political life was also largely complete. Using a variety of methods, of which overt force was only one and often not the most important, the military authorities had established themselves indisputably as the controlling power in the land.

It was essential to the survival of Reza Khan's regime that the new army's continued loyalty to its commander be guaranteed. The military structures were therefore systematically used to distribute material rewards in return for political support. Unlike his dynastic predecessors, Reza Khan's rise to power was not based on the support of a tribal group and, in a sense, his former Cossack comrades were allotted the role that had belonged in the previous period to the Qajar family. Reza Khan dispensed political patronage and financial rewards to his senior commanders and appointed them to rule over the provinces. They also suffered, however, from the same arbitrariness that had been such a notable feature of the Qajar shahs' treatment of their ministers and officials.

In his state-building efforts Reza Khan faced certain serious difficulties. The failure of reform and modernization in every area of government and society during the nineteenth century meant that, by the beginning of the twentieth century, the gap between Iran and Europe, which had experienced dramatic industrial and technological advance, was immense. Although it was consciousness of Iran's military vulnerability which especially informed the nationalist agenda, it was clear that the country's military weakness was intimately related to other forms of infrastructural weakness and to general, particularly economic, backwardness. By the 1920s Iran still lacked any industrial base and possessed inadequate roads and virtually no railways, poor communications, and very few modern educational, particularly scientific and medical, facilities.

Yet certain features of the period under review furnished Reza Khan with a more amenable context for his state-building project. The weakened condition of British imperialism in the post-war world and the preoccupation of the young Soviet state with its own survival, created more space for the consolidation of the Iranian state. Furthermore, Reza Khan was able to take advantage of the more favourable fiscal structure prevailing in the 1920s to avoid the dilemma facing reformers of the previous century – that of finding enough money to raise sufficient armed strength with which to enforce effective revenue collection and thus finance a wider programme of modernization. In the nineteenth century Iran had depended for nearly 90 per cent of its revenue on land tax, which was notoriously difficult to collect.[65] In the twentieth century the state's dependence on land tax was greatly reduced, and more easily collectable revenue from customs and other sources – notably oil – constituted the bulk of its revenue.[66] Although in the early 1920s oil revenues were both absolutely and relatively small, they were received entirely by the state and in fact nearly doubled in value between 1919 and 1926. Strikingly, the value of oil exports was particularly high in 1924–26, when Reza Khan made his bid for supreme power.[67] Throughout these years the needs and demands of the army had first call on all the resources of the state, both political and financial.

Yet the internal organization of the army and its relationship with the rest of society was characterized by many negative and counter-productive features. Internally, the new army continued to exhibit many of the defects from which the Qajar armies had suffered. Corruption, embezzlement and financial malpractice of every kind were tolerated, and even encouraged, by the regime as the price of political loyalty. Of more ominous significance for the future was another feature of the general situation starkly revealed by 1926. This was the successful completion, in outline, of the military ascendancy over all other significant political forces, on which Reza Shah was to base his dictatorship up to 1941. By 1926 many of the features that were to characterize the regime in its later years were already clearly in place. In the period 1921–26 the military authorities had demonstrated the arbitrariness, the disregard for constitutional procedures and legality in general, and the insistence on constituting the sole source of political activity and ideological influence, that were to typify the ensuing era. The few remaining checks on the power of the military authorities were easily removed. Dr Millspaugh, for instance, was finally forced to resign in 1927, having incurred the enmity of the Shah and the senior officers for resisting the army's insatiable demands for cash. Although institutions such as the Majlis and a civilian government continued to exist, their role, after 1926, was purely decorative and ornamental. Independent political activity would not resume until after the abdication of the Shah in 1941.

The successful establishment of Reza Khan's military regime heralded a general rearrangement of social and political relationships in the country, and the rise of a new elite component consisting of the upper echelons of the officer corps. Nevertheless, despite their ascendancy the military authorities were not able to command the legitimacy that had characterized the old ruling class which they had politically supplanted. The opinion was widespread throughout

Iranian society that the plebeian origins of both Reza Khan and his principal associates rendered them unfit for the highest offices.[68] This view predisposed the population to perceive the rule of the military authorities as oppressive. Furthermore, the fact that the senior commanders themselves had no experience or understanding of traditionally accepted limits in the exercise of power and the exaction of financial rewards led them into excess, encouraging accusations of extortion and tyranny. Regarding the army officers themselves, both Cossacks and Gendarmes, although they had come to power with a thorough contempt for the traditional ruling class and determined upon change, they nonetheless tended rather to become assimilated to the old socioeconomic order, and acquired a stake in its perpetuation.[69] The upper echelons of the officer corps, following the Shah's example, acquired great landed wealth and transformed themselves from despised *arrivistes* into an essential component of the ruling oligarchy, occupying the commanding heights of state and economic institutions.

In the early 1920s both Reza Khan personally and, specifically, his project of constructing a strong army, benefited from the support of a layer of secular nationalist intellectuals. In particular, many of the ex-Gendarmes were attracted to the new army because of the role allocated to it in building a modern Iran. However, as the 1920s became the 1930s, those elements who had initially welcomed Reza Khan's state-building efforts gradually became disillusioned, while the younger generation, both within and outside the army, began to be attracted to oppositional ideologies, sometimes fascism but more particularly various forms of communism, although – perhaps in an unconscious tribute to the Pahlavi regime itself – always those predicated upon the strong state.[70]

By 1926 the relationship between state and society in Iran had been radically transformed. The balance between Tehran and the provinces had been decisively altered in the former's favour and the authority of the state over other sources of power had been greatly augmented. In these processes, the role played by the new, centralized army had been crucial. Furthermore, the weight of the army *vis-à-vis* civil state institutions, the government, the Majlis, provincial civil governors, etc., had increased in a dramatic and wholly novel way. Although in becoming Shah, Reza Khan transformed what had been an incipient military dictatorship into a dynastic despotism, the regime over which he presided was nevertheless firmly marked by

THE ARMY, CIVIL SOCIETY AND THE STATE IN IRAN   161

its military origins and continued to exhibit many features typical of military rule.

Notes

[1] Several recent works have focused on Reza Khan's rise to power in this period. These include Stephanie Cronin, *The Army and the Creation of the Pahlavi State in Iran, 1921–1926* (London and New York: I. B. Tauris, 1997), and, of especial interest, Homa Katouzian, *State and Society in Iran: The Eclipse of the Qajars and the Emergence of the Pahlavis* (London and New York, 2000). Also useful are Cyrus Ghani, *Iran and the Rise of Reza Shah: From Qajar Collapse to Pahlavi Power* (London and New York: I. B. Tauris, 1998) and Houshang Sabahi, *British Policy in Persia 1918–1925* (London: Frank Cass, 1990). An interesting summary is provided by Nikki Keddie, *Qajar Iran and the Rise of Reza Khan, 1796–1925* (London and New York: Mazda, 1999).

[2] Said Amir Arjomand, *The Turban For The Crown, The Islamic Revolution in Iran* (New York: American Philological Association, 1988, p. 35), p. 35.

[3] Homayoun Katouzian, 'Nationalist Trends in Iran, 1921–1926', *International Journal of Middle East Studies*, vol. 10, 1979, p. 533.

[4] Ibid., pp. 533–4.

[5] Arjomand, *The Turban For The Crown*, p. 42.

[6] M. Reza Ghods, *Iran in the Twentieth Century* (Boulder, CO, 1989), p. 94.

[7] Katouzian, 'Nationalist Trends', p. 533.

[8] See Cronin, *The Army*.

[9] Ibid.

[10] For Pasyan, see Stephanie Cronin, 'An Experiment in Revolutionary Nationalism: the Rebellion of Colonel Mohammad Taqi Khan Pasyan in Mashhad, April–October 1921', *Middle Eastern Studies*, vol. 33, no. 4, October 1997, pp. 693–750; Kaveh Bayat, *Enqelab-e Khorasan, Majmu'eh Asnad va Madarek 1300 Shamsi* (Tehran, 1370).

[11] James A. Bill and Robert Springborg, *Politics in the Middle East* (New York, 1999), p. 184.

[12] See Cronin, *The Army*.

[13] For opposition to Reza Khan within the army, see Cronin, *The Army*, ch. 5.

[14] Norman to Curzon, 25 May 1921, FO371/6404/E6040/2/34.

[15] Intelligence Summary no. 7, 18 June 1921, FO371/6435/E9263/2004/34.

[16] IS no. 8, 25 February 1922, FO371/7827/E10107/285/34.

[17] Loraine to Curzon, 31 January 1922, FO371/7804/E3074/6/34.

[18] IS no. 40, 7 October 1922, FO371/7828/E13033/285/34.

[19] For an account of this episode, see Cronin, *The Army*, pp. 153–54.

[20] Ervand Abrahamian, *Iran Between Two Revolutions* (Princeton, 1982), pp. 131–32.

[21] For examples see Cronin, *The Army*, pp. 188–89.
[22] IS no. 30, 26 July 1924, FO371/10132/E7104/255/34.
[23] See Cronin, *The Army*, pp. 189–90.
[24] The Cossack Brigade was originally formed in 1879 as a bodyguard for Nasir al-Din Shah.
[25] Annual Report, 1923, Loraine to MacDonald, 4 March 1924, FO371/10153/E3362/2635/34.
[26] Cronin, *The Army*, pp. 157–67; 191–94.
[27] Havard, Diary of Events concerning the Republican Movement in Persia, Ovey to MacDonald, 1 April 1924, FO371/10145/E3743/455/34.
[28] For the role of the *ulema*, see Vanessa Martin, 'Modarres, Republicanism and the Rise to Power of Reza Khan, Sardar-i Sipah', in Stephanie Cronin, *The Making of Modern Iran: State and Society under Reza Shah, 1921–1941* (London, Curzon, 2003, pp. 65–77.
[29] IS no. 14, 5 April 1924. FO371/10132/E5166/255/34.
[30] Havard, Diary of Events concerning the Republican Movement in Persia.
[31] IS no. 15, 12 April 1924, FO371/10132/E5168/E5168/255/34.
[32] Ahmad Amirahmadi, *Khatirat-i Nakhustin Sipahbud-i Iran*, 2 vols (Tehran, 1373), vol. 1, pp. 231–33.
[33] Ovey to MacDonald, 18 April 1924, FO371/10145/E4644/455/34.
[34] Ibid.
[35] Ibid.
[36] IS no. 27, 5 July 1924, FO371/10132/E6700/255/34.
[37] For Imbrie's murder, see Michael P. Zirinsky, 'Blood, Power and Hypocrisy: The Murder of Robert Imbrie and American Relations with Pahlavi Iran, 1924', *International Journal of Middle Eastern Studies*, 18 (1986), pp. 275–92.
[38] IS no. 7, 14 February 1925, FO371/10841/E1583/82/34.
[39] Loraine to Chamberlain, 26 February 1925, FO371/10840/E1581/18/34.
[40] IS no. 27, 31 October 1925, FO371/10842/E7216/82/34.
[41] Loraine to Chamberlain, 21 November 1925, FO371/10840/E7540/18/34.
[42] Annual Report on the Persian Army, Fraser, Military Attache, to Loraine, 31 December 1925, FO371/11491/E760/326/34.
[43] IS no. 37, 13 September 1924, FO371/10132/E9346/255/34.
[44] Kaveh Bayat, 'Baladeyyah-e Nezami', *Ganjinah*, vol. 2, pp. 11–36.
[45] Mohammad Mosaddeq, *Musaddiq's Memoirs*, edited and introduced by Homa Katouzian (London: I. B. Tauris, 1988), p. 246.
[46] Fraser to Colonel Muspratt, 1 June 1924, FO371/10145/E5427/455/34.
[47] Chick, Shiraz, to Loraine, 26 July 1923, FO371/9043/E9303/1417/34.
[48] IS no. 13, 18 April 1925, FO371/10842/E2783/82/34.
[49] Chick, Shiraz, to Loraine, 9 June 1926, FO371/11502/E4323/4323/34.
[50] Annual Report on the Persian Army, Saunders, Military Attache, 15 November 1922, FO371/9021/E71/71/34.

THE ARMY, CIVIL SOCIETY AND THE STATE IN IRAN   163

[51] See Cronin, *The Army*, pp. 171–81.
[52] Ovey to FO, 15 May 1924, FO371/10124/E5496/26/34.
[53] Loraine to FO, 3 June 1926, FO371/11491/E3397/326/34.
[54] Loraine to Chamberlain, 15 June 1926, FO371/11491/E4063/326/34.
[55] See Stephanie Cronin, 'Reza Shah and the Disintegration of Bakhtiyari Power in Iran, 1921–1934', *Iranian Studies* (forthcoming), 2000.
[56] Documentary material relating to this campaign, consisting of a considerable quantity of correspondence passing between Amirahmadi and the General Staff, is reproduced in Amirahmadi, *Khaterat*, vol. 2. Further material on the Luristan campaigns may be found in Kaveh Bayat (ed.), *Amaliyyat-e Luristan: Asnad-e Sartip Mohammad Shahbakhti, 1303 va 1306 shamsi* (Tehran, n.d.).
[57] IS no. 20, 17 May 1924, FO371/10132/E5498/255/34.
[58] IS no. 22, 31 May 1924, FO371/10132/E5858/255/34.
[59] IS no. 21, 24 May 1924, FO371/10132/E5856/255/34.
[60] Sir A. T. Wilson, Extract from Ahwaz Diary for the period ending 4 June 1924, Ovey to MacDonald, 3 July 1924, FO371/10124/E6692/26/34.
[61] IS no. 13, 18 April 1925, FO371/10842/E2783/82/34; IS no. 14, 2 May 1925, FO371/10842/E3056/82/34.
[62] IS no. 11, 29 May 1926; Amirahmadi, *Khatirat*, vol. 1, p. 265.
[63] Consul Gilliat-Smith, Tabriz to Loraine, 20 March 1926, FO248/1376/6; Gilliat-Smith to Loraine, 8 April 1926, FO248/1376/8; Gilliat-Smith to Loraine, 12 May 1926, FO248/1376/10.
[64] For the campaign against conscription led by the *ulema* in 1927, see Hossein Makki, *Tarikh-e Bist Salah-e Iran*, 8 vols (Tehran: Elmi, 1323), vol. 4, pp. 415–39; Stephanie Cronin, 'Conscription and Popular Resistance in Iran, 1925–1941', In Erik Jan Zürcher's *Arming the State: Military Conscription in the Middle East and Asia, 1775–1925*. London: I. B. Tauris, 1999, pp. 145–68. For the tribal uprisings in 1929, see Kaveh Bayat, *Shuresh-e Asha'er-e Fars* (Tehran, Shirazeh 1372); Cronin, 'Reza Shah and the Disintegration of Bakhtiyari Power'.
[65] Arjomand, *The Turban for the Crown*, pp. 41–42.
[66] Ibid.
[67] Homa Katouzian, *The Political Economy of Modern Iran: Despotism and Pseudo-Modernism, 1926–1979* (London: McMillan, 1981), p. 93.
[68] Batatu has noted the same phenomenon in Iraq in relation to the ex-Sharifian officers, Hanna Batatu, *The Old Social Classes and the Revolutionary Movements of Iraq* (Princeton, 1978), p. 322.
[69] Ibid.
[70] See, for example, Stephanie Cronin, 'The Politics of Radicalism within the Iranian Army: the Jahansuz Group of 1939', *Iranian Studies*, vol. 32, no. 1, Winter 1999, pp. 5–25.

CHAPTER VII
The Army and the Founding of the Turkish Republic*

Dankwart A. Rustow

Modern Turkish history furnishes numerous examples of active participation by the military in politics.* The so-called 'Young Turk Revolution' of 1908, in fact, may well be regarded as the prototype of Near Eastern military coups of this century.[1] A decade later, Mustafa Kemal (Atatürk)[2] and other army officers took the lead in creating a nationalist Turkish Republic out of the ruins of the multinational Ottoman Empire. Since the proclamation of the Republic in 1923, however, the Turkish army has abstained from any such obvious role on the political stage. Indeed, during a period when military coups have become endemic in the newly independent countries of the Near East, Asia and Africa, Turkey has built up a unique record of a generation of civilian government by orderly constitutional procedures. Although the pendulum in the last 35 years has swung from a dictatorial one-party system toward competitive party politics and back again toward increasing restrictions on political expression, the Kemalist movement of 1919–23 has remained to date the military intervention to end all military interventions in Turkey.

In this chapter I propose to examine the circumstances which led first to the profound involvement of the army and of army officers

---

* The research on which this article is based was carried out mainly at the Hoover Library, Stanford, CA, under a grant from the Center of International Studies, Princeton University. A first draft was presented to the Princeton University Staff Seminar in Near Eastern Studies. I should like to express my gratitude to the Honorable Tevfik Bryikhoğlu, participant in and leading historian of many of the events here described, for his careful and critical reading of the present version. The writer alone is responsible for such errors of fact or interpretation as remain.

in Turkish politics after the First World War and later to their withdrawal from the political stage.

Historical background

The Young Turk military coup of 1908 was the culmination of a long series of antecedents in Near Eastern and Ottoman history. Islam arose in the seventh century A.D. as a conquering faith which unified, within a century after the Prophet's death, a vast region from the Pyrenees to the Pamirs and imposed on most of it a religious and cultural stamp which thirteen centuries have not deleted. Compared with other world religions, Islam in its theology and jurisprudence accords a high degree of legitimacy to warfare. The doctrine of *jihad*, or Holy War, for example, asserts that the true faith can be spread by conquest as well as by conversion; Muslim international law rests on a basic distinction between the Abode of War and the Abode of Islam; and *amir al-mu'minin*, or Commander of the Faithful, is one of the most frequently used titles of the Caliph.[3]

Within the early Islamic domain, the Ottoman state itself emerged as one of the many principalities founded by frontier warriors along the northern marches.[4] The Ottoman victory over Byzantium (1453) initiated a century of spectacular conquest that carried Ottoman rule as far as Algeria, Hungary, the Ukraine, Iraq and Yemen. Throughout Ottoman history the army, along with the Sultan's palace establishment, remained the largest, most elaborate and most expensive part of the Empire's 'ruling institution';[5] and the decline of Ottoman military fortunes in the protracted contest with the Habsburg and Romanov Empires only served to reinforce the military's central position. The impact of modern Europe on the Ottoman Empire was felt most acutely as a military impact – from the breaking of the second siege of Vienna (1683) to Bonaparte's invasion of Egypt (1798) and down to the Great War of 1914–18. The Ottomans' natural reaction was to try to borrow, first and foremost, the 'cutting edge' of Western civilization.[6] With the importation of European military instructors, which began in the late eighteenth century, and the substitution of a newly organized army for the dissolute Janissary corps (1826), the army officers became one of the most Westernized elements in the Empire. The officer corps had always had a wide base of social and geographic recruitment; as a result of the nineteenth-century reforms, it also became one of the most conspicuous channels for merit advancement within the Empire's social structure. The Ottoman Empire, as its name indicates, had been founded on the dynastic principle of loyalty to the House of Osman. The many linguistic and denominational groups within the Empire – Turks, Arabs, Greeks, Kurds, Bulgarians, and many others; Muslims, Christians of numerous distinct churches, and Jews – were held together by a loose-jointed system of administration which left considerable leeway for ethnic and local autonomy and by a system of ethnic division of labour which linked these groups in a multiple symbiotic relationship. The spread of political ideas of nineteenth-century Europe first to the Balkans and later to the Near East presented a twofold challenge to Ottoman traditions. Nationalism threatened the delicate adjustment among the Empire's polyglot subjects. Liberal ideas of representative government undermined the principle of dynastic absolutism. Within the Ottoman elite, army officers were among the first to be converted to these new ideas. In its social ethos, the reformed officers corps thus was much closer to the Bonapartist tradition of middle-class revolution than to the agrarian-conservative tradition of the Prussian *Junkers*. Nationalism, moreover, like military reform itself, was largely a response to repeated defeats. As late as the beginning of this century, the members of the Empire's ruling class were proud to consider themselves 'Ottomans', reserving the term 'Turk' for the unlettered peasant of Anatolia.[7] Modern nationalist consciousness was prepared by such patriotic proclamations as Namik Kemal's play *Vatan (The Fatherland)*, of 1873, which celebrated the defense of the Rumanian frontier fortress of Silistria two decades earlier; one of its first clear statements was the poem of Mehmed Emin [Yurdakul], 'Going to Battle' (i.e., against the Greek nationalist insurgents on Crete in 1896), which proudly – and, to polite Ottoman ears, shockingly – opened, 'I am a Turk, my faith, my race are sublime . . .'

Students at the military staff colleges, and particularly the medical cadets, became the centre of secret political organization within the Ottoman Empire from the mid-nineteenth century onward. The attempt of Sultan Abdülhamid II (1876–1909) to halt or reverse Westernizing innovations in many fields while allowing them to continue in the army pushed the officers further toward the forefront of social change. His practice of exiling political suspects supplied a steady stream of recruits to the centers of expatriate conspiratorial organization in Paris and Geneva.[8] The fact that these young revolutionaries adopted the name 'New Ottomans' indicates to what extent their thinking was still bounded by dynastic concepts. To Westerners they are known as 'Young Turks', a name bestowed on them by their European hosts and one that has found currency in Turkish only in the form of a French loan word, *Jön Türk*.

The Ottoman revolution of 1908 was largely inspired by these radicals in exile, though it was carried out by rebellious officers in various Macedonian garrisons. Like many later Near Eastern military coups it ushered in a period of political unrest, of ambitious attempts at socio-political reform jeopardized by even more ambitious foreign policy commitments. The immediate aim of the revolutionaries was the restoration of the parliamentary constitution of 1876, which had been shelved by Abdülhamid almost immediately upon its adoption. Their wider goal was the transformation of the decrepit Empire into a modern state based upon a common sense of allegiance among its citizenry and with sufficient military and political strength to halt the encroachments of European powers. Both goals eluded the Young Turks.

A year after the revolution, a mutiny of the İstanbul garrison which challenged the restored constitutional regime was suppressed by the Macedonian army's march on the capital. The ensuing wrangle between a centralist and a federalist faction among the 1908 revolutionaries set the stage for a party dictatorship of the centralists, known as the Committee of Union and Progress (CUP). The party's power increasingly came to be concentrated in the famous wartime triumvirate of Enver, Cemal, and Talât – the first two young army officers whom the revolution had launched upon meteoric political careers, the third a former telegraph clerk who had risen to control over the party's local apparatus. Among the three, Enver Pasha – Minister of War and deputy Commander in Chief (under the Sultan's nominal authority) – soon emerged as the most powerful figure. Thus negotiations leading to the secret alliance with Germany of 2 August 1914, which so disastrously involved the Empire in the First World War, were conducted by Enver with the knowledge of only two or three of his cabinet colleagues. Within a few years the lofty theory of parliamentary constitutionalism had been converted into the crude practice of partisan and personal dictatorship.

The ideal of a common Ottoman citizenship was undermined just as rapidly by the CUP's facile tendency to equate Ottomanism with Turkish nationalism and also by the secessionist inclinations of the major non-Turkish nationalities (as manifested in the Balkan Wars of 1912–13, the dealings of the Armenian nationalists with Czarist Russia during the First World War which prompted the much-publicized repressive measures of 1915–16, and the British-supported Arab revolt of 1916–18). Within the cultural and administrative spheres, the Unionists cabinets of Mehmed Said Halim (1913–17) and Talât (1917–18) undertook a number of far-reaching reforms – including the establishment of a modern university at İstanbul, a simplified orthography for the Arabic script then still used for Turkish, the elimination of the last vestiges of tax-farming from the Imperial revenue system, and a revision of Muslim family law whereby the marriage partners could contract for monogamy. But in the meantime Enver's grandiose and amateurish conduct of the war, which substituted political romanticism for strategic design and personal vanity for tactical calculation, cost the Empire scores of thousands of its best troops. The Russian Revolution of February 1917, which relieved the pressure on the northeastern front, delayed the impending disaster only briefly. The separate armistice which the Ottoman government saw itself forced to sign at Moudros (30 October 1918) put an end not only to Ottoman participation in the First World War but also to 600 years of Imperial history. Only three days later, Enver, Talât, Cemal, and other Young Turk leaders ignominiously fled beyond the borders of the Empire.[9]

The decade from 1908 to 1918 had established the army, in close alliance with the Union and Progress Party, as the dominant element on the political scene. The deposed Abdülhamid, confined first in Salonica and then until his death (1918) in Beylerbeyi palace opposite İstanbul, served as a living reminder of the power of party over sovereign.[10] His brother Mehmed V Reşad throughout his reign (1909–18) never lost sight of the possibility of another deposition.[11] In the meantime, seven years of almost uninterrupted hostilities (with Italy, 1911–12; in the Balkans, 1912–13; and in the First World War) brought the Ottoman Empire closer to being a garrison state than it had perhaps been at any time since its infancy.

The experience of the wars in Tripoli and the Balkans, moreover, gave the Ottoman leaders an opportunity to refine the Macedonian *komitadji* techniques so successfully employed in the Young Turk Revolution and to apply them to the attempted reconquest of lost territories. When the Ottoman forces in the Second Balkan War were retaking Edirne and other parts of Eastern Thrace up to the

Maritsa, local Turkish leaders formed a provisional government of Western Thrace in the region immediately beyond; and individual Ottoman officers, assisted by armed bands mainly of Circassian extraction proceeded to organize a militia for this provisional government.[12] Following the limited Ottoman victory in the second Balkan campaign, the boundary along the Maritsa was accepted and the Western Thrace government disbanded. But the following year Enver Pasha, presumably with War Ministry funds, set up a so-called Special Organization (*Teşkilâti Mahsusa*) – a combination, it would appear, of secret service and guerrilla forces – which over the next few years carried the irredentist struggle to other territories beyond the Ottoman borders. The first commander of this Special Organization, Süleyman Askerî, was an army captain who had been active in the campaign of the Western Thrace irregulars. During the early part of the World War, a number of officers from the Special Organization helped to organize the Sanusi order and other tribal elements in their continued fight against Italian colonial rule. A similar campaign was undertaken in 1918 in the Caucasus region, where the Ottoman guerrillas operated under the high-flown name of Army of Islam. Throughout this period Enver kept close personal control over these operations. Thus, the Army of Islam was headed by his brother Nuri (Killigil), an army major on whom Enver had earlier conferred the rank of honorary major general, and who from 1915 to 1918 had served with the Special Organization in Libya; it was attached to Enver's uncle Halil (Kut) in his capacity of commanding general in the Caucasus.[13]

If not the army, who else?

The importance of the army in Turkish politics, was greatly accentuated following the Empire's defeat in 1918. Under the terms of the armistice of Moudros, the Allies kept enough troops in İstanbul to deprive the Sultan of his freedom of action, but not enough in the hinterland to establish effective authority over Anatolia. Up to the time of the Greek landings in May 1919, Allied forces in the interior of Anatolia consisted chiefly of token detachments along the main rail line from İstanbul to Adana and at several Black Sea ports. Potential control over Anatolia thus remained in the hands of the seven army corps that had in large part been reconstituted from the Ottoman Empire's Caucasian, Syrian, and Mesopotamian armies.

Decimated though they were, these forces had never, throughout the World War, been deployed over so compact an area. Despite the general demobilization decreed at Moudros, the army preserved its discipline and its clear chain of command. Its telegraphic code could be used for instant and secret communication for political as well as military purposes.[14] In taking up the nationalist cause, the army would be able, where necessary, to resist by force any countermeasures on the part of the Allies or the Sultan. The successive encroachments by the Allies in the winter and spring of 1919, some made possible by the vague terms of the armistice and some in outright violation of it, led to early stirrings of national resistance. But this resistance was scattered and ill organized. To quote a participant of this period, 'This heroic [Turkish] people had only one defect – it was not yet linked to any organization.'[15] It was this defect which leadership by the army and its high-ranking commanders was ideally equipped to remedy.

Quite apart from historical antecedents and its own positive qualifications in the post-1918 situation, the army and its officer corps were propelled into action because all other political forces were, at least for the moment, disqualified from offering any effective initiative. Turkish citizens looking for leadership in the impending struggle for national independence could well ask (as did Gemal Abdel Nasser and his fellow-conspirators against the corrupt regime of King Faruq a generation later): 'If the Army does not do this job, who will?'[16] Several of these potential political forces deserve closer examination in this context.

The view of the Sultan was bounded by the intrigues of the capital and the palace. Few Ottoman Sultans of the late period would have qualified as leaders of a popular movement. Mehmed VI Vahideddin (who ruled from mid-1918 until the abolition of his throne in 1922) was less popular than most. According to a intimate and level-headed observer,

> He was nervous of disposition and irascible of temper and would now and then shout at people; but his ire quickly subsided . . . However polite Sultan Vahideddin might be in his apartment, toward outsiders he seemed very cool. When receiving in audience, he would bend his head forward on his way in and out and, without taking notice of anyone, pass with scowling face. When he received the ministers as a group he would close his eyes and,

taking a minute or two over each word, he would with bated breath make a few insulting remarks. Most ministers never quite believed that he could carry on a conversation at all, let alone speak fluently. But after he had received someone a few times and become accustomed to him he would gradually open up and sometimes talk continuously for an hour. In this manner he could not endear himself to outsiders.[17]

The Union and Progress Party, which had concluded the German alliance and manoeuvred the Empire into the war on the side of the losing Central Powers, was utterly discredited as a result of the defeat and of the cowardly flight of its top leaders. The party organization, four days after the armistice, resolved its own abolition, reconstituting itself as the Renewal Party, under the chairmanship of Mehmed Şemseddin (Günaltay), a liberal theology professor. The winter of 1918–19 brought a number of investigations and trials of the wartime Unionist leaders, and any overt or prominent association with them became a distinct political liability. Thus when Kemal (Atatürk) in the spring of 1919 was being considered for the inspectorate of the 9th Army, his friends were at pains to deny that he had ever been a Unionist.[18] Kemal himself in a statement to the press disclaimed any connection with the Renewal Party.[19] And the members of the Kemalist Congress of Sivas in the summer of 1919 swore that they 'would not work for the revival of the Society of Union and Progress'.[20]

On the other hand, a decade of Unionist hegemony had concentrated much of the country's political talent within the party and its affiliated organizations in the educational and cultural fields. Early in 1919 the Sultan complained to his secretary: 'I realize that [the ministers] are incompetent; but when are we to appoint in their places? If there are five or six people in this country who can get things done, [the Allies] object that they are Unionists.'[21] Halide Edib (Adıvar) in her recollections of this period only slightly overstated the case when she said, 'Every man in this country was once a Unionist in the past.'[22] The party had greatly extended the traditional base of political recruitment. Talât, who rose from telegraph clerk to First Minister and the rank of Pasha, once told his friend Dr Adnan (Adıvar): 'After I became minister everybody began nursing the same ambition.'[23] The tendency therefore was for dissident or second-rank members of the wartime Union and Progress regime to take the lead in the post-armistice period.

The composition of the cabinet which signed the armistice of Moudros clearly reflects this tendency. It was headed by Ahmed İzzet Pasha, a general in his mid-50s who enjoyed the highest professional respect among his fellow officers. After the 1908 revolution İzzet had served as army commander, Chief of Staff, and Minister of War. But he did not conceal his contempt of officers who, like Enver, used their political influence to compensate for their military ineptitude; as a result, he had been relegated to secondary assignments following the Balkan Wars.[24] The Minister of Marine (and one of the co-signers of the Moudros agreement) was Hüseyin Rauf (Orbay), who had won wide fame as a courageous naval commander during the war and was associated with the Young Turks without holding any prominent party post. The Interior portfolio was held by Ali Fethi [Okyar], a former army officer and one-time member of the Union and Progress executive committee who, in the closing months of the war, had been parliamentary leader of an opposition group within the party. The only holdover from Talât's outgoing cabinet was Cavid, the Finance Minister, who earlier had left the cabinet in protest against Enver's Germanophile war policy and only reluctantly re-entered it later. Ürgüblü Mustafa Hayri, who as Şeyhülislâm (Grand Mufti) in the Said Halim cabinet had signed the 1914 *fetva* calling for a Holy War and left the cabinet in 1916, partly in disagreement with Enver, this time reappeared as Minister of Justice.

Among the public figures who had participated in the early Young Turk movement, supported its ideal of nationalism and political regeneration, but sharply condemned the policy and strategy of the Enver-Talât regime, Mustafa Kemal (Atatürk) was by far the most prominent. He had been a cofounder in 1906 of the Fatherland and Freedom Society, a Young Turk group in Damascus, and three years later had taken a leading part in the action of the Macedonian contingent that suppressed the İstanbul counterrevolution. But he had kept aloof from Unionist Party politics, and within the army his rivalry with Enver was proverbial. In 1917 he had taken it upon himself to criticize the conduct of the war in great detail in an acrid and lengthy memorandum to the high command.[25] He had declined two different army commands, accompanied Crown Prince Vahideddin on a trip to Germany, and only shortly before the end of the war resumed active command on the Syrian front.

The return to office of dissident Unionists also occurred below the cabinet level. Reşid Pasha, a Unionist who had been dismissed as governor of Kastamonu for his criticism of the Talât government's Armenian pogrom policy, records that the Damad Ferid government had to bring men back from retirement in its attempt to purge the provincial administration of CUP supporters. Reşid himself owed his appointment as governor of Sivas (where he assumed a somewhat hesitant position between nationalists and antinationalists) only to his earlier differences with the Talât government.[26]

The anti-Unionist politicians of the capital were, by and large, men of small stature and dim vision. The Freedom and Accord Party (*Hürriyet ve İtilâf*, often translated as Liberal Entente) had been founded in 1911 by the federalist wing of the Young Turk movement and been dissolved two years later when it lost out to the centralist CUP. The Freedom and Accord group was reconstituted in 1919 and furnished the main political support of the five cabinets formed by Vahideddin's brother-in-law Damad Ferid Pasha (March to October 1919 and April to October 1920). But the new party had little more than the name in common with its predecessor.[27] The original programme of federalism among the various nationalities of the Empire was now largely inapplicable, and the Arab and Armenian followers of the old party no longer participated in Turkish politics. Some of the most capable members of the original Freedom and Accord Party and other anti-Unionist groups of the 1908–13 period, moreover, joined the Kemalist movement in Anatolia soon after its inception.[28] The new Freedom and Accord Party advocated a policy of abject collaboration with the victor powers in the hope of securing a lenient peace and retaining the appearance, if not the substance, of Ottoman suzerainty over Arabia and the Fertile Crescent as well as Anatolia. This policy was faithfully carried out by the various Damad Ferid governments, but the final Allied peace terms as announced in the spring of 1920 and signed by Damad Ferid's emissaries at Sèvres in August showed how utterly illusory a policy it had been.

The *civilian bureaucracy* proved to be far more consistent than the army in its loyalty to the Sultan and his cabinet, and hence more disinclined to take any pro-nationalist action that might smack of treason or insubordination. İstanbul Ministers of the Interior, such as Ali Kemal and Âdil, provided some of the most determined opposition to Mustafa Kemal's attempt to consolidate the Anatolian movement – at a time when the War Ministry and the General Staff still were solidly controlled by nationalist sympathizers. This divergence at the apex presumably accentuated, by means of contrasting appointment policies, the political differences between military and civilian officials at the provincial base. Most of the Anatolian governors and subgovernors (*valis* and *mutasarrifs*) in the summer and fall of 1919 seem to have been hostile, cool, or at best cautiously correct towards the nationalist cause. This was true in Ankara, Kastamonu, Samsun and Sivas.[29] Kemal had one of his narrowest escapes in late June 1919 when the newly appointed governor of Mamuretülaziz, Ali Galib, on instructions from İstanbul tried to arrest him in Sivas.[30] There were of course, exceptions. Hilmi (Uran), as subgovernor of Kars, was instrumental in launching the nationalist provisional government of Southwest Caucasia late in 1918. Bekir Sami, ex-governor of Beirut, İbrahim Süreyya (Yiğit), ex-subgovernor of İzmit, and Mazhar Müfid (Kansu), governor of Bitlis, were among the first civilians to join the Anatolian movement in mid-1919; all three were old personal friends of Kemal. The governor of Erzurum, Münir (Akkaya), in August 1919 refused to obey the İstanbul government's orders to arrest Kemal and Rauf [Orbay].[31] And Ebübekir Hâzım (Tepeyran), İstanbul Minister of the Interior early in 1920, was sentenced in August of that year by a court martial, headed by Nimrod Mustafa Pasha, for having aided the nationalists while serving as governor of Bursa. Yet, by and large, even the civilian support of the early Kemalist movement came from former Unionist politicians or other local notables rather than from the local representatives of central authority.

The various non-Turkish groups of the Empire, as might be expected, remained outside the nationalist movement. The larger groups – such as the Arabs, Armenians, and Greeks – were engaged in setting up or enlarging their own national political communities, and the latter two were soon engaged in military action against the Anatolian nationalists. Even the Kurds, encouraged by Allied promises, strove for regional autonomy. Some of the smaller Muslim nationalities supplied many of the most dedicated bitter-end supporters of the supranational Ottoman Empire, and hence many of the most determined opponents of the Kemalist movement; yet without solid support from the Turkish element, there was little prospect that these alone could save the Empire. İzzet Bey, a Kurdish governor of Van, was instrumental in giving an antinationalist orientation to the Tevfik Pasha cabinet (November 1918 to January 1919), in which he served as Minister of Pious Foundations. His brother-in-law, Nimrod Mustafa Pasha, as chairman of the aforementioned court martial, presided over one of the most sweeping purges of former Young Turks and other nationalist sympathizers. İzzet's nephew, Şerif Pasha, at the same time was presenting demands for Kurdish independence to the Allied diplomats in Paris. Seyyid Abdülkadir, chairman of the separatist *Kürdistan Teali Cemiyeti* (Kürdistan Resurrection Society), was a prominent member of the revived Freedom and Accord Party and a cabinet minister under Damad Ferid. Ahmed Anzavur, retired Gendarmerie-major and ex-subgovernor of İzmit, who in the fall and winter of 1919-20 took the field against the nationalists at the head of a force of irregulars, was a Circassian. So was Edhem, commander of the nationalists' irregular cavalry, who ultimately went over to the Greeks, Albanians were well represented in the İstanbul governments of 1918-22, although some of them, like Ahmed İzzet Pasha, adopted an attitude of benevolent neutrality toward Kemal. And throughout Anatolia, Circassian and Kurdish gangs or tribes took leading parts in the uprisings of the spring and summer of 1920 which challenged the authority of the nascent nationalist government at Ankara.[32] In contrast to these loyalist Circassians, other Ottoman citizens of Caucasian descent prominently joined the Anatolian movement – the most notable ones being Rauf [Orbay], who was Mustafa Kemal's closest political collaborator in 1919-1920, and Bekir Sami, the Ankara government's first Foreign Minister.[33]

Nationalist and Antinationalist Officers

It should not be assumed that the officer corps supported the nationalist cause to a man. Some high-ranking officers, in fact, remained loyal to the İstanbul government to the very end. A few staked their careers on the cause of resistance, risking demotion or the firing squad if they should fail. Some applied for retirement and thus avoided political involvement. Others spent much of the post-armistice period in voluntary or involuntary political exile. Most, especially in the lower ranks, simply carried out the orders of their immediate superiors. And many in the higher ranks manoevred carefully among conflicting directives from İstanbul and Ankara, cautiously awaiting some indication of the outcome. More research is required to establish fully and clearly the composition and activities of each of these groups. In the meantime, available data on the age and geographic origin of certain categories of civilian and military leaders during this transition period from Ottoman Empire to Turkish Republic allow us to compare in general terms those officers who remained loyal to İstanbul with those who joined the Anatolian movement, and also each of these with their civilian colleagues.

An examination of the figures in Table 1 reveals several striking features.

TABLE 1 Age and Regional Origin of Turkish Military and Civilian Leaders, 1914-1923*

| | Total | Total Known | BIRTH DATES | | | Total Known | BIRTHPLACES PER CENT BORN IN | | | | |
			Oldest	Median	Youngest		Macedonia, Thrace, &c.	Istanbul	Anatolia	Arab Countries	Caucasus
	1	2	3	4	5	6	7	8	9	10	11
1 Ottoman Army Commanders, 1914-18	17	17	1860	1876	1882	17	35	35	12	18	0
2 Istanbul Ministers, 1918-22	88	62	1838	1864	1881	66	15	47	24	6	8
3 Civilians	59	36	1838	1867	1880	40	20	48	23	5	5
4 Officers	29	26	1846	1860	1881	26	8	46	23	8	15
5 Ankara Ministers, 1920-23	35	35	1856	1881	1892	32	19	22	59	0	0
6 Civilians	26	26	1862	1880	1892	23	13	9	78	0	0
7 Officers	9	9	1856	1881	1884	9	33	56	11	0	0
8 Nationalist Commanders, 1919-22	25	25	1870	1880	1885	25	24	44	32	0	0

* *Definitions.* In tabulating the data for lines 4 and 7, 'officers' has been taken to include all active and retired military personnel, except for those who took up civilian careers after leaving the service. Hence Ali Fethi [Okyar], who left the army in 1912 to become a party official and diplomat, is included in lines 3 and 6; Hüseyin Rauf [Orbay], who resigned from the navy in May 1919 so as to join the Anatolian movement without official position, in lines 4 and 7.

In the breakdown of birthplaces, column 7 includes all European parts of the Ottoman Empire (Albania, Northern Greece, Macedonia, Bulgaria, Bosnia, the Dobruja, Crete, the Aegean Islands), as well as Cyprus. Column 9 includes the Asiatic parts of present-day Turkey. Column 10 includes Syria, Iraq and Egypt.

Sources. The lists of names on which the above calculations are based have been derived from the following sources:

Line 1: M. Larcher, *La Guerre Turque dans la Guerre Mondiale*, Paris, 1926, pp. 540, 596-99, occasionally supplemented by other sources.

ARMY AND FOUNDING OF THE TURKISH REPUBLIC

Lines 2 to 4: İbnülemin Mahmud Kemal İnal, *Osmanlı Devrinde Son Sadrazamlar*, 14 fascicles, İstanbul, 1940–1953, *passim*; Ali Fuad Türkgeldi, *Görüp İşittiklerim*, 2nd ed., Ankara, 1951, *passim*; and Gotthard Jäschke, 'Beiträge zur Geschichte des Kampfes der Türkei um ihre Unabhängigkeit', *Welt des Islams*, n.s., v (1957), pp. 61–62. In addition, incumbents of individual cabinet posts are listed in *Türk Ansiklopedisi*, Vols. I–ix (A to Cato), Ankara, 1946–1958 (Vols. I to IV published under the title *İnönü Ansiklopedisi*), I, p. 143 (Justice) and v, p. 64 (Navy); and *Harp Tarihi Vesikaları Dergisi*, II, No. 3 (March 1953), p. 4 (War). It is hoped that inaccuracies contained in each of these sources have been eliminated by collation with the rest.

Lines 5 to 7: *Türkiye Büyük Millet Meclisinin 25nci Yıldönümünü Anış*, Ankara, 1945, pp. 84–100; birthplaces and ages are listed in *ibid.*, pp. 1–73, *passim*. Appointments as acting ministers and other temporary posts have been disregarded.

Line 8: Cemal Nadir [Güler] and Naci Kasim, eds., *Ordumuzun Zafer Kitabeleri: Yunan Askerlerinin Yetim Bıraktığı Mahzun Analar İçin*, Şark Kitabevi [İstanbul, 1923?], pp. 97–148 (copy in Hoover Library). The selection of officers contained in a contemporary panegyric may be assumed to be representative for our purposes. Note, however, that one of the 25 officers listed – Cemal [Mersinli] – joined the Ankara Assembly without assuming any active military command in Anatolia.

I am greatly indebted to the officials of the War History Division of the Turkish General Staff for generously supplying me with biographical data, based on official records, for most of the officers included in the table or otherwise referred to in this article. Published information on birth dates and places will be found in the following works, which on occasion have been supplemented by individual biographies:

İbrahim Alâettin Gövsa, *Turk Meşhurları Ansiklopedisi*, İstanbul, 1946, for the better-known figures.

Türk Ansiklopedisi (see above) for those whose names start with A or B.

Obituaries in *Millî Nevsal* (annual) İstanbul, 1921–1925.

T. B. M. M. Yıllığı and *T. B. M. M. Albümü*, Ankara, published since the late 1920's – as a rule, once per legislative session – for those who later joined the parliaments of the Republic.

Ali Çankaya, *Mülkiye Tarihi ve Mülkiyeliler*, 2 vols., Ankara, 1954, for graduates of the civil service training school (Mülkiye), especially line 3.

Hasan Basri Erk, *Meşhur Türk Hukukcuları*, İstanbul, 1959(?), for prominent lawyers, especially line 3.

Muharrem Mazlum [İskora], *Erkâniharbiye Mektebi (Harp Akademisi) Tarihi*, İstanbul, 1930, for graduates of the General Staff College; and Silistreli Mehmed Es'ad, *Mir'at-i Mekteb-i Harbiye*, İstanbul, 1310 (i.e., 1894), for graduates of the officers' training school.

The last two sources, as well as Güler, give only birthplaces and summaries of military careers. For four officers on line 4, birth dates have been estimated

First, exactly two-and-a-half times as many persons served in the İstanbul cabinets from the end of the World War until the demise of the Sultan's government (four years and one month) as served in the various Ankara cabinets during the first Grand National Assembly (three years and four months). This is explained only in small part by the somewhat larger number of portfolios (13 to 15 in İstanbul as against 8 to 12 in Ankara; in addition, one İstanbul cabinet included as many as ten ministers without portfolio). The large turnover of ministers in İstanbul reflected both its hesitant political course and its difficulties in attracting qualified personnel.

Second, about half the İstanbul ministers were natives of the Imperial capital, whereas the Ankara governments, and especially their civilian membership, were overwhelmingly made up of men from Anatolia, whose defense the nationalists had undertaken. The military in each group represent a somewhat wider regional spectrum, with strong representation from Macedonia, especially among the Ankara officers. As might be expected, natives of the Ottoman Arab territories are represented in the civilian and military leadership of the late Empire, but are entirely absent from the Ankara governments; the same is true for natives of the Caucasus.

Third, and somewhat surprisingly, the proportion of military men actually was larger in the İstanbul than in the Ankara cabinets. Cabinet turnover in İstanbul was particularly rapid in the ministries of War and Marine, reflecting the conflicting pressures from Allies and nationalists under which these departments operated. (There were 15 changes of minister in the War Office and nine in the Navy Department, as against only six changes of Prime Minister; by contrast, only four persons occupied the two military posts – Minister of National Defense and Chief of the General Staff – in the Ankara cabinet.) In addition, İstanbul premiers demonstrated a penchant for military men as Minister of Public Works and of Commerce; but

by subtracting 23 years from their date of graduation from staff college as given by İskora. (The mean age for 73 graduates of the period 1876–1909 whose birth dates could be established independently was 23·5; 60 of them ranged in age from 21 to 25, so that the margin of error rarely will exceed two years.) For three officers on line 8, birth dates have been similarly estimated according to information given by Güler.

Finally, Messrs Tevfik Bıyıklıoğlu and Faik Reşit Unat have expertly helped me solve a number of remaining biographical puzzles, for which I should like to record my gratitude.

even such non-military departments as Education and Pious Foundations were at times headed by generals.

Fourth, a look at the age distribution of İstanbul and Ankara ministers confirms that the profusion of military ministers in İstanbul was very far from indicating solid army support for the Sultan's regime. The median age of İstanbul ministers was fully 17 years above that of their Ankara colleagues, the difference being even more pronounced among the military (21 years) than among the civilian component (13 years). Similarly, the military ministers in İstanbul were on the average 16 years older than the army commanders of the World War. With very few exceptions they were brought back from retirement, whereas officers on active duty overwhelmingly appear to have joined the Anatolian movement.

The age difference between the supporters of the Sultan and of Mustafa Kemal is by far the most remarkable contrast between the two groups, and numerous striking illustrations may be cited. The seven men who headed the eleven İstanbul cabinets of this period ranged from 54 to 75 years of age at the time of their appointment, averaging 66. The two youngest, Generals İzzet (Furgaç) (October–November 1918) and Salih Hulûsi (Kezrak) (March–April 1920), significantly also were the most sympathetic to nationalist aims. One of the elderly generals whom Damad Ferid selected as Minister of War replied to the Sultan's second urgent invitation: 'Don't let them latch on to me: I am headed straight for the grave.'[34] The İstanbul government's predilection for retired personnel on either side of the grave was even more starkly illustrated in November 1918, when the 73-year-old Premier-designate Ahmed Tevfik (Okday) 'appointed to the post of Şeyhülislâm the former Kadi of Egypt, Yahya Reşid Efendi, who, it was subsequently learned, had died two years before . . .'[35] The Ankara government, on the other hand, was headed by Mustafa Kemal, aged 39 in 1920, as President of the Grand National Assembly. Its first prime ministers were Fevzi [Çakmak] and Hüseyin Rauf (Orbay), aged 45 and 41 at the time of their respective appointments. Only three of the Ankara ministers were over 50 years of age; the oldest, İsmail Fazıl Pasha (1856–1921), had joined the nationalist cause as a result of the prominent role played in it by his son, Ali Fuad (Cebesoy) (b. 1882), a classmate of Kemal who, at 38, became the first commander of the nationalist Western front. The second oldest was Foreign Minister Bekir Sami (1862–1932). The youngest Ankara minister, Mahmud Esad (Bozkurt)

(1892–1943), had joined the Grand National Assembly at 28 – two years before reaching the statutory age for members of parliament. The age contrast between the rival governments became apparent at the London Conference in February 1921, to which the Allies had been careful to invite competing delegations from İstanbul and Ankara. The İstanbul delegation was headed by Premier Ahmed Tevfik Pasha, by then 76 and ailing, and that from Ankara by Bekir Sami, who was only 59. Tevfik Pasha, dragging himself out of bed with difficulty and barely able to make himself heard in the conference room, yielded the floor to the Ankara delegation at the very opening session, and thus helped the nationalists win their first important diplomatic victory.[36]

It should be stressed that the several categories of persons listed in Table 1 overlap. Thus four ministers (Orbay, Okyar, Çakmak, and Ahmed Ferid (Tek) served in both İstanbul and Ankara cabinets; significantly again, they were among the six youngest İstanbul ministers, although still above the Ankara average. Of the 17 Turkish army commanders of 1914–18, five later served in various İstanbul cabinet posts (especially in the early period up to the reinforced occupation of the capital on March 16, 1920), and six reappear on the list of nationalist commanders of 1919–22. Indeed, the post-armistice careers of these World War commanders illustrate vividly both the general political situation during the transition period from Empire to Republic, and the officer corps' part in that transition.

(a) Of the 17 generals in this group,[37] one, Hafız İsmail Hakkı Pasha (1879–1915), a prominent CUP politician (and, like Enver, married to a princess of the Imperial house), died of typhus early in the war.

(b) Nine of the generals – the majority – spent varying periods after the war in exile. Enver (1881–1922) and Ahmed Cemal (1872–1922), as noted earlier, fled soon after the armistice; both engaged in intense and complex political activities mainly in Moscow and in the Caucasus. They were soon joined by Halil (Kut), who earlier had been interned by the British at Batum and imprisoned during the İstanbul government's round-up of Young Turks, but who had escaped each time. Cemal and Halil Pashas seem to have done much to prepare the Bolshevik-Kemalist rapprochement that involved in due course a coordinated offensive against Armenia, and Russian shipments of gold and arms to Anatolia, and was to culminate in the Friendship Treaty of March 16, 1921. Enver, assisted by Halil and other former associates, attempted a comeback in Anatolia when

Mustafa Kemal's military fortunes seemed on the decline in the summer of 1921. Cemal was killed by an Armenian assassin's bullet in Tiflis in July 1922 – a fate that had overtaken Talât in Berlin and Said Halim in Rome the previous year. Two weeks later Enver lost his life in an ill-calculated military adventure in Turkestan, flamboyant and quixotic to the end. Vehib Pasha (1877–1940) was arrested in İstanbul in early 1919 – apparently for alleged financial irregularities during the war rather than for political reasons – and subsequently escaped to Europe.[38]

Ali İhsan (Sabis) (1882–1957) and Yakub Şevki (Sübaşı) (1876–1939), at the time of the armistice commander of the 6th and of the 9th Army (Iraq, Caucasus), respectively, were recalled to İstanbul at Allied insistence (March–April 1919). Ali İhsan was arrested upon his arrival at Haydarpaşa station and deported by the British to Malta, where he was soon joined by Mahmud Kâmil Pasha (1879–before 1930). Both of them escaped from internment in September 1921.[39] Yakub Şevki, Cemal (Mersinli) (1873–1940), and Cevad (Çobanll) (1870–1938) were included in the second wave of deportations to Malta in the spring of 1920, and were returned to Turkey in November 1921 as a result of the exchange agreement following Kemal's decisive victory on the Sakarya.[40] Mustafa Fevzi (Çakmak) (1876–1950) escaped deportation by fleeing to Ankara in April 1920. Çobanll and Çakmak, who from December 1918 to April 1920 alternated, with short interruptions, as Minister of War and Chief of Staff, contributed decisively to the launching of the nationalist movement by posting energetic younger commanders to Anatolia and by facilitating the smuggling of arms from İstanbul. Cemal [Mersinli], as Minister of War in the Ali Reza cabinet (October 1919), considered himself the official İstanbul representative of Kemal's provisional government (or 'Representative Committee').[41] Following their return from Malta, Ali İhsan, Yakub Şevki, and Cevad assumed various front commands in Anatolia in the final phase of the War of Independence; Cemal (Mersinli), who had applied for retirement prior to his deportation, served as deputy in the first Grand National Assembly. Mahmud Kâmil, a native of Damascus, seems to have been the only one of the Malta group who did not go to Anatolia; in fact, I have found no indication of his later activities.

(c) Three of the 17 – Mustafa Kemal (Atatürk) (1881–1938), Çakmak, and Nihad (Anılmış) (1878–1954) – proceeded from İstanbul to Anatolia at various times in 1919 and 1920.

(d) Hasan İzzet Pasha (1870–19—), a native of Damascus, resigned his army command just prior to the defeat at Sarıkamış (December 1914), was subsequently retired from the army (1915), and went to Syria in 1921.[42]

(e) The three remaining wartime commanders stayed in İstanbul and accepted leading posts in the government there. Esad (Bülkat) (1862–1952) briefly became Minister of Marine in March–April 1920. Ahmed İzzet (Furgaç) (1864–1937), in addition to his term as Premier in 1918, served as Minister of Interior and then of Foreign Affairs in the Sultan's last cabinet (October 1920–November 1922). And Zeki Baraz (1860–1942) during this same period was the last İstanbul Chief of Staff. As can be seen, these were the three oldest of the entire group of 17; in addition, Furgaç and Bülkat were of Albanian origin, and Baraz was a native of Syria.

These details confirm our earlier generalizations as to age and regional origin of the supporters of the Sultan and of the Anatolian nationalist movement. The eight generals who sooner or later joined the Anatolian movement and the five who remained in exile were all under 50 in 1920, averaging 44 and 42 respectively. The four who remained in İstanbul (or, in one case, went to Syria) were in their 50s, averaging 56; all four, moreover, were of non-Turkish origin.[43] The three generals who served first in İstanbul and then in Anatolia were all in their late 40s, averaging 47. All in all, for every top-ranking front commander who remained in İstanbul until the end, there were two who joined the Anatolian cause. If the five exiled or deceased Young Turk generals are added on the side of the seven Anatolians, it becomes clear that 12 of the 17 Turkish army commanders of the First World War were committed to the cause of Turkish nationalism (Anılmış, Atatürk, Cemal, Çakmak, Çobanı, Enver, Hafiz Hakkı, Kut, Mahmud Kâmil, Mersinli, Sabis, and Sübaşı), whereas only two (Baraz, Furgaç) served the Sultan until the end of his government.

The relative youth of the Anatolian commanders (see line 8 of Table 1, as well as the biographical data just reviewed) goes a long way toward explaining their readiness to support new political ideas. The typical retired officer who served in the İstanbul cabinet saw his last service at the front during the Balkan War débâcle, and before that had spent up to a quarter-century of his military career under Abdülhamid, accommodating himself in one way or another to the stagnant spirit of that despotic regime. Most of the top-ranking Anatolian commanders, on the other hand, received training as officers toward the turn of the century, when Young Turk agitation for liberal and constitutional principles was rife in the military schools. As political suspects, many of them were posted to remote assignments in the Balkans or Arabia, where they received painful object lessons in the Empire's military weakness, and where daily contact with the nationalist aspirations of the Empire's non-Turkish subjects reinforced their own nationalist sentiments. They actively participated in the thorough reorganization of the army undertaken by Young Turk and German officers in 1913–14; but further contact with German officers assigned to various Ottoman commands during the World War convinced many of them that only Turkish leadership could ultimately save the country.[44] Five of them (including Mustafa Kemal and Ali Fuad [Cebesoy] had served as military attachés in Europe, and at least two others spent varying periods on other official missions abroad. Most of them entered the war as captains or majors and had risen to the rank of colonel by 1918. At the time of the armistice only three were major generals (Galib, Fevzi (Çakmak), and Cemal (Mersinli), and seven other brigadier generals – of whom Kemal and two others had been promoted in 1916, the rest toward the end of the war).

Several eloquent statements by these youthful commanders may illustrate the spirit of nationalism which animated them. In March 1919 Yakub Şevki, faced with systematic British attempts to force Turkish evacuation of the Caucasian frontier provinces of Kars, Ardahan, and Batum, and attributing them to a general plan to occupy İstanbul and the rest of the country in clear violation of the armistice terms, said in a cable to the War Ministry:

> History has shown many times that resistance movements based on legitimate rights can force even strong states to change their aim and purpose. I consider it necessary to act, if only with this hope in mind. Otherwise compliance will result in annihilation. If it is asserted that the way of resistance is useless and leads to an abyss, at least in this way honor and dignity are preserved. The Turkish nation cannot come back to life by simply currying favor with the British. If the Turkish nation can find a way to win the favor and friendship, and hence the assistance, of the nations of the entire world, maybe then it can be saved. This, no doubt, is the way of honor, dignity, and firmness.[45]

A few years later, Cemal Pasha, former member of the wartime Young Turk triumvirate, defended the Turkish decision to enter the First World War against Russia and her allies in similar terms:

> in my view, rather than fall miserably under the yoke of the Russians, English, and French after the Russians had won, it was infinitely better to defend ourselves to the last drop of blood in the hope of freeing ourselves forever – the only alternative worthy of a brave and great nation – or at any rate to be able to say, *'Tout est perdu sauf l'honneur!'* and thus bring to a splendid close a national history which was established on honor and courage, and rich in fame and glory . . .
>
> Of course, my observations are addressed only to those who are ready to give their lives to defend their honor. The miserable creatures who are ready to endure anything if only they can prolong their wretched lives for a few days will certainly not appreciate my words.[46]

In his Six-Day Speech of 1927 Mustafa Kemal, in describing the thinking that prompted the formation of the Anatolian movement of 1919, echoed these same sentiments, expressing them in language harking back to the American War of Independence:

> The basic goal was that the Turkish nation should live in dignity and honor. This goal could only be achieved by the possession of complete independence. A nation deprived of its independence – however wealthy and prosperous it may be – is not regarded worthy, in the eyes of civilized humanity, of any treatment better than that of a slave . . . But in fact the Turk possesses honour, self-respect, and ability to a great and high degree. Rather than live in servitude it is better that such a nation should perish!
>
> Therefore: Independence or Death! This was to become the rallying cry of those who desired true salvation. Let us suppose for a moment that the application of this decision had been doomed to failure. What would have been the result? Slavery! Very well, gentlemen. In adopting the other proposals [such as that for an American mandate over Turkey] would not the result have been the same? With the difference – that a nation that defies death in its struggle for independence will be content

to make all the sacrifices required by human dignity and honor. And naturally its position in the eyes of friend and foe alike will differ from that of the abject and miserable nation which with its own hands puts the chain around its neck.[47]

And a comment by Kemal on Wilson's famous Fourteen Points, to which the nationalists referred in defining their political aims in the so-called National Pact, sharply throws into relief Kemal's conception of the relationship between might and right in history:

> I confess that I also tried to define the national border somewhat according to the humanitarian purposes of Wilson's principles. But let me make clear at once: On the basis of these humanitarian principles I defended boundaries which Turkish bayonets had already defended and laid down. Poor Wilson, he did not understand that lines which are not defended by the bayonet, by force, by honor and dignity, cannot be defended by any other principle.[48]

Organization of the Kemalist Movement

Important as are the biographical details reviewed in the preceding section, a mere group profile and its statistical analysis cannot adequately convey the intensity of the drama in which the formation of the Turkish national movement was enacted; they are also likely to obscure the decisive role which Mustafa Kemal Pasha played in that drama.

Kemal held a unique and unrivalled position among the commanders of the demobilized Ottoman army. In contrast to the dreary picture of incompetence, vainglory and disarray of the remainder of the Turkish war effort, he had built up a brilliant record of solid military accomplishment. His defense of Gallipoli against invading forces many times stronger had saved the Ottoman Empire from collapse and its capital from imminent occupation – and this at a time when Czarist Russia still stood powerful. Later he had stabilized the front in Eastern Anatolia, where many other generals had gone down in defeat, and converted the rout of Turkish armies in Syria into an orderly retreat. The defeat of 1918 seemed to justify fully his sharp condemnation of Enver and Enver's German strategic advisers.

No other military leader in 1919 could match Kemal's popularity of reputation of invincibility.[49]

The events of 1919, moreover, lead one to conclude that none of the highest army commanders, if given an opportunity for leadership in this highly delicate and at times desperate situation, could have equalled the personal courage, resoluteness, and even ruthlessness, combined with patience, foresight, and judgment, that Kemal was to display. Even Yakub Şevki, whose vigorous nationalist sentiments were quoted above, accepted the War Ministry's call to return to İstanbul, and thus relinquished the very position of potential leadership that local nationalists were urging upon him,[50] and which Kemal actively sought immediately afterward. Ali İhsan, who shortly before the armistice had allowed a large part of his army to be captured by the British, had accepted the summons to İstanbul – and ultimately to Malta – even earlier.

Unfortunately, the scanty contemporary documents that have so far come to light give little indication of how Kemal's plans took shape from the time of his recall from the Syrian front in November 1918 until his assignment to Anatolia the following May, and subsequent accounts must naturally be treated with a good deal of caution.[51] It is known that, even before his return, Kemal vainly tried to use his connections at the Sultan's place to secure the appointment of a moderately Unionist cabinet in which he would have held the crucial War portfolio[52] – a position from which Enver earlier had ruled Turkey as a virtual dictator. Somewhat later Kemal obtained a personal audience with Vahideddin.[53] There are several other references to unsuccessful attempts by Kemal to gain a position of power in the capital, whether by securing the parliamentary defeat of Tevfik Pasha's cabinet;[54] by forming a ministry under the Young Turks' dissident grand old man, Ahmed Reza;[55] or even by plans – quickly abandoned – for a *coup d'état*.[56]

In the early spring of 1919, developments were coming to a head. At the beginning of March the Freedom and Accord Party under Damad Ferid had come to power in İstanbul. In April, the victor powers gave their sanction to Greek annexation of İzmir. The Ferid government's round-up of Young Turks and British deportations of military commanders were clear signs of personal danger to Mustafa Kemal. Whether for these or other reasons, it seems that Kemal by this time was 'slowly come to the conclusion that nothing could be done in İstanbul'.[57] But just then the recall of Yakub Şevki from his

9th Army command in early April opened up a promising new opportunity. Of the three post-armistice army commands (then being converted into 'inspectorates'), the first, at İstanbul, included the Straits region, where pressure from the Allies and from an antinationalist cabinet would be irresistible. The second, at Konya, included the western and southern parts of Anatolia where Allied contingents held major rail centres, and where French military pressure from Syria (and later Greek pressure from the Aegean) would be strongest. By contrast, the 9th Army's territory in North-eastern Anatolia (roughly from the Kızılırmak to Lake Van) was almost free of Allied contingents; British and Armenian troops in the Caucacus were far weaker and had a far more precarious supply route than the British in Mosul or the French in Cilicia. Except for the line from Erzurum to the frontier, there was not a single railroad within the entire area. This lack of means of communication, together with the extreme inhospitality of much of the terrain, imposed great obstacles to any defense build-up, but far more formidable ones to any sudden attack.

Kemal's plans for heading a resistance movement in the Eastern Anatolian mountains must have taken final shape toward the middle of April. The General Staff's policy of posting its best commanders to Anatolia, Kemal's own connections at the palace dating back to his trip to Germany with Vahideddin, and a fortuitous acquaintance within the Ferid cabinet[58] enabled him to secure appointment as inspector of the 9th Army by the end of the month. Recent complaints of political agitation in the area and of friction between Muslims and non-Muslims along the Black Sea coast provided a welcome justification for conferring upon the 9th Army inspectorate broad civil powers, enabling it to give instructions to governors and subgovernors in its own region and to communicate directly with those immediately adjoining.[59] When, on May 19, the British representative, General Milne, asked for an explanation of why a new inspector with a large staff had been sent to an army command that had officially been abolished, Kemal and his entourage of 18 carefully chosen officers were just landing in Samsun. Another three weeks passed before the War Office, at Milne's insistence, requested Kemal's return on the first steamer; and it was not until July 20 that the İstanbul government, in view of Kemal's increasingly open defiance, terminated his powers.[60]

The two months' head start that Kemal had thus gained enabled him to lay the foundations of a well-organized nation-wide resistance movement. Kemal had become the first general to take up the nationalist cause courageously. The difference that his arrival on the scene made has been well summed up by Colonel Bıyıklıoğlu: 'Mustafa Kemal Pasha in Anatolia headed off a situation where every commander would have acted separately and according to his own lights. He united all front commanders and the civil and military authorities in Anatolia under his energetic leadership and in the pursuit of a definite national ideal; thus he prevented anarchy.'[61]

Kemal's first endeavour was to build a position of strength from which to resist any Allied scheme of partition or dismemberment of the defeated Empire within the armistice boundaries. Effective resistance clearly presupposed the co-operation of organized civilian groups. An army with a hostile or indifferent population in its rear would have little energy left to fight the external foe. While Allied officers in charge of supervising the demobilization provisions of the armistice kept their eyes fixed on the movements of army commanders and military units, civilian groups often enjoyed greater freedom of action.[62] Concerted agitation by nationalist committees, moreover, could be used in an attempt to force a more resolute policy on the Sultan and, if he should prove receptive, to strengthen his hand in dealings with the Allies. The experience of the Damad Ferid cabinets proved how vulnerable a government divorced from popular sentiment would be to foreign pressure. Considerations both of prudence and of democratic principle would make the Allies more circumspect in dealing with a movement based on strong and articulate popular support.

The military phase of the nationalist build-up in Anatolia continued to enjoy the full, if covert, support of the War Office and the General Staff in İstanbul. The Karakol ('Police Precinct') and Mim Mim societies, which took charge of the lively arms traffic from İstanbul to Anatolia, were largely staffed by demobilized officers[63] and are said to have been direct continuations of Enver's Special Organization.[64] Earlier, the War Ministry had confirmed plans for the transfer of the 20th Army Corps, under Ali Fuad (Cebesoy), from the main Anatolian rail line at Ulukışla to a more favourable Central Anatolian location at Ankara. Now, after Kemal's arrival, Ali Fuad Pasha (who was officially under the 2nd, rather than the 9th, Army Inspectorate) offered full co-operation to his old friend Kemal, thereby extending the nationalist sphere of control 200 miles westward. In the spring of 1920, as nationalists, loyalist troops of the

Sultan, and Greek invaders were readying themselves for the first major campaign of the War of Independence, Kemal's control was extended farther west and southwest to the 13th and 14th Corps at Bursa and Konya – but not until after a set of lengthy deliberations at Kemal's Ankara headquarters, to which each of the Corps commanders was brought under armed escort tactfully disguised as an honour guard.[65]

Nor did the civilian organizations which supported the nationalist resistance in Anatolia have to be created anew in a complete void. The Young Turk decade had initiated an unprecedented broadening of the circle of active political participants – a process that was to continue and indeed to find its first culmination in the War of Independence. Political rallies had become an accepted part of public life in the capital and even in the major provincial centres.[66] The circulation of newspapers had vastly increased, and CUP party locals had been founded even in the smaller country towns.

There is considerable evidence that the Union and Progress leaders in the closing weeks of the World War tried to transform this loose network of popular organizations into the nucleus of a national resistance movement. Enver in 1917 and 1918 had concentrated some of the Empire's best remaining troops on the northeastern front. His immediate purpose was to take advantage of the military vacuum in the wake of the Czarist collapse for operations in Caucasia and, beyond that, in Turkestan, focus of Panturanian dreams. But he also seems to have hoped to prepare a centre of resistance in Eastern Anatolia in case the Empire lost the war on the Balkan and Arab fronts. In this connection he is said to have envisaged a provisional Turkish government at Baku.[67] As a result of the Moudros armistice and subsequent Allied pressure, Ottoman forces were required to evacuate not only Transcaucasia, but also the Kars-Ardahan border region. But Yakub Şevki Pasha delayed his evacuation of Kars by two months, and in the interval civilian and military authorities jointly encouraged the formation of a provisional Turkish government for Southwest Caucasia with headquarters at Kars.[68]

Similar developments took place in Eastern Thrace. As early as September 1918 Talât, judging the war lost after a visit to Berlin, urged his friends in Edirne 'to found a popular organization'. Immediately before his flight in November he gave more specific instructions to Faik (Kaltakkıran), Unionist leader from Edirne, who promptly organized the Society for the Defense of Rights of Thrace and Paşaeli.[69] Other Defense of Rights societies were founded in early December for İzmir and for Eastern Anatolia (the latter at first with headquarters in İstanbul) and these were to become the prototype of numerous similar patriotic resistance societies that spread throughout Anatolia in 1919.[70] Popular outrage at the Greek landings in İzmir in May 1919 and the gradual French advance from Syria into Southern Turkey swelled the ranks of the movement. Everywhere former Unionist politicians and army officers seem to have co-operated with local notables in forming this network of organizations. The movement behind the Kars provisional government was composed of 'local landowners, lawyers, and school teachers, reinforced by some Muslim officers of the former Russian Imperial Army'.[71] Later, İzzet Pasha was to characterize the entire Anatolian movement in strikingly similar terms as one 'made up for the most part of military commanders and their staffs, of country notables and landowners, and of intellectuals'.[72]

The successful Anatolian movement of 1919–20 in many ways resembled the abortive irredentist operations in Western Thrace in 1913. The Thrace movement had attempted to regain by popular protest and guerrilla activity what had been lost on the battlefield and at the conference table. In view of Allied partition plans, the whole of Anatolia was now in danger of becoming a single irredenta and thus provided ample room for operations in a twilight zone between diplomacy, planned popular uprising, guerrilla, and open warfare. The very slogans of 'national defense' and 'national forces' which now received wide currency in Anatolia had been first been used in Western Thrace in 1913; and several veterans of that campaign reappeared on the scene in 1918–1919. Among these were Cihangiroğlu İbrahim (Aydın), who headed the Kars provisional government; Hüsrev Sami (Kızıldoğan), a close friend of Kemal from their Syrian days and now a member of the Representative Committee elected by the Kemalist Congress of Sivas; the Circassian brothers Reşid and Edhem, guerrilla leaders in Thrace and now in Anatolia; İhsan (Eryavuz), the Ankara government's first Minister of Marine, and others.[73]

Generally there was a greater continuity of personnel between the Young Turk and Kemalist periods than is often acknowledged[74] – and it was this circumstance more than anything else that led to the persistent suspicion of contemporary critics that the Kemalist movement was a continuation of the Union and Progress war effort in a different guise.[75] But it should not be overlooked that Kemal had ample reason to fear the rivalry of the exiled Young Turk leaders: Enver, for one, seemed poised to take charge in Anatolia as soon as Kemal should suffer any serious reversal at the fronts.[76] A more balanced examination would indicate that Kemal, while defining his own aims and means, made use of all the rudimentary organization and of much of the experienced personnel left behind by the fugitive Unionists. The location of the first Kemalist parliament may be taken to symbolize this relationship. The Grand National Assembly convened in the former Ankara headquarters of the Union and Progress Party – not because of any predilection for overt association with the discredited Unionists, but rather because in all of Ankara this was the only large building available for the purpose at the time.

Disengagement of the Military

The personal and organizational connections between Unionists and Kemalists should not be allowed, therefore, to obscure their fundamental differences in outlook and purpose. Nothing perhaps exemplifies that contrast better than the divergent development of civil-military relations under the two regimes. The Young Turks, swept into power as champions of constitutional and parliamentary government, proceeded to concentrate power increasingly in military hands. Both the professional integrity of the army and the constitutional integrity of the political process suffered severely as a result. The Kemalist movement, starting from a military apex, worked hard to provide itself with a solid civilian base. During the War of Independence, it not only registered striking military successes in the most trying of circumstances but also gave Turkey its first genuine experience of government by discussion.

The elaboration of civilian institutions of government in Anatolia preceded even the launching of full-scale military operations, and later went apace with it. Immediately upon arrival in Eastern Anatolia in 1919, Kemal made plans to hold a national congress that would consolidate the many local Defense of Rights and Rejection of Annexation societies. Learning that a similar congress had already been scheduled on a more limited regional scale in Eastern Anatolia, he agreed to hold both meetings *seriatim*, one at Erzurum and the other at Sivas.[77] It was at the Sivas Congress that the resistance groups merged into a nationwide Society for the Defense of Rights of Anatolia and Rumelia (i.e., Asiatic and European Turkey). The resignation of Damad Ferid Pasha and the announcement of new elections by his successor (October 1919) gave rise to temporary hopes that the nationalist programme might be accepted as the Sultan's official policy. Vigorous and skilful electioneering by the Defense of Rights societies, often supported by local army commanders,[78] produced a solid nationalist majority. The new House of Representatives in İstanbul lost little time in adopting the Kemalist 'National Pact', which stoutly asserted the right to national independence of the 'Ottoman-Muslim' (i.e., Turkish and Kurdish) parts of the Empire. With the reinforcement of the Allied occupation of İstanbul, the deportation of leading nationalists, and the return of Damad Ferid to the İstanbul premiership, the focus of nationalist activity shifted entirely to Ankara, where, in April 1920, a Grand National Assembly convened at Kemal's invitation.

In the complex struggle which Kemal now faced, he systematically set out to minimize and postpone internal differences while taking on his external enemies one at a time – uniting his followers and dividing his antagonists. The Allied occupation of İstanbul provided a convenient pretext for carrying on the nationalist struggle in the name of the Sultan, and for discounting the Sultan's antinationalist acts and proclamations as having been obtained under duress. The official statements that emanated from Ankara during this period were all couched in terms of monarchist loyalty, and frequently blended a religious-Muslim with a nationalist-Turkish appeal.[79] Simultaneously Kemal tried to make use of vague pro-Communist and pan-Islamic leanings among some of his followers in a bid for moral and material support from Russia and from foreign Muslims, particularly in India.

In the meantime jealousy and indecision among the Allies allowed Kemal to concentrate his slim but growing resources on one front at a time, and diplomatic recognition went hand in hand with military success. Kemalist armies defeated the Armenians in the east and repelled the French advance in the south (1920–21). Bekir Sami in London negotiated separate agreements with France and Italy, while Ali Fuad (Cebesoy) in Moscow signed a formal friendship treaty with Soviet Russia (March 1921). Only the Greeks now continued the anti-Kemalist campaign. By the end of 1922 the last shattered remnants of the invading Greek armies embarked across the Aegean, and the Allies arranged for the speedy evacuation of their troops (and also of the Sultan) from İstanbul. The following year the peace treaty of Lausanne provided recognition for that national independence which had been so tenaciously asserted on the battlefield.[80]

It was during the years of the War of Independence that a dividing line between civil and military institutions first was drawn. The experience with Enver's wartime regime, which based advancement in the army on political intrigue while laying the civilian administration open to interference by corrupt army personnel, had left Kemal and his associates with a set of strong convictions as to the desirability of a clear separation of the two spheres. As early as 1909, Mustafa Kemal at a Unionist Party congress had advocated the withdrawal of army officers from partisan politics, and later Kemal was to state categorically:

> 'Commanders, while thinking of and carrying out the duties and requirements of the army, must take care not to let political considerations influence their judgment. They must not forget that there are other officials whose duty it is to think of the political aspects. A soldier's duty cannot be performed with talk and politicking . . .'[81]

But specific developments during the War of Independence and later helped to crystallize the army's withdrawal from politics. In July 1919, Kemal, having exhausted all subterfuge in resisting the İstanbul government's orders to return to the capital, had announced his resignation from the army. He forthrightly stated that he had found that to continue his beloved military career would hinder him in his service to the nation, and that he therefore would continue the struggle 'in the bosom of the nation as an individual fighter for the cause'.[82] The immediate practical effect of this step was only slight: both Kâzim Karabekir, whom İstanbul had designated as his replacement, and other commanders continued to follow his directives; and soon the Erzurum and Sivas congresses, by making Kemal the head of their Representative Committee, placed him, in effect, at the head of a provisional nationalist government. But the moral significance of Kemal's decision was immense. It testified to his conviction that an army career was not an end in itself, but must at every point be subordinated to wider considerations of service to the nation; and that a time might come when political and military functions could not legitimately or effectively be combined in the same person.

Somewhat later, in December 1920, the arrogance and insubordination of Çerkes Edhem, commander of the nationalists' irregular cavalry, precipitated a showdown with the regular army. The result was the complete integration of these guerrilla forces into the army's more disciplined command structure. Edhem's subsequent treason did much to destroy the legend of the *komitadji* – half bandit and half national hero – which the early Kemalists had inherited from the Macedonian Young Turk movement and which, while its spell lasted, blurred any dividing line between civilian and military authority.

The Grand National Assembly of 1920–23 included a large number of higher officers on active duty, but in practice they were kept fully occupied at the front or at headquarters in Ankara. Kemal's energies, on the other hand, were largely devoted to careful manoeuvring in the proud, faction-ridden, and intractable Assembly. Only during the critical phases of the military contest with Greece did Kemal at the Assembly's insistence, assume personal direction of operations, and the cautious legislators in each case renewed his powers as Commander in Chief for only three months. The special Independence Tribunals with which the Ankara regime established to try cases of treason or rebellion were no courts-martial but rather civilian tribunals composed of members of the Grand National Assembly. The provisional constitution of 1921, the law proclaiming the Republic in 1923, and the definitive constitution of 1924 all confirmed the principle of legislative supremacy which the political situation of 1920 had at first made mandatory. Kemal, to be sure, induced the Assembly to dispense with its original method of electing and dismissing individual ministers by majority vote and to adopt instead a cabinet system based on presidential selection and collective responsibility to the legislature. But even as President of the Republic he could not persuade the Assembly to surrender such normal executive powers as dissolution of the legislature or the granting of amnesties and pardons. In 1924 the Chief of the General Staff was excluded from the cabinet to which he had earlier belonged. In 1923 the earlier Defense of Rights Society was converted into the Republican People's Party, which for the next 27 years was to control the destiny of the Republic.

A growing cleavage between Kemal and his earliest political and military associates precipitated the formal divorce of the military from political activity. Shortly after the proclamation of the Republic, Kemal, suspecting an incipient plot against him among some of his army commanders, obtained passage of a law that made membership in the National Assembly incompatible with active military service. The generals who sided with Kemal left parliament and retained their military assignments. The dissidents who preferred to retain their legislative seats resigned, or were removed, from their army commands;[83] they were to furnish the nucleus of the Progressive Republican Party (November 1924), the first organized opposition under the Republic.

Although many details of the contest between Kemal and the Progressives still remain obscure, the nature of the underlying tension may be gathered from the personnel of the opposition group. There were generals Kâzi Karabekir, Ali Fuad [Cebesoy], and Refet [Bele]; there were Rauf [Orbay], Bekir Sami, Colonel Kara Vasıf and Dr Adnan (Adıvar) – in short, the most prominent military and civilian associates who had joined Kemal in the crucial days of 1919. There had been a growing estrangement between Kemal and these old comrades-in-arms, due generally to Kemal's increasing tendency toward purely personal leadership and to his friends' reluctance to accept such leadership without discussion. ('Who are your apostles now?' Ali Fuad once asked, and Kemal replied airily: 'I have no apostles. Those who serve the country and the nation and show merit and ability for service, those are apostles.'[84]) There also were more specific irritations. Rauf and Kemal had differed on the tactics to be applied within the last İstanbul House of Representatives (where Rauf was the nationalist floor leader), and Rauf's exile in Malta had kept him out of touch with the Anatolian movement in its most formative stage. There had been further friction between Rauf and İsmet (İnönü) when the former served as Prime Minister and the latter as chief negotiator at Lausanne. Ali Fuad had been relieved of his command of the Western front after an initial military setback. Bekir Sami's London agreement of 1921 had been rejected by the Assembly because of a number of economic concessions that it made to France. Rauf and others considered Kemal's move to abolish the Caliphate precipitate and unfortunate. Another group of Progressives comprised Cavid, İsmail Canbulat and Ahmed Şükrü, who had served in Talât's cabinet of 1917–18 and re-entered politics in 1923 and who, after the deaths of Talât, Cemal and Enver in 1921–22, probably were the most prominent surviving ex-Unionist leaders. In short, the Progressive Party included all political figures who might have become serious rivals to Kemal or who might in some respects be considered his equals. Among the top-ranking generals in particular, only the late arrivals from İstanbul – Fevzi (Çakmak), İsmet (İnönü), and, with some hesitation, Cevad (Çobanlı) – sided with Kemal in the 1924 dispute.[85]

Kemal was about to embark on his resolute programme of sweeping Westernization, including the closing of religious schools and orders, the substitution of European codes for traditional precepts of Muslim law, and the replacement of Arabic by Latin letters.[86] His tactic was to announce these measures at some carefully chosen moment of suspense, and to carry them through rapidly without giving the potentially overwhelming opposition a chance to crystallize. In preparing for this rapid reform effort, he preferred to surround himself with followers junior to him in prestige and experience, who were willing to give him unquestioning loyalty. The suppression of the Progressive Party early in 1925 confirmed the break with his old associates. Although the dispute between Kemal and this early opposition was not, on either side, a military bid for power, it had the effect of removing from the political scene nearly all the military leaders whose personal and political stature could have enabled them to stand up to Kemal.

Developments Under the Republic

The exclusion of officers on active duty from any formal role in politics which was laid down in the early years of the Kemalist movement has been maintained to the present. Kemal Atatürk and İsmet İnönü chose to administer the country as civilian rather than as military rulers. They were not seen in uniform after the end of the War of Independence. They drew their political support from the Republican People's Party, the Grand National Assembly, and, increasingly, the bureaucracy.

On the other hand, the separation of military and civilian spheres under the Republic has never been complete or watertight. Kemal's and İsmet's military prestige was the best guarantee that the armed forces would be content with the non-political role these leaders assigned to them. In return, Fevzi Çakmak, Ankara Chief of Staff for a quarter-century (1921–1944), by virtue of his early association with Kemal and İsmet enjoyed great autonomy in his handling of military affairs. Military considerations are known to have loomed large in the shaping of the Republic's economic development programme in the 1930's. Although no longer a cabinet minister, the

Chief of Staff regularly appears to have attended cabinet meetings at which supreme matters of war and peace were discussed, and it may well be that military spokesmen were consulted on other occasions as well. At the regional level, division or corps commanders during the 1920's at times combined their military posts with the governorship of frontier provinces, much as they had in Ottoman days.[87] The proclamation of states of siege for important regions and prolonged periods (e.g., the Kurdish Provinces after the uprisings of the 1920's and 1930's and İstanbul during the Second World War) similarly put regional army commanders in charge of civil administration. To this day charges of high treason, including Communist conspiracy, are generally tried in camera by military tribunals.

Furthermore, officers after their resignation or retirement from the army have continued to be recruited into parliament, the cabinet, and other high civilian offices – although the proportion of them in public life has diminished steadily since the War of Independence. The ratio of former army officers in the Grand National Assembly, which was about one-sixth in 1920, still stood at about one-eighth in 1943, but went down to one-twentieth after the Democratic landslide of 1950. Of the twenty-five nationalist commanders in the War of Independence included in our earlier statistical profile, as many as 20 entered parliament subsequently, nearly all of them after retirement.[88] Since 1923 men of military background have served as President of the Republic (17 years), Prime Minister (16 years), Minister of Defense (16 years), of Public Works (15 years), of Communications (9 years), and in other cabinet posts. The first ministry in which no ex-officers participated was that of Hasan Saka in 1948. Former officers also were prominent among the Ankara government's early diplomats.[89] Marshal Çakmak, forced into retirement early in 1944, was returned to the Assembly as an independent Democrat in 1946, and a few years later became the leader of the newly formed religious-conservative Nation Party. In the 1954 elections, colonels and generals who had served with the Turkish Brigade in Korea figured prominently on several party tickets.

Despite this continued recruitment of ex-officers into legislative and cabinet positions, the supremacy of the civilian arm over the military has never to date been challenged in the thirty-six years of the Turkish Republic. More particularly, Turkey has been spared the recurrent military coups so familiar to the rest of the Near East.

*

The history of the Ottoman Empire and of the Turkish War of Independence goes a long way toward explaining both the decisive role which the officer corps played in the formation of the Republic and its subsequent disengagement from direct or overt political activity. From the origins of Islam to the Young Turk dictatorship of Enver Pasha, the importance of the military mounted steadily. The Ottoman Empire rose by the sword and fell by the sword. Both its chronic ailment from the late seventeenth century onward and its mortal crisis of 1918 were brought on by military defeat. Both, at the most obvious level, were military problems. Hence the army became Ottoman society's natural instrument for effecting a regeneration. The remedy, it turned out, was the creation of the Turkish Republic.

The imminent threat of national extinction which Kemal and his associates faced after 1918 was a situation without parallel in previous Turkish history, and it resulted in a radical departure from both Ottoman and Young Turk precedents. The immediate target of the Young Turk revolutionaries of 1908 was a series of internal antagonists – Abdülhamid, with his network of spies and palace retainers, the counterrevolution of 1909 and various dissidents in the Young Turks' own ranks. On all sides the movement was caught in the contradictions between its programme and its performance. The CUP's Turkish nationalism contributed decisively to eroding the earlier ideal of Ottoman brotherhood; its ruthless partisanship gave a hollow ring to its professions of liberal constitutionalism. Meanwhile external involvements such as the Balkan and World wars were deliberately exploited to suppress opposition and to enhance the power of Unionist leaders and of officers like Enver. Yet the Unionists' grandiose foreign adventures only served to underline the contrast between the Empire's patent weakness and the pan-Turanian-pan-Islamic romanticism of its leaders.

Mustafa Kemal, under the impact of the defeat of 1918, resolutely cast aside all dreams of imperial glory – whether of the Ottoman, Panturkish, or Panislamic variety. While domestic failures had propelled the Young Turks into ill-calculated foreign and military gambles, considerations of military and foreign policy prompted the Kemalists to strengthen the domestic cohesion and civilian organization of the Turkish body politic. The Young Turks measurably hastened the collapse of the Empire which they had set out to save with such swashbuckling bravado. Kemal, disposing of far slimmer material resources but realistically limiting Turkish political aims, tapped latent moral energies which enabled him to erect an enduring political structure. The Young Turks, proclaiming the restoration of the Empire's civilian constitution, rapidly converted it into a military dictatorship. Kemal's movement, born of the need for military defense at a moment of supreme national crisis, fashioned a set of civilian institutions to which the military were increasingly subordinated.

Notes

[1] The earlier coup of Urabi Pasha in Egypt was suppressed in an embryonic stage by the British occupation of 1882. For a general survey of Near Eastern military coups since that time, see Majid Khadduri, 'The Role of the Military in Middle East Politics', *American Political Science Review*, XLVII (1953), pp. 511–24; reprinted as 'The Army Officer: His Role in Middle Eastern Politics', in Sydney N. Fisher, ed., *Social Forces in the Middle East*, Ithaca, NY, 1955, pp. 162–84.

[2] Throughout this article, family names adopted by Turks in accordance with a law of 1934 are given in square brackets. Kemal's last name was bestowed on him by special action of the Grand National Assembly.

[3] Cf. Majid Khadduri, *War and Peace in the Law of Islam*, Baltimore, 1955.

[4] Cf. Paul Wittek, *The Rise of the Ottoman Empire*, London, 1938.

[5] The phrase is that of Albert H. Lybyer (*The Government of the Ottoman Empire*, Cambridge, Mass., 1933). For a more recent survey of Ottoman military and civil administration up to the eighteenth century, see Hamilton A. R. Gibb and H. L. Bowen, *Islamic Society and the West*, I, Part i–ii, London, 1950–1957.

[6] In Lewis V. Thomas' apt phrase; see L. V. Thomas and R. N. Frye, *The United States and Turkey and Iran*, Cambridge, MA, 1951, p. 51. On the Ottoman reform attempts, see the suggestive interpretation given in the many writings of Arnold J. Toynbee (e.g., *The World and the West*, London, 1953, ch. 3; and A. J. Toynbee and K. P. Kirkwood, *Turkey*, London, 1926), and Bernard Lewis, 'Turkey: Westernization,' in Gustave E. von Grunebaum, ed., *Unity and Variety in Muslim Civilization*, Chicago, 1955, pp. 311–31.

[7] On the rise of Turkish national consciousness, cf. Bernard Lewis, 'History-Writing and Nationalist Revival in Turkey,' *Middle Eastern Affairs*, IV (1953), pp. 218–27.

[8] The exile movement is described in detail by Ernest Edmondson Ramsaur, Jr., *The Young Turks: Prelude to the Revolution of 1908*, Princeton, NJ, 1957.

[9] A detailed examination of the internal political development of the Ottoman Empire from 1908 until 1918 remains one of the urgent desiderata

of modern historiography. Ahmed Emin [Yalman], *Turkey in the World War*, New Haven, CT, 1930, may serve as an introduction for the English-speaking reader. Yusuf Hikmet Bayur, *Türk İnkılâbi Tarihi*, İstanbul and Ankara, 1940—, emphasizes international politics and also treats the period largely in terms of what it contributed to later developments under the Republic. Ali Fuad Türkgeldi's modest, conscientious, and detached memoirs, *Görüp İşittiklerim*, 2nd ed., Ankara, 1951, are limited mainly to the small, if crucial, segment of public affairs of which he had official knowledge as secretary to the Sultan. The Turkish war effort is thoroughly and competently treated by M. Larcher, *La Guerre Turque dans la Guerre Mondiale*, Paris, 1926; see also the memoirs of the Austrian military plenipotentiary, Joseph Pomiankowski, *Der Zusammenbruch des ottomanischen Reiches*, Leiptzig, 1928. Finally, Uriel Heyd, *Foundations of Turkish Nationalism*, London, 1950, systematically examines the philosophical ideas of the leading Union and Progress theorist, Ziya Gökalp.

[10] Depositions had been frequent in Ottoman history. The earlier ones, however, had been due to intrigues in the palace and the capital; Abdülhamid's was the first prompted by popular and partisan action. Cf. Anthony D. Alderson, *The Structure of the Ottoman Dynasty*, Oxford, 1956, pp. 71f.

[11] Türkgeldi, *op. cit., passim.*

[12] For a detailed and well-documented account of the Western Thrace episode, see Tevfik Bıyıklıoğlu, *Trakyada Millî Mücadele*, Ankara, 1955–1956, I, pp. 75ff.; cf. Djemal Pasha, *Memories of a Turkish Statesman*, London, 1922, pp. 49ff., and [Ahmed İzzet Furgaç], *Denkwürdigkeiten des Marschalls İzzet Pascha*, tr. by Karl Klinghardt, Leipzig, 1927, p. 215. A decade earlier Mustafa Kemal is said to have been greatly impressed by the course in guerrilla tactics offered at the General Staff College by Trabzonlu Nuri (see Enver Behnan Şapolyo, *Kemal Atatürk ve Millî Mücadele Tarihi*, 3rd ed., İstanbul, 1958, pp. 54f.).

[13] On the formation of the Special Organization, see Bıyıklıoğlu, *op. cit.*, pp. 135, 193) refers to General Staff preparations for popular resistance in lost areas such as Macedonia and Libya. On the Army of Islam and its operations in the Caucasus, see Tevfik Bıyıklıoğlu, *Osmanlı ve Türk Doğu Hadut Politikasi*, İstanbul, 1958, p. 18; W. E. D. Allen and Paul Muratoff, *Caucasian Battlefields*, Cambridge, Eng., 1953, pp. 468, 479, 490ff.; and Pomiankowski, *op. cit.*, pp. 172f., 388. On Nuri [Killigil], see Samet Ağaoğlu, *Babamın Arkadaşları*, İstanbul, 1959, pp. 30–34. The fullest account yet published of the Special Organization, by one of Askerî's successors, unfortunately bears all the earmarks of historical sensationalism rather than of detached reporting. See Hüsameddin Ertürk, *İki Devrin Perde Arkası*, ed. by Samih Nafiz Tansu, İstanbul, 1957.

[14] When asked by a journalist in 1922, 'How did you win this victory?' Mustafa Kemal is said to have replied, 'With the telegraph wires.' (Şapolyo,

ARMY AND FOUNDING OF THE TURKISH REPUBLIC 201

op. cit., p. 349.) For details of the struggle which developed in the summer of 1919 between Kemalist forces and the İstanbul government over control of the telegraph stations, see Ali Fuad Cebesoy, *Millî Mücadele Hâtıraları*, İstanbul, 1953, p. 149.

[15] Cevat Dursunoğlu, *Millî Mücadelede Erzurum*, Ankara, 1946, p. 27.
[16] Gemal Abdel Nasser, *Egypt's Liberation*, Washington, DC, 1955, p. 31.
[17] Türkgeldi, *op. cit.*, pp. 274f.
[18] See, e.g., Cebesoy, *Millî Mücadele*, pp. *34ff*.
[19] Tarik Z. Tunaya, *Türkiyede Siyasî Partiler*, İstanbul, 1952, pp. 413f., quoting Kemal's letter of January 1919 to the İstanbul paper *Söz*. In October 1919 Kemal, when asked, 'Is it possible that the Unionists will influence the National Forces?' replied: 'Our National Forces are under the influence only of the nation and of the supreme national aims. Aside from this no individual or society can exercise any influence upon them.; ([Kemal Atatürk], *Nutuk*, İstanbul, 1934, III, pp. 169f., document 144.) Four years later he was to state more candidly: 'We were all members [of the Society of Union and Progress] . . . Most of the members of that society and of the Renewal Party . . . joined, or participated in, the Society for the Defense of Rights of Anatolia and Rumelia . . .' (Kemal Atatürk, *Söylev ve Demeçler*, İstanbul-Ankara, 1945–1954, III, p. 62.) And earlier he had declared, 'If there must needs be some Unionism in this business, then the entire nation stands accused of Unionism.; (*Ibid.*, III, p. 2.)
[20] German translation of oath in A. Fischer, 'Der türkische Nationalismus and der Sturz des dritten Kabinetts Damad Ferid Pascha', *Der neue Orient*, VII, No. 3 (1920), p. 98.
[21] Türkgeldi, *op. cit.*, p. 176.
[22] Halide Edib, *The Turkish Ordeal*, New York, 1928, p. 39. Similarly İzzet Pasha was to recall of the time of his premiership: 'The Committee of Union and Progress, despite its many faults and failures, still was a force not to be neglected in the country as a whole and in İstanbul in particular. All the police officers [were] their own people . . .' (Quoted by İbnülemin Mahmud Kemal İnal, *Osmanlı Devrinde Son Sadrıazamlar*, İstanbul, 1940–1953, p. 1983.)
[23] Quoted in *ibid*, p. 1962.
[24] On İzzet's relations with the Unionists, see Furgaç, *op. cit.*, pp. 202, 215, 217, and *passim*.
[25] The target of Kemal's sharpest criticism was General von Falkenhayn, his superior as commander of the *Yıldırım* group of armies on the Syrian front. The memorandum was first made public in the İstanbul paper *Tasviri Efkâr* during the 1919 election campaign. It is reprinted in Hüseyin Hüsnü Emir [Erkilet], *Yıldırım* (supplement to *Mecmua-yi Askeriyye*, İstanbul, 1337 [i.e., 1921]), pp. 78ff. A number of related documents have recently been published by Hikmet Bayur, 'Mustafa Kemal'ın Falkenhayn'la Çalışmasıyle İlgili Henüz Yayınlanmamış Bir Raporu,' *Belleten*, XX (1956), pp. 619–32.

[26] See [Reşid Pasha], *Reşit Paşa'mn hatıraları*, ed. by Cevdet R. Yularkıran, İstanbul, 1939, p. 13.

[27] On the leadership and program of the two Freedom and Accord parties, see Tunaya, *Türkiyede Siyasî Partiler*, pp. 315-44, 447-56.

[28] Among these may be named the nationalist writers Rıza Nur, Ahmed Ferid [Tek], and Akçuraoğlu Yusuf; the prominent İstanbul lawyer Celâleddin Ârif, the last speaker of the Ottoman House of Representatives before its dissolution in March 1920; Nihad Reşad [Belger], who served as one of the first diplomatic representatives of the Ankara government; and Cami [Baykurt], former Undersecretary of the Interior and co-founder in December 1918 of the Ottoman Defense of Rights Society of İzmir. In the Ankara cabinet of 1920, Ârif, Cami, Ferid, and Rıza Nur served, respectively, as Minister of Justice, Interior, Finance, and Education. On the earlier party affiliations of these men, see *ibid.*, pp. 239, 244, 290, 358.

[29] See Cebesoy, *Millî Mücadele*..., pp. 49, 77, 84f., 110f., 143; *Açıksözcü Hüsnü, İstiklâl Harbinde Kastamonu*, Kastamonu, 1933, pp. 13ff.; Hasan Umur and Adil Pasin, *Samsun'da Müdafaai Hukuk*, İstanbul, 1944, p. 9. For Sivas we have the governor's own, naïvely candid, testimony: Reşid Pasha, *op. cit.*, passim.

[30] Atatürk, *Nutuk*, I, pp. 27ff. It should be added that Ali Galib was a former colonel on the General Staff.

[31] Cf. *Tarih Vesikaları*, I, No. 16 (August 1955), pp. 7ff.

[32] Cf. Nami Malkoç, *920 Yılının Kurtuluş Savaşları* (Askerî Mecmua Tarih kismi, No. 48) İstanbul, 1937, pp. 33ff.

[33] On plans to make İzzet Pasha Prince of Albania in 1913, see İnal, *op. cit.*, p. 1979, and Furgaç, *op. cit.*, p. 231.

On Bekir Sami's descent, see Allen and Muratoff, *op. cit.*, pp. 546f. His father, Musa Kundakov, Czarist and later Ottoman general, in 1865, had led a large group of Ossetian and Chechen refugees from the Caucasus to the Tokat region of North-Central Anatolia. Orbay's father, Admiral Mehmed Muzaffer Pasha, likewise had immigrated from the Caucasus. The İstanbul cabinets included some Circassians who took a moderately benevolent attitude toward the Anatolian cause – such as Salih Hulûsi [Kezrak] Pasha, Premier for three weeks early in 1920 and repeatedly Minister of Marine, whose father, Dilâver Pasha, had commanded a Circassian auxiliary corps in the Ottoman-Russian war of 1877 (İnal, *op. cit.*, p. 2118); and Ahmed Abuk Pasha, Minister of War and of Works in 1919-20. Other Circassians, such as War Minister Ömer Yaver Pasha, who was to accompany Sultan Vahideddin into exile, were known for their antagonism to the nationalist cause.

[34] Türkgeldi, *op. cit.*, p. 211. Marshal Mehmed Şakır, the minister in question, died two months later, in June 1919, at the age of 65, while serving as minister without portfolio.

[35] Ibid., p. 163.
[36] İnal, op. cit., p. 1735.
[37] Four other commanders of Ottoman armies or army groups had been Germans. Of these, Field Marshal Colmar von der Goltz died in 1916, whereas Liman von Sanders, Kress von Kressenstein, and von Falkenhayn (along with Enver's deputy during the closing months of the war, von Seeckt) left Turkey by the end of 1918. None of these is included in the above summary or in Table I.
[38] On Enver's final days, see Ahmed Zeki Velidi [Togan], *Bugünkü Türkistan ve Yakın Mazisi* (old Turkish script), Cairo, 1940, pp. 408–38; idem, *Bugünkü Türkili Basmatchis (1917–1924)*, Paris, 1928. On his attempt to return to Anatolia, Sami Sabit Karaman, *Trabzon ve Kars Hâtıralart: İstiklâl Mücadelesi ve Enver Pasha*, İstanbul, 1949; and Ali Fuad Cebesoy, *Siyasî Hâtıraları*, İstanbul, 1957, pp. 25f. On Halil, see Gotthard Jäschke and Erich Pritsch, *Die Türkei seit dem Weltkriege: Geschichtskalender, 1918–1928*, Berlin, 1929, p. 19; Larcher, op. cit., p. 665; Jäschke, 'Beiträge', pp. 47f. On Cemal's and Halil's mediation between Moscow and Ankara, see Ali Fuad Cebesoy,, *Moskova Hâtıraları*, İstanbul, 1955, passim. On Vehib and his adventurous career abroad (including service in Ethiopia against the Italians in 1935–36), see Jäschke and Pritsch, op. cit., pp. 15, 34; Larcher, op. cit., pp. 223, 674; Allen and Muratoff, op. cit., p. 375; Gövsa, op. cit., p. 397; and *Oriente Moderno*, XX (1940), p. 52.
[39] Ali İhsan Sabis, *Harb Hâtıralarım*, v, İstanbul, 1952, pp. 24, 34ff.
[40] The release of prisoners from Malta had begun as early as April 1921. Among the earlier returnees were the poet Ziya Gökalp, and Ali Fethi [Okyar], a close friend of Mustafa Kemal and Interior Minister at the time of armistice and later in Ankara. Of those exchanged in November, ten asked to be repatriated to İstanbul, the rest to Anatolia (see Açıksözcü, op. cit., pp. 105ff., who lists 59 in all; and Nurettin Peker, *1918–1923 İstiklâl Savaşının Vesika ve Resimleri . . . İnebolu ve Kastamonu Havalisi*, İstanbul, 1955, p. 384, who gives only 55 names). The latter included, in addition to the three generals mentioned above, Hüseyin Rauf [Orbay], who had been the nationalist floor leader in the İstanbul parliament of 1920, and Colonel Kara Vasıf, chief Anatolian representative in İstanbul in 1919–1920.
[41] See Rahmi Apak, *İstiklâl Savaşında Garp Cephesi Nasıl Kuruldu?*, İstanbul, 1942, p. 45 (commanders to Anatolia); İnal, op. cit., p. 2113 (Allies force Çobanli and Mersinli to resign after large nationalist raid on French-guarded ammunitions depot); and Atatürk, *Nutuk*, II, pp. 150–55 (Mersinli and Representative Committee).
[42] İskora, op. cit., p. 228; communication from the War History Division of the General Staff.
[43] There were exceptions with regard to age, as well as to ethnic origin (see above). Among the aged generals who showed some nationalist leanings

may be cited Marshal Fuad Pasha (1835-1931; known as 'Crazy Fuad'), who at 84 called in person on the Sultan to transmit the Anatolian nationalists' petition for dismissal of Damad Ferid (Türkgeldi, *op. cit.*, p. 244); and Ali Rıza Pasha (1854-1921; known as Topçu Rıza or Livanai Rıza, and not to be confused with Prime Minister Ali Rıza Pasha [1860-1932]), who demonstratively abstained from the vote by which the Privy Council approved the Sèvres Treaty in July 1920 (İnal, *op. cit.*, p. 2063); as well as İsmail Fazıl Pasha (see above).

[44] On Kemal's criticism of German leadership on the Syrian front, see above, pp. 522-23. Yakub Şevki in 1916 had to be transferred from his command of the Turkish contingent in Galicia because he refused to communicate with German headquarters in any language but Turkish (Larcher, *op. cit.*, p. 142).

[45] Cable of March 6, 1919, quoted in Tevfik Bıyıklıoğlu, 'Mondros Mütarekenamesinde Elviyei Selâse İle İlgili Yeni Vesikalar', *Belleten*, XXI (1957), p. 577.

[46] Djemal Pasha, *op. cit.*, pp. 125f.

[47] Atatürk, *Nutuk*, I, pp. 9f. (my translation). The English version published in 1927, apparently a retranslation from the French or German, unfortunately is both inaccurate in detail and inadequate in style. (See *A Speech Delivered by Ghazi Mustapha Kemal, President of the Turkish Republic*, Leipzig, 1929.) Contrast with this statement the notion that 'a weak existence is preferable to total annihilation', by which the Sultan's Privy Council justified its acceptance of the Sèvres peace terms (see Jäschke and Pritsch, *op. cit.*, p. 37).

[48] *Büyük Gazinin Hatıralarindan Sahifeler*, No. 26. These reminiscences of Mustafa Kemal were first published in the semi-official newspapers *Hakimiyeti Milliye* (Ankara) and *Milliyet* (İstanbul) from March 13 to April 12, 1926; a French translation, somewhat condensed, was made by Jean Deny ('Souvenirs du Gâzi Moustafa Kemâl Pacha', *Revue des Etudes Islamiques*, I, 1927, pp. 117-36, 145-222, 459-63; the above quote appears on p. 174). A continuation, covering the crucial period until May 1919, was published by Falih Rıfkı Atay (*19 Mayıs*, Ankara, 1944, pp. 5-30). A readaptation of the entire series of memoirs will be found in Falih Rıfkı Atay, ed., *Atatürk'ün Bana Anlattıkları*, İstanbul, 1955, which, however, omits the quote on Wilson.

[49] Cf. Tevfik Bıyıklıoğlu, 'Başkumandan Atatürk'ün Kısa Bir Portresi', *Belleten*, XX (1956), p. 713.

[50] Dursunoğlu, *op. cit.*, p. 42; and Fahreddin Erdoğan, *Türk Ellerinde Hatıralarım*, Yeni Matbaa [Ankara?], 1954, pp. 199f.

[51] 'Die lange Zeit, die Mustafa Kemal nach seiner Abberufung aus Adana in İstanbul verbrachte..., ist zum grossen Teil noch in geschichtliches Dunkel gehüllt und von Legenden umrankt.' Jäschke, 'Beiträge...', p. 27.

[52] October 1918. Kemal's cable to his friend Naci [Eldeniz], adjutant to

the Sultan, is reprinted in Hikmet Bayur, '1918 Bırakışmasından Az Önce Muştafa [sic] Kemal Paşa'nin Başyaver Naci Bey Yulo [sic – i.e., Yolu] İle Padişaha Bir Başvurması,' *Belleten*, XXI (1957), pp. 561–63. Kemal's proposal cabinet was far more definitely Unionist in complexion than that which was in fact appointed. In addition to İzzet as premier, Fethi, Rauf, and Hayri (cf. above, p. 522), it was to have included İsmail Canbulat (Justice Minister under Talât), Azmi (the Unionist police chief of İstanbul who a month later fled with the triumvirate to Berlin), and Tahsin [Uzer] (a provincial governor under the CUP administration).

53 December 20, 1918. Jäschke-Aksu, *op. cit.*, I, p. 28.
54 November 18, 1918; see *Büyük Gazinin, op. cit.*, Nos. 33–34 (Deny, *op. cit.*, pp. 203–6; Atay, *Atatürk'ün*, pp. 84ff.).
55 March 23, 1919. See Kâzim Karabekir, *İstiklâl Harbimizin Esasları*, İstanbul, 1951, p. 34; cf. Atay, *Atatürk'ün*, pp. 106f.
56 *Ibid.*, pp. 94f.
57 Jäschke, 'Beiträge . . . ,' p. 29.
58 Mehmed Ali, Damad Ferid's Minister of Posts and Telegraphs, earlier that year had given his daughter in marriage to the elder brother of Ali Fuad [Cebesoy] and had met Mustafa Kemal at Cebesoy's parental home. See Cebesoy, *Millî Mücadele*, p. 34.
59 Kemal's instructions are reprinted in facsimile and transliterated in *Harp Tarihi Vesikaları Dergisi*, I, No. I (September 1952), doc. 3. Mehmed Ali, who happened to be Acting Minister of Interior in mid-May, drew attention to a geographic oversight in that document: The *mutasarrıflıks* of Kayseri and Maraş also bordered on the 9th Army's area; should they have been included in the list? By all means, was the War Office's reply. (*Ibid.*, docs. 12–13.)
60 *Ibid.*, docs. 15ff., and I, No. 2, docs. 35ff. The War Minister's cable requesting Kemal's immediate return (June 6) was followed by a postscript from the head of the General Staff's first section, indicating that British pressure was at work (doc. 19); Kemal's dilatory reply three days later referred to lack of coal and gasoline (doc. 20). That there was continued collusion between Kemal and the War Office is clearly indicated by the opening passage of the first cable which the new War Minister, Ali Ferid Pasha, sent Kemal on June 30: 'Since I, like you, rely on my powers of judgment, I can assert that there is no one who understands the deepest recesses of your mind as well as I do . . .; (*Ibid.*, doc. 28.)
61 Bıyıklıoğlu, 'Mondros . . . ,' p. 579.
62 Military authorities and civilian groups alike co-operated in the systematic evasion of the demobilization regulations; for specific examples, see Cebesoy, *Millî Mücadele*, p. 31, and the colourful account of Colonel A. Rawlinson, one of the British control officers (*Adventures in the Near East*, London, 1923, p. 221).

[63] The Karakol Society's leaders included Colonel Kara Vasif (cf. note 40, above), and Colonel Kemaleddin Sami, who had distinguished himself in the Caucasus campaign of 1918 and later became a brigadier general in the Kemalist forces. See *Halide Edib, op. cit.*, p. 21; Bıyıklıoğlu, *Trakyada*, I, p. 391; Tunaya, *Türkiyede*, p. 520. On the Mim Mim group, see Kemal Koçer, *Kurtuluş Savaşlarımızda İstanbul*, İstanbul, 1946. The extent of the latter group's activities is indicated by a contemporary statistical rèsumè, published in Hüseyin Dağtekin, 'İstiklâl Savaşında Anadolu'ya Kaçırılan Mühimmat ve Askerî Eşya Hakkında Tanzim Edilmis Mühim Bir Vesika', *Tarih Vesikaları*, n.s., I, No. 1 (August 1955), pp. 9–15.

[64] Şapolyo, *op. cit.*, p. 281; Ertürk, *op. cit.*, p. 200; Süleyman Külçe, *Mareşal Fevzi Çakmak*, 2nd ed., 2 vols., İstanbul, 1953, I, p. 91.

[65] See Cebesoy, *Millî Mücadele*, pp. 332ff.

[66] For an anthology of speeches at nationalist rallies in İstanbul during this period, see Kemal Arıburnu, *Millî Mücadelede İstanbul Mitingleri*, Ankara, 1951.

[67] Cebesoy, *Millî Mücadele* . . . , pp. 8, 42.

[68] See the account of Fahreddin Erdoğan, who, as the fledgling republic's Foreign Minister, established contact with Turkish nationalists and military authorities at Erzurum (*op. cit.*, pp. 168–207); cf. Kırzıoğlu M. Fahreddin, *Kars Tarihi*, I, İstanbul, 1953, pp. 556–58; Bıyıklıoğlu, *Osmanlı ve Türk Doğu Hudut Politikası*, pp. 24f.; Jäschke, 'Beiträge,' pp. 24f.; Dursunoğlu, *op. cit.*, pp. 42ff.; Allen and Muratoff, *op. cit.*, p. 497.

[69] Bıyıklıoğlu, *Trakyada*, I, pp. 123ff.

[70] For a detailed listing of these societies, see Tunaya, *Türkiye'de*, pp. 481ff.; *for the role of local Unionists, cf. Açiksözcü, op. cit.*, pp. 13–15; Reşid Pasha, *op. cit.*, p. 37; Dursunoğlu, *op. cit.*, p. 27.

[71] Allen and Muratoff, *op. cit.*, p. 497.

[72] Quoted by İnal, *op. cit.*, p. 1996.

[73] On the slogans of 1913, see Bıyıklıoğlu, *Trakya'da*, I, pp. 66, 77, 81. For brilliant biographical sketches of İbrahim Aydın and İhsan Eryavuz, see Ağaoğlu, *op. cit.* (note 13), pp. 112–16 and 44–61; note that the subject of each biography in this work is identified by a sobriquet rather than by name.

[74] The impressive list of political leaders of the Republic who won their political spurs within the Young Turk movement includes two of three Presidents (Atatürk, cf. above, p. 522, and Bayar); four of ten Premiers (Okyar, Bayar, Saracoğlu, and Günaltay); Atatürk's long-time Foreign and Interior Ministers, Tevfik Rüştü Aras and Şükrü Kaya; prominent newspapermen such as Yunus Nadi Abalıoğlu and Falih Rıfkı Atay, and many others. As early as 1923 the Kemalists included in their Lausanne delegation two ex-ministers of Talât's wartime cabinet – Cavid and Mustafa Şeref [Özkan]. The exact relationship between Kemalists and Unionists, however, as well as the exile activities of the Unionist leaders and their attempts at a

comeback, need much fuller study. Generally it is true that those who held first rank in the CUP at best held second rank in the Kemalist movement, and vice versa. Following the 1926 assassination attempt on Kemal, a number of the surviving CUP leaders, including Cavid, Ahmed Şükrü, and İsmail Canbulat, were executed – but their trial was presided over by Ali [Çetinkaya], himself one of the original Macedonian conspirators of 1908. By the 1930's many prominent surviving Unionists were allowed to return to political activity and to parliament.

[75] For a pointed expression of that suspicion, see, e.g., the remark which Reşid Pasha attributes to the Sivas leader of the Freedom and Accord Party: 'Mustafa Kemal Pasha keeps exerting himself to encourage the Union and Progress movement ... Enver, Talât, and the others, before their flight, selected him as their replacement and put several hundred thousand pounds at his disposal. They ordered him to go to Anatolia and to revive Unionism there ...' (Op. cit., p. 31.)

[76] See Ali Fuad Cebesoy, Siyasî Hâtıralar, pp. 25f.; and Karaman, op. cit., passim.

[77] On the Erzurum Congress, see Dursunoğlu, op. cit. pp. 107ff., 155ff.; on the Sivas Congress, Vehbi Cem Aşkun, Sivas kongresi, Sivas, 1945.

[78] For a specific instance, see, e.g., Umur and Pasin, op. cit., p. 19; for the army's role in the selection of the Sivas Congress, see Cebesoy, Millî Mücadele ... , p. 111. The political struggle in and around the last İstanbul House of Representatives is analyzed by Tarik Z. Tunaya, 'Osmanlı İmparatorluğundan Türkiye Büyük Millet Meclisi Hükümeti Rejimine Geçis,' in Muammer Raşit Seviğ'e Armağan, İstanbul, 1956, pp. 373–94.

[79] For a fuller discussion of the religious attitude and policies of the early Kemalist movement, see Dankwart A. Rustow, 'Politics and Islam in Turkey, 1920–1955,' in Richard N. Frye, ed., Islam and the West, 's-Gravenhage, 1957, especially pp. 69ff.

[80] On the foreign policy of the Kemalist movement, see Dankwart A. Rustow, 'The Foreign Policy of the Turkish Republic', in Roy C. Macridis, ed., Foreign Policy in World Politics, Englewood Cliffs, NJ, 1958, pp. 295–322. For the War of Independence period, see also Roderic H. Davison, 'Turkish Diplomacy from Moudros to Lausanne', in Gordon A. Craig and Felix Gilbert, eds., The Diplomats, 1919–1939, Princeton, NJ, 1953, pp. 172–209.

[81] Atatürk, Nutuk, II, p. 43. The 1909 episode is recounted in a letter from Kemal to his friend Behiç [Erkin] of July 29, 1912, first published by Kemal's order in 1925. See Behiç Erkin, 'Atatürk'ün Selânik'teki Askerlik Hayatına Ait Hatıralar', Belleten, xx (1956), pp. 599f.

[82] This particular wording appears in Kemal's letter to the vilâyet of Erzurum of July 9, 1919; see Faik Reşit Unat, 'Atatürk'ün Askerlikten İstifası ve Erzurum'da Tevkifi Teşebbüsü İle İlgili Bazı Vesikalar', Tarih

Vesikaları, n.s., I, No. 1 (August 1955), p. 5. Other related documents will be found in *Harp Tarihi Vesikaları Dergisi*, I, No. 2 (December 1952), doc. 37; and Atatürk, *Söylev*, I, p. 27.

[83] See Atatürk, *Nutuk*, II, pp. 303ff., for Kemal's account of this episode. The fourth volume of General Cebesoy's memoirs, in press at the time of writing, may be expected to shed additional light on these and subsequent developments.

[84] Atatürk, *Nutuk*, II, p. 261. General Cebesoy, in response to the writer's query, was kind enough to comment in some detail on this episode (personal letter, February 3, 1959). He confirms that the conversation took place (probably in early August 1923) as reported by Kemal, and explains that a divergence of views on the selection of cabinet ministers and parliamentary officers formed the immediate background.

[85] Of the other World War I army commanders who fought with Kemal in Anatolia, Cemal [Mersinli] had joined an even earlier, informal opposition in the Assembly known as the Second Group, and later withdrew from politics until after Atatürk's death. Ali İhsan [Sabis] had fallen out with İnönü while the latter was his superior as commander of the western front; he was elected to the Assembly in 1950 on a Democratic ticket. Nihad [Anılmış] became a Republican People's Party deputy after his retirement from the army in 1942. Yakub Şevki [Sübaşı] appears to have taken no part in the politics of the Republican period.

[86] For systematic accounts of the Kemalist reforms, see Lewis V. Thomas, 'Turkey', in Thomas and Frye, *op. cit.*; and Geoffrey L. Lewis, *Turkey*, London, 1955.

[87] For an instructive account of this blending of military and political functions, see Karaman, *op. cit.*, *passim*.

[88] Similarly, at least half of the 18 officers who went with Kemal to Samsun in 1919 later joined the legislature – only one waiting until retirement, the remainder imitating Kemal's switch from a military to a political career. Most prominent among these were two military surgeons, Dr Refik Saydam, later Minister of Health and Premier; and Dr İbrahim Tali Öngören, party organizer and diplomat. For a list of the eighteen, see Mehmed Arif, *Anadolu İnkılâbı*, İstanbul, 1340 [i.e., 1924], p. 25; cf. *Harp Tarihi Vesikaları Dergisi*, I, No. 1 (September 1952), pp. 9f.

[89] Cf. Gotthard Jäschke, 'Die Diplomatie der Ankara-Regierung', *Mitteilungen der Ausland-Hochschule an der Universität Berlin*, xli (1938), Part ii, pp. 161–70.

CHAPTER VIII

Dress Codes for Men in Turkey and Iran

Houchang Chehabi

The hat, it must constantly be borne in mind, should not be lightly spoken of.[1]

The similarities in the cultural modernization policies of Mustafa Kemal Atatürk and Reza Shah have often been noted, but seldom analyzed comparatively.[2] This chapter examines one of the most visible aspect of the modernization efforts of the two states in the 1920s and 1930s, namely, the westernization of menswear that was enshrined in a series of dress codes between 1925 and 1935.[3]

Dress codes are not a distinctive feature of modernizing societies, and are in fact more typical of traditional societies. But in the latter, they usually aim at maintaining distinctions among groups, and serve as outward markers of ethnic, tribal, class or religious identity,[4] whereas the sartorial policies introduced in the inter-wars in Turkey and Iran sought to render people's appearance uniform and to bring it in line with European practice, rather like Peter the Great's reforms of outward appearance in Russia.[5]

After presenting the dress policies in chronological rather than country-by-country order, which serves to highlight the mutual influences, it will be argued that the parallel sartorial policies of Turkey and Iran were motivated by similar concerns about nation-building and the two countries' standing in international society.[6]

Westernization of Dress in the Nineteenth Century

As in other fields, westernization reached the sphere of clothing through the military, as elements of European-style uniforms were deemed more functional than traditional ones. The Europeanization of clothing flew in the face of the religious injunction against dressing like infidels,[7] and predictably aroused the ire of the *ulema*. Opposition to uniforms sparked (but did not cause) the rebellion that led to the ouster of Sultan Selim III in 1807,[8] and in Iran some *ulema* opposed Abbas Mirza's introduction of boots, which made washing one's feet before prayers cumbersome.[9]

In the civilian realm, the westernization of clothing began at Court: Sultan Mahmud II (r. 1808–39) in the Ottoman Empire and Mohammad Shah (r. 1834–48) in Iran were the first rulers routinely to prefer Western suits to traditional garments.[10] They were followed by the men, and to a lesser extent the women,[11] of the elite in a pattern similar to that discerned for the case of Europe by Norbert Elias.[12] As the nineteenth century advanced, an increasing number of Ottoman and Iranian Muslims adopted European clothing, prompted by travel abroad, the example of non-Muslim subjects in their midst and the new fashions at Court, for al-nasu'ala suluki mulukihim, 'people follow the ways of their kings'.[13] Traditional opinion was opposed to the Europeanization of dress, and clothes became an important issue in the discursive conflict between modernists and traditionalists, who called the former *şapkalı* (hat-wearer) in the Ottoman Empire and *fokkoli* (from the French *faux col*) in Iran.

Until the mid-1920s male headgear was exempt from the gradual Europeanization of menswear. The turban, believed to have been the Prophet's habitual head covering, enjoyed special respect among Muslims. According to a tradition ascribed to Mohammad, the turban is the barrier between unbelief and faith,[14] and Europeans associated it with Islam too: John Locke spoke of Muslims as the 'turbaned nations'.[15] Therefore the introduction in 1829 of a uniform hat for all male subjects of the Ottoman Empire, irrespective of religion, met with the opposition of traditionalists.[16] This new hat was the fez (*fes* in Turkish, *tarbush* in Arabic, *fineh* in Persian), whose origin has been variously surmised to be North African, Greek or Venetian.[17]

Initially, Sultan Mahmud wished to add a small leather rim in front of the fez to protect the eyes from the glare of the sun, but the *ulema* opposed this innovation, as it prevented a Muslim from touching the ground in prayer:[18] traditionally, Muslims covered their head while praying. Its reformist and secularist origins notwithstanding, the fez later in the nineteenth century gradually came to symbolize a man's membership in the Islamic community, and it was adopted by Muslims from India to South Africa.

In Qajar Iran a rimless cap (*kolah*) made of lambskin (astrakhan) or felt, a token, perhaps, of the Qajars' Turkoman origins, replaced the turban as the main headgear of urban Iranian men by the middle of the nineteenth century;[19] only the *ulema* and members of other learned professions remained loyal to the turban, whose religious significance was thereby underscored.[20] As the standard headgear of urban men, the *kolah* played roughly the same role as the Ottoman fez, although unlike the latter it was not imposed by official decree.[21]

It was not only the shape of their headgear that distinguished Muslims from Europeans, but also the etiquette associated with it. According to European custom a man removes his hat as a sign of respect and when indoors,[22] whereas according to the rules of Muslim *adab* he keeps it on.[23] This led to incongruities at official ceremonies involving European diplomats in the East and Muslim diplomats in the West.

By the early twentieth century, the fez had come to symbolize reaction in the eyes of Ottoman modernists, and headgear became a political issue in the Ottoman Empire. The Young Turks wore European-style brimmed hats in Europe to blend into the crowd and escape the attention of Sultan Abdülhamid's spies,[24] and the Padişah outlawed the wearing of hats by Muslims.

After the revolution of 1908, the *kulturkampf* between traditionalists and modernists intensified and men's headgear became a hotly contested issue. Turkish nationalists disdained the fez, which for them symbolized Hamidian pan-Islamism, and wore a fur cap, *qalpaq*, inspired by Central Asian and Caucasian headgear.[25] This choice reflected their pan-Turanist proclivities, but it also helped sustain the boycott of Austrian goods begun after Austria-Hungary's annexation in 1908 of Bosnia-Herzegovina, which was a major manufacturer of fezes.[26] The *qalpaq* differed from the Iranian *kolah* in that it was wider rather than narrower at the top. Nothing exemplifies the political symbolism attached to headgear in the twilight years of the House of Osman better than the so-called 'tassel affair', instigated by the educational reformer Ismail Hakkı. In numerous lectures he would argue that the tassel (*püskül*) attached to the fez was wasteful, unaesthetic and useless, ending his speech by cutting off his own fez's tassel – a performance for which he earned the sobriquet *püskülsüz* (tassel-less).[27]

The dress codes of the 1920s and 1930s

Coming out of the Young Turk tradition, Mustafa Kemal and other members of the Ankara regime also wore the *qalpaq*. But it 'smacked of Asia' and thus did not accord with Mustafa Kemal's project for the new Turkey.[28]

Following the abolition of the Caliphate in March 1924, in February 1925 the Şeyh Said rebellion broke out in Eastern Anatolia.[29] In response, the government promulgated the 'Law for the Maintenance of Order' in early March 1925, giving it dictatorial powers for two years. Feeling threatened by what he perceived to be forces of reaction, Mustafa Kemal in the summer of that year began an all-out assault on traditionalism by focusing his attention on the most immediately visible symbol of Turkish separateness from the Western world: the fez.

The connection between the fez and reaction was one that Mustafa Kemal felt very deeply. As a young man he had travelled in Europe, and had felt humiliated by his headgear, which he came to consider a mark of his inferiority. In the months leading to the abolition of the fez, he revealed that he had dreamt of it three times, adding: 'whenever I did so, Ismet [Pasha] knocked at my door in the morning to report a reactionary movement somewhere in the country'. The press was instructed to prepare public opinion for the abolition of the fez, but instead of the word *şapka*, which had a negative connotation due to its association with the 'infidels', – in fact, *şapka giymek*, 'to put on a hat', meant becoming a turn-coat[30] – he used euphemisms such as 'civilized headgear', 'protector from sunshine', or 'headcover with a brim' (*şemsiperli serpuş*, from Persian *sarpush*, 'headcover').

As with Mahmud II a century earlier, the introduction of European headgear began in the military. In May 1925 the navy was given orders to switch to a cap with a visor.[31] A former officer remembers:

> Just prior to Atatürk's abolition of the fez the Military were issued with a small cap that had the suspicion of a peak on it. The peak, we were told, was to guard the eyes against the sun. It was so small however that the idea of it being able to guard against anything, let alone the sun, was laughable. We had always previously worn a fez with a Turkish moon and stars woven into the front and we were now very much ashamed to be seen with our new headgear, which was really, we thought,

too much like the hat the Christians wore. So we carried the offensive hat in our hands as often as we dared and the few boys who were brave enough to keep it on were called 'Gavur' – an epithet relating to a Christian in an unsavoury way.[32]

Encouraged by the navy's decision, many men in Istanbul took to wearing European hats. This was aided by a declaration of Rifat Bay, the president of the Directorate of Religious Affairs, to the effect that there was no verse of the Koran and no hadith that prescribed a special type of clothing, and that therefore a Muslim was free to dress as he liked, provided it was not his intention to imitate the infidels.[33]

A few months later, Mustafa Kemal decided to extend the introduction of brims and visors to the civilian population. To announce his policies, he chose Kastamonu (ancient Paphlagonia), a coastal province north of Ankara then known both for its religious conservatism and its contribution to the War of Independence; the idea was to strike at 'reaction' at its heart but in a place where the Ghazi enjoyed considerable personal legitimacy.

The whole affair was carefully staged, with a sense for drama. Kemal set out from Ankara in a car and dressed in a white suit, bare-headed. He alighted from the car in a few villages on the way, and his entry into one of them was remembered thus by a student:

When the President walked slowly down the street, greeting the crowds, there was not a sound. The clean-shaven Gazi was wearing a white, European-style summer suit, a sports shirt open at the neck, and a Panama hat. The few officials applauded frantically, urging on those near them, but a flutter of hand-clapping was all they would muster, so great had been the shock.[34]

In Kastamonu itself, Mustafa Kemal attended a number of meetings, but left his major policy statement for the port of Inebolu. The town had been richly decorated, the people celebrated their leader and sacrificed sheep for him, and school children processed before him crying 'Long live our father'. On 28 August 1925, the third day of his stay, he delivered a speech wearing a Panama hat:[35]

Gentlemen, the Turkish people who founded the Turkish republic are civilized . . . but . . . the truly civilized people of

Turkey must prove in fact that they are civilized ... also in their outward aspect.

He then asked the audience: 'Is our dress national?', to which they roared: 'No!' He continued: 'Is it civilized and international?' and received the same answer. He concluded:

> I agree with you ... My friends, there is no need to seek and revive the costume of Turan. A civilized, international dress is worthy and appropriate for our nation, and we will wear it. Boots or shoes on our feet, trousers on our legs, shirt and tie, jacket and waistcoat – and of course, to complete these, a cover with a brim on our heads. I want to make this clear. This head-covering is called a 'hat' (şapka).[36]

The word was out – no more euphemisms. After his return to Ankara a number of decrees and laws made Mustafa Kemal's personal choice obligatory for the rest of the country. On 2 September a cabinet decree (qararname) banned the wearing of religious vestments and insignia by persons not holding a recognized religious office (i.e., state-appointed muftis, imams, hatibs or village religious teachers), and an order was given to all civil servants to wear the 'costume common to the civilized nations of the world', namely the suit (elbise) and the hat – only military officers and judges, who were to be given special uniforms, were exempt.[37] On 4 September another decree enjoined that hats be taken off indoors, and that salutes be performed outdoors by doffing the hat and inclining the head.[38] When the tekkies were dissolved by a decree of 30 September, the wearing of the dervishes' distinctive dress also became a criminal offence.[39]

For the time being, ordinary citizens were exempt from these rules, but on 25 November 1925 Law no. 671, titled 'Law Concerning the Wearing of the Hat', required all men to wear hats and made wearing of the fez a criminal offence. It read:

> Art. 1. Members of the Grand National Assembly and officials and employees of central and local administration and of all institutions are obliged to wear the hat, which the Turkish nation has assumed. The general headdress of the Turkish people also is the hat, and the government forbids the continuation of any practice that is incompatible with this.

Art. 2. This Law has effect from the date of its publication.
Art. 3. This law will be implemented by the Grand National Assembly and the Council of Executive Ministers.[40]

A few days later, on 30 November, Law no. 676 established a one-year prison sentence for the wearing of religious garb by unauthorized persons.[41] The law for the restoration of order was in force, allowing the state to nip any opposition in the bud. In parliament, a deputy of Bursa, Nurettin Pasha, a military man who had been one of the first to rally to Mustafa Kemal's nationalist cause, introduced a motion against the wearing of hats, asserting that such a law was a 'contradiction of the fundamental rights of the national sovereignty and of the principle of the integrity of personal freedom', and concluding:

> we have condemned the oppressive policies of Abdülhamid II for [infractions on personal liberty] much less grave than this one. We must therefore not introduce into the world an innovation which has not been introduced into any other country, nor must we strike at the heart of liberty.

But only one other deputy voted for the motion, and the hat law passed easily.[42]

The elites immediately followed Mustafa Kemal's lead. Among non-elite groups, reaction was mixed. Some resigned themselves to the innovation in deference to the *ghazi*, but there were not enough hats for everybody, and men often had to improvise before local hat factories came into full production.[43] In Istanbul, some 30 people were arrested for publishing and distributing a tract titled *Hats and Imitating the Frank*.[44] In the East, there were serious disturbances. Between 22 and 26 November 1925 demonstrations against the hat took place in Kayseri, Erzurum, and Maraş. In Kayseri they were led by a naqshbandi sheikh, Mekkeli Ahmed Hamdi, who incited the crowds with the rumour that the government would soon outlaw the veil and prohibit possession of the Koran. In Maraş, the protest began when a treatise condemning the change in headgear was discovered on a mosque door: after prayers, a crowd marched under a green banner shouting 'we don't want hats'. Mekkeli Ahmed Hamdi and four others were eventually sentenced to death, while the total number of those from Maraş who were executed may be over 20. In

Erzerum the scale of the disturbances was much larger: on 24 November a group of 20 to 30 men, led by one Şeyh Osman Hoca, marched on the government buildings to petition the governor to allow them to wear the local headgear (*ağniye*, *kabalak*), better suited for the cold winters of eastern Anatolia than the hat. When the governor dismissed the petition and tried to have the leaders arrested, the crowd, which had grown to over 2,000, grew restless. Local gendarmes opened fire and killed 23 protestors. Alarmed, the government declared martial law around Erzurum for a month, and between 20 and 30 'reactionaries', including Şeyh Osman Hoca, were executed.[45]

Between the two extremes of compliance and resistance a third group tried to adapt as best as they could. A British observer wrote a few years after the reform:

> [A] religious significance attached to the wearing of the fez, and it went hard with the conservative population to be forced by law to give it up. Besides, the Turks do not like the hat and it does not suit them. They have evolved a way of wearing it which makes it look as much like their old headgear as possible. I am speaking, of course, of the peasants. The smart young man about town in Angora and Istanbul is turned out like a European. So the men of Turkey are now wearing any and every kind of hat. I have seen the Muezzin give the call to prayer in a bowler hat.[46] I have seen men go into mosques to say their prayers wearing tweed caps turned back to front, so that the peak may not be in the way when they bow their head to the ground.[47]

Another observer relates that 'one of the most learned men in Turkey never wore a hat and that when he left his library at night, he bundled up his head with a bandage as though he had a terrible tooth-ache. To observers he was obviously in no condition to wear a hat.'[48]

But the new policy did have its supporters too, and so scuffles sometimes broke out over the new headgear:

> The men indignantly refused to throw away the fez and it became a usual sight to see fighting taking place between the supporters of the new order and the diehards of the old. Government officials were the first to give way to Atatürk.

They were forced into this position by reason of their work, and the streets became full of bowler hats worn with a self-conscious air. The children used to throw stones after them and the police arrested men who still persisted in wearing the fez, and the street sellers in desperation put fancy paper hats on their heads and added a note of unusual gaiety to the market-places. And out in the country places and the villages the men even wore women's hats in order to evade arrest. The old men took to tying handkerchiefs on their heads, placing the offending Christian hat over this, but the police became wise to this ruse and promptly arrested them. Arrested men were hauled to the police stations in such great numbers that they could not be dealt with and the white handkerchiefs were pulled off the bald plates, the insulting head-gear being firmly clamped over the naked, uneasy heads.[49]

By 1930 opposition against the hat was still smouldering: when Fethi Bey, the leader of the Free Republican Party, an opposition party briefly tolerated by Mustafa Kemal from August to November of that year, visited Izmir, he gave a speech in which he mentioned hats. (Wrongly) anticipating an outburst against it, 'thousands of people took off their hats and threw them on the ground', much to the dismay of Mustafa Kemal.[50] As late as 1947, a total of 579 arrests were made for infringements of the 1925 and 1934 laws,[51] and in the 1950s in a distant part of Turkey villagers expressed anger at a man who sat indoors bareheaded.[52] For their prayers, some observant Muslims took to carrying little skullcaps (*takke*) with them, substituting it for the hat while praying.[53]

Iran followed Turkey two years later. In 1927 relations between the two nations were strained, due to Iranian claims that the Turkish government pursued Kurdish rebels into Iranian territory. An anti-Turkish campaign was unleashed in the Tehran press, which afforded an opportunity to poke fun at the hat laws, to wit the following example:

We are not much surprised by the unfriendly incursions into Persia to which the Turks incite the Kurds, for the change from the Caliphate to the Republic, from the fez to the hat, from Islam to Christianity, has in no way changed the mentality of the Young Turks, true sons of their be-turbanned fathers, who lost what they had in Europe and are now trying to pick quarrels with Persia.[54]

But only a few days later, in early August 1927, the Iranian cabinet decided to institute the 'Pahlavi hat', similar to the French kepi, as the official hat for Iranian men.[55] The introduction of the new hat coincided with the passage of the conscription law and the secularization of the judiciary, all of which led to widespread unrest in the country. Objection to the Pahlavi hat centered on its visor, which impeded touching the ground in prayer. Some Tehran *ulema* took sanctuary in Qom, and the bazaars closed in protest. By a mixture of concessions and repression, however, the government brought the situation under control, and after a few months felt secure enough to change the rest of men's clothing. But before this could happen, women's veiling became an issue in state–society relations for the first time, when the new Shah's female relatives decided to celebrate the Iranian new year, *Nowruz*, at the holy shrine in Qom, and for this donned transparent chadors. Some clergymen protested, whereupon Reza Shah drove to Qom from Tehran the next day, entered the shrine with his boots on, and personally manhandled a number of clerics, much to the indignation of traditionalists.[56]

After his consolidation of power, Reza Shah began to carry out the cultural agenda of Iranian modernists in his drive to bring progress to Iran, and this included Europeanizing Iranian clothes. In the autumn of 1928 there were rumours that Western dress would be made obligatory for everyone,[57] and in Rasht local tailors were given one month to complete existing orders, after which they were to cut in the new fashion only.[58] Throughout November, slogans were printed in the local press, like 'People who do not strive for uniformity of dress cannot claim to be patriots'.[59] Finally, on 28 December 1928 the first dress code was passed into law by the recently convened seventh Majles, which had been stacked with regime supporters and from which all opposition had been banned. Nevertheless, a number of deputies did oppose the law, especially Sayyed Ya'qub from Yazd, who observed that in the times of Darius, Iran was vast and populated, forms of dress were varied, and yet Iran had enjoyed total independence. He argued that national sentiment and solidarity would be better created by the diffusion of knowledge than by standardizing dress.[60] But others spoke in favour of the law, and the law passed easily. Its final text was as follows:

Article I. All male Iranian subjects who are [not] required to wear special clothing in conformity with service in the government shall wear uniform clothing within the country; and all government employees whether civil or judicial shall, when on government duty, wear civil or juridical clothing, as officially prescribed, and at other times they shall wear the uniform attire.

Article II. The following eight classes are exempt from the prescriptions of the law:
1) The *mojtahed*s in possession of *ijazah*s furnished by the sources of emulation, and engaged in spiritual matters.
2) Religious authorities in villages and districts who have passed a specified examination.
3) Sunni muftis who should possess licenses from two recognized religious authorities of the Sunni sect.
4) The leaders of prayers who are in charge of a *mihrab* of a mosque.
5) Preachers of the religious traditions relating to the Prophet, after their knowledge has been certified by two *mojtahed*s.
6) Students of *feqh* and *osul* who are able to pass an examination in their field of study.
7) Teachers of the Muslim law and theology.
8) Non-Muslim clerics living in Iran.

Article III. Residents of towns who are delinquent in the observance will be subject to a fine of from one to five tomans or from one to seven days' imprisonment, and in cases where they do not live in towns they will be liable to imprisonment of from one to seven days by virtue of a sentence by a court. The funds which accrue as a result of the fines collected in any given locality in conformity with this article shall be used by the municipality for the purchase of uniform clothing for the poor of the locality.

Article IV stipulated that the law would become effective between March 1929 and 1930 (the Iranian year 1308).[61]

On 26 January 1929 the ministry of the interior issued regulations that explicated the meaning of 'uniform dress' and defined more precisely the clerical exceptions to it. Article I defined it as a Pahlavi hat and a European suit; Article II outlawed the wearing of any other form of dress; and Article V held parents responsible for their male offspring's compliance with the code. Local authorities tried to implement these rules. In Kerman, for instance, the local chief of police ordered that men not wearing the new clothes be prohibited from attending any public entertainment or being served in coffee shops.[62]

There was some resistance to the measure, especially in the tribal areas, but anti-government agitation resulted more from the contemporaneous introduction of conscription than from the dress codes *per se*,[63] in fact, both were aspects of the Pahlavi state's increasing meddling with people's lives. In tribal areas men clung to their traditional clothes longest, especially Kurds and Arabs.[64] But even within the regime some did not like the new policy. Reza Shah's then prime minister, the deeply religious Mehdiqoli Hedayat (Mokhber al-Saltaneh), remembers: 'I resisted for a while, until one day during a cabinet meeting the Shah took me by the collar and asked whether he should have a suit made for me. I said now that it is your pleasure, I'll see to it myself.'[65] But in 1929 the ouster of King Amanullah of Afghanistan slowed down the pace of reforms, and the Shah even tried to mend his relations with the clergy.[66] As a British report observed:

> [The Shah] has learnt that he can neither interfere with tribal customs nor upset religious observances in the manner so disastrously attempted by Amanullah. Both his Majesty and his Minister of Court have been brought to realise that the old maxim of 'Festina Lento' is a wise one, even if Mustafa Kemal may appear to have succeeded by other methods.[67]

Soon, however, the Turkish example began to reassert itself at the expense of the Afghan one – a continuation of a trend going back to Ottoman times.[68] As we saw earlier, in the 1920s relations between the two countries had been somewhat tense, but the appointment of the respected Iranian statesman and man of letters Mohammad-Ali Foroughi (Zoka' al-Molk) as ambassador to Ankara paved the way for an improvement in relations. Foroughi was quite aware of the sartorial dimension of his new appointment. He happened to be in Paris when he learnt of it, and immediately rushed out to buy himself a dinner jacket, tails and a morning coat.[69] In Turkey, he got along well with

Mustafa Kemal and Ismet Pasha, and saw them often.[70] But it was not easy for a man of Forughi's urbanity to have to keep his Pahlavi hat on while all other diplomats were bareheaded, and so on 28 April 1928 he sent a secret letter to Taimurtash, in which he pressed the powerful court minister to work for the adoption of the European hat, since that would standardize etiquette inside and outside Iran and make life easier for Iranian diplomats.[71] Forughi returned to Iran in 1930, but his work endured. By 1932 bilateral negotiations had led to a marked improvement in Irano-Turkish relations; an official visit by the Shah was to crown this achievement.[72]

In June 1934 Reza Shah travelled to Turkey on a state visit, the only one of his reign. In the words of Hasan Arfa', who accompanied Reza Shah, 'the Iranian reformer had come to visit his Turkish counterpart to learn' and 'profited much more from the progress accomplished in Turkey then he would have done by visiting a more advanced country . . . and on his return he set to work immediately to apply what he had learnt there.'[73] It was the social functions he witnessed on that occasion that induced Reza Shah to speed up the pace of Europeanization.[74] Atatürk showed Reza Shah the example when, during a joint railway trip, he saw a turbaned cleric among the well-wishers on the platform. He threw a tantrum, ordered the man to be seized as he was an 'enemy of the people', but the cleric disappeared into the crowd. The next day Atatürk ordered that clerics of all religions should be forbidden to wear their clerical garb outside houses of worship.[75]

Yahya Dowlatabadi writes that since Atatürk had accepted an invitation for a return visit, Reza Shah wanted Iran to modernize rapidly until the date of his visit so that Atatürk would not witness Iran's comparative 'backwardness'. Again according to Dowlatabadi, Reza Shah sent a telegram to his government while still in Turkey, ordering that peasants wear hats with full brims, because they had to labour in the sun.[76] Isa Sadiq, for his part, reports that upon returning from Turkey Reza Shah ordered dustmen in Tehran and carriage drivers in Mashad to wear full-brimmed hats.[77]

In Turkey, meanwhile, the last element of the dress code for men was put in place when on 3 December 1934 the Grand National Assembly passed a law that forbade the clergy of all faiths to wear religious dress, except in places of worship and during religious ceremonies, and that also prohibited the wearing of foreign uniforms and insignia by foreigners.[78] Exceptions to this law were granted in

June 1935, when the ministry of the interior released a list of seven religious leaders who were provisionally authorized to wear religious garb outside religious ceremonies: the chairman of the office of religious affairs in Ankara, five orthodox clerics and the chief rabbi of Istanbul. In other words, one Muslim and six non-Muslims.[79]

Back in Iran, by the mid-1930s Reza Shah's regime had become so autocratic that Reza Shah's remaining dress reforms were promulgated not as laws but as decrees. In late May 1935 the Shah told his assembled ministers that Iranians had to become Western, and as a first step they had to put on *chapeaux* (European felt hats), beginning with the forthcoming opening of the tenth Majles on 6 June. On that day, all men present came with Western brimmed hats, and took them off during the proceedings,[80] in violation of custom. On 8 July the brimmed hat was made obligatory by cabinet decree. All state employees were ordered to wear the new hat, or be put on unpaid leave.

While in Tehran the new policies met with a measure of approval among the new middle class, matters were different in the provinces. For one thing, there were not enough hats for all Iranians. As one traveller observed a few years later:

> In Sultanabad the great men of the village each had their Pahlevi hat, but amongst the other lesser people there seemed to be one communal hat ... borrowed ... by ... the lesser fry when they went in to Kasvin.
> Before we left Persia the order came from the Shah *ferengi* hats ... and, driving through the villages on my way to Baghdad, I could see piles of discarded pillboxes outside each police post, where the unfortunate owners had been made to leave them, while each went into the town to provide himself with more conventional headgear. I didn't see the universal change before I left; only a few in Tehran had succeeded in getting felt hats ... *Ferengi* hats were quickly at a premium, and everyone was sold out.[81]

Directives were sent from the ministry of the interior to the provinces, providing detailed rules of etiquette for state employees, such as what kinds of hats could be worn at what time of the day and year, who had to tip his hat in greeting first, etc.[82] While traditional Iranian men could grudgingly accept the imposition of the so-called Pahlavi hat in the interest of national unity (see below), the new official hat was explicitly called 'international' (*bein al-melali*) and thus no longer connoted national specificity.

To respond to the new wave of what they considered anti-religious measures, the *ulema* in turn began holding semi-secret meetings. In Meshad the *ulema*, under the leadership of Aqa Hosein Qomi, protested openly and sent telegrams to the Shah. Qomi decided to go to Tehran personally to negotiate with Reza Shah in the hope of changing the monarch's mind. Upon reaching the capital, however, Qomi was snubbed by the authorities, and went on to Najaf. Around this time, meetings had begun to be held openly at the Gowharshad mosque in Mashad, which adjoins the shrine of Imam Reza. At these meetings preachers and *ulema*, chief among them Bohlul, spoke against the international hat and unveiling, and Qomi's treatment radicalized these gatherings. It was summer, and so a high number of pilgrims were camping out in the courtyard if the shrine of Imam Reza, whose sanctity they expected the security forces to respect.

But on Friday, 13 July 1935 (20 Tir, 1314) security forces stormed the shrine and the mosque, shot at the demonstrators, killed some, but, failing to dislodge them, withdrew. Now people from all over the city and the surrounding countryside converged on the shrine to protest and listen to the preachers' fiery speeches. The next day troops went into position all over the city, and in the late evening attacked the mosque and put an end to the whole affair amid much bloodshed. The following day the dead were buried in mass graves, and most senior *ulema* in the city were arrested and exiled from Mashad. The press played down the incident, and in fact the chief topic in July was the enthusiastic reception of the new hat by the population everywhere in the country.[83] It was after this incident that Reza Shah decided to ban the veil, a measure Atatürk never adopted as a general policy applicable to all women.[84]

As for men's dress codes, the most contentious issue was defining those who were exempt from it. Pre-Reza Shah Iran had been, like all pre-industrial societies, relatively undifferentiated socially, or, in Roy Mottahedeh's words, a 'world of numberless, ill-defined, and overlapping degrees of status',[85] where men who had other occupations would sometimes engage in some religious activity. By defining those who were entitled to a 'turban licence' narrowly, many not very learned habitual turban wearers had to give up their traditional clothes. Many switched to Western dress, while a few older provincial ones preferred to stay at home or, if they could afford it, bribed officials into granting a licence. In response to the restrictions, the high-ranking *ulema* liberally granted *ijazahs* for *ijtihad*.[86] In Hamadan, for instance, all 135 turbaned men were elevated in this way and thus received government turban licences.[87] But in the face of this unanticipated consequence, the government began applying the rules ever more restrictively, and the number of turbaned men declined until the end of Reza Shah's reign.[88] For the clergy, having to depend on the government's goodwill for wearing their traditional garb was humiliating enough, but perhaps even worse was the fact that according to the law non-Muslim clerics were subjected to the same treatment, which to the Shi'ite clergy signalled an intolerable equivalence between their religion and those of the minorities.

A decade after the European hat was introduced in Turkey, it again caused controversy, this time in Alexandretta, an area under French control as part of the Syrian mandate in which Turks and Arabs were about equal in numbers.[89] In the mid-1930s Turkish men took to wearing the hat, to which Arab men responded by wearing the *faisaliyyah*,[90] which King Faisal had introduced in Iraq as his nation's distinctive headgear.[91] To forestall a Turkish alliance with Germany, however, the French accepted to cede the territory to Turkey, after first organizing a plebiscite which the Arab and Armenian communities boycotted. In the years running up to the plebiscite, the fez became a symbol of Arab, and the hat a symbol of Turkish nationalism, leading to occasional fisticuffs. A Turkish song from the region had this text: 'Our juridical school is Kemalism, we are modern Hatayanis, we wear hats and berets, and tear up the fez, symbol of slavery.' Consequently, when the autonomous government of Hatay, as the Turks called it, was constituted by the Turkish community in 1938, one of the first laws to be passed by the assembly made the hat the official headgear of the nation.[92] Soon thereafter Hatay was absorbed by Turkey. Now all Turks wore hats – except in British Cyprus, where the fez survived Atatürk's laws.[93]

Sartorial standard of civilization

With the benefit of hindsight, the dress policies of Atatürk and Reza Shah look somewhat silly. The question arises as to why these two leaders were so adamant about changing their citizens' outward appearance.

One reason was anticlericalism. For both Atatürk and Reza Shah, the *ulema* symbolized backwardness and reaction, and by giving the state the right to declare who was an *alim* and who was not, they hoped to reduce the total number, and thus the overall influence, of the clergy, for, as a British diplomatic report put it, '[i]t was the minor turbaned gentry, the hangers-on and sycophants of the big priests who were accustomed to create clerical agitation, and their compulsory adoption of the Pahlavi cap and short coat will put an effective stop on their tricks'.[94]

In the long run, however, this policy had an unanticipated consequence, for the irony is that by instituting an outward distinction between laymen and *ulema*, the Pahlavi state unwittingly contributed to the creation of a clearly bounded clergy with an *esprit de corps*, a group that would four decades later preside over the dynasty's downfall. A similar effect obtained in Turkey, where 'the Ulema, which had until that time been only one among several medieval orders, became singled out as a class of clergymen distinguishable from laymen through their conservatism and insistence upon retaining their medieval attire'.[95]

But anticlericalism was not the only motivation for the dress codes; nationalism and nation-building also played major roles. Among all Muslim nations, only Turkey and Iran witnessed sustained sartorial social engineering; Afghanistan and Albania imitated the two but did not go as far. It is no coincidence that of all Muslim states, only Turkey and Iran retained their full sovereignty throughout the heyday of European imperialism. However, the two countries' membership in this society was fragile, and therefore full acceptance by the other members as true equals rated very high on the agenda of nationalists. Unlike India, say, where national dress became a symbol of nationalism that distinguished local people from the Europeans present on their soil, in Iran and Turkey Europeanization was seen as a precondition for emancipation and equality within a system of nations of which the country was already a member, albeit a precarious one. In this, Turkey and Iran differed from the model posited by Partha Chatterjee, where a colonized nation's culture became the most sacrosanct aspect of it, one that had to be defended against outsiders who already controlled the political and economic realms.[96]

Nationalism had two closely connected dimensions: internally a strong state had to be built to withstand the onslaught of the West, and externally the emancipation of the nation *vis-à-vis* Europe had to be secured. The first provided the impetus for standardization, the second for Europeanization.

State building had to entail nation building, which was begun in light of the Jacobin tradition of equating unity with uniformity.[97] Standardization of clothing was less of a problem in Turkey than in Iran, as the fez had already accomplished that task in Ottoman times, except that by 1925 many men wore a turban or a *qalpaq*. Besides, the new Turkey was ethnically less diverse than Iran. Nevertheless, in late November 1925 riots had taken place in Rizeh, in which opposition to the new hat laws had become mixed up with the grievances of the local, largely Laz population against the central government.[98] On 19 January 1927 a member of the Council of the Vilayet of Rizeh proposed that the veil and the traditional Laz costume, the *sübkah*, be banned in the region.[99]

In Iran, by contrast, standardization was a crucial to the nation-building project of the Pahlavi state. Ali-Akbar Siasi, who as long-time minister of education and rector of Tehran University played an important part in Iranian cultural life, summed up the link between nation building and dress codes in his 1931 doctoral dissertation about 'Iran and the West' submitted to Paris University. In a chapter titled 'The Emancipation and Consolidation of National Sentiment' he began by chastising the clergy for their reactionary attitudes and their hypocrisy, factors that explained their diminishing moral authority in Iranian society. The fusion of religious and national sentiment that had assured Iran's survival as a nation having become obsolete with the abolition of the Ottoman Caliphate in 1924 and the weakening of religious sentiment in Iran, nationalism had to be encouraged. To this end, the author averred, a number of measures were taken by Reza Shah. The first was the military centralization of the country, and the second the uniformization of dress. The reasoning concerning the latter is worth quoting at length:

> We know that the ten to twelve million Persians, although of the same race and, with few exceptions [*sic!*], of the same language and religion, used to form groups that were rendered heterogeneous by the large distances that separated them and by the bad state of roads. Every one of them had its own mores, customs, and costumes. The Lurs, Kurds, Turkomans, Shahsavans, Baluchis, Bakhtiaris etc. dressed so differently that

it was difficult for them to consider each other as belonging to the same country.

Admitting sarcastically that Reza Shah's dress policy deprived European travellers of local colour, Siasi continued that the measure reflected Reza Shah's psychological acumen in that

> it rests on the principle of the reciprocal influence of the physical and moral [realms]. The national Persian costume, constantly worn by a tribal man, in a distant region, will give him the sentiment of belonging to a vast national unit and not to a particularist clan. Also, this common trait, precisely because it is superficial and visible, will bring together the different groups of Persians – the Turks of Azerbaijan, the Kurds, the Lurs, the Arabs of Khuzistan, the Baluchis etc. – who used to treat each other sometimes as adversaries, and will help to create sympathy among them. Furthermore, if the Armenian, Zoroastrian, and Jewish minorities used to feel uneasy in their relations with each other and with their Muslim compatriots, this was a little bit because of the visible particularities of their respective clothes ... Finally, and this is, we think, the main reason of this policy, and main social problem being the europeanization of the Persian, it was felt that the imitation of [the Europeans'] external appearance would not fail to facilitate the adoption of [European] ideas; that the Persian, by abandoning his long robe, his cloak, his bonnet, all of which seemed to serve as a refuge for traditionalism, would definitely capitulate to the advance of Western civilization, to which he would thenceforth abandon himself without shame or constraint. And in fact, dressed in a short jacket and a hat with visor, he seems indeed less ill at ease in his march towards modern progress.[100]

In sum, Iranians would be more willing to imagine each other as a community, to paraphrase Benedict Anderson,[101] if they all looked alike.

Regarding the international dimension, Kenneth Waltz has pointed out how the international society of states exerts pressure on individual states to conform to successful practices.[102] But states have no volition of their own, and are run by individuals, who interact with individuals from other countries.[103] For the leaders of

Turkey and Iran, emancipation could best be achieved by showing the Europeans that one was worthy of their company in the society of nations. And what better way to prove this than to become physically like them? The hat symbolized the superiority of the Europeans for both Turks and Iranians. In Turkey there was a saying to the effect that 'behind the hat there are warships', meaning that whoever got into a conflict with a Western şapkalı (hat-wearer) would provoke a diplomatic incident, that would, because of the capitulary rights European powers enjoyed, lead to a humiliation for the Ottomans.[104] Atatürk himself, on his travels in Europe, had felt very annoyed when Europeans made fun of the fez he and his friends wore.[105] In his famously long speech of 1927, he mentioned the hat laws only briefly, but his justification of the measure is telling:

> Gentlemen, it was necessary to abolish the fez, which sat on our heads as a sign of ignorance, of fanaticism, of hatred to progress and civilisation, and to adopt in its place the hat, the customary headdress of the whole civilised world, thus showing, among other things, that no difference existed in the manner of thought between the Turkish nation and the whole family of civilised mankind.[106]

As for the international dimension of dress reform in Iran, Reza Shah himself admitted the link that existed, in his mind, between Europeanization and international emancipation. According to Isa Sadiq, the monarch felt that European clothes induced an inferiority complex in Iranians, and the Shah decreed the wearing of these clothes to give his subjects self-confidence.[107] Other accounts seem to show that it was above all Reza Shah himself who had an inferiority complex. On 8 July 1935, the day the decree instituting the international hat was issued, he received a number of Majles deputies and told them:

> The new hat has nothing to do with religion, but it does have something to do with nationality. Previously those who wore it thought that this headgear conferred on them superiority over those who were not wearing it. We do not want those others to think that they are superior to us because of a minor difference in head covering.[108]

In private, he was even more candid: in a meeting with Hedayat at which he criticized the latter's insufficiently modern hat, he reacted to his former prime minister's feeble defense by saying that he wanted Iranians to become like everybody else so that they would not be made fun of.[109] Others were less apologetic, and after the *kepi* was replaced with the fedora in 1935 one official hailed the international hat as the ancestral headdress of Iran, stating that during the Sasanian period the Iranians had worn similar brimmed hats.[110]

In the case of Iran, the obvious gap between the European model and the Muslim reality of society could be bridged by reclaiming the country's pre-Islamic heritage, of which European scholars had discovered that it shared a common ancestry with European culture – a path Atatürk explicitly rejected when in his speech, quoted earlier, he dismissed a return to the 'costume of Turan'. In the minds of the Iranian modernists, Europeanization was thus not an alienation but a return to the true self; mimicry of Europe and national particularism could go hand in hand.[111] The obsession of these two countries' elites with sartorial westernization can thus be understood as a deep-seated desire to satisfy, as it were, a cultural standard of civilization.[112] This is confirmed by the fact that the dress policies were almost contemporaneous with the abolition of the capitulations, the most visible sign of the inequality of these nations in international society. In Turkey it was the Treaty of Lausanne of July 1923 that abolished them, and in Iran they were ended in 1928.[113]

Conclusion

The dress codes of inter-war Turkey and Iran are a text-book example of modernization from above. Both Atatürk and Reza Shah wanted their nations to join 'civilization', and for that a 'new man' had to be created, one who would leave the outmoded ways of Ottoman Turkey and Qajar Persia behind and adapt to the dominant culture of the West. Given the wide gap between the two south-west Asian countries and the West, and the urgency to bridge it, there was no time for this 'new man' to emerge gradually, as had happened in the West: hence the decision to force the pace of social change by drastic state action.[114] The dress codes were only one aspect of this westernization, albeit the most immediately visible one.

What one must not forget, however, is that in both countries these policies did not result merely from the whims of their two rulers but met with the approval of certain segments of the population. Given the greater proximity of Turkey to Europe and the greater intensity of its interactions with it, the native constituency for change was greater in Turkey than in Iran. Moreover, Atatürk could at least take a centralized state for granted, whereas Reza Shah had first to create it. In some ways, then, Reza Shah was the Iranian counterpart not only of Atatürk, but also of Mahmud I.[115] It took almost a century for the first uniform headgear of the Ottomans, the fez, to yield to the international hat, but in Iran less than a decade separated the functional equivalent of the fez, the Pahlavi hat, from the *chapeau*.

In both Turkey and Iran the dress codes were internalized by the male population, and after World War II only women's headgear would emerge from time to time as a political issue. In Iran, veiling became compulsory after the Islamic revolution of 1979, and in Turkey it became a major issue in the *kulturkampf* between secularists and Islamists in the 1980s.[116] Although the Islamic Republic's lay officials kept to Western attire minus the tie, the events of the 1930s were not forgotten: after the revolution, octogenarian General Iraj Matbu'i, who had led the charge at the Gowharshad mosque 44 years earlier, was arrested and executed in the autumn of 1979,[117] there being no statute of limitations in revolutionary justice.

Notes

[1] George Augustus Sala, *The Hats of Humanity, Historically, Humorously, and Aesthetically Considered: A Homily* (Manchester: J. Gee, hatter, 1880), p. 14.

[2] See John R. Perry, 'Language Reform in Turkey and Iran', *International Journal of Middle East Studies*, 17 (1985), pp. 295–311, for an exception. See pages 238–259 in this volume.

[3] For other studies on the reform of menswear in that period, see John Norton, 'Faith and Fashion in Turkey', and Patricia L. Baker, 'Politics of Dress: The Dress Reform Laws of 1920–1930s Iran', in Nancy Lindisfarne-Tapper and Bruce Ingham (eds), *Language of Dress in the Middle East* (London: Curzon, 1997); Dr Orhan Koloğlu, *Islamda Başlilc* (Ankara: Türk Tarih Basimevi, 1978); and Matthew Elliot's forthcoming book. The reform of menswear also seems to have exercised the minds of quite a few people in England at the time: see Barbara Burman and Melissa Leventon, 'The Men's Dress Reform Party 1929–37', *Costume* 21 (1987).

[4] For the Ottoman case, see Donald Quataert, 'Clothing Laws, State and

Society in the Ottoman Empire, 1720–1829', *International Journal of Middle East Studies*, 29 (1997), pp. 407–12.

[5] Evgenii V. Anisimov, *The Reforms of Peter the Great: Progress through Coercion in Russia*, trans. John T. Alexander (Armonk, NY: M. E. Sharpe, 1993), pp. 218–19.

[6] The concept of 'international society' is used as in Hedley Bull, *The Anarchical Society: A Study of Order in World Politics* (London: Macmillan, 1977).

[7] Bernard Lewis, *The Middle East: A Brief History of the Last 2,000 Years* (New York: Scribner, 1995), pp. 3–7. For a full discussion see Marius Canard, 'Coiffure européenne et Islam', *Annales de l'Institut d'Etudes Orientales* 8 (1949–59), pp. 220–29.

[8] Stanford Shaw, *Between Old and New: The Ottoman Empire under Sultan Selim III 1789–1807* (Cambridge, MA: Harvard University Press, 1971), pp. 376–79.

[9] Mohamad Tavakoli-Targhi, 'Refashioning Iran: Language and Culture During the Constitutional Revolution', in *Iranian Studies* 23 (1990): 83.

[10] For Mahmud II, see Niyazi Berkes, *The Development of Secularism in Turkey* (Montreal: McGill University Press, 1964), pp. 122–26; Bernard Lewis, *The Emergence of Modern Turkey* (Oxford: Oxford University Press, 1969), pp. 100–02; and Quataert, 'Clothing Laws', pp. 412–17. For Mohammad Shah, see Mohamad Tavakoli-Targhi, 'Refashioning Iran: Language and Culture During the Constitutional Revolution', in *Iranian Studies* 23 (1990), p. 83.

[11] According to Nancy Micklewright, in the 1860s and 1870s elite women in Istanbul were wearing Western dress. 'London, Paris, Istanbul, and Cairo: Fashion and International Trade in the Nineteenth Century', *New Perspectives on Turkey* 7 (1992), p. 129. In Iran, a certain Europeanization of women's dresses began after Nasereddin Shah's visit to Europe in 1873, but fashions remained unmistakably Iranian. See Dust-Ali Moʻayyer al-Mamalek, *Yaddashtha'i az Zendegani-ye Khosusi-ye Naser al-din Shah* (Tehran: Elmi, n.d.), pp. 44–45.

[12] Norbert, Elias, *The Civilizing Process* (Oxford: Blackwell, 1978–82).

[13] Or, to use the Persian expression, *har cheh Khosrow bekonad shirin ast*, i.e., whatever the King may do is sweet.

[14] Hamid Algar, 'Amāma', *Encyclopaedia Iranica* (London: Routledge, 1985), pp. 219–21.

[15] Nabil Matar, 'John Locke and the "Turbaned Nations"', *Journal of Islamic Studies* 2:1 (1991), pp. 67–77.

[16] For traditional Ottoman headgear, see Hans-Peter Laqueur, 'Die Kopfbedeckung im osmanischen Reich als soziales Erkennungszeichen, dargestellt anhand einiger Istanbuler Grabsteine des 18. und 19. Jahrhunderts', *Der Islam* 59 (1982). For the opposition of the *ulema* to the new hat, see Uriel

Heyd, 'The Ottoman Ulema and Westernization in the Time of Selim III and Mahmud II', in Uriel Heyd (ed.), *Studies in Islamic History and Civilization* (Jerusalem: Magnes Press, the Hebrew University, 1961).

[17] For a good history of the fez see Patricia L. Baker, 'The Fez in Turkey: A Symbol of Modernization?', *Costume* 20 (1986).

[18] James E. De Kay, *Sketches of Turkey in 1831 and 1832* (New York: J. and J. Harper, 1833), p. 226, as quoted in Lewis, *Emergence*, pp. 124–25.

[19] On clothing in the nineteenth century, see 'Clothing X. in the Safawid and Qajar Periods', *Encyclopaedia Iranica*; and Jacob Eduard Polak, *Persien, das Land und seine Bewohner* (Hildesheim: Georg Olms Verlag, 1976, first published 1865), chapter IV, Book I.

[20] Abdollah Mostowfi, *Sharh-e zendegani-ye man, ya tarikh-e dow eh-ye Qajar* (Tehran: Elmi, 1945).

[21] In nineteenth-century Iran there was less state intervention in the way men dressed than in the Ottoman Empire, except in one instance: the original *kolah* was high, and large sums of money were therefore spent to procure sufficient quantities of lambskin abroad. This provoked Naser al-Din Shah on a number of occasions to order men to wear shorter caps, and at one time he even ordered policemen pitilessly to cut off the extra inches from the hats of passers-by. But the resistance of his courtiers defeated the Shah's sartorial orders, and it was only after the expeditions against Herat and the Turkomans that the *kolah* became shorter. Polak, *Persien*, pp. 140–41.

[22] For the development of this rule, see Penelope J. Corfield, 'Dress for Deference and Dissent: Hats and the Decline of the Hat Honour', *Costume* 23 (1989).

[23] Removing one's head-cover was actually a sign of distress. See Ignaz Goldziher, 'Die Entblöjung des Hauptes', *Die Welt des Islams* 6 (1916).

[24] Şrafettin Turan, *Türk Kültür Tarihi: Türk Kültüründen Türkiye Kültürüne ve Evrenselli* (Ankara: Bilgi Yayinevi, 1990), p. 221, as quoted in Selçuk Esenbel, 'The Anguished of Civilized Behavior: The Use of Western Cultural Forms in the Everyday Lives of the Meiji Japanese and the Ottoman Turks During the Nineteenth Century', *Nichibunke Japan Review* 5 (1994), p. 169.

[25] See C. J. Charpentier, 'The Making of Karakol-caps', *Afghanistan Journal* 4 (1977), pp. 76–78, for a description of this type of hat, whose origin is ancient: Francis Weiss, 'When Man Covered his Head', *Costume* no. 13 (1979), p. 18.

[26] See Baker, 'The Fez in Turkey', p. 78.

[27] Niyazi Berkes, *The Development of Secularism in Turkey* (Montreal: McGill University Press, 1964), pp. 403–04.

[28] Judge Pierre Crabites, 'Mustafa Kemal Ghazi and His Hat', *The Moslem World* 18:4 (1928), pp. 389–90.

²⁹ Robert W. Olsen and William F. Tucker, 'The Sheikh Sait Rebellion in Turkey (1925)', *Die Welt des Islams* 18 (1978), pp. 195–211.
³⁰ Lewis, *The Middle East*, p. 4.
³¹ Gotthard Jäschke, *Der Islam in der neuen Türkei: Eine rechtsgeschichtliche Untersuchung* (Leiden: E. J. Brill, 1951), p. 25n; *Oriente Moderno* 5 (1925), p. 288.
³² Irfan Orga, *Portrait of a Turkish Family* (London: Victor Gollancz, 1950), p. 222.
³³ *Oriente Moderno* 5 (1925), p. 351.
³⁴ Latimer, quoted by Lord Kinross, in *Atatürk: the Rebirth of a Nation* (London: Weidenfeld & Nicolson, 1964), p. 414.
³⁵ The above is from Kinross, *Atatürk*, pp. 413–15. Chapter 50 of this book is titled 'Revolution in Headgear'.
³⁶ Bernard Lewis, *Emergence*, pp. 268–69.
³⁷ Jäschke, *Der Islam in der neuen Türkei*, pp. 45–46.
³⁸ Religious officials could keep their turban or fez while saluting, but had to take it off when they saluted the flag. Count Léon Ostrorog, *The Angora Reforms* (London: University of London Press, 1927), pp. 73–74.
³⁹ Ostrorog, *The Angora Reform*, p. 73.
⁴⁰ Mustafa Baydar, *Atatürk ve Devrimlerimiz* (Istanbul: Celtut Matbaacilik, 1973), p. 208. I am grateful to Professor G. L. Lewis for translating this law for me.
⁴¹ Jäschke, *Der Islam in der neuen Türkei*, p. 46.
⁴² *Oriente Moderno* 5 (1925), pp. 630–31.
⁴³ Lord Kinross, *Atatürk*, p. 416.
⁴⁴ Baker, 'The Fez in Turkey', p. 82.
⁴⁵ This account of popular resistance is from Gavin D. Brockett, 'Collective Action and the Turkish Revolution: Towards a Framework for the Social History of the Aratürk Era, 1923–38', in Sylvia Kedourie (ed.), *Turkey before and after Atatürk: Internal and External Affairs* (London: Frank Cass, 1999), pp. 49–50. See also Mete Tuncay, *Tek-Parti Y netimi'nin Kurulması (1923–1931)* (Ankara: Yurt Yayıncılık, 1981), pp. 149–59.
⁴⁶ Another observer noted a muezzin wearing a Homburg. Sir Harry Luke, *The Old Turkey and the New: From Byzantium to Ankara* (London: Geoffrey Bles, 1955), p. 226.
⁴⁷ Sir A. Telford Waugh, 'Nine Years of Republic in Turkey', *Journal of the Royal Central Asian Society* 20 (1933), p. 56.
⁴⁸ Quoted in Richard D. Robinson, *The First Turkish Republic: A Case Study in National Development* (Cambridge, MA: Harvard University Press, 1963), p. 84.
⁴⁹ Orga, *Portrait*, p. 223.
⁵⁰ Metin Heper, *İsmet İnönü: The Making of a Turkish Statesman* (Leiden: E. J. Brill, 1998), p. 179, quoting from İnönü's memoirs.

51 Baker, 'The Fez in Turkey', p. 82.

52 Mahmut Makal, *A Village in Anatolia*, trans. Sir Wyndham Deedes (London: Vallentine, Mitchell, 1954), p. 113.

53 Barbro Karabuda, *Goodbye to the Fez: A Portrait of Modern Turkey* (London: Dennis Dobson, 1959), p. 48.

54 *Shafaq-e sorkh*, 29 July 1927, as quoted in 'Appendix to Intelligence Summary No. 14/1927', reprinted in R. M. Burrell (ed.), *Iran Political Diaries 1881–1965*, Volume 8, 1927–1930 (London: Archive Editions, 1997), p. 36.

55 The choice may have fallen on the French hat because the French army, unlike the British or Russian, had no history of imperialist involvement in Iran. Sattareh Farman Farmaian writes, however, that her father, Prince Farmanfarma, had designed a cap to which Reza Shah had then (almost exactly one century after Sultan Mahmud II had unsuccessfully tried a similar measure) 'stuck a visor'. *Daughter of Persia* (New York: Crown, 1992), p. 54. For an exhaustive study of visors, see G. LaForge, *Visors: Their Uses and Abuses* (San Francisco: S. F. A. Press, n.d.).

56 Ne'matollah Qazi, *Elal-e soqut-e hokumat-e Reza Shah* (Tehran: Asar, 1993), pp. 28–29; and 'Intelligence Summary No. 7, 7 April 1928', in Burrell (ed.), *Iran Political Diaries 1881–1965*, Volume 8, 1927–1930, p. 182.

57 'Intelligence Summary No. 21, 20 October 1929', in Burrell, ibid., p. 239.

58 'Intelligence Summary No. 23, 25 November 1928', in Burrell, ibid., p. 245.

59 'Intelligence Summary No. 24, 10 December 1928', in Burrell, ibid., p. 251.

60 *Oriente Moderno* 9 (1929), pp. 74–75.

61 This English translation is based, almost verbatim, on Donald Wilber, *Reza Shah Pahlavi: The Resurrection and Reconstruction of Iran 1878–1944* (Hicksville, NY: Exposition Press, 1975), pp. 138–39.

62 'Intelligence Summary No. 3, 3 February 1929', in Burrell, *Iran Political Diaries*, p. 349.

63 See Stephanie Cronin, 'Conscription and Popular Resistance in Iran', *International Review of Social History* 43:3 (1998).

64 See the declaration of the governor of Azerbaijan, dated Dey 26, 1307 (January 16, 1929), in *Vaqe'eh*, pp. 58–59; and 'Intelligence Summary No. 24, 10 December 1928', in Burrell, *Iran Political Diaries*, p. 250.

65 Mehdqoli Hedayat Mokhber al-Saltaneh, *Khaterat va khatarat* (Tehran: Rangin, 1950), p. 488.

66 'Intelligence Summary No. 5, 2 March 1929', in Burrell, *Iran Political Diaries*, p. 354. For instance, in Mashaad, police showed tact in enforcing the dress codes and made exemptions for clerics and villagers. 'Intelligence Summary No. 9, 4 May 1929', in Burrell, (ed.), p. 365.

67 'Annual Report, 1929', in Burrell, p. 442.

[68] See Anja Pistor-Hatam, *Iran und die Reformbewegung im osmanischen Reich: Persische Staatsmönner, Reisende und Oppositionelle unter dem Einfluj der Tanzimat* (Berlin: Klaus Schwarz, 1992) and Th. Zarcone and F. Zarinebaf-Shahr (eds), *Les iraniens d'Istanboul* (Paris: Institut Français de Recherche en Iran, 1993).

[69] Baqer Aqeli, *Zokal-Molk Forughi va Shahrivar-e 1320* (Tehran: Entesharat-e Mohammad Ali 'Elmi, n.d.), p. 38.

[70] His cook prepared Iranian dishes for the Turkish leaders, which they enjoyed, and they would sometimes play backgammon. Ibid., pp. 250-51.

[71] Bager Aqeli, *Taimurtash dar Sahneh-ye Siyasate Iran* (Tehran: Javidan, 1992), , pp. 251-52.

[72] For a discussion of Irano-Turkish relations in this period, see Ahmad Mahrad, *Iran unter der Herrschaft Reza Schahs* (Frankfurt: Campus, 1977), pp. 239-64.

[73] General Hassan Arfa, *Under Five Shahs* (New York: William Morrow & Co., 1965), pp. 246, 252.

[74] An eye-witness account by Iran's then ambassador to Turkey corroborating this direct influence is quoted in Sadiq, *Yadegar*, pp. 304-05.

[75] Arfa, *Under Five Shahs*, p. 250.

[76] Dowlatabadi, *Hayat-e-Yahya*, vol. 4, p. 431.

[77] Sadiq, *Yadegar*, p. 305.

[78] *Oriente Moderno* 14 (1934), p. 575.

[79] *Oriente Moderno* 15 (1935), p. 314.

[80] Wilber, *Reza Shah*, p. 165.

[81] Alice Fullerton, *To Persia for Flowers* (Oxford: Oxford University Press, 1938), pp. 157-58. I am grateful to Guive Mirfendereski for pointing this book out to me.

[82] This directive is reproduced in Sina Vahed, *Qiam-e Gowharshad* (Tehran: Publications of the Ministry of Culture and Islamic Guidance, 1987), pp. 47-48.

[83] 'Intelligence Summary No. 14 for the Period ending July 13, 1935,' in Burrell (ed.), *Iran Political Diaries 1881-1965*, Volume 10, 1935-1938, p. 28. Sadr al-Ashraf, who was minister of justice at the time, writes in his memoirs that even cabinet members were left in the dark about the details of the repression. Sadr, *Khaterat*, p. 304.

[84] For a discussion see H. E. Chehabi, 'The Banning of the Veil and its Consequences', in Stephanie Cronin (ed.), *The Making of Modern Iran: State and Society under Shah, 1921-1941*, London: Curzon, 2003.

[85] Roy Mottahedeh, *The Mantle of the Prophet: Religion and Politics in Iran* (New York: Pantheon Books, 1985), p. 234.

[86] Sadr al-Ashraf speaks of a 'flood of ijazahs from Najaf to Iran.' Sadr, *Khaterat*, p. 305.

[87] *Vaqe'eh*, p. 70.

⁸⁸ *Khoshunat*, p. 24.
⁸⁹ For the census data of 1933, see *Oriente Moderno*, 16 (1936): 618.
⁹⁰ *Oriente Moderno*, 15 (1935): 517.
⁹¹ On the national headgear of Iraq see Canard, 'Coiffure européenne et Islam': 204n, 217.
⁹² *Oriente Moderno*, 18 (1938): 432, 433, 554.
⁹³ Luke, *The Old Turkey*, p. 226.
⁹⁴ 'Annual Report, 1928', in Burrell, *Iran Political Diaries*, p. 283.
⁹⁵ Berkes, *Secularism in Turkey*, p. 124.
⁹⁶ Partha Chatterjee, *Nationalist Thought and the Colonial World: A Derivative Discourse* (London: Zed Books, 1986).
⁹⁷ See the various articles in the issue on 'La révolution française, la Turquie et l'Iran', *Cahiers d'études sur la méditerranée orientale et le monde turco-iranien*, no. 12 (1991), especially Marcel Ahano, 'L'image de la Révolution française lors de la modernisation de la Turquie et de l'Iran contemporains'.
⁹⁸ Brockett, 'Collective Action and the Turkish Revolution', pp. 52–53.
⁹⁹ *Oriente Moderno* 7 (1927): 13.
¹⁰⁰ Akbar Siasi, *La Perse*, pp. 203–06.
¹⁰¹ Benedict Anderson, *Imagined Communities: Reflections on the Origin and Spread of Nationalism* (London: Verso, 1983).]
¹⁰² Kenneth N. Waltz, *Theory of World Politics* (New York: Random House, 1979), p. 128.
¹⁰³ See Carlos Escudé, 'The Anthropomorphic Fallacy in International Relations Discourse', Center for International Affairs, Harvard University, Working Paper No. 94–96, 1994.
¹⁰⁴ Karl Klinghardt, *Angora-Konstantinopel: Ringende Gewalten* (Frankfurt: Frankfurter Societöts-Druckerei, 1924), p. 94. One might add that in the early years of the Italian occupation of Tripoli, a popular distich said: *Ya Trablus, yaumm al-bruj al-tawila, ba'ùki li l-Tuly an bu-bartilah* (Oh Tripoli, with your long fortification walls, they have sold you to the Italians, wearers of hats.) *Oriente Moderno* 5 (1925): 631.
¹⁰⁵ Esenbel, 'Anguish': 180.
¹⁰⁶ *A Speech Delivered by Ghazi Mustapha Kemal, President of the Turkish Republic, October 1927* (Leipzig: K. F. Koehler, 1929), pp. 721–22.
¹⁰⁷ Sadiq, *Yadegar*, vol. 2, p. 306.
¹⁰⁸ National Archives. American Legation Despatch 505, July 11, 1935. As quoted in Wilber, *Reza Shah*, p. 166.
¹⁰⁹ Hedayat, *Khaterat*, p. 520. Hedayat adds that at that moment it occurred to him that what would be made fun of was what was under the hats, i.e., unthinking imitation.
¹¹⁰ Wilber, *Reza Shah*, p. 166.
¹¹¹ On this point see Amin Banani, *The Modernization of Iran 1921–1941* (Stanford, CA: Stanford University Press, 1961), pp. 44–51.

[112] Gerrit W. Gong, *The Standard of 'Civilization' in International Society* (Oxford University Press, 1984).

[113] For the case of Iran see Michael Zirinisky, 'Reza Shah's 1927–28 Abrogation of Capitulations', in Cronin (ed.), The Making of Iran.

[114] Ahano, 'L'image de la Révolution française', pp. 15–16.

[115] Jean-François Bayart, 'Republican Trajectories in Iran and Turkey: a Tocquevillian Reading', in Ghassan Salamé (ed.), *Democracy without Democrats?* (New York: St Martin's Press, 1994), pp. 282–301.

[116] Elisabeth Özdalga, *The Veiling Issue, Official Secularism and Popular Islam in Modern Turkey* (London: Curzon, 1998).

[117] Vahed, *Qiam-e Gowharshad*, pp. 82–84.

CHAPTER IX

Language Reform in Turkey and Iran*

John R. Perry

I.

Of all man's cultural badges, that of language is perhaps the most intimately felt and tenaciously defended. Even chauvinists who are prepared to concede under pressure that language, race and culture are not the same thing – that their national ethnicity may be mixed, their religion imported, their culture synthetic to a degree – will still cling to the national language as the last bastion of irrational totemic pride. Hence, one of the most controversial features of the programmes of westernization and modernization fostered by Kemal Atatürk in Turkey and Reza Shah in Iran was that of state-sponsored language reform, characterized chiefly by attempts to 'purify' Turkish and Persian of their centuries-old accretion of Arabic loanwords. A case study of this process also affords some insight into the differing attitudes to national social reforms in Turkey and in Iran, and among the respective regimes, intelligentsia and masses, which might help to explain why on balance one 'succeeded' while the other 'failed'.

Linguistic engineering is a particularly perilous branch of sociopolitical experimentation, the more so since it is not so exact an applied science as, say, genetic engineering. The latter is at least in the hands of professionally qualified biologists who, one hopes, know how to juggle recombinant DNA to best effect. By contrast linguistic engineering in modern times – as attempted to varying extents in virtually all the countries of the Middle East and in many others, such as Norway, Hungary, Indonesia and China – has been practiced mainly not by linguists but by generals, politicians, social ideologues and other amateurs. Their efforts have often been feared by scholar and layman alike as the harbingers of an Orwellian 'News-

* Reprint from *International Journal of the Middle East Studies*, 17 (1985), pp. 295–311.

peak'. So-called language reform is thus primarily a socio-political, not a linguistic and cultural, process, although its effects remain to colour the speech and literature of succeeding generations. For present purposes I shall focus on the genesis and activities of the Persian Academy (the *Farhangestān*), founded in 1935, the official body charged with implementing language reform in Iran, as compared with its counterpart the Turkish Language Society (Türk Dil Kurumu, or TDK), founded at Atatürk's instigation in 1932.

Deliberate linguistic engineering did not of course begin, for either Persian or Turkish, in the 1930s. The situation of literary Persian and Turkish in the eleventh and twelfth centuries – that of a language quite suddenly endowed with a novel and greatly expanded cultural field (Islam) and a new writing system (Arabic script) in which to express it – closely parallels that of the same languages, especially Turkish, in modern times. In both cases the initial impetus was toward lexical transparency, i.e., foreign words for foreign concepts had to be translated into more familiar native equivalents before percolating down from the specialists to the lay population. Hence, almost a thousand years ago Iranian scholars like Avicenna (Ibn Sinā) and al-Biruni, when writing scientific and philosophical treatises in the vernacular (which was a language revolution itself), did not merely adopt the ready-made Arabic terminology but devised Persian equivalents and coined neologisms from Persian roots and formatives; such were *peydā'i*, 'phenomenon' for Arabic *ẓohur*, and *seh-su*, 'triangle' ('three-sides') for Arabic *mosallas*.[1] Early Turkish scholars, too, in interpretive and didactic works, found native glosses and calques for Arabic (and Persian) models, e.g., *bulḡaq*, 'temptation; trouble, disorder' for Arabic *fetna*.[2] It was not until the thirteenth century, for Persian, and somewhat later in the case of Turkish, that a massive influx not only of lexical loans but also of grammatical adjuncts such as the broken plural and adjectival concord produced the highly Arabicized literary dialects that became the *bête noire* of the purists.

In the later nineteenth-century Ottoman Empire, attempts were made in the context of the Tanzimat reforms by Namık Kemal, Ziya Pasha, and other modernists to simplify the legal and administrative language, chiefly by imposing a moratorium on the coining of new terms from Arabic or Persian sources. Under the Young Turks, from about 1908, much was done to simplify the newspaper language (with an eye to propagating Pan-Turkism both at home and in other

Turkish-speaking countries) by eliminating alien 'grammatical baggage' such as the Perso-Arabic izafet construction. From 1911 the literary movement known as the Genç Kalemler ('Young Pens') reinforced the trend away from an artificial literary language toward a written version of everyday speech.[3]

In Iran, the antecedents of modern language reform were fewer and less palpably influential. From the middle of the nineteenth century various writers, including some Qajar princes and even Naṣer al-Din Shah in his foreign travel diaries, employed a simpler and less Arabicate style than is found in the pseudo-chancellery verbiage of most of their contemporaries. At least one Iranian scholar has seen in this the influence of the contemporary post-Tanzimat purist movement in the Ottoman Empire.[4] But these works commanded a small and still elite circulation, and could hardly have exercised a broad influence on their contemporaries and successors. Lexical influences from Ottoman Turkish during the nineteenth century were, if anything, counter-reformist. Technical and political-administrative terms such as *eḥṣā'iyeh*, 'statistics', *mawāadd-e awwaliyeh*, 'raw materials' and *amniyat*, 'security' were coined first by Ottoman journalists and intellectuals by dint of injecting French concepts and derivational models into Arabic morphological moulds to produce something that was often as foreign to Arabic as English *television* or

TABLE 1 *Examples of early 'military' relexification (c. 1924) in Turkey and Iran*

Meaning	Turkish replacement	Arabicate loan	Persian replacement
Equipment	donatı[m] 'equip-ment'	← *tajhīz-āt* 'preparation-s'	→ *basij* 'mustering: gear'
To mobilize	donatmak 'to equip, fit out'	← { *tajhīz etmek* / *tajhīz kardan* } 'to prepare, fit out, equip'	→ *basijidan, b. dādan* 'to muster, equip'
Mobilization	donatma 'outfitting'	← *tajhīz* 'preparation, outfitting'	→ *basij*[*idan*] 'mustering'
Airplane	uçak 'fly-craft'	← *tayyāreh* 'fly-craft'	→ *hawā-peymā* 'air-rover'
Airfield	uçak alanı 'flycraft field'	← { *t. meydāni* / *meydān-et* } 'f-c. field'	→ *forud-gāh* 'down-place'

gastroenteritis are to classical Latin and Greek; these were then exported into Persian,[5] and in some cases even into modern Arabic.

It was only from the time of the Constitutional Revolution of 1906 up to World War I (a period contemporary with the Young Turks and *Genç Kalemler* in the Ottoman Empire and the *Jadids* in Central Asia) that literary societies arose in Tehran and the provinces with the purpose of promoting modern ideas and coining Persian words to express them. These gave birth to publications such as the scholarly biweekly *'Aṣr-e Jadid* at Mashhad (1912) and the first purist periodical, *Nāmeh-ye Pārsi*, at Maragha in Azerbaijan (1906–8).[6]

II.

As in the case of social and political reforms, the impetus for concerted government action in the field of language came initially – both in Turkey and in Iran – from the military. By 1924, following Gazi Mustafa Kemal's establishment of a Turkish republic after a bitter war of independence, and Reza Khan's rise to power as minister of war in the crumbling Qajar kingdom, the needs of the military in both countries were seen as paramount. These included the modernization of hardware, tactics and administration, together with new terminology and simplified language for the manuals. Thus certain Arabic loanwords having to do with warfare, transportation and administration were definitively replaced by Turkish or Persian terms, even before the official language reform institutions (which in some cases indignantly disowned these coinages) came into existence.[7] In Iran, a committee formed (logically enough) from the Ministries of War and of Education, produced between November 1924 and December 1925 a list of 300 neologisms that included French loans (*bomb*) and calques (*wā-basteh-ye neẓāmi* from 'attaché militaire') and the coinages illustrated in Table 1.

A brief morphosemantic examination of a few of these cases where the earlier term was, *mutatis mutandis*, the same in both languages, will demonstrate some of the principles that, consciously and unconsciously, guided the language reformers in reawakening the somewhat different geniuses of their respective languages.

In the broad English glosses of the terms in Table 1, the glosseme '-craft' indicates an instrumentative formative of whatever kind (an internal root-modification in Arabic, a suffix in Turkish) that in this instance connotes a vehicle. The other glosses represent simplified analogies with English morphological devices. All the replacement morphs are native except Persian *hawā*, 'air', which is an Arabic loan. The simplest procedure is that of loan-translation, i.e., replacing the Arabic expression by a native gloss. Hitherto the usual terms for '(military) equipment, outfitting' and 'equipping, mobilizing; mobilization' in both Turkish and Persian had been based on the Arabic loanword *tajhīz*, an action noun originally denoting the preparation and outfitting for any structured undertaking such as a wedding, funeral, journey or raid. The Turkish and Persian roots best corresponding to the semantic range, respectively *donat-* (*tunāt*) and *basij-*, were both archaic and either too specialized (Turkish) or too general (Persian) in meaning: *donat-* was used chiefly in relation to maritime outfitting and naval ordnance, and *basij-*, while primarily military in connotation, also meant 'purpose, intention' in general. Nevertheless, these neoclassical veterans were pressed into service in the world of tanks and submarines, and are still soldiering on.

The Turkish replacements for 'aeroplane' and 'airfield' remain loan translations of their Arabicate antecedents. Semantically, the Ottoman and Persian *meydān*-compounds were evidently inspired by the French/English Grecism *aerodrome* [i.e., a place where air(craft) run], coined airily by those daring young men – or, in cavalier fashion, by their ground crew – on the analogy of *hippodrome*; the existing Turkish and Persian calques on 'hippodrome' (*at meydanı* and *meydān-e asb-dawāni*) perhaps reinforced the further calque on 'aerodrome'. It is interesting to note that the English loan-coinage *aerodrome* was later 'purified' in the same way to *airfield*, using two English morphs. To replace *ṭayyāreh* (which, like its Turkish calque, shows the influence of German *Flugmaschine/Flugzeug*), Persian chose a calque, shows the influence of German *Flugmaschine/Flugzeug*), Persian chose a calque of the French/English Grecism *aeroplane* (literally 'air-wanderer'), using the naturalized Arabic loanword *hawā*, 'air', and the appropriate form of a Persian verb meaning 'to tread, rove'. For 'airfield' someone revived the classical *forudgāh*, 'halt, campsite'. This is an uncomfortable ellipsis for *forud-āmadan-gāh*, 'alighting-place' (*foru/forud* is primarily a directional, not a locational, adverb, and combines directly with verbs of motion rather than locatives like *gāh*). The semantic impulse was evidently supplied by French *terrain d'atterrissage* or the English *landing strip* (compare Persian *forud āmadan*, 'to come down; to land'), or indirectly through Arabic *mahbeṭ*, 'alighting-place; airstrip'.

III.

With this precedent, the language purists in both countries began to flex their muscles. From 1928 the *öz Türkçe* ('pure Turkish') movement became linked officially to the revolutionary secularizing policy of Atatürk's regime, mirroring the nationalist spirit rampant in other academic fields, particularly that of history, and marching in step with political and social reforms. Thus the committee to Romanize the writing system was set up in June 1928, at the same time as Mehmet Fuat Köprülü suggested that the language of the ritual prayer be changed from Arabic to Turkish. On 12 July 1932, right after the First Turkish Historical Congress, Atatürk personally encouraged the formation of the Society for Turkish Language Research (*Türk Dili Tetkik Cemiyeti*), which soon afterward reformed its own title to become the Türk Dil Kurumu. With a brand-new Latin alphabet to wield, the language bureaucrats set out to give the new state a practical national language of which to be proud. Its stated goals and procedures may be summarized as: (1) to collect and publish Turkish vocabulary from the popular language and old texts, (2) to define principles of word formation and to create words from Turkish roots in conformity with them, and (3) to propose and propagate genuine Turkish words to replace foreign terms in the (written) language. In September the Society held a large and widely publicized congress, and was soon publishing in the daily press lists of suggested Turkish replacements for Arabic and Persian loanwords scheduled for oblivion.[8]

In Iran, meanwhile, the teacher-training college (*dār al-moʻallemin-e ʻāli*) in 1933 formed a society to suggest new terms in the arts and sciences; of the 3,000 words resulting, some 400 were later used by teachers and educators in their publications. This body continued to function until 1941, overlapping with the Farhangestān by five years. In 1934 the Ministry of Education collaborated with the medical college to look into the collection, translation and standardization of medical vocabulary.[9]

The summer of 1934 was perhaps the high point of Atatürk's secularizing measures, and a crucial period for both Turkish and Persian language reform. The Aya Sofya mosque was turned into a museum, and the weekly holiday was transferred from Friday to Sunday. The Turkish Language Society issued its first dictionary, the *Osmanlicadan-Türkçeye Söz Karşıkları Tarama Dergisi*, in which were collected 30,000 suggested substitutes for some 7,000 proscribed Perso-Arabic loans. And between 2 June and 10 July, Reza Shah paid a state visit to Atatürk and his republic. The two old soldiers got along famously, reviewing troops and playing with new trains, planes and gunboats; the Shah was sufficiently impressed with Atatürk's social reforms that he cabled instructions from Istanbul to his Prime Minister to decree the wearing of a brimmed European-style hat in Iran, in emulation of Atatürk's hat law.[10]

During the same period the language purists in Iran, encouraged by secularist and chauvinistic agitation in other fields and aware of developments in Turkey, became more vociferous. The press campaign began with a moderate traditionalist view, a plea in Eṭṭelāʿāt of 25 and 27 Mordad/16 and 18 August for resistance to creeping European calques, e.g., use of the word enteqād in the neutral or approbatory sense of 'critique', instead of its traditional meaning in Persian of '(adverse) criticism'. On 21 and 22 Shahrivar/12 and 13 September, the newspaper reported on the Second Turkish Language Congress, held the previous month. Iranian readers learned that Atatürk and İsmet İnönü attended the conference in person, and that the proceedings included not only 11 papers on language reform topics, but some bold nationalist philology (probably further garbled in its passage through the Persian press) claiming that most Semitic words had a Turkish root, and that all the postulated Uro-Altaic loans in Indo-European were Turkic in origin. The Sun-Language Theory was lurking just below the horizon.

These and other events in Turkey during this year were reported in Eṭṭelāʿāt's news pages without overt comment. Some concomitant editorials, however, such as that on the duty of women in (Iranian civic) life, which appeared on 26 Azar/17 December next to a translation of İnönü's speech on the election of women to the Turkish parliament, make clear that the Turkish experience was being closely followed by Iranian intellectuals, and that Reza Shah and his government were more than willing to condone and even feed this interest to prepare the way for similar reforms at home.

A month after the Second Turkish Language Congress came Iran's equivalent academic orgy of nationalistic pride – the Ferdawsi Millennium. Eminent foreign scholars, including Turkey's Fuat Köprülü, converged on Tehran to see the Shah unveil the poet's new mausoleum and to exchange speeches on Persian literature and culture. In the course of its reporting on this event (and on Ferdawsi celebrations throughout the world), Eṭṭela'at printed on 21 Mehr/ 13 October an address by Professor Rezāzādeh Shafaq that was, in effect, the manifesto of the moderate wing of the Persian language reform movement. To summarize: Ferdawsi's *Shahnameh*, as a conscious polishing of the national identity badge in reaction to the Arab conquest and the near-victory of the Arabic language, was as much a restoration and preservation of the Persian language as of Iranian national epic poetry. Ferdawsi had consciously avoided using Arabic vocabulary except in dire necessity, preferring, for example, *basij* to *taheyeh* when mustering a mythical army (compare Table 1). He urged teachers and writers to learn from this example and, while praising in principle the efforts of the purists, recommended Ferdawsi's 'measured path' (*rāh-e sanjideh*) in preference to their noisy fulminations and ill-conceived experiments.

The overwhelmingly literary-historical context of Shafaq's challenge is itself indicative of the secondary and peripheral role played by the question of language reform in modern Iran, compared with its central importance in Turkey, where the classical literature was heavily derivative and readily seen as itself the corrupter, not the saviour, of the national language. The first and most decisive reform of Turkish had been the replacement of the Arabic by the Latin alphabet; in Iran this step was never seriously considered. An editorial in *Eṭṭela'at* of 8 Bahman 1313/28 January 1935 illustrates the extent to which the nationalistic ire of many Iranians was directed even then against Western influences, rather than against the Arabic and Islamic tradition that the Shah, like Atatürk, sought to promote as the universal scapegoat. The writer deplores the plague of foreign words (*loḡāt-e bigāneh*) that 'like noxious germs' had invaded the public noticeboards and popular press. By these he evidently referred not to Arabic loans, or even to French or English loanwords as such, but to proprietory names and advertising copy reproduced in Latin characters – a symptom of decadence for many Iranians that continued to prompt letters to the editor into the 1970s.

In the six months after Shafaq's challenge, *Eṭṭela'at* printed more than a dozen articles and letters on the language question, most of them front-page exchanges between purists and moderates. Each is immediately identifiable by his prose style. Nationalist sentiments were uppermost, and attacks on loanwords ranged from a mild plea for the replacement of the Gallicism *mādmuāzel*, 'Miss', and the

Turkicism *xānom*, 'Mrs', by Persian *doxt* and *bibi*, respectively (11 Esfand 1313/2 March 1935), to a tirade against the Arab conquerors of Iran, who had invaded in the wake of their insidious secret agents, the 'Semitic words', and destroyed a glorious Persian culture (3 Esfand/24 February). The position of the purists may be summed up as follows: Persian has no need of foreign (especially Arabic) words; newspapers in particular should strive to use language that is (1) readily comprehensible to the masses, (2) the language of Ferdawsi, and (3) the purists' proffered version of 'pure Persian' (*fārsi-ye sareh*). The moderates pointed out scathingly that these three qualities were manifestly incompatible, and that the many assimilated Arabic loanwords in current Persian were more familiar to the masses than the resurrected or invented 'Persian' of the purists.[11] This was essentially the same argument as advanced by language-reform moderates in Turkey, who were likewise on the defensive at this period.

IV.

The purists appeared to have won royal support when, in February 1935, on the anniversary of his 1921 coup and seven months after his visit to Turkey, Reza Shah personally charged into the language battle. At dinner with his officers, the Commander-in-Chief addressed them for the first time as *afsarān-e man*, using the new word *afsar*, 'officer', in place of the Arabicate collocation *ṣāḥeb-manṣab*. The faithful *Eṭṭela'at* took its cue to espouse the purist cause with an editorial titled *soxan-e šāh šāh-soxam ast* (roughly, 'A Persian King Speaks the King's Persian'), crying shame that Persian words should be forced into foreign moulds such as the Arabic broken plural (as *dahāqin* for the plural of *dehqān*, 'peasant'; laws should henceforth be drafted by our *kangāśestān* (the purism for *majles*, 'parliament', which never caught on) in pure Persian, and the only foreign words allowed should be indispensable European technical terms.[12] The writer's position is virtually identical with that of the hardliners of the TDK at this same time.

The keyword *afsar* (later disowned by the Farhangestān) was ostensibly a classical word meaning 'diadem, crown', although subjected here to a mind-boggling semantic somersault; in fact it is a phonetic calque on English 'officer' processed through Urdu (it was in use in India from at least the middle of the nineteenth century).[13] It thus represents much the same process seen in the contemporaneous Turkish neologism *okul*, 'school', out of *oku-*, 'to read' and a distinctly arbitrary Turkish suffix that together produce a vowel-mutated phonetic calque on French *école*.[14] This kind of blend, fixed by popular etymology, is not uncommon in lexical innovation; it may also be seen in English *compound* in the sense 'enclosure' (from Malay *kampong*). *Afsar* was soon promoted and generalized: it appeared again in *Eṭṭelā'āt* of 21 Farvardin 1314/10 April 1935 with reference to Hitler's army staff (though the Turco-Persian *qošun* 'army' had not yet been replaced by *artesh*).

The editor of *Eṭṭelā'āt* was more prescient than others of his colleagues. At the Nawruz reception a month later, the Shah publicly upbraided the journalists present for not expunging Arabic words from their editorials.[15]

The language bazaar was now wide open. Younger employees of various agencies, publishing houses and ministries began enthusiastically to coin their own, often mutually incomprehensible, neologisms to replace Arabic loans. The Ministry of War's commission on military terminology sought to extend its purview to other fields and to publicize its vocabulary selections – with royal assent virtually assured – through the press. Caught between the Scylla of bureaucratic chaos and the Charybdis of military fiat, the moderates at the Ministry of Education and the Prime Minister, Moḥammad 'Ali Forughi, neatly outflanked both perils: they gained the Shah's ear and a *farmān* was issued for the formation of a Persian language academy, a body of scholars in coordination with the Ministry of Education to oversee the whole realm of language reform and put an end to sporadic and ill-informed experimentation.[16] Thus on 29 Ordibeheŝt 1314/19 May 1935 – to a muted fanfare in *Eṭṭelā'āt* the following month (12 Khordad/2 June) – was born the Farhangestān.

V.

The charter of the new academy committed it, inter alia, to compiling a list of classical and dialect words and, ultimately, a Persian dictionary; standardizing the derivational morphology, i.e., setting rules by which to coin new terms; proposing necessary neologisms; and pruning Persian of unsuitable foreign words.[17] All these corresponded closely with the expressed aims of the TDK.

Meanwhile, even the Turkish Language Society's truculent purism had somewhat abated by November 1935, when it published its selection of the best 'substitute vocabulary' so far collected in two pocket dictionaries, the *Osmanlıcadan-Türkçeye Cep Kılavuzu* and vice versa. Its stated goals – and the actual results, insofar as could be judged – were not so much to maintain the racial purity of the language as to eliminate diglossia, i.e., to bring the written language into concordance with the spoken, for the practical purpose of expanding education at all levels. Thus many assimilated loanwords had, sensibly, been retained; this was unashamedly rationalized in the Society's journal with the claim that etymological research had proved many words formerly thought to be foreign loans to be really Turkish in origin. This attitude, crystallized after the Third Language Congress of August 1936 in the Güneş-Dil Teorisi or 'Sun-Language Theory', had the salutary result that it was 'no longer necessary to sacrifice any word needed in our language and familiar to the people'. Some Turkish writers have surmised that Atatürk himself launched this ultranationalistic and blatantly unscientific piece of hokum, tongue in cheek, specifically to pull the rug from under the extremists of the purist movement.[18] If so, this manoeuvre is a worthy parallel to that of Prime Minister Forughi and the moderates of the Persian language reform movement in coopting the royal patronage for their antipurist Farhangestān.

Whatever its origins, the plan worked. Atatürk himself set the tone by rehabilitating Arabic loanwords such as *millet*, 'nation', in his speeches from the late 1935 on, having previously used the purist replacement *ulus*. With the death of Atatürk in 1938 the Sun-Language Theory dipped below the westernizing horizon and, under İnönü's patronage, purism briefly flared anew in the Society's list of grammatical, philosophical, pedagogical and sociological terms published in March of 1942. As in Iran, the verbal slugging match continued between moderate academics, concerned with practical gains in literacy and comprehensibility, and the ultranationalists, determined to wave the banner of a purified language at all costs. But university professors, schoolteachers and the educated public at large were by now less willing to accept the Society as their lexical dictator. In 1948 the Teachers' Association (*Muallimler Birliği*) formed its own language association (*dil encümeni*), proclaiming by its use, in the very titles of these institutions, of Arabic and Persian loanwords combined with Turkish words (*birlik* and *dil*) a moderate, pragmatic approach to lexical standardization. In 1951 the TDK lost its official status and half its revenues when its government subsidy was cut off. *Pari passu* with political democratization and relaxation of the more draconian antireligious measures of the Atatürk period, language policy has in general come under the control of moderates since World War II.[19]

The Farhangestān meanwhile published in its dozen years of active life some lists of the scientific and technical terms it had agreed should be added to the language or should supplement existing loans (*wāžeh-hā-ye now*, 1318/1939 and 1319/1940); some glossaries of regional terms and other studies of dialect and classical lexica; and its journal, *Nameh-ye Farhangestan* (1322/1943–1326/1948). This at first included a few good scholarly articles on aspects of Persian language and literature, but soon degenerated into a catalogue of minutes of meetings, obituaries, eulogies, etc. The promised dictionary and grammar never appeared. Another of the Academy's duties was, in the careful phrasing of its constitution (Article 2), 'to study [proposals for] the reform of the Persian writing [system]'. Sayyed Ḥasan Taqizadeh had in November 1928 published a pamphlet recommending the adoption of a modified Latin alphabet of 40 letters, to replace Arabic script over a period of 40 years; but his cautious approach to language reform in general put him on Reza Shah's blacklist.[20] Although the Shah was anxious to push relexification as fast as Atatürk, romantization on the Turkish model was never officially endorsed, for reasons given below (see Section VII). The nearest the Academicians got to their modest interpretation of this goal appears to have been an article on Persian orthography, which was descriptive rather than prescriptive. For reasons examined below, the Farhangestan came nowhere near the impressive record of publication and propagation established by the TDK. Coincidentally, the Persian Academy's chronology of crisis shows parallels to that of its Turkish counterpart: in April 1938 it was temporarily dissolved by Reza Shah, who was annoyed with its lack of progress,[21] and by 1948, toward the end of the less autocratic period that followed Reza Shah's abdication in 1941, it was moribund.

VI.

An up-to-date assessment of the linguistic results achieved by either of these movements or institutions is far beyond the scope of this presentation. Successes and failures in specific lexical fields may in general be accounted for. In both countries, new military terms caught on rapidly and usually permanently, since the armed forces are a perfect captive speech community: any subordinate who failed to learn the Commander-in-Chief's new words fast enough might find himself scrubbing Arabic graffiti off the latrine walls with a toothbrush. Government administration is hardly less subject to dictatorial fiat. Table 2 shows five terms in this field where an Arabic loan common to both languages was replaced by revived archaic or specialized literary words.

It may be noted, in Table 2, that *wāli* (vali) in Turkish and *mo'assaseh* in Persian are still common in popular and semiofficial usage, and that *welāyat* survives in both languages in its historical and generalized senses of '(earlier) administrative division; home (province); outlying region', as distinct from a current administrative unit. Also of note are the French loan *enstitü* and the Persian loan *encümen*, which in Turkish preceded, and to an extent coexist with, the purist replacements. The Turkish replacement for 'prime minister' is, syntactically speaking, modelled on the Arabic (strictly, Arabicate Ottoman) original, while the Persian replacement is a calque on the corresponding European expressions (compare French *premier ministre*). No attempt was made in Persian to replace *wazir*, probably because this word, although Arabic in form, is generally considered to be a borrowing in Arabic from middle Persian.

With adequate statistics, a sliding scale of 'replacement success' could be continued through medical, scientific, social-scientific and educational vocabulary down into the everyday language, the least specialized and most impervious to official fiat, where a host of Arabic loanwords and even collocations – the purists' greatest bugbear – still hold their own. Table 3 illustrates a few common expressions in each language where an Arabic loan has survived (broken arrow) or even overcome (reverse arrow) its purist replacement.

While stylistic, contextual and other variables make it difficult to quantify the effects of language reform on the current Turkish lexicon as actually used, we may nevertheless be certain that 'the reform

TABLE 3 *Examples of unsuccessful or partially successful relexification*

Meaning	Turkish replacement	Arabicate loan	Persian replacement
Precedent	geçmiş-te suç 'in-past crime'	↔ sābeqeh 'preceding + *subst.*'	↔ pišineh 'prior + *subst.*'
Civil servant, official	iş-yar 'work-apt'	↔ ma'mur 'appointed'	–→ kār-mand [-e dawlat] 'work-endorsed'
Congratulate	kut-lamak 'luck + *vb.*'	←– { tabrik etmek / tabrik goftan } 'do/say blessing'	↔ šād bāš goftan 'say be-happy,
Experience Experiment, test	(tecrübe) deney[im], deneme ←	{ tajrobeh₁ / tajrobeh₂ }	(tajobeh) → āzmāyeš

has obviously influenced the relationship between spoken and written Turkish ... [It] fulfilled its purpose of bringing the literary language closer to colloquial Turkish.'[22] In comparing the style and lexical content of the Persian press, news broadcasts, official announcements and much nonfiction writing with the spoken language and its representation in modern fiction, one feels much less sure that Persian language reform has had any such result. It seems fair to assert that, particularly in the realm of less specialized vocabulary, the Persian attempts at relexification were not nearly so thoroughgoing, widely propagated, and ultimately successful as those of the Turkish. Why this difference?

VII.

The reasons why the Persian purist movement as a whole, and the Farhangestān in particular, were less successful than their Turkish counterparts may be summarized under the rubrics of linguistic, cultural-ideological and methodological factors, which merge one into another.

The strictly linguistic factors are well known. The nature and history of the languages made the need for reform less urgent in Persian. Literary, and especially bureaucratic, Ottoman Turkish had become a Perso-Arabic lexical (and partly morphological) hybrid, held together by varying amounts of basic Turkish syntax. It had lost more of its productive native morphology than any other contemporary Turkic language and, most significant, was in practice a different language from the spoken Turkish of Istanbul or Anatolia.

Literary Persian, on the other hand, had been assimilating its Arabic loan vocabulary longer and more successfully than Turkish, and had only Arabic loanwords to consider in any question of stylistic variation or relexification. It had also retained much more of its productive morphology, and overt Arabic or Turkish syntactic influence was confined to names and titles and similar frozen collocations. Diglossia between the written and spoken norms was a relatively straightforward question of lexical variation.

TABLE 2 *Examples of administrative relexification (1930s) in Turkey and Iran*

Meaning	Turkish replacement		Arabicate loan		Persian replacement
Province	il 'territory'	←	welāyat 'governor-ate'	→	ostān (Middle Persian) 'province'
Governor general	il-bay 'territory-magnate'	←	wāli √ 'governor'	→	ostān-dār 'province-holder'
Prime minister	baş-bakan* 'head-looker'	←	ra'is ol-wozarā' 'head of viziers'	→	naxost-wazir 'first-vizier'
Foundation, institute	kurum – (enstitü) 'set-up + *subst.*'	←	mo'assaseh 'based + *subst.*'	→	bon-gāh 'base-place'
Association, society	dernek – (encümen) 'gathering, assembly'	←	jam'iyat 'gathering'	→	anjoman 'crowd, assembly'

*Bakan is a direct calque from Arabic 'Nazir', the Ottoman term for 'Minister'.

The Arabic writing system, in particular, was less well adapted to Turkish, with its eight-vowel system, than to Persian, where the six native vowel qualities were adequately represented by the three long (overt) and three short (covert) vowels of Arabic. For the Turkish purists, abandoning the Arabic script meant cutting the umbilical cord to a suspect literary past and clearing the way for a maximal assimilation of other non-Arabic elements; in Persian, the much greater quantity and value of the literature enshrined in Arabic script – even for the purists – made its abandonment unthinkable, and thus the retention of Arabic letters facilitated the preservation of other entrenched Arabic elements. At the lexical level, Arabic loans clothed in Latin script soon lose their etymological and stylistic identity; Arabic words still embedded in Arabic script stand out against Persian neologisms and European loans alike, which has a distinct advantage for survival.

An important consideration was what we might call cultural-literary ideology. For Ottoman Turkish, the classical literary models were in Persian, and to a lesser extent in Arabic; the 'Classics' were thus neither a practical nor an ideological model for a modern Turkish language. Between classical and modern Persian, by contrast, lay an unbroken linguistic and literary continuity, and the Classics – paradoxically, and with blatant selectivity! – provided models of 'good Persian' for both purists and moderates.

From the standpoint of sociopolitical ideology, the Turkish-speaking territory was at this period consciously undergoing a traumatic transformation from multilingual empire to monolingual nation state. The new language had to serve both as a practical tool for a new kind of citizen and as a major, or even the main, badge of this new nationality. Iran, however, was still in practice – and implicitly in theory – a multilingual empire. Persian, although long the supraregional contact vernacular and prestige language of the state, took second place as a cultural badge to an Iranian ethos usually expressed paralinguistically by reference to history, literature (as in the Ferdawsi Millennium), and the cult of the Shah and/or the Shi'a. After 1921 an Arab or Greek Ottoman citizen could not become a Turk; an ethnolinguistic Arab or Turk in Iran, however, remained an Iranian.

Atatürk's formula for modernization called for immediate, uncompromising westernization and a concomitant rejection of traditional Islamic structures and systems; independent nationalist props in legend, history, literature and language were not yet available in sufficient quantity to play a leading role in this transformation. Hence Western loanwords such as *psikoloji* were accepted, or at least tolerated, until an ethnic Turkish lexicon could be reinvented. Reza Shah's plan called more for a spearhead of chauvinism based on the revival of readily available pre-Islamic Iranian cultural symbols; this found an echo among many Iranian intellectuals, even some who disagreed with his westernizing policies, so that Iranian linguistic xenophobia was as likely to find expression in obsessive loan translation (e.g., *rawānšenāsi*, 'psychology') and denunciation of French and English loans as in condemnation of Arabisms. As we have seen, 'foreign words' for the Iranian purist may refer not to *madraseh* and *qanāt*, but to *mādmuāzel* and rolls razor.

Ultimately, the personalities and attitudes of the instigators of and participants in the respective language reform institutions determined their practical results. Atatürk personally initiated the TDK as an arm of his modernizing policies, although his subsequent actions reveal him as a pragmatist rather than a committed purist. İsmet İnönü, however, was active in the language movement and the Society as a purist, presiding over several of the language congresses and employing neologisms in his speeches. Both these leaders made an effort to involve all classes of people in this, as in other aspects of social reform, explaining their reasons and urging solidarity and participation.[23]

Reza Shah, as we have seen, was less immediately concerned with the inauguration and proceedings of the Farhangestān. According to the Academy's official history, the Shah was impressed by his observation of language reform at work in Turkey, and personally set up the military relexification commission that preceded the Farhangestān; Wilber, too, sees Reza Shah as 'personally responsible for the movement to purify the Persian language of Arabic and other foreign words ... In 1935, in the early stages of the "scientific revision" of the language, he himself went over the Persian words and roots that were to replace Arabic words in common usage, approving some and rejecting others.' Anxious before the birth of his daughter Ashraf's first child, he was visibly pleased when the obstetrician used the 'pure Persian' term *naxost-zā* in referring to his patient as a first-time mother-to-be.[24] Certainly the Shah was conscious of the importance of language reform as an aspect of his policy, and gave it a memorable boost with his *afsarān* speech. But Reza Shah's naive purism was far from Atatürk's shrewd management of the purist movement. The former colonel of Cossacks had nothing of the intellectual dilettante; he remained sensitive to his lack of formal education, and his written Persian revealed mistakes in spelling and grammar. More important, after he became Shah in 1925 he had little contact with the common people and made no attempt to explain his plans for Iran or to mobilize popular support for them.[25] For him the masses were still the torpid medieval *ra'iyat*, to be led or prodded to a *fait accompli* rather than aroused and persuaded to work for their own salvation.

The members of the TDK were – in principle and, initially at least, in practice—purists committed to a thorough purging of the language. Their opponents, the moderates, were *ipso facto* outside the Language Society and tried to act as a brake on its more disturbing flights of lexicobatics, so that in general there ensued a straightforward and profitable dialectic. The leading members of the Farhangestān, however – such as Prime Minister Forughi and the Poet Laureate, Bahār –

were avowed moderates; indeed, the Academy had been conceived as a way to check the activities of the extreme purists. Forughi's manifesto in the first issue of the Academy's journal, *Farhangestan čist?* provided a more conservative blueprint than the Shah had in mind; as a result the institution periodically fell foul of its patron and other more ardent nationalists.[26] Ironically, the embattled Academicians were just as bitterly attacked by the more conservative of their literary colleagues, such as Moḥammad Qazvini, Sayyed Ḥasan Taqizadeh and 'Abbas Eqbal, who regarded them as cryptopurists or incompetent meddlers.[27] The language debate in Iran, once institutionalized, thus became a rather pointless round of mutual recrimination.

The Iranian purists active outside the Farhangestān included Aḥmad Kasravi, who sought to put unproductive morphemes to work. For instance, on the analogy of a few verbal derivatives such as *xōrāk*, 'food', and *pušāk*, 'clothing', he proposed to expand the realm of the suffix *-āk* to product, for instance, *āmuzāk*, 'instruction' (from *āmuxtan*, 'to teach') and *xwāhāk*, '(object of) desire, request' (from *xwāstan*, 'to wish, etc.').[28] But his awkward *-āk* words have never caught on. Other ill-considered purisms involved the arbitrary use of archaic concrete terms in more abstract or specialized modern senses, to produce phrases such as *dar-yābeh-ye āmiğhā-ye barahneh*, which was intended to translate 'perception of abstract realities', but actually means something more like 'discovery of naked copulations'.[29]

The nature of the language reform organizations and their methods reflected this fundamentally different approach in the two countries. The Turkish purists, and hence many members of the TDK, were influenced (and still are, as the existence of the next note demonstrates) by the purist movement in Germany. Problems of derivation and composition and techniques of loan translation were remarkably similar in German and Turkish. These approaches were preferred in both languages over straight borrowing from foreign sources, since they appealed both to the nationalistic ideology and to the genuine lexical potential of morphologically transparent languages. The Allgemeine Deutsche Sprachverein, the German purist organization of the turn of the century, was not an academic committee but a broadly based society with a membership of hundreds of university professors, teachers, writers, politicians and other intellectuals.[30] Membership of the TDK was even more broadly based, being open to any adult Turk with an interest in his language.

By contrast, the Farhangestān was tacitly modelled on the Académie française (founded in 1635), as is shown by the article in Eṭṭela'at of 16 Farvardin 1314/5 April 1935 celebrating the 300th anniversary of the French Academy, by the short history of the same body published in the second issue of Nameh-ye Farhangestan, and by the setting of the number of permanent members of the Farhangestān at 41 – one more than the 'Forty Immortals' of the Académie française. Like similar imitations of the French body in Italy and Spain, the Persian Academy was to be a circumscribed committee of distinguished native and foreign scholars, cut off from the broader repercussions of language reform. Its corresponding members included the eminent expatriate Moḥammad 'Ali Jamalzadeh, four Egyptian scholars (testifying to the Academy's recognition of the continuing importance of Arabic) and the European orientalists Arthur Christensen, Henri Massé and Jan Rypka.

Apart from its showpiece congresses, the TDK took practical steps to solicit feedback and enlist active public participation in its reform programme. In the early stages it published in the newspapers daily lists of ten to 20 Perso-Arabic loanwords and invited suggestions for Turkish replacements; this met with a lively response. The collection of vernacular and regional dialect words was achieved with the cooperation of schoolteachers and other literates throughout the country, and it is claimed that every single form thus generated was duly processed. What was missing in linguistic expertise was more than made up in enthusiasm. The results were propagated widely through the media of government publications and the state news agency, the radio, the Turkish Encyclopedia and a whole range of dictionaries, several of which continue to be reprinted and updated.[31] Whatever the results, the Turkish Language Society can never be accused of not trying.

No such efforts appears to have been made by the Farhangestān. Individual members were certainly competent and diligent scholars, but the glossaries they produced were not widely distributed, public feedback was not actively sought and the collection and analysis of lexical material was the sporadic work of individuals or small committees. The endeavour was not coordinated with any educational or literacy campaign, and no dictionary was published. In short, Turkey's language reform, like its other programmes, was comparatively focused and persistent; Iran's was diffuse and vacillating.

VIII.

All this points to one general difference between the respective modernization programmes of Turkey and Iran. Turkey's problems were, or were seen to be, simple. There was one villain – the Islamic Ottoman past; one goal – independent westernization; and one method – to persuade the masses to see things just as simply. Neither Reza Shah nor the Iranian intellectuals managed to simplify Iran's problems like this, either for themselves or for the masses. The catalogue of villains included Britain and Russia as well as traditional Islam, but none of them could be antagonized outright; the goals of national independence, westernization and modernization were in practice incompatible; and the various methods that were tried largely ignored or misjudged the masses.

Both in Turkey and Iran, however, the language reform movements and the efforts of their related institutions did have positive results that went beyond a mere stockpiling of neologisms or jettisoning of selected Arabic loanwords. They sparked an active interest in questions of the national language and of language and society in general, resulting in some useful scholarly studies and linguistic aids. And they fostered – or perhaps merely accelerated – a trend in both languages toward increased transparency of the lexicon and a concomitant ease of assimilation and dissemination of new concepts and terms, albeit more readily in Turkey than in Iran. This same trend has been evident in modern Western languages, especially English, since World War II: where Victorian scientists and their successors devised such portentous opacities as pantechnicon, phonograph/gramophone, homosexuality, and arteriosclerosis for their awed clientele, our age has preferred to think up such words as blackout, black hole, trade-off, trade-in, spin-off and software for immediate distribution to the functionally literate. It is not so much the 'genius' of a particular language that prefers loan translations or other native devices to prepackaged loanwords, or vice versa, but rather it is the spirit of an age of discovery, reappraisal and popularization that periodically prompts the speakers of any language to revive dormant morphology in an effort to understand what they are talking about instead of merely parroting the past.

In 1349/1970 Reza Shah's son and successor revived the Farhangestān under the title *Farhangestan-e zaban-e Iran*, 'Iranian Language Academy', with much the same charter. It was still active up to 1979, and appeared to have learned something from the mistakes of its predecessor and, perhaps, from the relative success of the Turkish Language Society. Its membership was larger, and its appeal to the public was expanded. It saw its main task as the provision of necessary technical terminology (a report in the newspaper *Kayhān-e Hawā'i* of 11 Mordād 2537/2 August 1978 quoted its president as stating that Persian stood in need of one million new words), and tried a more democratic approach to the problem: the Academy's word selection centre issued a series of glossaries of technical terms in English with proposed Persian equivalents, under the heading *pišnehād-e šomā čist?* 'What do you suggest?'

The ultimate answer to such a leading question was soon given in more than merely linguistic terms; Mohammad Reza was no more able than his father had been to inculcate a broad condemnation of the Arabic-Islamic past and stem the pervasive undercurrent of antiwesternizing sentiment. As a result of the recent revolution, the next stage of language reform in Iran may take a rather different turn.

Author's Note: This is an expanded version of a paper presented at the Atatürk Centennial Symposium organized by the Center for Middle Eastern Studies, University of Chicago, 5 June 1982. Transliteration of Persian, Arabic and Ottoman Turkish for convenience follows a system based on Persian. Modern Turkish is given in the current orthography.

Notes

[1] See A. Shakoor Ahsan, *Modern Trends in the Persian Language* (Islamabad, 1976), pp. 7–8.

[2] A. Bodrogligeti, 'Islamic Terms in Eastern Middle Turkic', *Acta Orientalia* (Budapest), 25 (1972), 359.

[3] Uriel Heyd, *Language Reform in Modern Turkey* (Jerusalem, 1964), pp. 10–12, 16–17; Emin Özdemir, *Dil Devriminiz*, TDK Yayınları 269 (Ankara, 1968), pp. 20–30.

[4] See Ahsan, p. 103.

[5] Compare Moḥammad Taqi Bahar, *Sabkšenasi*, vol. 3, 2nd ed. (Tehran, 1337/1959), pp. 403–4; Khosraw Farshidvard, *'Arabi dar Fārsi*, 2nd impression (Tehran, 1348/1969), pp. 60–61.

[6] Ahsan, pp. 103–4.

[7] Compare Heyd, p. 18; *Nameh-ye Farhangestan*, 1(1), (1322/1943–4), 11.

[8] Heyd, pp. 25–26; Özdemir, pp. 42–46.

[9] *Nameh-ye Farhangestan* 1(), 2–3; Ahsan, p. 112.

[10] See Donald N. Wilber, *Reza Shah Pahlavi: The Resurrection and Reconstitution of Iran* (New York Exposition, 1975), pp. 160 ff.
[11] See, typically, the exchange in *Eṭṭelā'āt*, 12 and 13-Esfand 1313/March 3 and 4, 1935, between Qahramāni and 'h. h.'
[12] *Eṭṭelā'āt*, 3 Esfand 1313/February 22, 1935. The placing of this editorial next to advertisements in Roman characters for CONQUEROR and ROLLS RAZOR shaving blades is probably fortuitous.
[13] See J. R. Platts, *A Dictionary of Urdu, Classical Hindi, and English* (Oxford, 1884).
[14] See Karl Steuerwald, *Untersuchungen zur türkischen Sprache der Gegenwart*, vol. 1 (Berlin–Schöneberg: Langenscheidt, 1936), p. 110.
[15] Wilber, p. 104.
[16] Compare Ahsan, pp. 113–14. This brief but valuable account of the genesis of the Farhangestān – the only one I know of outside the Persian sources-suffers from faulty chronology and excessive reliance on self-serving publications by the Academicians.
[17] See *Nameh-ye Farhangestan* (1), 15 ff.
[18] Heyd, p. 34; see also Özdemir, pp. 52–53. The official Turkish version of the Sun-Language Theory, with diagrams, is reproduced in Steuerwald, pp. 71–76.
[19] Heyd, pp. 36–49; Özdemir, pp. 53–54; Steuerwald, pp. 45–47.
[20] Wilber, pp. 160, 169.
[21] Ibid., p. 148.
[22] Luděk Hřebíček, 'The Turkish Language Reform and Contemporary Lexicon', *Archiv Orientální*, 45 (1977), 137–38; see also Heyd, pp. 97 ff; Özdemir, pp. 54–55.
[23] Heyd, pp. 36–37.
[24] Wilber, p. 235 (the term does not translate as 'first birth').
[25] Ibid., pp. 237–38.
[26] Ibid., p. 169.
[27] See, e.g., 'Abbas Eqbal Ashtiyani, '*Baz ham Farhangestan*', *Yadgar*, 3, 6–7 (1947), 1–7.
[28] See Ahmad Kasravi, *Zaban-e Pak*, 3rd impression (Tehran, 1339/1960), pp. 42–43, 53, 54.
[29] See Ahsan, pp. 105, 106.
[30] Vural Ülkü, *Sprachreinigungsbestrebungen in Deutschland* (Ankara: University Press, 1975), pp. 17–18; Heyd, p. 108.
[31] Heyd, pp. 29–30, 52–54.

CHAPTER X

Putting the Record Straight: Vosuq al-Dowleh's Foreign Policy in 1918/19

Oliver Bast

Vosuq al-Dowleh (Mirzâ Hasan Khân) is one of the most-hated figures in the collective memory of the Iranian nation. As the person responsible for the Anglo-Persian Agreement of 1919, he has been usually portrayed as a traitor who sold his fatherland to the British.[1] Up to the present day, the Agreement signed by Vosuq al-Dowleh has been utterly condemned by authors of all political and ideological inclinations.[2] As a whole, Persia in 1918/19 is seen as a helpless victim of foreign, mainly British, machinations. Persia's diplomacy is thought to have been either inefficient or corrupt. The sources, however, tell a different story of Vosuq al-Dowleh's foreign policy in 1918/19. This chapter, therefore, intends to put the record straight.

I

> The outcome of this conference will have far-reaching consequences that will not cease to make an impact for long years to come. The deliberations of this conference will decide whether Persia will survive as an independent state or whether she will agonise and eventual die in political slavery. After this conference, there will be no judge left to which we could turn and plead for our just cause ... It is therefore an absolute necessity that the government thinks very carefully about the composition of the delegation that it wants to sent there.[3]

In late October 1918, the Persian Minister in The Hague used these dramatic terms in order to make sure that the government in Tehran was sufficiently aware of the crucial importance of the forthcoming peace conference. Yet Persia's foreign policy-makers had been already aware since summer 1917 that the peace settlement, which was to follow the current war, would be of utmost importance for the fate of their nation.[4] Although Persia had not been a belligerent, they hoped that it would be able to gain admission to a future peace conference by emphasising that its neutrality had been violated severely during the war. Indeed, neutral Persia suffered more damage and losses than some of the nominally belligerent nations did.

Thus, as early as 23 June 1917, the Cabinet 'Alâ' os-Saltana established a special institution, the so called Commission for the Assessment of Damages (*Komisiyun-e ta'yin-e khesârât*).[5] This interdepartmental institution, led jointly by the Foreign Ministry and the Ministry of the Interior, had the task of assessing systematically the moral, financial and physical damage suffered by the different regions of the country as a result of foreign intervention. Sub-commissions were established in the provincial capitals, and the public was invited to report their damages and losses, filling in specially prepared forms.[6]

Given the administrative weakness of Persia and the persisting foreign occupation of some regions, the task of the *Komisiyun-e ta'yin-e khesârât* proved to be extremely difficult, so that gathering 100 per cent exact data was nearly impossible. Nevertheless, this impressive effort of a systematic, farsighted and complex preparation of a diplomatic initiative would provide a major argument for Persian diplomats when addressing the Paris peace conference with the demand for reparations.

However, the issue of reparations was not the principal reason for Persian diplomats to hasten their preparations for the forthcoming conference. What the Persian foreign-policy makers seem to have anticipated was an opportunity to settle the Persian Question once and for all. By participating in the peace conference, Persia would be able to anchor itself firmly within the framework of the new world order that was expected to be established after the war.

In this context, the famous Fourteen Points stipulating the right of the small nations to self-determination that US President Woodrow Wilson had proclaimed in January 1918 could offer a *point d'appui* for Persian diplomacy. Persia's foreign-policy makers were indeed aware of the new role and the increasing importance of the United States. On 10 October 1918, for instance, the Persian chargé d'affaires in Washington, 'Ali Qoli Khan (Nabil al-Dowleh), informed Tehran about the latest measures taken by the Wilson administration in order to realise the American 'peace aims'.[7]

In a report dated 13 October 1918, the Persian Minister in London referred explicitly to Wilson's Fourteen Points (*nokât-e châhârdagâneh*). He informed the government in Tehran that the end of the war was near and that peace was going to be concluded on the base of the new Wilsonian principles, which prohibited secret or unfair arrangements. The Minister also reported the existence of a project to establish a League of Nations, which would guarantee the independence and territorial integrity of all member states. He emphasised that all these elements were creating an extremely favourable occasion for Persia to secure her rights; an occasion, he underlined, that must not be missed. Hence, the Persian Minister finished by urging his government to establish a special mission comprising of a number of high-ranking, respected and capable individuals. This mission should then be sent immediately to Washington, where the Persian Minister thought the League of Nations would be convened.[8] 'Abd al-Samad Khan (Momtaz al-Saltaneh), the Persian Minister in Paris, also underlined the importance of the United States in his reporting to Tehran. Nevertheless, he not only informed his government, but started holding talks with his American counterpart in Paris in order to win American support for the Persian cause.[9]

The government in Tehran was fully aware of the specific potential of the situation. As early as on 8 October 1918, Vosuq al-Dowleh, who had become Prime Minister for the second time in August 1918, underlined the absolute necessity to take adequate measures immediately, although the war was not yet over. According to Vosuq al-Dowleh, the point was to be ready to act immediately when the moment would come for a peace conference to be convened. Vosuq al-Dowleh also came up with concrete proposals as to the composition of the Persian delegation. Furthermore, he informed the Foreign Ministry that a draft list of demands as well as a detailed map concerning Persia's territorial claims had been already established.[10]

Even so, these measures did not satisfy Moshâver al-Mamâlek ('Ali Qoli Khân Ansâri), the Foreign Minister. In a memorandum for the Cabinet, he reproached the Prime Minister for not taking seriously enough the issue of getting ready for a future peace conference, and proposed a special commission composed of five well-known academics, who would elaborate Persia's peace aims.[11]

It seems as if the proposed commission of experts was actually never established. Nevertheless, when Nosrat al-Dowleh (Prince Firuz Firuz), the Minister of Justice, informed the British chargé d'affaires in Tehran of Persia's mere intention to create such an institution, it was enough to alarm the Foreign Office, especially Lord Curzon. The latter hoped that it would be possible for Britain to acquire an exclusive position in Persia after the collapse of Tsarist Russia and the defeat of the Central Powers.[12]

As far as the Persian Cabinet is concerned, they had been well aware of the risk that Britain could obtain a nearly incontestable hegemony in the region. Thus, after the war in the Middle East had ceased (the armistice of Mudros on 30 October 1918), Persian diplomacy intensified its activities. In early November 1918, Vosuq al-Dowleh tried to exploit the increasing post-war Franco-British rivalry when he simultaneously contacted the British and the French Ministers in Tehran in order to press for Persia's admission to the future peace conference.[13] In their first reaction, the British tried to temporise. On 7 November 1918 they informed the Persian government that because the forthcoming peace conference was an Allied venture, Britain could not decide alone whether Persia could be admitted or not. But the British chargé d'affaires told the Persian government that a Persian mission would be welcome, and a consultation with the Persian delegates would be possible if and when an occasion developed.[14] These promises having been given, now the Shah as well urged the British to help Persia gain admission to the forthcoming peace conference. On 17 November 1918, in an audience granted to the British chargé d'affaires, Ahmad Shah Qajar emphasised the absolute necessity of Persia's participation.[15]

Meanwhile in France, the Persian Minister in Paris managed to bring together a number of high-ranking French foreign-policy makers in a special promotional meeting held at the Persian Legation in Paris on 18 November 1918. The French Foreign Minister, the directors of the different departments of the Quai d'Orsay and the newly assigned French Minister to Tehran, who was about to leave for Persia, took part in it.[16] On 24 November 1918, all these various diplomatic efforts culminated in a memorandum detailing Persia's demands in an eight-point catalogue, which was submitted at the same time to the governments of France, Great Britain and the United States.[17] Vosuq al-Dowleh's cabinet asked for:

1. Representation at the peace conference.
2. Abrogation of treaties and concessions prejudicial to Persia's independence and integrity, as well as undertakings from the signatories of the final treaty of peace ensuring Persia's status.
3. Reparation for losses suffered during the war.
4. Economic liberty.
5. Revision of treaties still in effect and annulment of the capitulation to all powers.
6. New commercial treaties, and especially new custom tariffs, within the principle of commercial liberty.
7. Support for a revision of existing concessions to foreign citizens.
8. Readjustment of the Persian frontiers.

How did the Allied powers react when faced with Vosuq al-Dowleh's demands? French diplomacy categorically rejected the idea of Persia's admission to the deliberations of the peace conference. They also objected to the annulment of the capitulations, and to the revision of treaties still in effect and of existing concessions. On the other hand, the Quai d'Orsay saw a possibility of negotiating new commercial treaties and of granting economic liberty to a certain extent. The French also believed that Persia was entitled to reparations. They could even envisage giving way to at least some of the Persian territorial claims, as these could be used to weaken the Ottoman Empire.[18] However, as a whole the Quai d'Orsay decided to discourage the Persians from sending a delegation to the peace conference and, the French Minister in Tehran was instructed to tell the Persian government to drop the project of a mission to Paris.[19]

As far as the British were concerned, the submission of the eight-point catalogue of claims must have made them aware of how seriously the Persians were pursuing their objective of getting admission to the peace conference. Thus, the light-hearted promise to welcome a Persian delegation became increasingly embarrassing for the Foreign Office, which regarded it indeed as extremely undesirable that Persia would get access to the conference, and stressed the necessity to do everything necessary to keep the Persians out. The Foreign Office suggested that in case the Persians nevertheless managed to gain access to the conference, Britain should try to subvert the Wilsonian discourse and aim for a transformation of Persia into a mandate of the League of Nations. The responsibility for this mandate was then to be given to Britain, or at least to a compliant state. The Government of India and in part the India Office objected to this scheme, but the Foreign Office succeeded in imposing its views.[20] Thus, on 17 December 1918 the Foreign Office outlined the agreed policy designed to prevent the Persians from sending a mission to the conference in a long memorandum titled, 'Memorandum Regarding the Policy of his Majesty's Government Towards Persia at the Peace Conference'.[21] However, the British were somewhat late; ironically, on that same day, 17 December 1918, the Persian delegation left Tehran for Paris.

In the meantime, Persian diplomacy had not wasted time waiting for a response from the Allies. On 28 November 1918, the Persian Minister in Paris once again urged his government to send a competent delegation to Paris as fast as possible. Referring to the professional lobbying efforts undertaken by other small nations, especially the Armenians, 'Abd al-Samad Khan underlined the absolute importance of having exact and detailed information concerning questions of geography, history, language, religion and ethnicity in order to justify the Persian claims in an accurate and serious manner.[22] In other words, what the Persian Minister in Paris expected his government to do was nothing less than prepare, plan and justify its foreign policy in a rational and academic way, as for instance the Americans had done with the 'Inquiry'. This is a good example of how the pressures resulting from the forced Persian involvement in the war obliged the country's diplomats to consider a modernisation of their working methods.

The Persian Minister in Paris finished his urgent report with a dramatic appeal, inviting the whole nation to unite in order to seize the unique occasion that the peace conference offered to Persia. At the same time, 'Abd al-Samad Khan again did not limit his actions to patriotic appeals. In view of the forthcoming arrival of President Wilson in Paris, he intensified his talks with the American Ambassador. These led 'Abd al-Samad Khan to invite his government to contact the Wilson Administration in Washington as soon as possible, in order to make sure that the Persian Question would figure on the American agenda at the conference.[23]

The process of forming the Persian delegation in early December 1918 caused some political tension in the capital. There seems to have been a power struggle between the different factions in the

Cabinet. Nevertheless, a Cabinet crisis was avoided. While the Prime Minister succeeded in consolidating his position, the Foreign Minister became head of the Persian delegation to Paris.[24] This delegation, headed by Moshaver al-Mamalek, comprised the following members:[25]

- Mohammad 'Ali Forughi (Zoka' al-Molk), the well-read former tutor of Ahmad Shah.
- Mirza Hossein Khan 'Alâ' (Mo'in al-Vozara), the very capable British-educated, but nevertheless radically nationalist, son of the venerable 'Ala' al-Saltaneh.
- Adolphe Perny, the French juridical adviser to the Persian government.
- Nasrollah Entezam (Entezam al-Molk).
- 'Abdol Hoseyn Khan (Mas'ud Ansari), Moshaver al-Mamalek's son.

The composition of the delegation was strongly denounced both by the Foreign Office,[26] who highlighted in particular the radical anti-British attitude of Mirzâ Hoseyn 'Alâ', and by the Quai d'Orsay, which had been alerted by the French Minister in Tehran. Raymond Lecomte had informed Paris of the 'dangerous and deplorable' personality of Moshaver al-Mamalek, whom he reproached for having openly collaborated with the enemy during the war.[27] However, now that the mission had become a fact, the French government ordered the French authorities in Constantinople to offer all necessary assistance to accommodate its journey.[28] After travelling with a French vessel from Constantinople to Toulon, the Persian delegation reached Paris on 23 January 1919, five days after the official opening of the peace conference.[29]

II

Since the final report of the *Komisiyun-e ta'yin-e khesarat* was still not ready when the delegation arrived in Paris,[30] the Foreign Ministry in Tehran decided to assist the efforts of the mission by publishing at least some figures concerning the damages in the capital's papers. In view of this, even the usually extremely critical French Minister had to admit that it would be unjust to reject the Persian claims for reparations out of hand. However, he did not miss the occasion to denounce the large number of inaccuracies in the list of damages presented.³¹ In another attempt to support the effort of the Persian mission in Paris, Tehran published a compilation of diplomatic documents dating from the beginning of war, the so-called *Green Book on Persian Neutrality*. A draft version in Persian of this publication was submitted to the Allied legations in Tehran at the end of January 1919. The *Green Book* was to prove that Persia observed strict neutrality when the war broke out and when foreign intervention began.³² Nevertheless, only a few days after the mission had arrived in Paris, the Prime Minister instructed its head to refrain from any official approach to the conference until further instructions had been given.³³

While waiting for these further instructions, the delegation made various efforts to win support for the Persian case amongst influential people. Thus, the mission held numerous meetings with journalists (*Le Temps*), Members of Parliament, businessmen, industrialists and high-ranking officers. The Persian Minister in Paris, as well as Nabil al-Dowleh, the Persian chargé d'affaires in Washington, who had come to Paris on the trail of the American delegation, helped the mission with this task. Instructed not to approach the peace conference on an official basis, the mission engaged in a number of informal talks. During his first days in Paris, Moshaver al-Mamalek held talks with Colonel House (8 February 1919), Lord Balfour, the British Foreign Secretary (7 February 1919) and Vittorio Emmanuelle Orlando, the Italian Prime Minister (10 February 1919). As far as the French were concerned, the head of the Persian mission met twice with Stéphen Pichon, the French Foreign Minister (1 and 2 February 1919), but he also conferred with Raymond Poincaré, the French President (5 February 1919).³⁴ However, Moshaver al-Mamâlek did not succeed in his attempts to meet Georges Clemenceau, the French Prime Minister, who had become the President of the peace conference.³⁵

On 11 February 1919, the Persian delegation finally received the promised further instructions.³⁶ Vosuq al-Dowleh not only gave the delegation the green light to officially approach the peace conference, but he also urged it to make a maximum effort to achieve admission and to press for the realisation of Persia's claims as stipulated in the eight-point catalogue of demands. The Persian delegation in Paris hastened to carry out these instructions. Thus, on 12 February 1919, the Persian Minister in Paris organised a formal reception at the

Persian Legation, which was attended by a number of French Cabinet members, MPs and influential journalists. Furthermore, on that same day, Moshaver al-Mamalek met with President Wilson, who is said to have clearly encouraged the Persian mission to pursue their aims. Since Wilson was about to leave Paris for Washington, he promised to instruct Robert Lansing, the Secretary of State, to continue to co-operate with the Persian mission in order to help it get access to the conference.[37]

As instructed by Vosuq al-Dowleh, on 14 February 1919 the Persian delegation submitted Persia's official request for admission to the peace conference.[38] Thanks to the successful promotion campaign that the delegation had carried out during its first days in Paris, Persia's official request did not go unnoticed. On 18 February 1919, the Italian delegation put the Persian demand on the agenda of the Council of Ten.[39] Nevertheless, the British delegation strongly opposed this proposal and the Council of Ten postponed the discussion about Persia's request.[40] The next day, Moshaver al-Mamalek had a long meeting with Lansing, who again assured him that the Americans would support Persia's request.[41]

On 20 and 21 March 1919, the Persian mission participated in a session attended by the delegates of 13 neutral states. This meeting was held in order to discuss the project of a League of Nations with the representatives of those non-belligerent states that were supposed to be admitted to the League.[42] Thus, Persia belonged to the founding nations of the League right from the beginning.

On 23 March 1919, the Persian delegation submitted a second official memorandum outlining its claims in greater detail. Unsurprisingly, the claims that had been already made in the eight-point catalogue of demands submitted on 24 November 1918 reappeared, slightly modified. In the first part of the memorandum the Persians demanded:

1. Abrogation of the Anglo-Russian convention of 1907 (equals point 2 of the eight-point catalogue),
2. Freedom to hire foreign advisers without needing to ask Russian or British permission (equals point 4 of the eight-point catalogue),
3. Annulment of the capitulations (equals point 5 of the eight-point catalogue),
4. The withdrawal of all foreign troops still present in Persia,

5. A revision of the existing concessions made to foreign citizens (equals point 6 of the eight-point catalogue),
6. A revision and modification of the existing customs tariffs (equals point 6 of the eight-point catalogue).

The second part presented Persia's territorial claims in detail. Persia demanded the territories ceded after the two Russo-Persian wars at the beginning of the nineteenth century. It also claimed large parts of Transcaspia and the whole Ottoman Kurdistan, that is, a territory much larger than the district of Soleymanieh, which Persia had ceded to the Ottomans in the Treaty of Erzeroum in 1847 (point 8 of the eight-point catalogue). The memorandum's third part, based on the work of the *Komisiyun-e taʿyin-e khesarat*, detailed Persia's demand for reparations (equals point 3 of the eight-point catalogue).[43]

When this memorandum did not immediately have the desired feedback, the Persian delegation launched a new diplomatic initiative in the first days of April 1919. On one hand, the mission resubmitted its memorandum to the French,[44] and on the other, Moshaver al-Mamalek once again addressed himself directly to President Wilson, demanding American support for the Persian claims.[45]

How did the Allied powers react to the renewed efforts of the Persian mission? The Quai d'Orsay, although it had been informed of the negative attitude of the Foreign Office, did not adopt the British policy of total obstruction to the Persian demands. Although the French were resisting Persia's admission to the conference, they continued to consider it possible that the Persian mission could at least be heard consultatively.[46]

As for the Americans, on 23 April 1919, President Wilson raised the question of Persia's admission during a meeting with Clemenceau and Lloyd George. However, the British immediately blocked the proposal and successfully managed to get it off the agenda.[47] On 7 May 1919, Wilson brought up the topic for the second time, but Lloyd George succeeded once again in temporising and the discussion of the issue was again postponed.[48] When the American Secretary of State raised the issue in talks with the British Foreign Secretary, he encountered the same obstructive reaction.[49]

From what has been said so far, it is obvious that by May 1919 the Persian delegation had succeeded at least in attracting the attention of the powers to their claims. Furthermore, in contrast to the very obstructive attitude of the British, France as well as the US were at least in favour of a consultative hearing of the Persian delegates. However, at the end of May 1919, after a serious clash between Lloyd George and Clemenceau concerning the partition of the Ottoman Empire, Clemenceau simply refused to have any further discussions of Middle Eastern issues with the British. For an indefinite time, an important topic that might have touched Persian affairs disappeared from the conference agenda.[50]

On 27 June 1919, the talks with the Ottoman delegation, which could have brought about a new opportunity for the Persian delegates to be consulted, ended abruptly and with no result. The powers decided to postpone the solution of the Turkish Question, thus further minimising the potential for a consultation with the Persian delegation in the near future.[51] The next day Wilson left Paris for the United States and the first part of the Paris conference had come to an end.[52] The Persian delegation had not been able either to gain admission to the deliberations or even to be heard consultatively.

III

Was it a fiasco? Had the Persian mission to the peace conference failed? Had all the diplomatic efforts been made in vain? Did Persia in Paris once again become the helpless victim of the big powers' expansionist policies? As mentioned at the beginning of this chapter, until the present day the historiography of modern Iran has tended to see it like that. Normally, the signing of the infamous Anglo-Persian Agreement of 9 August 1919 is seen as the epitome of the mission's failure. The Persian delegation is normally portrayed as having been stabbed in the back by Vosuq al-Dowleh, who had opened negotiations with the British behind the mission's back.

However, if one places the genesis of these negotiations into the context of the efforts undertaken by the Persian mission in Paris, it becomes clear that such a view cannot no longer be sustained. Admittedly, whilst the Persian mission was on its way to Paris, Vosuq al-Dowleh had indeed approached the British and indicated that he was willing to consider an exclusive arrangement with Britain behind the back of the Persian delegation.[53] The prevailing orthodoxy has usually portrayed this as an act of treason that completely deceived the Persian mission to Paris.[54]

However, there are a number of curious coincidences. In early February 1919, just after the Persian delegation had arrived in Paris and the first measures meant to support the mission's efforts had been taken in Tehran (submission of the *Green Book*, publication of the lists elaborated by the *Komisiyun-e ta'yin-e Khesarat*), an apparently sudden desire occurred to the Shah. He declared that he wished to travel to Europe and demanded that the British accommodate his journey. Although he denied that he would like to assist the Persian delegation in Paris, the Foreign Office regarded it as extremely embarrassing for the Shah to come to Europe at that time.[55] Of course, it was by no means certain that the Shah, once in Europe, would not use his imperial reputation to back the efforts of the Persian mission in Paris.

Further, a couple of days later, after the mission in Paris had submitted the first official memorandum (14 February 1919), Vosuq al-Dowleh asked the British to honour his inclination to seek an exclusive arrangement by granting him a number of concessions. He first asked for support to carry out some measures of modernisation. What is more important, however, is that Vosuq al-Dowleh also demanded that the Allied powers as a whole (!), that is to say, France, the USA and Italy as well as Britain, would:

1. guarantee Persia's independence,
2. support efforts to secure reparations from the Turks and the Russians,
3. agree in principle to a revision of the custom's tariff and
4. assist in the possible recovery of some lost territories.[56]

If one compares the list of demands that Vosuq al-Dowleh presented to the British with Persia's initial eight-point catalogue of claims, it becomes obvious that Vosuq al-Dowleh's list was nothing more than a slightly modified and condensed version of those points. As mentioned above, the Persian delegation in Paris was pressing to achieve exactly those eight points. However, it was the none other than Vosuq al-Dowleh himself who had instructed the mission to do this shortly before he approached the British!

It very much looks as if Vosuq al-Dowleh had succeeded in carrying out a diplomatic pincer movement. He tried to dictate his terms to the British by causing them anxiety by the spectre of a Persian admission to the peace conference. In this light, the Shah's not so 'sudden' wish to travel to Europe must be seen as part of the game. Indeed, the situation must have turned out to be quite a dilemma for the Foreign Office. On one hand, the Persian delegates to Paris had started to deploy their efforts and there seemed to be a real risk that they would succeed in getting French and American support. Thus, the best way to contain the mission's efforts seemed to be an exclusive arrangement with Vosuq al-Dowleh. On the other hand, however, his proposals did not really differ from what was being pressed for by the Persian delegation in Paris!

Meanwhile, the Shah seemed to get nervous too. For the British, however, the Shah's complicity was necessary to reach a successful exclusive agreement. Thus, they could not simply refuse to help with his 'sudden' wish to travel, but at the same time it was highly dangerous to have him in Europe. Finally, the British decided to link the question of support for the Shah's journey to conditions concerning the preparation of an exclusive agreement. The Foreign Office also considered making some concessions according to Vosuq al-Dowleh's list of claims, if this was needed would bring about an exclusive arrangement.[57] Nevertheless, the British did not want to comment specifically on the point concerning territorial claims, because they feared that the Persian delegation in Paris could make use of it if they did.[58] Indeed, the British had indications that information passed to the Persian Cabinet found its way to Paris.[59]

In this context, a look at the Persian diplomatic offensive of early April 1919 is equally revealing. We have seen that at the beginning of April 1919, after their initial request for admission to the peace conference had not been answered satisfactorily, the Persian delegation in Paris again approached both the French and the Americans. Yet it was exactly during those first days of April 1919 that Vosuq al-Dowleh simultaneously came up with a detailed draft for an exclusive agreement with Britain.[60] Can the timetabling of these two initiatives be coincidence? What is even more striking, is that the draft for an agreement submitted by Vosuq al-Dowleh, although it made some considerable concessions to the British, still contained no less than five of the all too well-known Persian claims![61]

At this stage, it is worth remembering that both the French and the Americans had responded rather positively to the Persian initiative of early April 1919. The French, although aware of the obstructive British stance, had stated that they could still envisage a consultative hearing of the Persian delegation. Furthermore, both President Wilson and the US Secretary of State had raised the Persian issue on more than one occasion. Thus, the Foreign Office still had to be concerned that the Persian mission could succeed at least partly in its efforts. It must therefore have been in the British interest to reach an agreement as soon as possible.

William J. Olson, in his analysis of the Anglo-Persian relations, points out that the terms of Vosuq's draft were remarkably similar to the proposals put forward by several former Persian governments. He wonders why the British baulked at these terms when presented by a supposedly unfriendly cabinet, whereas in April 1919, after the same terms had been presented by a cabinet that appeared to be cooperative, they were prepared to consider them favourably.

To me, it seems that the subtle diplomacy of double pressure pursued by Vosuq al-Dowleh *forced* the British to consider his proposals of April 1919 favourably, even though they were so similar not only to some demands of former cabinets, but especially to the claims that the Persian delegation in Paris tried to get accepted. It really looks as if the Vosuq al-Dowleh cabinet exercised pressure on the British by continually pushing identical claims from two different sides. By playing this double game from the beginning of the peace conference, the Persians had succeeded in leaving all doors open for themselves to choose how to reach to their objectives.

However, while these options allowed Persian diplomacy a rather comfortable position, they must have disturbed the Foreign Office. The situation was such that in mid-May 1919, Curzon had no other choice than to disclose his plans to the Americans. He approached Colonel House to inform the Americans that the Foreign Office was carrying out secret negotiations with the Persian Prime Minister. He then implored the American delegation to refrain from helping the Persian delegation in their effort to obtain admission to the Conference.[62] The fact that Lord Curzon had to take the risk of revealing his plans, which were highly incompatible with the new Wilsonian principles, to none other than to Wilson himself (in the form of the American delegation) perfectly illustrates the success that the Persian diplomacy had achieved by constantly alarming the British with the spectre of an admission of Persia to the peace conference.

The Americans made no specific answer to the British demand of complicity. Thus at the end of May 1919 the British still had to hurry to reach a result in their negotiations with Vosuq al-Dowleh. It must have been for that reason that, inexplicably for Olson, they showed themselves to be rather conciliatory when negotiating the outline of the proposed agreement with the Persian Prime Minister.[63]

As described above, by summer 1919 the circumstances for any kind of Persian admission to the Conference had begun to look much less favourable. Thus, at the end of the day, before being totally stripped of any means to exercise pressure, Vosuq al-Dowleh opted for the exclusive agreement with Britain, which seemed to be the second-best way of achieving at least a part of Persia's claims. Indeed, the text of the agreement signed on 9 August 1919 follows nearly word for word the draft submitted by Vosuq al-Dowleh in April that year, which in turn – and this cannot be repeated often enough – was nearly identical to what the Persian delegation in Paris tried to achieve.[64] Admittedly, the agreement made considerable concessions to the British. This is especially true of the second point proposing that the British alone would supply 'whatever' expert advisers who might be considered necessary for the Persian administration.

Nevertheless, it must be noted that the agreement still meant the achievement of the five most important objectives that the Persians had been trying to secure at the peace conference. Indeed, the Anglo-Persian accord, including the two supplementary letters exchanged between Vosuq-al-Dowleh and the British chargé d'affaires that formed an integral part of the agreement, foresaw:

1. A guarantee of Persia's independence.
2. A revision of all treaties and agreement still in effect.
3. A revision of customs tariffs, with a view to their adaptation to the needs of Persia.
4. The possibility of a readjustment of the Persian frontiers, at least at certain points.
5. British support for Persian claims for reparations for losses suffered at the hands of other belligerents, i.e., Russia and the Ottoman Empire.

Against this background, one has to see the effort made by the Persian mission in Paris and the negotiations, into which Vosuq al-Dowleh entered at the same time, as two elements of a single manoeuvre. The Paris delegation's memorandum listing the Persian claims, on one hand, and the draft of an exclusive agreement submitted simultaneously by Vosuq-al-Dowleh on the other, should be seen as the two versions, maximal and minimal, of the same foreign policy. This policy had one common objective: to settle the Persian question once and for all by anchoring Persia within the framework of the new world order that was expected to be the outcome of the peace conference.

The Persian mission to the peace conference is therefore far from a failure; it has to be seen as an integral part of Vosuq's cleverly exercised diplomatic strategy, which ultimately achieved its objective. Curiously, it was not the Anglo-Persian Agreement itself that led to the realisation of that objective. This was done by the strong attacks of the French and American diplomacies on the agreement. By loudly denouncing the Anglo-Persian Agreement, they made themselves, consciously or not, the most ardent defenders of Persia's independence and territorial integrity, thus ultimately confirming the country's status as a fully recognised, independent member of the international community.

Notes

[1] For some directly related studies, see W. J. Olson, *Anglo-Iranian Relations During World War I*, London, Cass, 1984, Houshang Sabahi, *British Policy in Persia 1918–1925*, London, Cass, 1990 and especially Iraj Zowqi's otherwise very informative article, 'Chegunegi-ye shekast-e ma'muriyat-e nemayandegan-e Iran dar konferans-e solh-e Paris', in *Barresi-ha-ye tarikhi*, X, 5 (1354/1975), pp. 65–92. Text books and works of reference also reflect the negative view of Vosuq al-Dowleh and the Anglo-Persian Agreement of 1919. See for instance Nikki Keddie's in *The Cambridge History of Iran*, vol. 7, Cambridge, Cambridge University Press, 1991, p. 209 or the ninth edition of Donald N. Wilber, *Iran: Past and Present*, Princeton, NJ, Princeton University Press, 1981, p. 72.

[2] For details concerning this unanimous condemnation, see Homa Katouzian, 'The Campaign Against the Anglo-Iranian Agreement of 1919', *British Journal of Middle Eastern Studies*, XXV,1 1998, pp. 5–46, here pp. 5–7. One has to note that Katouzian is one of the very rare authors who has been calling for a more objective and rational view on the Agreement since long ago. See his study, *The Political Economy of Modern Iran*, London, Macmillan, 1981, p. 77–79, where Katouzian demonstrates that the implementation of the Agreement could have had a positive influence on the economic development of Iran. At least two other authors, Mansura Ettehâdiya and Vladimir Volodarsky, also take a more objective view on Vosuq al-Dowleh and the Agreement. See Ettehâdiya's article on Nosrat al-Dowleh and the Agreement in Oliver Bast (ed.), *La Perse et la Grande Guerre*, Tehran and Paris, IFRI, 2002, pp. 427–437 and Vladimir Volodarsky, *The Soviet Union and its Southern Neighbours Iran and Afghanistan, 1917–1933*, Ilford,

Cass, 1994, pp. 24–32. Nevertheless, no one has so far attempted to look systematically at Persia's policy regarding the Paris peace conference from a strictly Persian point of view. This chapter tries to do this by synthesising the evidence scattered over archival material from Paris, a number of recent Iranian and other document publications, long known memoirs and Olson's otherwise excellent study, which takes a British point of view.

³ The Persian Minister at The Hague to the Persian Minister of Foreign Affairs, The Hague, 3 Moharram 1337q (29 October 1918), Mohammad Nader Nassiri-Moqadam (ed.), *Gozida-ye asnad-e dariya-ye khazar va manateq shomâli Irân dar jang jahâni avval*, Tehran, Daftar-e motâle'ât-e siyâsi va beyn al-mellali – Edara-ye enteshar-e asnad, 1374 (1995), document no. 231, p. 573.

⁴ Already on 12 Safar 1336q (27 November 1917), the Persian Minister of Foreign Affairs had submitted a memorandum to the Cabinet asking the government to take immediate action in order to prepare systematically Persia's participation in a future peace conference. See the reference to this earlier memorandum in a note submitted to the Cabinet by the Persian Ministry of Foreign Affairs, Tehran, 12 Moharram 1337q (18 October 1918), Mohammad Hasan Kavusi-'Erarqi (ed.), *Gozida-ye asnad-e Iran va 'osmani, jeld-e haftom 1905–1924*, Tehran, Daftar-e motale'at-e siyasi va beyn ol-mellali – Edâra-ye enteshâr-e asnâd, 1375 91996), document no. 1540, p. 818.

⁵ The Persian Ministry of Foreign Affairs, Commission for the Assessment of Damages, to the Persian Ministry of the Interior, Tehran, 3 Ziqa'da 1335q (20 August 1917). Behruz Qotbi (ed.), *Asnad-e jang-e avval-e jahani dar Irân*, Tehran, Nashr-e qarn/Sazman-e chap va entesharat-e vezarat-e farhang va ershad-e eslami, 1370 (1991), p. 276–77.

⁶ See the facsimile of a poster distributed by the sub-commission for the province of Isfahan published in Ebrahim Safa'i, *Chehel khatera az chehel sal*, Tehran, Entesharat-e 'elmi, 1373 (1994), p. 23.

⁷ The Persian chargé d'affaires in Washington to the Persian Ministry of Foreign Affairs, Washington, 4 Moharram 1337q (10 October 1918), Archives of the Iranian Ministry of Foreign Affairs (AIMFA), *box 67, dossier 17, 1338q*. In his report the Persian chargé d'affaires referred in particular to a session of the Senate, which preceded the departure for Paris (17 October 1917) of Colonel Edward Mansell House, Wilson's *homme de confiance*, who would become the most influential member of the American delegation at Versailles. On his role in general, see Inga Floto, *Colonel House in Paris*, Aarhus, Universitetsforlaget i Aarhus, 1973.

⁸ The Persian Minister in London to the Persian Ministry of Foreign Affairs, London, 8 Moharram, 1337q (13 October 1918), Kâvusi-'Erârqi (ed.), *Gozida-ye asnad-e Iran va 'osmani*, op. cit., document no. 1539, p. 815.

⁹ The Persian Minister in Paris to the Persian Ministry of Foreign Affairs, Paris, undated [September/October 1918?], Nassiri-Moqadam (ed.), *Gozida-ye asnad-e dariya-ye khazar va monateq shomali*, op. cit., document no. 219, p. 545.

[10] The Persian Prime Minister to the Persian Ministry of Foreign Affairs, Tehran, 3 Moharram 1337q (8 October 1918), Kâvusi-'Erârqi (ed.), *Gozida-ye asnad-e Iran va 'osmani*, op. cit., document no. 1538, p. 813.

[11] The Persian Minister of Foreign Affairs to the Persian Cabinet, Tehran, 12 Moharram 1337q (17 October 1918), Kâvusi-'Erârqi (ed.), *Gozida-ye asnad-e Iran va 'osmani*, op. cit., document no. 1540, p. 818.

[12] Olson, *Anglo-Iranian Relations*, op. cit., p. 217.

[13] See Frederick Stanwood, *War, Revolution and British Imperialism in Central Asia*, Ithaca Press, London, 1983, p. 191 for the turn to the British. For the approach of the French see the French Minister in Tehran to the French Ministry of Foreign Affairs, Tehran, 15 November 1918, Archives of the French Ministry of Foreign Affairs (AMAEF), AS 18–40, *Perse–Iran*, vol. 24, f°97.

[14] Olson, *Anglo-Iranian Relations*, op. cit., p. 217.

[15] Olson, *Anglo-Iranian Relations*, op. cit., p. 217.

[16] The Persian Minister in Paris to the Persian Ministry of Foreign Affairs, Paris, 14 Safar 1337q (19 November 1918), Nassiri-Moqadam (ed.), *Gozida-ye asnad-e dariya-ye khazar va manateq shomali*, op. cit., document no. 236, p. 585.

[17] See Olson, *Anglo-Iranian Relations*, op. cit., pp. 220–21 for the Persian turn towards the British government. For the French government, see French Minister in Tehran to the French Ministry of Foreign Affairs, Tehran, 24 November 1918, AMAEF, AS 18–40, *Perse–Iran*, vol. 24, f° 139. The list with the Persian demands was submitted at the same time to the Quai d'Orsay by the Persian Minister in Paris, see AMAEF, AS 18–40, *Perse–Iran*, vol. 24, f° 142. For the USA, see United States, Department of State (ed.), *Papers relating to the Foreign Relations of the United States 1919: The Paris Peace Conference*, vol. 1, Washington, DC, Government Printing Office, 1942, p. 265, cited in Zowgi, Chegunegi-ye shekast-e ma'muriyat-e nemâyandegân-e Iran, in *Barresi-ha –ye tarikhi*, X, 5 (1354/1975), op. cit., p. 75.

[18] The French Minister in Tehran to the French Ministry of Foreign Affairs, Tehran, 15 November 1918, AMAEF, AS 18–40, *Perse–Iran*, vol. 24, f° 97 and idem, Tehran, 26 November 1918, AMAEF, AS 18–40, *Perse–Iran*, vol. 24, f° 136.

[19] Charles Bonin, *Note sur les demandes de la Perse à la conférence de la Paix*, Paris, 10 December 1918, AMAEF, série Paix, sans sous-série, microfilm no. 1597, f° 1.

[20] Stanwood, *War, Revolution and British Imperialism*, op. cit., pp. 203f, and Olson, *Anglo-Iranian Relations*, op. cit., p. 218. The Persian diplomacy had been actually fully aware of the risk that such a scenario could take place. Already in October 1918, the Persian Minister in London had made it perfectly clear that on one hand Persia had to complain loudly over the violations of its neutrality and the losses and damages encountered, but on the other hand it had to be careful not give the impression that Persia was

too hopeless, so that it would not be accepted as a fully fledged member to the expected League of Nations but placed under the tutelage of a foreign power. The Persian Minister in London to the Persian Ministry of Foreign Affairs, London, 23 Moharram 1337q (29 October 1918). Compare Nassiri-Moqadam (ed.), *Gozida-ye asnad-e dariya-ye khazar va manateq shomali*, op. cit., document no. 230, p. 570.

[21] Compare Olson, *Anglo-Iranian relations*, op. cit., pp. 221–24.

[22] The Persian Minister in Paris to the Persian Minister of Foreign Affairs, Paris, 23 Safar 1337q (28 November 1918), Kâvusi-'Erârqi (ed.), *Gozida-ye asnad-e Iran va 'osmani*, op. cit., document no. 1546, p. 832.

[23] The Persian Minister in Paris to the Persian Minister of Foreign Affairs, Paris, 29 Safar 1337q (4 December 1918). Compare Nassiri-Moqadam (ed.), *Gozida-ye asnad-e dariya-ye khazar va manateq shomali*, op. cit., document no. 241, p. 596.

[24] Moshaver al-Mamalek describes the formation of the delegation in an account of his mission to Persia intituled *Ketâb-e siyâh*. 'Abdol Hossain Khan (Mas'ud-Ansari), Moshaver al-Mamalek's son, who himself was a member of the delegation, later published this account as well as a part of the journal kept by his father during this period. See the first volume of 'Abdol Hossain Khan memories. 'Abdol Hossain Mas'ud-Ansari, *Zendegani man va negahi be tarikh-e mo'aser-e Iran va jahan*, vol. 1, Tehran, Ebn-e Sina, sans date, p. 269–82.

[25] The French Minister in Tehran to the French Ministry of Foreign Affairs, Tehran, 15 December 1918, AMAEF, AS 18–40, *Perse–Iran*, vol. 24, f° 150.

[26] Compare Olson, *Anglo-Iranian Relations*, op. cit., p. 220.

[27] The French Minister in Tehran to the French Ministry of Foreign Affairs, Tehran 6 December 1918, AMAEF, AS 18–40, *Perse–Iran*, vol. 24, f° 146.

[28] The French Ministry of Foreign Affairs to the French Ministry of the Navy, Paris, 16 December 1918. Compare AMAEF, AS 18–40, *Perse–Iran*, vol. 24, f° 186.

[29] Moshâver al-Mamâlek's son gives a detailed description of the journey via Baku, Tiflis, Batum and Constantinople in his memoirs, 'Abdol Hoseyn Mas'ud-Ansari, *Zendegani man*, op. cit., pp. 282–291. The Persian mission had left Constantinople for Toulon on 16 January 1919 on board of the French battleship *Diderot*. The mission arrived there on 22 January 1919 and took the train for Paris, The *Préfet maritime de Toulon* to the French Ministry of the Navy, Toulon, 22 January 1919. Compare AMAEF, AS 18–40, *Perse–Iran*, vol. 24, f° 216.

[30] On 29 January 1919, the Persian Ministry of Foreign Affairs urged the Ministry of the Interior to exercise pressure on the provincial governors to send the collected data to Tehran as soon as possible in order to produce a

detailed breakdown of the damages; the Deputy Minister of Foreign Affairs of Persia to the Persian Ministry of the Interior, Tehran, 26 Rabi' al-sani 1337q (29 January 1919), Qotbi (ed.), *Asnad-e jang-e avval-e jahani*, op. cit., p. 283.

[31] The French Minister in Tehran to the French Ministry of Foreign Affairs, Tehran, 29 January 1919. Cf. AMAEF, AS 18–40, Perse–Iran, vol. 24, f° 220. See also Mansoura Ettehâdiya, Gozareshi darbara-ye khesarat vâreda de boluk-e Maragha dar jang-e jahani-e avval, in: *Barresi-ha-ye tarikhi*, XII/28 (1356/1977), p. 110–126.

[32] The French Minister in Tehran to the French Ministry of Foreign Affairs, Tehran, 1 February 1919. Compare AMAEF, *série Paix, sans sous-série, microfilm no. 1597*, f° 12.

[33] The Persian Prime Minister to the Persian Minister of Foreign Affairs, received Paris, 29 January 1919, Moshaver al-Mamalek included the text of this telegram in his *ketab-e siyah* published by 'Abdol Hoseyn Khân. See 'Abdol Hossain Mas'ud-Ansari, *Zendegani man*, op. cit., p. 260 (journal of Moshaver al-Mamalek) and p. 272 (*ketab-e siyah*).

[34] For the campaign of promotion launched jointly by the Persian delegation, 'Abd al-Samad Khân, and Nabil al-Dowleh, see Moshaver al-Mamalek's journal for the period between 30 January 1919 and 11 February 1919, Mas'ud-Ansari, *Zendegani man*, op. cit., pp. 261–66.

[35] For Moshaver ol-Mamalek's attempts to meet with Clemenceau, see the Persian Minister in Paris to the French Ministry of Foreign Affairs, Paris, 29 January 1919, AMAEF, AS 18–40, Perse–Iran, vol. 24, f° 225. See also a non-signed note probably prepared by *sous-direction Asie-Océanie* of the French Ministry of Foreign Affairs, Paris 30 June 1919. Compare AMAEF, *série, microfilm no. 1597*, f° 50.

[36] The Persian Prime Minister to the Persian Minister of Foreign Affairs, received Paris, 12 February 1919. It is very likely that this crucial document, which somewhat clears Vosuq al-Dowleh, is authentic because Moshâver ol-Mamâlek's account is otherwise very much anti-Vosuq al-Dowleh. Thus there is no reason why Moshaver al-Mamâlek should have invented this telegram. See *ketâb-e siyâh* in 'Abdol Hossain Mas'ud-Ansari, *Zendegani man*, op. cit., p. 278.

[37] See journal of Moshâver al-Mamalek, 12 February 1919, in ibid., p. 267.

[38] Requête adressée par le Gouvernement Persan à la Conférence des Préliminaires de Paix à Paris afin d'être admis à y participer, AMAEF, *série Paix, sans sous-série, microfilm no. 1597*, f° 17.

[39] United States, Department of State (ed.), *Papers relating to the Foreign Relations of the United States 1919: The Paris Peace Conference*, vol;. 4, Washington DC, Government Printing Office, 1942, p. 57. Cited in Iraj ZOWQI, Chegunegi-ye shekast-e ma'muriyat-e nemâyandegân-e Irân, *Barresi-ha -ye tarikhi*, X, 5 (1354/1975), op. cit., pp. 84f.

The Council of Ten united the heads of government and the Foreign Ministers of the five most important *Entente* states: France, Britain, Italy, Japan and the United States.

[40] The motivation for the Italian initiative has yet to be discovered. It might have been related to what became known as the 'Adriatic crisis' concerning the partition of Dalmatia, Istria and Fiume between Italy and the newly established SHS state, the future Yugoslavia. The Italians, aware that the British did not like to see the issue on the agenda, might have brought it up in an attempt to increase their pressure on the British, but this is speculation. See H. James Burgwyn, *The Legend of the Mutilated Victory, Italy, the Great War, and the Paris Peace Conference*, Westport, CT, Greenwood, 1993. (Contributions to the Study of World History, 38), p. 256f.]

[41] The Persian Minister of Foreign Affairs to the Persian Prime Minister, Paris, 20 February 1919. Moshâver al-Mamâlek has included this telegram in his *Ketâb-e siyâh*, see 'Abdol Hossain Mas'ud-Ansari, *Zendegani man*, op. cit., p. 281.

[42] Compare David Hunter Miller, *The Drafting of the Covenant*, vol. 1, New York and London, Putnam, 1928, pp. 303–09.

[43] The Persian Minister of Foreign Affairs to the French Minister of Foreign Affairs, Paris, 23 March 1919. Compare AMAEF, *série Paix, sans sous-série, microfilm no. 1597*, f° 16.

[44] *Direction des Affaires politiques et commerciales* of the French Ministry of Foreign Affairs to *Secrétariat de la Conférence de Paix*, Paris, 14 April, AMAEF, *série Paix sans sous-série, microfilm no. 1597*, f° 44.

[45] The Persian Minister of Foreign Affairs to the President of the United States, Paris 8, April 1919. Compare Arthur S. Link (ed.), *The Papers of Woodrow Wilson*, vol. 58, Princeton, NJ, Princeton University Press, 1988, p. 21.

[46] The Quai d'Orsay responded to the Persians on 13 May 1919. See the reference to this response in a letter of the Persian Minister of Foreign Affairs to the President of the peace conference, Paris, 17 June 1919, AMAEF, *série Paix, sans sous-série, microfilm no. 1597*, f° 46.

[47] See the summary of the meeting established by Paul Mantoux, the official interpreter of the Council of Four, Paul Mantoux, *Les délibérations du Conseil des Quatre*, vol. 1, Paris, CNRS, 1955, p. 341f.

[48] United States, Department of State (ed.), *Papers relating to the Foreign Relations of the United States 1919: The Paris Peace Conference*, vol. 5, Washington DC, Government Printing Office, 1942, p. 153. Cited in Iraj Zowqi, Chegunegi-ye shekast-e ma'muriyat-e nemâyandegan-e Iran, in *Barresi-ha -ye târikhi*, X, 5 *(1354/1975)*, op. cit., p. 85.

[49] The American Secretary of State to the American Ambassador in London, Washington, 20 August 1919, Arthur S. Link (ed.), *The Papers of Woodrow Wilson*, vol. 62, Princeton, NJ, Princeton University Press, 1990, pp. 427f.]

[50] See Arthur Walworth, *Wilson and his Peacemakers, American Diplomacy at the Paris Peace Conference 1919*, New York, Norton, 1986, pp. 494f. and Christopher M. Andrew and A. S. Kanya-Forstner, *France Overseas, the Great War and the Climax of French Imperial Expansion*, London, Thames & Hudson, 1981, pp. 196–199.

[51] Compare Paul C. Helmreich, *From Paris to Sèvres, The Partition of the Ottoman Empire at the Peace Conference of 1919–1920*, Columbus, OH, Ohio State University Press, 1974, pp. 109–11.

[52] Compare Arthur Walworth, *Wilson and his Peacemakers*, op. cit., p. 495–96.

[53] Olson, *Anglo-Iranian relations*, op. cit., pp. 228–29.

[54] For this orthodoxy, see note 1.

[55] Olson, *Anglo-Iranian relations*, op. cit., pp. 230–31.

[56] *Ibid.*, p. 231.

[57] *Ibid.*, pp. 231–32.

[58] *Ibid.*, p. 232.

[59] *Ibid.*

[60] *Ibid.*, pp. 234–36.

[61] *Ibid.*, pp. 235.

[62] See the entry for 20 May 1919 in the journal of Colonel House, Arthur S. Link (ed.), *The Papers of Woodrow Wilson*, vol. 59, Princeton, NJ, Princeton University Press, 1988, pp. 317f.

[63] Olson, *Anglo-Iranian Relations*, op. cit., p. 236.

[64] For Vosuq al-Dowleh's draft, see Olson, *Anglo-Iranian Relations*, op. cit., pp. 234–46 as mentioned above. For the text of the Anglo-Persian Agreement, see H. W. V. Temperley (ed.), *A History of the Peace Conference of Paris*, vol. VI, London, Oxford University Press, p. 212–13.

Index

Afshar, Mahmud, 7, 9, 20
Ahmad Shah, 53–54, 66, 78–79, 139–140, 144–146, 263, 266
Ali, Mehmet
Anatolia, 100, 166, 169, 173, 175, 178, 180–182, 186–191, 216, 251
Ankara, 50–52, 57, 59–60, 102, 107, 110, 113, 174–175, 178–181, 188, 190–192, 194, 196–197, 213–214, 220, 222
Anti-clericalism, 9
Arab countries, 11
Arab lands, 2
Arabs, 8
Atabaki, Touraj, 1, 11, 44
Authoritarian Modernization, 5, 11, 61
Ayandeh, 7
Azerbaijan, 8, 16, 50, 56, 136, 148–149, 156, 227, 241

Balkan War, 5
Balkans, 5
Bast, Oliver, 12, 260
Bayar, Celâl, 115–118
Bolshevik Russia, 15
Bonaparte, 2
Büchner, Ludwig, 5
Büchnerian biological materialism, 4
Bureaucratism, 120
Byzantine, 9
Byzantium, 165

Centralism, 120
Chehabi, Houchang, 11, 209
Civil society, 2, 130, 139, 152

Clive, Robert, 70, 73, 75–76, 79–80, 81–83
Colonialism, 2
Committee of Union and Progress (CUP), 49, 99, 103, 167, 173, 180, 189, 198
Comte, Auguste 5
Constitutionalism, 38, 130, 132–133, 167, 198
Coup d'état, 11, 26, 38, 53, 68, 131, 134, 139–140, 147, 186
Cronin, Stephanie, 11, 130
Curzon, Lord, Nathaniel 15–17, 263, 273

Darwin, Charles 5
Darwinism, 5
Davar, Ali Akbar, 20–21, 25, 30, 60, 71, 73, 76, 82–83
Durkheim, Émile 5

Egalitarianism, 3, 6
Egypt, 2, 12, 165, 179
Elliot, Matthew, 11, 65, 110
Emancipation, 226, 228
Emrouzi budan, 6
Enlightened men, 4
Enver Pasha, 7, 167–169, 172, 180–181, 185–186, 188–189, 191, 193, 195, 198
Enzeli, 16
Erzurum, 50, 174, 187, 191, 193, 215–216, 269
Etatisme, 32, 45–46, 60
Ettela'at, 70, 76, 244–247, 256
Europe, 1, 4, 7, 20, 26, 47, 54, 56, 66, 73, 99, 106, 110, 124,

Europe – *cont.*
139–140, 143, 158, 165–166, 181, 183, 210–212, 218, 228–230, 270–272
Europeanization, 221, 225–229

Farhangestan, 35, 239, 243, 246–249, 251, 254–257
Ferid Pasha, Damad, 51, 173, 175, 179, 186, 188, 192
Firuz, 16, 21, 30, 71, 263
Foreign Office, 17, 264–266, 269, 271–273
Forughi, Mohammad 'Ali (Zoka' al-Molk), 27–28, 31, 33, 35, 38, 70, 78–80, 220–221, 247–248, 254–255, 266
France, 1, 5, 15, 48, 52–53, 124, 192, 195, 263, 269–271

Genghiz Khan, 8
Gilan, 16, 49–50, 135, 148
Gökalp, Mehmet Ziya, 5, 9, 49, 52
Gozashteh-Emruz-Ayandeh, 7
Great Britain, 16, 26–27, 53, 124, 163, 257, 263–265, 270–272, 274
Gulestan Treaty, 2

Hüseyn Cahit, 6

Imperialism, 2, 20, 26, 158, 225
Individualism, 1–2, 11, 61
İnönü period, 11, 113, 119, 121, 123
İnönü, İsmet, 105, 113–119, 121–127, 195–196, 212, 244, 248, 254
International Institute of Social History, 11
Iran, 1–2, 4, 6–13, 15, 25–26, 35, 37, 39, 44–47, 49, 53–57, 59–61, 65, 67, 84, 98, 110, 130–133, 138, 146, 150, 153, 158, 160, 209–210, 217–219, 221–222, 225–226, 228–230, 238–241, 243–246, 248, 253–258, 270
Iran-e Now, 65, 67–71, 73–77, 82–84

Iranian Constitutional Movement (1905–1911), 5
Iranian Constitutional Revolution (1905–1911), 13–14, 24, 34, 38, 48, 65–66, 131, 241
Iranshahr, 7
Iraq, 21, 165, 181, 224
Islam, 4, 45, 48–49, 58, 60, 133, 155, 165, 217, 238, 257
Istanbul, 5, 47, 51–53, 100, 102, 113, 167–169, 172–176, 178–183, 186–188, 190, 192–193, 195–197, 215–216, 222, 251
Italy, 67, 109–110, 124, 192, 256, 271

Japan, 1

Katouzian, Homa, 11, 13, 131
Kaveh, 7
Kazemzadeh, 7, 9
Kemal Pasha, Mustafa (Atatürk) 4, 6–12, 21, 29, 45–46, 50–54, 57, 59–61, 68, 84, 98–99, 102–106, 109–111, 113–119, 121–123, 126, 133, 164, 171–175, 179, 181–191, 193–196, 198–199, 209, 212–217, 220–221, 223–225, 228–230, 238–239, 241, 243–245, 248–249, 253–254
Kemalism, 45, 121, 133, 224
Kemalist movement, 164, 173–174, 185, 190–191
Kemalist reform, 9
Kemalist Republic, 11, 98–99, 103
Kemalist State, 100, 103
Kemalist Turkey, 9, 110
Khuzestan, 8
Koçak, Cemil, 11, 113
Komisiyun-e ta'yin-e khesarat, 261, 266, 269, 271
Küçük Kaynarca Treaty, 2
Kurdish insurrection, 5
Kurds, 8

LeBon, Gustave, 5
Liberalism, 3, 6

INDEX

Linguistic and cultural nationalism, 6
Lors, 8, 153–155, 226–227

Majles, 7, 14, 18, 20–25, 27–32, 36, 38, 46, 49–50, 55–58, 61, 66, 68–69, 72, 76–80, 82–84, 131, 134, 136–143, 145–146, 152, 154, 159–160, 218, 222, 228
Man of order, 5, 60
Medeniyet, 9
Mehmed Ali Pasha, 2
Menemen incident, 5
Meritocratism, 7
Middle East, 2, 5, 65–66, 238, 263
Middle Eastern intellectuals, 5
Middle Eastern modernisers, 2
Millspaugh, Arthur C., 77, 137, 148–149, 159
Modarres, Sayyad Hasan, 15, 20–22, 24, 27–29, 56–58, 79–80, 143
Modernization, 1–3, 5, 8, 11, 23–24, 44–45, 100, 109, 130, 133, 151, 158, 209, 238, 241, 257, 271
Moluk al-tavayef, 8
Mosaddeq, Muhammad 7, 18–19, 21–22, 26–29
Moudros, 168–170, 172, 189, 263
Muasirlaşma, 6
Mussolini, Benito, 5, 68

Nameh-e Farhangestan, 7, 249, 256
Nation and state, 6
Nationalism, 45–46, 56, 103, 106, 130, 132, 134, 149–151, 166–167, 172, 182, 224–226
Nation-building, 209, 225–226
Nation-state, 6

Ottoman Empire, 2, 4, 45–46, 49–50, 52, 54, 84, 98–99, 102, 164–166, 169, 174, 176, 185, 198, 210–211, 239–241, 264, 270, 274

Pahlavi dynasty, 61, 146
Paris, 4, 15, 35, 46–47, 166, 175, 220, 261–268, 270–274

Peker, Recep, 109–110, 114, 121
Perry, John R., 11, 238
Persia, 5, 65–68, 71–72, 78, 80, 82, 84, 217–218, 222, 260–265, 267–270, 273–275
Political authoritarianism, 6
Populism, (*halkçılık*), 45–46
Positivism, 4–5
Putsch, 66

Qajar dynasty, 54–55, 61, 65, 140, 145
Qajar Empire, 99
Qajar State, 131
Qajar, 22, 47, 55, 98, 145–146, 158, 211
Qajars, 19, 22–23, 25, 36, 65, 140, 145–146
Qashqa'is, 8, 31
Qazvin, 16–17
Qom, 21, 58, 75, 141, 218

Rasht, 16, 23, 145, 151, 156, 218
Rationalism, 11
Reform, 3–4, 6, 65, 132–134, 158, 166, 238, 244, 253–255, 257–258
Reformers' Party, 138
Reforming pasha, 12
Renan, Ernest 5
Republican People's Party (RPP) (Halk Fırkası), 54, 68, 98, 103–111, 114–115, 118–123, 125–127, 133, 194, 196
Repulicanism, 44–46, 48–49, 54, 56–60, 103, 134, 140–141, 144
Reza Khan Pahlavi (Reza Shah Pahlavi) 7, 9–13, 17–21, 23–27, 29–31, 33, 36–39, 45–46, 51, 53–54, 56–61, 65–71, 73, 75, 77–84, 98, 110–111, 130–147, 149–160, 209, 218, 220–225, 227–230, 238, 241, 244, 246, 249, 253–254, 257
Romantic nationalism, 3
Russia, 2, 4, 68, 184, 192, 209, 257, 263, 274

Russo-Turkish War, 2
Rustow, Dankwart A., 11, 164

Sardar-e Sepah, 7, 19, 135, 151
Scientism, 4–5
Secularism, 7, 44–46, 59, 103
Solidarism (tesanütçülük), 6
Soviet Union, 36, 67–68, 109, 114, 124
Spencer, Herbert 5
State-building, 9, 98, 131, 133, 158, 160, 226

Tabriz, 16, 22, 35, 73–74, 145
Tadayyon, Sayyed Mohammad, 20, 25, 56, 73–76, 82–84
Taimurtash, 21, 25, 30, 67–69, 71, 73–77, 82, 84, 110, 221
Tamurlane, 8
Taqizadeh, Sayyed Hasan, 7, 9, 18, 22, 26–27, 31–32, 35, 249, 255
Taraqqi, 65, 67–70, 76–77, 83–84
Tehran, 5, 15–17, 21–24, 27–28, 31, 34, 51, 53, 56–58, 70, 73–75, 137, 139–147, 150–151, 156, 60, 217–218, 221–223, 241, 244, 260, 262–267, 270–271
Territorial nationalism, 3, 6
Tönnies, Ferdinand 5
Treaty of Lausanne (1923), 101, 113, 193, 229
Tsarist Empire, 2
Türk Dil Kurumu (TDK), 239, 243, 246–249, 253–256
Turkey, 1, 4, 6–7, 9–12, 21, 44–46, 51–54, 57, 59, 61, 67–68, 84, 98–100, 104–105, 109–110, 113, 118–119, 122–126, 133, 164, 181, 184, 186, 190–191, 197, 209, 212, 214, 216–217, 220–221, 224–226, 228–230, 238, 241, 244–246, 254, 256–257
Turkey's Grand National Assembly (TGNA), 50–52, 57, 59, 116–117, 122–123, 125–126, 178–181, 191–192, 194, 196–197, 214–215, 221
Turkification of religion and language, 9
Turkish Republic, 164, 176, 197–198
Turkmanchay Treaty, 2
Turkmen, 8
Turks, 8

Ulema, 21–22, 24, 33, 58–59, 71, 73–75, 83, 150, 155–157, 210–211, 218, 223–225
United States, 15, 70, 124, 261–264, 269–271

Vosuq al-Dowleh (Mirza Hasan Khan), 12, 14–16, 27–28, 79, 260, 262–264, 267–268, 270–275

Westernism, 7
Westernists (*garbcilar*), 9
Westernization, 196, 209–210, 229, 238, 253, 257
Wilson, Woodrow, 185, 261–262, 265, 268–269, 272–273
World War I, 5, 12,14, 49, 66, 100–101, 113, 124, 131, 165, 167–170, 178, 180, 182–184, 189, 241
World War II, 12, 119, 123–124, 133, 197, 230, 249, 257

Young Turks, 3, 6, 9, 47, 100, 133, 167–168, 172, 175, 180, 183–184, 186, 189–191, 194, 198–199, 211, 217, 239, 241

Zanzibar, 7
Zürcher, Erik Jan, 1, 11, 98

www.ingramcontent.com/pod-product-compliance
Ingram Content Group UK Ltd.
Pitfield, Milton Keynes, MK11 3LW, UK
UKHW021912220326
469209UK00005B/28